The
Oxford Book of
Scottish Verse

The Oxford Book of Scottish Verse

Chosen by

John MacQueen

and

Tom Scott

Oxford

At the Clarendon Press

1966

Oxford University Press, Ely House, London W.1

GLASGOW NEW YORK TORONTO MELBOURNE WELLINGTON
BOMBAY CALCUTTA MADRAS KARACHI LAHORE DACCA
CAPE TOWN SALISBURY NAIROBI IBADAN
KUALA LUMPUR HONG KONG TOKYO

PRINTED IN GREAT BRITAIN

ACKNOWLEDGEMENTS

THE editors wish to thank all those who have kindly given their permission to include copyright material. They are:

Miss Rhoda Spence, Sir Alexander Gray, Helen B. Cruickshank, Mrs. Willa Muir, Miss Bessie J. B. Macarthur, Miss Margaret Winefride Simpson, Dr. C. M. Grieve (Hugh MacDiarmid), Miss Edith Anne Robertson, Mr. Joe Corrie, Mrs. William Jeffrey, Mr. Robert Rendall, Miss Alice V. Stuart, Mr. Joseph Gordon MacLeod (Adam Drinan), Dr. William Montgomerie, Mr. A. D. Mackie, Mr. J. K. Annand, Mr. Robert MacLellan, Miss Kathleen Raine, Mr. Robert Garioch, Mr. George Bruce, Mr. T. A. Robertson (Vagaland), Mr. Norman MacCaig, Mr. T. S. Law, Dr. Douglas Young, Mr. R. Crombie Saunders, Mr. G. S. Fraser, Mr. Sydney Goodsir Smith, Mr. George Campbell Hay, Mr. W. S. Graham, Mr. Maurice Lindsay, Mr. W. J. Tait, Mr. Thurso Berwick, Mr. Hamish Henderson, Mr. Alexander Scott, Mr. Sydney Tremayne, Mr. Edwin Morgan, Mr. George Mackay Brown, Mr. W. Price Turner, Mrs. James Burns Singer, and Mr. Iain Crichton Smith.

They wish also to thank the staffs of the National Library of Scotland, the Library of the University of Edinburgh, and of the Scottish Section of the Edinburgh Public Library. In particular, Miss Dickson of the last named has been most helpful.

We are also indebted to the following publishers:
The Centaur Press Ltd. for the poem by James Thompson; Messrs. Rupert Hart-Davis Ltd. for the poems by Robert Louis Stevenson and Andrew Young; Messrs. John Baker Ltd. for the poem by John Davidson originally published by the Unicorn Press; the Orcadian Press for the poems by Robert Rendall; *Country Life* for a poem by Violet Jacob; Messrs. Constable & Co. Ltd. for the poem by Charles Murray; Messrs. Oliver & Boyd Ltd. for a poem by Violet Jacob, and a poem by Sydney Goodsir Smith; Messrs. Faber & Faber Ltd. for the poems by Marion Angus, Alexander Gray, and Joe Corrie; Messrs. Faber & Faber Ltd. and Oxford University Press Inc. New York for the poems by Edwin Muir; Messrs. W. & R. Chambers Ltd. for the poem by Margaret Wine-

ACKNOWLEDGEMENTS

fride Simpson; the Macmillan Co. New York for the poems by Hugh MacDiarmid; M. MacDonald for the poems by Edith Anne Robertson, Thurso Berwick, Alexander Scott, Sydney Goodsir Smith, and R. Crombie Saunders; the National Library of Scotland for the poems by William Soutar; the Fortune Press Ltd. for the poems by Adam Drinan; the Bodley Head Ltd. for four poems by William Montgomerie; William MacLellan for poems by William Montgomerie, Sydney Goodsir Smith, George Campbell Hay, Robert MacLellan, Douglas Young, and George Bruce; the Arts Council of Great Britain for a poem by A. D. Mackie; Messrs. Thomas Nelson & Sons Ltd. for poems by A. D. Mackie, Robert Garioch, Douglas Young, and Alexander Scott; the Hogarth Press Ltd. for poems by Norman Cameron, Norman MacCaig, and George MacKay Brown; the Burns Federation for the poem by J. K. Annand; Messrs. Hamish Hamilton Ltd. for the poems by Kathleen Raine; Peter Russell for three poems by Sydney Goodsir Smith; the Saltire Society for a poem by George Bruce; *The New Shetlander* for poems by T. A. Robertson and William J. Tait; Messrs. Routledge & Kegan Paul Ltd. for the poem by J. F. Hendry; Contemporary Poetry, Baltimore, for a poem by R. Crombie Saunders originally published in *Contemporary Poetry XV*, copyright Mary Owings Miller, 1955; Messrs. Ivor Nicholson and Watson Ltd. for the poems by G. S. Fraser, and a poem by W. S. Graham; the Chalmers Press for a poem by Sydney Goodsir Smith; Messrs. Robert Hale Ltd. for a poem by Maurice Lindsay; Messrs. Chatto & Windus Ltd. for the poem by Sydney Tremayne; *Peace News* for the poem by Edwin Morgan; the Manchester University Press for the poem by William Drummond; Messrs. Secker & Warburg for the poems by Burns Singer; Messrs. Eyre & Spottiswoode Ltd. for the poems by Iain Crichton Smith.

In one or two cases it has proved impossible to contact a poet, or his executors, or a publisher: in any such case where we seem to offend we offer our sincere apologies.

Special thanks are due to the Scottish Text Society; to Mrs. A. West and Mr. Robert Garioch for their help in compilation of text and glossary; and to the National Library of Scotland for the text of Mark Alexander Boyd's *Sonet*.

PREFACE

MOST of the principles underlying this anthology will reveal themselves to those who read it. The title has been taken seriously: we have tried to bear in mind throughout that this is a book of verse, not of some other alleged kind of 'poetry'; that it is Scottish verse; and that the Scottish verse should be chosen and presented according to principles consonant with the traditions of the great series of Oxford Books which this anthology now, rather belatedly, joins.

We have not presumed to write down to the reader. We have tried to discover the best texts, and make them available with the minimum of tampering, in all cases stating our sources.

A few concessions to present-day conventions have been made, where not to do so would have been merely pedantic. The main ones are:

For poems up to about the beginning of the seventeenth century all contractions have been expanded.

The forms *u*, *v*, *w*, *i*, *j*, and *y* have been normalized. Punctuation has been normalized.

Capitals, other than those which seem to mark emphasis, have been removed, where they appeared to be superflous.

Where applicable, the same principles have been carried into the later period, but the use of capitals in the eighteenth-century period has been regarded as deliberate, and a strict adherence to the best available text has been aimed at. For Burns, for example, the Kilmarnock edition has been preferred where relevant, as the poet emended this text only under duress: and for Fergusson the Scottish Text Society edition has been strictly adhered to. In rare instances, where many versions of an anonymous poem exist and none seems to be more authoritative than the others, some editorial freedom has been taken.

In choosing from the rich Medieval-Renaissance period the editors have tried to be representative, though not immune from editorial preferences. This is also true for the later period, but the bulk of our limited space has been given to the major figures at the expense of minor, where minor works abound and major is scarce. Among living poets the editorial preference may have been followed at the expense of the policy of full representation. But the editors have tried throughout to hold the balance between the claims of tradition and those of innovation. In the best work there is no conflict: in lesser, but still significant work, the claims tend to quarrel. Here we have been guided by the title—'Scottish Verse'. This has meant the exclusion, or only nominal representation, of one or two poets whose work seems to be more at home—like that of Drummond—in the English tradition than in the Scottish.

It has been impossible to include all the good poets now living, and where the poet is something of a one-poem man, the preference has gone to another whose work is more sustained, even if at a slightly lower level of intensity. There are at least four or five good poets whom we regret not having found room for. Some poems which the editors found it impossible to include, on grounds of quality, were urged upon them with such partisan pressure that the task of rejection was less than usually painful. No poet born after

1930 is included, for a number of obvious reasons, though this too is regretted.

A truly comprehensive selection of Scottish verse would have to include a large proportion of Gaelic and Latin verse, from the earliest times, but this was beyond the scope of the book. The editors hoped, in compiling this anthology, that before long it would be complemented by an anthology of Gaelic Verse, so essential a part of the Scottish tradition, and they would like to think that this present venture will emphasize its desirability.

The editors cannot hope to have pleased everybody; nor did they expect to. But where they cannot command agreement with their reading of Scottish tradition they at least hope to have stimulated dissenting opinion. An anthology cannot do more, by its nature, and too many do less.

SOME FEATURES OF PRONUNCIATION

IN the middle period the consonant *l* is often vocalized after a vowel and before another consonant or at the end of a word (cf. English *half, talk*). Double *ll* after *a* rounds the vowel and lengthens it, so that, e.g. *fall* becomes *faa*, with a sound like that in *law* but more open. In some words where it is not original it indicates vowel length, as *chalmer* (French *chambre*) pronounced as if *chahmer* or *chawmer*. After *o* and before certain consonants *l* becomes the second element of a diphthong like that usually spelt *ow*: *folk* (fowk), *gold* (gowd), *goldin* (gowdin).

The consonant *v* between vowels is lost in many words such as *devil, even, never*, which become *deil, een, neer*; in consequence *evil* is sometimes confused with *ill*, which is etymologically distinct. The letter *f*, or *ff*, when final is sometimes pronounced as *v*: so *haif* (have), *belyf* (belive).

In *shall* and *should* the initial consonant is usually *s* instead of *sh*: *sal(l), sould*. (But the use of *sedill* instead of *schedule* is not related to this; the French etymon was *cedule*.) In a few words the relation is the opposite, especially *schir* for 'sir', sometimes *schemit* 'seemed', etc.

Initial *h* is not sounded in some words, such as *harmony, habit, habitakle*, as well as those still familiar such as *honour*. The sound written *wh*, pronounced in Scots *hw*, is usually written *quh-* in the middle period.

Some words of French origin have spellings indicating palatalized *l* and *n*: *tailyeour, fenyeit*.

The letter *i* is sometimes written after *a* or *o* to indicate that the vowel is long, not that it is a diphthong: *mair, moir, gloir*, etc.

The eighteenth–nineteenth century conventions are well enough known—the peppering of apostrophes reveals the misunderstanding of Scots common in the period, when Scots forms were read as corruptions of English ones.

The twentieth-century convention of the so-called Lallans makars is a standardization of the true Scots forms used in the middle period. They are mostly self-explanatory, but the value of double *oo* given to the *ou* spelling should be noted—*house* in Lallans is pronounced *hoose*, *mouse*, *moose*, etc. The medieval distinction between gerundial and participial forms is maintained. The gerund *hunting* in the middle period is *huntin* in the modern; the participle *huntand* is *huntan*; and the past participle is much the same, ending in *-it* or *-t*—*lowpit*, *lowpt* (leapt). In this period too, *ay* means yes, *aye* means always. In the earlier periods they were interchangeable. The forms *ae* and *yae* mean *a* (unspecified) and *a* specified. For *one*, the forms *ane* or *yin*, the former preferred.

Here is a phonetic transcript of the first stanza of 'The Twa Corbies':

> əz a wəz waːkən aː əlen,
>
> ə hard twaː korbɪz makən ə men;
>
> ðə ten ʌntə ðə tɪðər seː,
>
> 'ʍaːr sal wi gaŋ ən dəin ðə deː?'

SOME FORMS

Verbs. The word *gar*, 'make', 'cause', 'compel', is frequent at all periods: 'I'll gar you run'; 'the king gart the beggar kneel'; 'gar a man bring him here'.

The present participle in the earlier period ends in *-and*: 'she was comand up the hill'. In modern Scots the *-d* is dropped and the form is *coman*. The verbal noun (or gerund), on the other hand, historically ends in *-ing*: 'Ha, ha, the wooing o't'—though in typical eighteenth-century use this becomes *-in*. At this period, and even earlier, there is a tendency for this form to supplant the participial *-an(d)*; but one of the editors has still heard *a dyand man* spoken by a farm-worker, with even the *-d* preserved.

The past tense and past participle of weak verbs often end in *-t* (cf. English *went*, *spelt*, etc.) or *-it*: 'he loutit low doun on his knee'; 'the bairn kent his faither'; 'he was a larnit man, and muckle had he larnt'. But the ending -(e)d is used in some forms, especially after vowels: 'he loued her weel'; 'the snaw it snawed aa nicht'.

Nouns. The commonest plural ending is -*is* or -*ys*, which in the middle period is also used for the genitive singular. This is usually pronounced simply as -*s*, but in verse the full syllable is sometimes sounded for the sake of metre.

Pronouns. The typical forms corresponding to English *who* are, according to period, *quha*, *quhae* or *wha*, *whae*, The formal equivalent of *which* is *quhilk*, but in relative function Scots uses *that* much more than English. The equivalent of *whose* is *quhais*, *quhase*, *whase*, and the like.

Demonstratives. The plural of *this* is *thir*, of *that* is *thae*, *tha*, or *thai*.

Articles. The definite article is used in some phrases where English has the preposition *to*, as *the day* 'today'. This begins in late middle Scots and is common in the modern period. The indefinite article is in early use *a*, but *ane* as well in middle Scots —the latter a literary affectation. The forms *ae*, *yae* are used as intensives, as 'ae day it chanced', meaning a particular day.

Prepositions. *Til(l)* is often used, besides *to*, as the equivalent of English *to*. In modern Scots *tae* is also used, but more commonly it is the equivalent of *too*.

CONTENTS

CONTENTS

CONTENTS

xv

CONTENTS

CONTENTS

CONTENTS

CONTENTS

xix

CONTENTS

CONTENTS

CONTENTS

CONTENTS

CONTENTS

CONTENTS

CONTENTS

CONTENTS

CONTENTS

CONTENTS

CONTENTS

? THOMAS OF ERCELDOUNE

c. 1225–*c.* 1300

From *SIR TRISTREM*

1

Tristrem and the Hunters

THE forest was fair and wide,
  With wilde bestes ysprad.
The court was ner bi side;
The palmers thider him lad.
Tristrem hunters seighe ride,
Les of houndes thai ledde;
Thai token in that tide
Of fat hertes yfedde
In feld.
In blehand was he cledde;
The hunters him beheld.

Bestes thai brac and bare,
In quarters thai hem wrought,
Martirs as it ware
That husbond men had bought.
Tristrem tho spac thare
And seyd wonder him thought:—
'Ne seighe Y never are
So wilde best ywrought
At wille.
Other,' he seyd, 'Y can nought,
Or folily ye hem spille.'

ysprad: well-stocked   seighe: saw   les: leash   blehand:
a kind of cloth   brac: broke   hem: them   martirs: cattle
slaughtered at Martinmas for winter provision   tho: then   are:
before   folily: foolishly   spille: kill

Up stode a serjaunt bold
And spac Tristem ogain:—
'We and our elders old,
Thus than have we sain.
Other thou hast ous told:
Yond lith a best unflain,
Atire it as thou wold,
And we wil se ful fain
In feld.'
In lede is nought to lain,
The hunters him biheld.

Tristrem schare the brest,
The tong sat next the pride;
The heminges swithe on est
He schar and layd bi side;
The breche adoun he threst,
He ritt and gan to right;
Boldliche ther nest
Carf he of that hide
Bidene;
The bestes he graithed that tide,
As mani seththen has ben.

The spande was the first brede,
The erber dight he yare,

serjaunt: servant   ogain: against   sain: seen   unflain: not flayed   atire: dress (of the quarry)   lede: people   lain: dispute   schare: cut   pride: spleen   heminges: pieces of deer-hide   swithe: quickly, soon   on est: ? by favour, by grace   threst: thrust   ritt: cut up   right: adjust   nest: next   bidene: at once   graithed: dressed   seththen: since   spande: shoulder   brede: breadth   erber: first stomach of ruminants   dight: prepared   yare: quickly

To the stifles he yede
And even ato hem schare;
He right al the rede,
The wombe oway he bare,
The noubles he yaf to mede.
That seighen that ther ware
Also.
The rigge he croised mare,
The chine he smot atwo.

The forster for his rightes
The left schulder yaf he,
With hert, liver and lightes
And blod tille his quirre;
Houndes on hyde he dightes,
Alle he lete hem se;
The raven he yave his yiftes,
Sat on the fourched tre,
On rowe;
'Hunters, whare be ye?
The tokening schuld ye blowe.'

He tight the mawe on tinde
And eke the gargiloun;
Thai blewen the right kinde
And radde the right roun.
Thai wist the king to finde
And senten forth to toun

---

stifles: kneecaps   yede: went   rede: entrails   noubles:
numbles, internal organs   yaf: gave   mede: reward   rigge:
back   croised: cut across   mare: more   quirre: quarry
dightes: lays out   yiftes: gifts   tokening: horn-call   tight:
fastened   tinde: ? branch   gargiloun: gullet, throat   radde:
set forth   roun: horn-call

And teld him under linde
The best, hou it was boun
And brought.
Marke, the king with croun,
Seyd that feir him thought.

teld: told   linde: lime tree   boun: prepared

ANONYMOUS

14th century

2   *The Death of Alexander*

QUHEN Alexander our kynge was dede,
That Scotlande lede in lauche and le,
Away was sons of alle and brede,
    Off wyne and wax, of gamyn and gle.
Our golde was changit in to lede.
    Crist, borne in virgynyte,
Succoure Scotlande, and ramede,
    That is stade in perplexite.

lauche: law   le: peace, quiet   sons: abundance   alle: ale
gamyn: amusement, mirth

JOHN BARBOUR

c. 1320–1395

From *THE BUIK OF ALEXANDER*

3   *Prologue to the Avowis of Alexander*

IN mery May, quhen medis springis,
  And foullis in the forestis singis,
And nychtingalis thare notis newis,
And flouris spredis on seir kin hewes,
Blew and burnat, blak and bla,
Quhite and yallow, rede alswa,
Purpit, bloncat, pale and pers,
As Kynd thame colouris gevis divers,
And burgeons of thare brancheis bredis,
And woddis winnis thare winfull wedis,
And everilk wy hes welth at waill,
Than ga I boundin all in baill
For ane, the lustyest that is wrocht,
That I have luffit, all lyke hir nocht,
Na never gat thing of my will
Bot tene, ay sen I tuik hir till,
Sa that my travell and my pane
I se weill all is set in vane.
For-thy I will set myne intent
To get lessing of my torment,

newis: renew   on seir kin: in many kinds of   burnat: dark brown   blak: pale   bla: dark blue   alswa: also   bloncat: light blue   pers: blue   Kynd: Nature   burgeons: buds   winfull: pleasant   everilk: every   wy: man   waill: choice   all lyke hir nocht: although (my love) does not please her   till: to   for-thy: therefore   lessing: lessening

For to translait in Inglis leid
Ane romains quhilk that I hard reid,
Of amourus, armis and of droury,
Of knicht-heid and of chevalry.
For wise men sais, he that in wit
Settis his intent and followis it,
It garris him oft-tymes leif foly,
And all murning of musardy.

leid: language   droury: love   garris: causes   musardy:
idle dreaming

From *THE BRUCE*

4   *[Incipit liber]*

Incipit liber compositus per magistrum Ihoannem Barber, Archi-
diaconum Abyrdonensem: de gestis, bellis, et virtutibus domini
Roberti de Brwyss, regis Scocie illustrissimi, et de conquestu regni
Scocie per eundem, et de domino Iacobo de Douglas.

STORYS to rede ar delitabill,
  Suppos that thai be nocht bot fabill;
Than suld storys that suthfast wer,
And thai war said on gud maner,
Have doubill plesance in heryng.
The fyrst plesance is the carpyng,
And the tothir the suthfastnes,
That schawys the thing rycht as it wes;

nocht: nothing   and: if, provided that   carpyng: story,
narrative   schawys: shows

And suth thyngis that ar likand
Tyll mannys heryng, ar plesand.
Tharfor I wald fayne set my will,
Giff my wyt mycht suffice thartill,
To put in wryt a suthfast story,
That it lest ay furth in memory,
Swa that na lenth of tyme it let,
Na ger it haly be foryet.
For aulde storys that men redys,
Representis to thaim the dedys
Of stalwart folk that lyvyt ar,
Rycht as thai than in presence war.
And, certis, thai suld weill have prys
That in thar tyme war wycht and wys,
And led thar lyff in gret travaill,
And oft in hard stour off bataill
Wan richt gret price off chevalry,
And war voydyt off cowardy.
As wes king Robert off Scotland,
That hardy wes off hart and hand;
And gud Schyr James off Douglas,
That in his tyme sa worthy was,
That off hys price & hys bounte
In fer landis renownyt wes he.
Off thaim I thynk this buk to ma;
Now God gyff grace that I may swa
Tret it, and bryng it till endyng,
That I say nocht bot suthfast thing!

likand: pleasing, acceptable giff: provided that thartill: there-to
furth: henceforth swa: so let: hinder, consign to oblivion
ger: cause foryet: forgotten ar: before prys: praise
wycht: rigorous stour: combat price: praise voydyt: free from
ma: make

Quhow the lordis of Scotland tuk the King of Ingland to be
arbitar at the last.

Quhen Alexander the king wes deid,
That Scotland haid to steyr and leid,
The land sex yer, and mayr perfay,
Lay desolat eftyr hys day;
Till that the barnage at the last
Assemblyt thaim, and fayndyt fast
To cheys a king thar land to ster,
That off auncestry cummyn wer
Off kingis, that aucht that reawte,
And mayst had rycht thair king to be.
Bot envy, that is sa feloune,
Amang thaim maid discencioun.
For sum wald haiff the Balleoll king;
For he wes cummyn off the offspryng
Off hyr that eldest systir was.
And othir sum nyt all that cas;
And said, that he thair king suld be
That wes in alsner degre,
And cummyn wes of the neist male,
And in branch collaterale.
Thai said, successioun of kyngrik
Was nocht to lawer feys lik;
For thar mycht succed na female,
Quhill foundyn mycht be ony male
That were in lyne evyn descendand;
Thai bar all othir wayis on hand,

barnage: assembly of barons   fayndyt: attempted   cheys:
choose   aucht: possessed   reawte: royal blood   nyt:
denied   alsner: as near   feys: fiefs   bar . . . on hand: strongly
asserted

For than the neyst cummyn off the seid,
Man or woman, suld succeid.
Be this resoun that part thocht hale,
That the lord off Anandyrdale,
Robert the Brwys, Erle off Carryk,
Aucht to succeid to the kynryk.
The barounys thus war at discord,
That on na maner mycht accord;
Till at the last thai all concordyt,
That all thar spek suld be recordyt
Till Schyr Edward, off Yngland king;
And he suld swer that, but fenyeyng,
He suld that arbytre disclar,
Off thir twa that I tauld off ar,
Quhilk suld succeid to sic a hycht;
And lat him ryng that had the rycht.
This ordynance thaim thocht the best,
For at that tyme wes pes and rest
Betwyx Scotland and Ingland bath;
And thai couth nocht persave the skaith
That towart thaim wes apperand;
For that at the king off Ingland
Held swylk freyndschip and cumpany
To thar king, that wes swa worthy,
Thai trowyt that he, as gud nychtbur,
And as freyndsome compositur,
Wald have jugyt in lawte;
Bot othir wayis all yheid the gle.

Anandyrdale: Annandale aucht: ought kynryk: kingdom
spek: discussion recordyt: reported but fenyeyng: without deceit
disclar: decide thir: those quhilk: which sic: such
hycht: height ryng: reign skaith: harm, injury for that at:
because swylk: such lawte· truth, fidelity yheid: went
gle: game

JOHN BARBOUR

5

[Fredome]

A! FREDOME is a noble thing!
Fredome mays man to haiff liking;
Fredome all solace to man giffis:
He levys at es that frely levys!
A noble hart may haiff nane es,
Na ellys nocht that may him ples,
Gyff fredome failyhe; for fre liking
Is yharnyt our all othir thing.
Na he, that ay has levyt fre,
May nocht knaw weill the propyrte,
The angyr, na the wrechyt dome,
That is couplyt to foule thyrldome.
Bot gyff he had assayit it,
Than all perquer he suld it wyt;
And suld think fredome mar to prys
Than all the gold in warld that is.
Thus contrar thingis evir-mar
Discoveryngis off the tothir ar.
And he that thryll is has nocht his,
All that he has enbandownyt is
Till hys lord, quhat evir he be.
Yheyt has he nocht sa mekill fre
As fre liking to leyve, or do
That at hys hart hym drawis to.
Than mays clerkis questioun,
Quhen thai fall in disputacioun,
That gyff man bad his thryll owcht do,
And in the samyn tym come him to

---

mays: makes   liking: choice   yharnyt: yearned for, desired
our: over, above   angyr: affliction   thyrldome: thralldom
assayit: tried   perquer: by heart, thoroughly   to prys: to be
praised   enbandownyt: subjected   owcht: anything

5

His wyff, and askyt hym hyr det,
Quhethir he his lordis neid suld let,
And pay fryst that he awcht, & syne
Do furth his lordis commandyne;
Or leve onpayit his wyff, and do
It that commaundyt is him to?
I leve all the solucioun
Till thaim that ar off mar renoun.
Bot sen thai mak sic comperyng
Betwix the dettis off wedding,
And lordis bidding till his threll;
Ye may weile se, thoucht nane yow tell,
How hard a thing that threldome is;
For men may weile se, that ar wys,
That wedding is the hardest band
That ony man may tak on hand.
And thryldome is weill wer than deid;
For quhill a thryll his lyff may leid,
It merrys him, body and banys;
And dede anoyis him bot anys.
Schortly to say, is nane can tell
The halle condicioun off a threll.

det: debt, conjugal rights   fryst: first   comperyng: com-
parison   merrys: harms

6   *[Before Bannockburn]*

I

THE worthy kyng, quhen he has seyn
   His host assemblit all bedeyn,
And saw thame wilfull to fulfill
His liking, with gud hert and will;

bedeyn: at once

And to maynteym weill thair franchis,
He wes rejosit on mony wis;
And callit all his consell preve,
And said thame, 'lordingis, now ye se
That Ynglis men with mekill mycht
Has all disponit thame for the ficht,
For thai yon castell wald reskew.
Tharfor is gud we ordane now
How we may let thame of purpos,
And swa to thame the wayis clos,
That thai pas nocht but gret lettying.
We haf heir with us at byddyng
Weill thretty thousand men and ma.
Mak we four battalis of all thai,
And ordane us on sic maner,
That, quhen our fayis cummys neir,
We till the New Park hald our way ;
For thair behufis thaim pas, perfay,
Bot gif that thai beneth us ga,
And our the marras pas; and swa
We sall be at avantage thair.
For me think that richt speidfull war
To gang on fut to this fechting,
Armyt bot in-to licht armyng.
For schupe we us on hors to ficht,
Syn that our fais ar mar of mycht,
And bettir horsit than ar we,
We suld in-to gret perell be.
And gif we ficht on fut, perfay
At avantage we sall be ay;

franchis: freedom   consell preve: Privy Council   disponit: disposed
but gret lettyng: without great hindrance   ma: more   battalis:
battalions, hosts   marras: morass, marsh   speidfull: advantageous
schupe: attempted

For in the park emang the treis
The hors men alwais cummerit beis,
And the sykis alswa thair doune
Sall put thame to confusioune.'
All thai consentit to that saw,
And than, in-till ane litill thraw,
Thair four battalis ordanit thai;
And to the erll Thomas, perfay,
He gaf the vaward in leding;
For in his nobill governyng
And in his hye chevelry
Thai had assouerans, trast trewly!
And, for to maynteym his baner,
Lordis that of gret worschip wer
War assignit with thair menye,
In-till his battale for till be.
The tothir battale wes gevin to lede
Till hym that douchty wes of dede,
And prisit of gret chevelry,
That wes schir Edward the worthy;
I trow he sall manteyme him swa,
That how sa evir the gammyn ga,
His fayis to plenye sall mater haf.
And syne the thrid battale he gaf
To Waltir Stewart for to leid,
And till Douglas douchty of deid.
Thai war cosyngis in neir degre,
Tharfor till hym betaucht wes he,
For he wes young; and, nocht-for-thi,
I trow he sall sa manfully

---

cummerit: encumbered   sykis: trenches   thraw: throw, space of
time   assouerans: assurance   menye: company   gammyn:
game   plenye: complain   betaucht: committed

Do his devour, and wirk so weill,
That hym sall neyd no mair yeymseill.
The ferd battale the nobill kyng
Tuk till hym-self in governyng,
And had in-till his company
The men of Carryk all halely,
And of Argile and of Kentyre,
And of the Ylis, quhar-off wes syre
Angus of Ylis and But, all tha.
He of the playne-land had alswa
Of armyt men ane mekill rout;
His battale stalward wes and stout.
He said, the rerward he wald ma,
And evyn forrouth hym suld ga
The vaward, and on athir hand
The tothir battalis suld be gangand
Behynd, on syde a litell space;
And the kyng, that behynd thaim was,
Suld se quhar thair war mast mystir,
And relief thaim with his baneir.

devour: duty   yeymseill: tutoring, supervision   syre: lord
tha: those   forrouth: before   mystir: need

7   *[Before Bannockburn]*

II

'LORDYNGIS,' he said, 'we aucht to luf
Almychty God that sittis abuf,
That sendis us so fair begynnyng.
It is ane gret disconfortyng
Till our fais, that on this wis

luf: praise

14

Sa soyn reboytit has beyn twis.
For quhen thai of thair host sall heir,
And knaw suthly on quhat maneir
Thair avaward, that wes so stout,
And syne yon othir joly rout—
That I trow of the best men war
That thai mycht get emang thame thar—
War reboytit so suddandly,
I trow, and knawis it all cleirly,
That mony ane hert sall waverand be
That semyt ere of gret bounte.
And fra the hert be discumfite,
The body is nocht worth a myt.
Thar-for I trow that gud ending
Sall follow till our begynnyng.
The quhethir I say nocht this you till,
For that ye suld follow my will
To ficht, for in you sall all be;
For gif ye think spedfull that we
Fecht, we sall ficht; and gif ye will
We leiff, your liking to fulfill,
I sall consent on alkyn wis
Till do richt as yhe will devis;
Tharfor sais on your will planly.'
Than with ane voce all can thai cry—
'Gud king, forouten mair delay,
To-morn, als soyn as ye se day,
Ordane yow haill for the battale,
For dout of ded we sall nocht fale;
Na nane payn sall refusit be
Till we have maid our cuntre fre.'

reboytit: repulsed   avaward: vanguard   the quhethir: nevertheless   spedfull: advantageous   alkyn: every   forouten:
without   dout: fear

Quhen the king herd thaim so manly
Spek to the ficht and hardely,
Saying, that nouther life nor dead
To sik discomfort sould them lead
That they sould eschew the feghting,
In heart he had great rejoycing;
In hert gret gladschip can he ta,
And said, 'lordyngis, sen ye will sa,
Schapis tharfor in the mornyng
Swa that we, be the sonne-rysing,
Haf herd mes, and be buskit weill,
Ilk man in-till his awne yscheill,
Without the palyownys arayit,
In battale with baneris displayit.
And luk yhe na way brek aray;
And, as ye luf me, I you pray,
That ilk man for his awne honour
Purvay hym a gud baneour.
And quhen it cummys to the ficht,
Ilk man set his hert and mycht
To stynt our fais mekill pryd.
On hors thai sall arayit ryd,
And cum on you in weill gret hy;
Meit thame with speris hardely,
And wreik on thame the mekill ill
That thai and tharis has done us till,
And ar in will yeit for till do,
Gif thai haf mycht till cum thar-to.
And, certis, me think weill that we,
For-out abasyng, aucht till be

ta: take	schapis: contrive	buskit: prepared	yscheill:
squadron	without: outside	palyownys: tents	baneour:
banner-bearer	stynt: stop, stay	in weill gret hy: in very great haste,	
with great fury	for-out abasyng: without cowardice		

JOHN BARBOUR

Worthy and of gret vassalage;
For we have thre gret avantage.
The first is, that we haf the richt;
And for the richt ilk man suld ficht.
The tothir is, thai ar cummyn heir,
For lypnyng in thair gret power,
To seik us in our awne land,
And has broucht her, richt till our hand,
Riches in-to so gret plentee,
That the pouerest of you sall be
Bath rych and mychty thar-with-all,
Gif that we wyn, as weill may fall.
The thrid is, that we for our lyvis
And for our childer and our wifis,
And for the fredome of our land,
Ar strenyeit in battale for to stand,
And thai for thair mycht anerly,
And for thai leit of us lichtly,
And for thai wald distroy us all,
Mais thame to ficht; bot yet ma fall
That thai sall rew thar barganyng.
And, certis, I warne you of a thing,
To happyn thame (as God forbeid!)
Till fynd fantis in-till our deid,
Swa that thai wyn us oppynly,
Thai sall haf of us no mercy.
And sen we knaw thar felloune will,
Me think it suld accorde till skill
To set stoutnes agane felony,
And mak swagat ane juperdy.

---

worthy: brave   vassalage: prowess   lypnyng: trust
strenyeit: constrained   anerly: only   leit: think   fantis:
cowardice   skill: reason   felony: cruelty   swagat: thus
juperdy: bold attempt

17

Quharfor I you requeir and pray
That, with all mycht that evir ye may,
Yhe pres you at the begynnyng,
But cowardis or abaysyng,
To meit thame that first sall assemmyll
So stoutly that the henmast trymmyll.
And menys on your gret manheid,
Your worschip and your douchty deid,
And of the joy that yhe abyd,
Gif that us fallis, as weill may tyd,
Hap to vencus the gret battale.
In-till your handis, for-outen faill,
Ye ber honour, pris, and riches,
Fredome, welth, and gret blithnes
Gif ye conteyn you manfully;
And the contrar all halely
Sall fall, gif yhe let cowardis
And wikkidnes your hertis suppris.
Yhe mycht haf lifit in-to thrildome;
Bot, for ye yarnit till haf fredome,
Yhe ar assemblit heir with me;
Tharfor is neidfull that yhe be
Worthy and wicht, but abaysyng.

but: without   assemmyll: advance to battle   menys on:
remember

ANDREW OF WYNTOUN

c. 1350—c. 1425

8

Macbeth

IN till this tyme that I of tell,
That this tressoune in Ingland fell,
In Scotland fell neire the like cais
Be Fynlaw Makbeth that than was,
Quhen he had murtherist his aune eme
Throu hope at he had of a dreme,
That he saw forow that in sleping,
Quhen he wes dwelland with the king,
That tretit him fairely and weill
In all that langit him ilk deill;
Becaus he wes his sister sone,
His yarnying oft he gert be done.

A nycht him thocht in his dremyng
That he wes sittand neire the king,
At a seit in hunting swa,
And in a lesche had grewhundis twa.
Him thocht, till he wes sa sittand,
He saw thre women by gangand,
And thai thre women than thocht he
Thre werd sisteris like to be.
The first he herd say gangand by:
'Lo, yonder the thayne of Crumbaghty!'
The tother sister said agane:
'Off Murray yonder I see the thayne.'

eme: uncle   at: that, which   forow: before   langit:
pertained to   ilk deill: in every way   werd sisteris: witches
(? fates)   Crumbaghty: Cromarty

The thrid said: 'Yonder I se the king.'
All this herd he in his dremyng.
Sone efter that, in his youth heid,
Off thai thayndomes he thayne wes maid;
Than thocht he nixt for to be king,
Fra Duncanis dais had tane ending.

   And thus the fantasy of this dreme
Muffit him for to sla his eme,
As he did falsly in deid,
As ye have herd befor this reid;
Syne with his awne emys wif
He lay, and with hir led his lif,
And held hir baith his wif and quene,
Rycht as scho forouth that had bene
Till his eme the king liffand,
Quhen he wes king with croune regnand
For litill taill that tyme gaif he
Off the greis of affinite.
And thusgatis quhen his eme wes dede,
He succedit in his steid,
And xvii. winter wes regnand
As king with croune in till Scotland.
Yit in his tyme thar wes plente
Off gold and silver, catall and fee.
He wes in justice rycht lauchfull,
And till his liegis rycht awfull.
Quhen Leo the tend wes pape of Rome,
In pilgrimage thidder he come,
And in almus he sew silver
To pure folkis that had gret mistere;
Yit usit he oftsys to wirk
Proffitably till haly kirk;

forouth: before	taill: account	greis: degrees	awfull:
imposing	sew: sowed, scattered	mistere: need	oftsys: often

Bot as we fynd in his storyis
That he wes gottin on selcouth wis.

His moder to woddis wald oft repair
For the delite of hailsum aire.
Sa, as scho went apon a day
To wod all be hir ane to play,
Scho met of cais with a faire man,
Never nane sa faire, as scho thocht than,
Sa mekle, sa strang, sa faire by sycht,
Scho never nane befor, I hecht,
Proportiound weill in all mesour,
Off lyme and lyth a faire figour.
In sic aquayntans thare thai fell
That, schortly tharof for to tell,
Thare in thare gamyn and thare play
That persone by that woman lay,
And on hir that tyme a sone gat,
This Makbeth, that efter that
Grew to gret stait and to hicht,
And to gret powere and to mycht,
As befor ye haif herd said.
And fra this persone had with hir plaid,
And had the jurnay with hir done,
And gottin had on hir a sone,
He said he a devill wes at him gat,
And bad hir nocht be fleit of that,
For he said at his sone suld be
A man of hie stait and pouste,
And na man suld be borne of wif
Off power to reif him his lif;

---

selcouth: strange   of cais: by chance   hecht: promise   lyth:
limb, joint   jurnay: journey   fleit: frightened   pouste:
power   reif: rob

And thare apon in takynnyng
He gaif his lemman thare a ring,
And bad at scho suld keip it weill,
And for his luf had that joweill.
And efter that oft usit he
To deill with hir in prevate,
And tald hir mony things suld fall
That scho trowit suld haif bene all.

JAMES I

1394–1437

From *THE KINGIS QUAIR*

9 [*Stanzas 1–13*]

HEIGH in the hevynnis figure circulere
   The rody sterres twynklyng as the fyre;
And, in Aquary, Citherea the clere
   Rynsid hir tressis like the goldin wyre,
   That late tofore, in fair and fresche atyre,
Through Capricorn heved hir hornis bright;
North northward approchit the mydnyght:

Quhen as I lay in bed allone waking,
   New partit out of slepe a lyte tofore,
Fell me to mynd of many divers thing,
   Off this and that; can I noght say quharfore,
   Bot slepe for craft in erth myght I no more;
For quhich as tho coude I no better wyle,
Bot toke a boke to rede apon a quhile:

late tofore: not long before   mydnyght: meridian   lyte:
little   for craft: by any contrivance   coude: knew

Off quhich the name is clepit properly
  Boece, efter him that was the compiloure,
Schewing counsele of philosophye
  Compilit by that noble senatoure
  Off Rome, quhilom that was the warldis floure,
And from estate by fortune a quhile
Forjugit was to povert in exile:

And there to here this worthy lord and clerk,
  His metir swete, full of moralitee;
His flourit pen so fair he set awerk,
  Discryving first of his prosperitee,
  And out of that his infelicitee;
And than how he, in his poetly report,
In philosophy can him to confort.

For quhich thogh I in purpos at my boke
  To borowe a slepe at thilke tyme began,
Or ever I stent my best was more to loke
  Upon the writing of this noble man,
  That in himself the full recover wan
Off his infortune, povert, and distress,
And in tham set his verray sekerness.

And so the vertew of his youth before
  Was in his age the ground of his delytis:
Fortune the bak him turnyt, and therfore
  He makith joye and confort that he quit is
  Off their unsekir warldis appetitis;
And so aworth he takith his penance,
And of his vertew maid it suffisance:

clepit: called   Boece: Boethius (A.D. 480–524)   forjugit:
condemned   discryving . . . of: describing   poetly: poetical
can: began   borowe: i.e. produce   stent: stopped   best: best
course   sekerness: security   aworth: at its worth, for what it is worth

With mony a noble resoun, as him likit,
   Enditing in his fair Latyne tong,
So full of fruyte and rethorikly pykit,
   Quhich to declare my scole is over yong;
   Therefore I lat him pas, and, in my tong,
Procede I will agayn to my sentence
Off my mater, and leve all incidence.

The long nyght beholding, as I saide,
   Myn eyne gan to smert for studying;
My buke I schet, and at my hede it laide;
   And doun I lay bot ony tarying,
   This mater new in my mynd rolling;
This is to seyne, how that eche estate,
As fortune lykith, thame will translate.

For sothe it is, that, on hir tolter quhele,
   Every wight cleverith in his stage,
And failyng foting oft, quhen hir lest rele,
   Sum up, sum doun; is non estate nor age
   Ensured, more the prynce than the page:
So uncouthly hir werdes sche devidith,
Namly in youth, that seildin ought providith.

Among thir thoughtis rolling to and fro,
   Fell me to mynd of my fortune and ure;
In tender youth how sche was first my fo
   And eft my frende, and how I gat recure

as him likit: as it pleased him   rethorikly pykit: rhetorically
embellished   my scole is over yong: i.e. my rhetorical training is in-
sufficiently advanced   sentence: main subject-matter   bot ony tarying:
without any delay   translate: transform   tolter: tottery   cleverith:
climbs   stage: rank, position   uncouthly: strangely   werdes:
fates   devidith: allots   namly: especially   providith: foresees
ure: fate

Off my distress, and all myn aventure
I gan ourhayle, that langer slepe ne rest
Ne myght I nat, so were my wittis wrest.

Forwakit and forwalowit, thus musing,
  Wery, forlyin, I lestnyt sodaynlye,
And sone I herd the bell to matyns ryng,
  And up I ras, no langer wald I lye:
  Bot now, how trowe ye? suich a fantasye
Fell me to mynd, that ay me thoght the bell
Said to me, 'Tell on, man, quhat the befell.'

Thoght I tho to myself, 'quhat may this be?
  This is myn awin ymagynacioun;
It is no lyf that spekis unto me;
  It is a bell, or that impressioun
  Off my thoght causith this illusioun,
That dooth me think so nycely in this wis:'
And so befell as I schall you devis.

Determyt furth therewith in myn entent,
  Sen I thus have ymagynit of this soun,
And in my tyme more ink and paper spent
  To lyte effect, I tuke conclusioun
  Sum new thing to write; I set me doun,
And furthwithall my pen in hand I tuke,
And maid a ✠, and thus begouth my buke.

---

ourhayle: think over   forwakit: tired with being awake   forwalowit: tired with tossing about   matyns: mattins (sung at
2 a.m.)   lyf: person   nycely: foolishly   devis: tell

[*Stanzas 22–45*]

NOGHT fer passit the state of innocence,
   Bot nere about the nowmer of yeris thre,
Were it causit throu hevinly influence
   Off Goddis will, or othir casualtee,
   Can I noght say; bot out of my contree,
By thair avis that had of me the cure,
Be see to pas tuke I myn aventure.

Purvait of all that was us necessarye,
   With wynd at will, up airly by the morowe,
Streight unto schip, no longer wold we tarye,
   The way we tuke, the tyme I tald to-forowe;
   With mony 'fare wele' and 'Sanct Johne to borowe'
Off falowe and frende; and thus with one assent
We pullit up saile, and furth oure wayis went.

Upon the wavis weltering to and fro,
   So infortunate was us that fremyt day,
That maugre, playnly, quhethir we wold or no,
   With strong hand, by fors, schortly to say,
   Off inymyis takin and led away
We weren all, and broght in thair contree;
Fortune it schupe non othir wayis to be.

Quhare as in strayte ward and in strong prisoun,
   So fer forth of my lyf the hevy lyne,
Without confort, in sorowe abandoun,
   The secund sister lukit hath to twyne,
   Nere by the space of yeris twis nyne;

state of innocence: the first seven years of life   casualtee: cause
to-forowe: before   Sanct Johne to borowe: Saint John be your protection   fremyt: unlucky   maugre: in spite of, no matter
the secund sister: Lachesis, the second Fate   twyne: twist, spin

Till Jupiter his merci list advert,
And send confort in relesche of my smert.

Quhare as in ward full oft I wold bewaille
  My dedely lyf, full of peyne and penance,
Saing ryght thus, quhat have I gilt to faille
  My fredome in this warld and my plesance?
  Sen every wight has thereof suffisance,
That I behold, and I a creature
Put from all this—hard is myn aventure!

The bird, the beste, the fisch eke in the see,
  They lyve in fredome everich in his kynd;
And I a man, and lakkith libertee;
  Quhat schall I seyne, quhat resoun may I fynd,
  That fortune suld do so? thus in my mynd
My folk I wold argewe, bot all for noght:
Was non that myght, that on my peynes rought.

Than wold I say, 'Gif God me had devisit
  To lyve my lyf in thraldome thus and pyne,
Quhat was the caus that he me more comprisit
  Than othir folk to lyve in swich ruyne?
  I suffer allone amang the figuris nyne,
Ane wofull wrecche that to no wight may spede,
And yit of every lyvis help hath nede.'

The long dayes and the nyghtis eke
  I wold bewaille my fortune in this wis,

---

advert: turn towards (me)   relesche: relief   quhat have I
gilt: how have I sinned   to faille: lose   comprisit: laid
hold of   amang the figuris nyne: i.e. (probably) 'among the multitude of other creatures'

For quhich, agane distress confort to seke,
   My custum was on mornis for to rys
   Airly as day; o happy exercis!
By thee come I to joye out of turment.
Bot now to purpos of my first entent:

Bewailing in my chamber thus allone,
   Despeired of all joye and remedye,
Fortirit of my thoght and wo begone,
   Unto the wyndow gan I walk in hye,
   To se the warld and folk that went forby;
As for the tyme, though I of mirthis fude
Myght have no more, to luke it did me gude.

Now was there maid fast by the touris wall
   A gardyn fair, and in the corneris set
Ane herber grene with wandis long and small
   Railit about; and so with treis set
   Was all the place, and hawthorn hegis knet,
That lyf was non walking there forby,
That myght within scars ony wight aspye.

So thik the bewis and the leves grene
   Beschadit all the aleyes that there were,
And myddis every herber myght be sene
   The scharp grene suete jenepere,
   Growing so fair with branchis here and there,
That, as it semyt to a lyf without,
The bewis spred the herber all about;

And on the small grene twistis sat
   The lytill swete nyghtingale, and song

hye: haste   herber: arbour   twistis: twigs

So loud and clere the ympnis consecrat
  Off lufis use, now soft, now loud among,
    That all the gardyng and the wallis rong
Ryght of thair song, and on the copill next
Off thair suete armony, and lo the text:

Cantus

'Worschippe, ye that loveris bene, this May,
  For of your bliss the kalendis ar begonne,
And sing with us, away, winter, away!
  Cum, somer, cum, the swete sesoun and sonne!
  Awake for schame that have your hevynnis wonne,
And amorously lift up your hedis all,
Thank lufe that list you to his merci call.'

Quhen thai this song had song a lytill thrawe,
  Thai stent a quhile, and therewith unaffraid,
As I beheld and kest myn eyne alawe,
  From beugh to beugh thay hippit and thai plaid,
  And freschly in thair birdis kynd arraid
Thair fetheris new, and fret thame in the sonne,
And thankit lufe, that had thair makis wonne.

This was the plane ditee of thair note,
  And therewithall unto myself I thoght,
'Quhat lyf is this, that makis birdis dote?
  Quhat may this be, how cummyth it of ought?
  Quhat nedith it to be so dere ybought?

ympnis: hymns   among: at intervals   copill: couplet,
stanza   kalendis: first day   thrawe: time   stent: stopped
alawe: down   hippit: hopped   fret: preened   makis:
mates

It is nothing, trowe I, bot feynit chere,
And that men list to counterfeten chere.'

Eft wald I think; 'O Lord, quhat may this be?
　That lufe is of so noble myght and kynde,
Lufing his folk, and swich prosperitee
　Is it of him, as we in bukis fynd?
　May he oure hertes setten and unbynd?
Hath he upon oure hertis swich maistrye?
Or all this is bot feynyt fantasye!

For gif he be of so grete excellence,
　That he of every wight hath cure and charge,
Quhat have I gilt to him or doon offens,
　That I am thrall, and birdis gone at large,
　Sen him to serve he myght set my corage?
And gif he be noght so, than may I seyne,
Quhat makis folk to jangill of him in veyne?

Can I noght elles fynd, bot gif that he
　Be Lord, and as a God may lyve and regne,
To bynd and lous, and maken thrallis free,
　Than wold I pray his blisfull grace benigne,
　To hable me unto his service digne;
And evermore for to be one of tho
Him trewly for to serve in wele and wo.'

And therewith kest I doun myn eye ageyne,
　Quhare as I sawe, walking under the tour,
Full secretly new cummyn hir to pleyne,
　The fairest or the freschest yong floure
　That ever I sawe, me thoght, before that houre,

seyne: say　　　　hable: fit, make competent　　　digne: worthy
pleyne: play, amuse herself

For quhich sodayn abate, anon astert,
The blude of all my body to my hert.

And though I stude abaisit tho a lyte
  No wonder was, forquhy my wittis all
Were so overcom with plesance and delyte,
  Onely throu latting of myn eyen fall,
  That sudaynly my hert become hir thrall
For ever of free wyll; for of manace
There was no takyn in hir suete face.

And in my hede I drewe ryght hastily,
  And eftsones I lent it forth ageyne,
And sawe hir walk, that verray womanly,
  With no wight mo bot onely women tweyne.
  Than gan I studye in myself and seyne,
'A! swete, ar ye a warldly creature,
Or hevinly thing in likeness of nature?

Or ar ye god Cupidis owin princesse,
  And cummyn ar to lous me out of band?
Or ar ye verray Nature the goddess,
  That have depaynted with your hevinly hand
  This gardyn full of flouris, as they stand?
Quhat sall I think, allace! quhat reverence
Sall I minster to your excellence?

Gif ye a goddess be, and that ye like
  To do me payne, I may it noght astert;
Gif ye be warldly wight, that dooth me sike,
  Quhy lest God mak you so, my derrest hert,
  To do a sely prisoner thus smert,
That lufis you all, and wote of noght bot wo?
And therefore, merci, swete! sen it is so.'

abate: drew away   astert: returned   manace: threat
takyn: token   astert: escape   that dooth me sike: who causes me
to sigh

11 **[*Stanzas 152–165*]**

QUHARE, in a lusty plane, tuke I my way,
    Endlang a ryver, plesant to behold,
Enbroudin all with fresche flouris gay,
    Quhare, throu the gravel, bryght as ony gold,
    The cristall water ran so clere and cold,
That in myn ere maid contynualy
A maner soun, mellit with armony;

That full of lytill fischis by the brym,
    Now here, now there, with bakkis blewe as lede,
Lap and playit, and in a rout can swym
    So prattily, and dressit tham to sprede
    Thair curall fynnis, as the ruby rede,
That in the sonne on thair scalis bryght
As gesserant ay glitterit in my sight:

And by this ilke ryversyde alawe
    Ane hye way fand I like to bene,
On quhich, on every syde, a long rawe
    Off treis saw I, full of levis grene,
    That full of fruyte delitable were to sene,
And also, as it come unto my mind,
Off bestis sawe I mony divers kynd:

The lyoun king, and his fere lyonesse;
    The pantere, like unto the smaragdyne;
The lytill squerell, full of besyness;
    The slawe as, the druggar beste of pyne;
    The nyce ape; the werely porpapyne;

enbroudin: embroidered	mellit: mingled	curall: coral
gesserant: armour	fere: companion, mate	smaragdyne: emerald
druggar: drudger = drudging	nyce: foolish	werely: warlike

The percyng lynx; the lufare unicorne,
That voidis venym with his evour horne.

There sawe I dress him new out of haunt
   The fery tiger, full of felonye;
The dromydare; the standar oliphant;
   The wyly fox the wedowis inemye;
   The clymbare gayte; the elk for alblastrye;
The herknere bore; the holsum grey for hortis;
The hair also, that oft gooth to the wortis.

The bugill, drawar by his hornis grete;
   The martrik, sable, the foynyee, and mony mo;
The chalk-quhite ermyn, tippit as the jete;
   The riall hert, the conyng, and the ro;
   The wolf, that of the murthir noght say 'ho!'
The lesty bever, and the ravin bare;
For chamelot the camel full of hare;

With mony an othir beste divers and strange,
   That cummyth noght as now unto my mynd.
Bot now to purpos—straucht furth the range
   I held a way, ourhailing in my mynd
   From quhens I come, and quhare that I suld fynd
Fortune, the goddess, unto quhom in hye
Gude Hope, my gyde, has led me sodeynly.

And at the last, behalding thus asyde,
   A round place wallit have I found;
In myddis quhare eftsone I have spide

---

voidis: drives out   gayte: goat   alblastrye: cross-bow archery
herknere: hearkening   grey: badger   hortis: hurts, wounds
bugill: ox   martrik: marten   foynyee: beech-marten   conyng:
rabbit   chamelot: cloth of hair   ourhailing: going over

Fortune, the goddess, hufing on the ground;
   And ryght before hir fete, of compas round,
A quhele, on quhich clevering I sye
A multitude of folk before myn eye.

And ane surcote sche werit long that tyde,
   That semyt to me of divers hewis,
Quhilum thus, quhen sche wald turn asyde,
   Stude this goddess of fortune and of glewis;
   A chapellet with mony fresche anewis
Sche had upon her hed; and with this hong
A mantill on hir schuldris, large and long,

That furrit was with ermyn full quhite,
   Degoutit with the self in spottis blake:
And quhilum in hir chier thus a lyte
   Louring sche was; and thus sone it would slake,
   And sodeynly a maner smylyng make,
And sche were glad; at one contenance
Sche held noght, bot ay in variance.

And underneth the quhele sawe I there
   Ane ugly pit depe as ony helle,
That to behald thereon I quoke for fere;
   Bot o thing herd I, that quho therein fell
   Com no more up agane tidingis to telle;
Off quhich, astonait of that ferefull syght,
I ne wist quhat to done, so was I fricht.

Bot for to se the sudayn weltering
   Off that ilk quhele, that sloppar was to hold,
   It semyt unto my wit a strong thing,

hufing: waiting	clevering: climbing	glewis: destinies
anewis: rings, small wreaths	degoutit: spotted	sloppar:
slippery		

JAMES I

So mony I sawe that than clymben wold,
  And failit foting, and to ground were rold;
And othir eke, that sat abone on hye,
Were overthrawe in twinklyyng of an eye.

And on the quhele was lytill void space,
  Wele nere ourstraught fro lawe to hye;
And they were war that long sat in place,
  So tolter quhilum did sche it to-wrye;
  There was bot clymbe and ryght dounward hye,
And sum were eke that fallyng had sore,
Therefore to clymbe thair corage was no more.

I sawe also that, quhere sum were slungin,
  Be quhirlyng of the quhele, into the ground,
Full sudaynly sche hath up ythrungin,
  And set thame on agane full sauf and sound:
  And ever I sawe a new swarm abound,
That to clymbe upward upon the quhele,
In stede of thame that myght no langer rele.

ourstraught: straight over   to-wrye: turn about   ythrungin:
thrust   rele: roll

SIR RICHARD HOLLAND

? 1420–? 1485

12   *From The Buke of the Howlat*

THE roye Robert the Bruss the rayke he avowit,
   With all the hart that he had, to the haily graif;
Syne quhen the dait of his deid derfly him dowit,
With lordis of Scotland, lerit, and the laif,
As worthy, wysest to waile, in worschipe allowit,
To James lord Douglas thou the gre gaif,
To ga with the kingis hart; thairwith he nocht growit
Bot said to his soverane: 'So me God saif!
Your gret giftis and grant ay graciouss I fand;
Bot now it movis all ther maist,
That your hart nobillast
To me is closit and cast,
Throw your command.

'I love you mair for that loiss ye lippyn me till,
Than ony lordschipe or land, so me our Lord leid!
I sall waynd for no wye to wirk as ye will,
At wiss, gif my werd wald, with you to the deid.'

---

rayke: pilgrimage   avowit: vowed   haily graif: Holy
Sepulchre   syne: then   dait: destiny   deid: death   derfly:
sternly   dowit: saddened   lerit: learned (the clerks)   laif:
rest of the people   waile: choose   allowit: commended
gre: honour   ga: go   growit: shuddered   fand: found
all ther maist: most of all   cast: encased   loiss: honour
lippyn: entrust   me till: to me   waynd: hesitate   wye: man
wiss: (your) wish   werd: fate   wald: would

SIR RICHARD HOLLAND

Thar with he lowtit full lawe; tham lykit full ill,
Baith lordis and ladyis, that stude in the steid.
Off commoun nature the courss be kynd to fulfill,
The gud king gaif the gaist to God for to reid;
In Cardross that crownit closit his end.
Now God for his gret grace,
Set his saull in solace!
And we will speike of Douglace,
Quhat way he couth wend.

The hert costlye he couth clos in a cler cace,
And held all hale the behest he hecht to the king:
Come to the haly graf, throw Goddis gret grace,
With offerandis and urisons, and all uthar thing;
Our Salvatouris sepultur, and the samyn place,
Quhar he raiss, as we reid, richtuiss to ryng;
With all the relykis raith, that in that roume was,
He gart hallowe the hart, and syne couth it hyng,
About his hals full hende, and on his awne hart.
Oft wald he kiss it, and cry:
'O flour of all chevalry!
Quhy leif I, allace! quhy?
And thou deid art!'

'My deir,' quoth the Douglass, 'art thou deid dicht!
My singuler soverane, of Saxonis the wand!
Now bot I semble for thy saull with Sarazenis mycht,
Sall I never sene be into Scotland!'

---

lowtit: bowed tham lykit ... ill: they were displeased steid:
place kynd (be kynd): of nature reid: judge couth
(wend): did (go) hecht: promised urisons: orisons
samyn: same ryng: reign raith: quickly gart: made
hals: neck hende: respectfully leif: live dicht: put
wand: rod, scourge semble: assemble, meet

Thus in defence of the faith he fure to the fecht,
With knychtis of Christindome to kepe his command.
And quhen the batallis so brym, brathly and bricht,
War joyned thraly in thrang, mony thousand,
Amang the hethin men the hert hardely he slang,
Said: 'Wend on as thou was wont,
Throw the batell in bront,
Ay formast in the front,
Thy fays amang.

'And I sall followe the in faith, or feye to be fellit;
As thy lege man leile, my lyking thou art.'
Thar with on Mahownis men manly he mellit,
Braid throw the battallis in bront, and bur thaim backwart.
The wyis quhar the wicht went war in wa wellit;
Was nane so stur in the steid micht stand him a start.
Thus frayis he the falss folk, trewly to tell it,
Aye quhil he coverit and come to the kingis hart.
Thus feile feildis he wan, aye worschipand it.
Throwout Cristindome kid
War the deidis that he did;
Till on a time it betid,
As tellis the writ.

batallis: bodies of troops   brym: strong   brathly: strong,
impetuous   thraly: fiercely   feye: (be) doomed   mellit:
joined in battle   braid: sprang, rushed   bront: onset
wyis: men   wellit: plunged   stur: strong   steid: place, spot
(battle-field)   start: moment   frayis: frightens, terrifies
coverit: gained ground   feile: many   kid: known

ANONYMOUS

15th Century

13   *King Berdok (? c. 1450)*

SYM of Lyntoun, be the ramis horn,
   Quhen Phebus rang in sing of Capricorn,
And the mone wes past the gussis cro,
Thair fell in France ane jeperdie forlo,
Be the grit king of Babilon, Berdok,
That dwelt in symmer in till ane bowkaill stok;
And into winter, quhen the frostis ar fell,
He dwelt for cauld in till a cokkil schell:
Kingis usit nocht to weir clayis in tha dayis,
Bot yeid naikit, as myne auctor sayis;
Weill cowd he play in clarschocht and on lute,
And bend ane aiprim bow, and nipschot schute;
He wes ane stalwart man of hairt and hand;
He wowit the golk sevin yeir, of Maryland,
Mayiola, and scho wes bot yeiris thre,
Ane bony bird, and had bot ane e;
Nevirtheless king Berdok luvit hir weill,
For hir foirfute wes langar than hir heill.
The king Berdok he fure our se and land,
To reveis Mayok the golk of Maryland,
And nane with him bot ane bow and ane bowtt;
Syne hapnit him to cum amang the nowtt,

rang: reigned   sing: sign   gussis: a young sow   cro: pen
forlo: forlorn, unlucky; ? furlough   bowkaill: cabbage   clayis:
clothes   clarschocht: clarsach   aiprim: ? apron   nipschot:
backwards   wowit: wooed   golk: cuckoo   bowtt: bolt
nowtt: cattle

And as this Berdok about him cowd espy,
He saw Mayok milkand hir muderis ky,
And in ane creill upoun his bak hir kest;
Quhen he come hame it wes ane howlat nest,
Full of skait birdis, and than this Berdok grett,
And ran agane Meyok for to gett.
The king of Fary hir fader then blew out,
And socht Berdok all the land about,
And Berdok fled in till a killogy;
Thair wes no grace bot gett him or ellis die;
Thair wes the kingis of Pechtis and Portingaill,
The king of Naippillis and Navern alhaill.
With bowis and brandis with segis they umbeset him,
Sum bad tak, sum slay, sum bad byd quhill thay get him;
Thay stellit gunis to the killogy laich,
And proppit gunis with bulettis of raw daich:
Than Jupiter prayit to god Saturn,
In liknes of ane tod he wald him turn;
Bot sone the gratiouss god Mercurius
Turnit Berdok in till ane braikane bus;
And quhen thay saw the bus waig to and fra,
Thay trowd it wes ane gaist, and thay to ga:
Thir fell kingis thus Berdok wald haif slane,
All this for lufe, luvaris sufferis pane,
Boece said, of poyettis that wes flour,
Thocht lufe be sweit, oft syis it is full sour.

howlat: owl   skait birdis: Richardson's skua   grett: wept
killogy: the open space in front of the fireplace in a kiln   umbeset:
besieged   stellit: placed, set   laich: low   proppit: primed
daich: dough   tod: fox   fell: murderous   Boece: Boethius
syis: times

14   From *Colkelbie Sow* (? *c.* 1450)

THE penny lost in the lak
   Wes fundin and uptak,
And he that fand it did by
With the samyn penny
A littill pig for his prow
Off Kolkelbeis sow.
A harlot wynnit neir by,
And scho wald mak a mangery,
And had no substance at all
Bot this pur pig stall,
To furnis a gret feist,
Withouttin stufe, bot this beist.
And yit scho callit to hir cheir
On apostita freir,
A perverst perdonair
And practand palmair,
A wich and a wobstare,
A milygant and a mychare,
A fond fule, a fariar,
A cairtar, a cariar,
A libbar and a lyar,
And riddill revar,
A Tuttivillus, a tutlar,
And a fanyeit flatterar,
A forfarn falconar,
A malgratious millare,
A berward, a brawlar,

prow: profit   wynnit: lived   mangery: feast   stall: stole
wobstare: weaver   milygant: bad person (O.Fr. male-gent)
mychare: thief   libbar: sow-gelder   riddill revar: ? riddle-
robber, fortune-teller, magician   Tuttivillus: devil, imp   tutlar:
? tippler   forfarn: worn-out   berward: bear-leader

And ane aip ledar,
With a cursit custumar,
A tratlar, a tinklar,
And mony uthir in that hour
Off all evill ordour.
First with a fulisch flour,
An ald monk, a lechour,
A drunkin drechour,
A double toungit counsalour,
A trumpour, a trucour,
A hangman, a hasardour,
A tyrant, a tormentour,
A truphane, a tratlour,
A faynit nigramansour,
A japer, a juglour,
A lase that lufis bot for lour,
And a man merrour,
An evill wyffis mirrour,
In all thair semblance sour
With a noyefull nychtbour,
A lunatik, a sismatyk,
An heretyk, a purspyk,
A lumbard, a lolard,
Ane usurar, a bard,
Ane ypocreit in haly kirk,
A burn grenge in the dirk,
A schipman on se and sand,
That takis lyfe and gud on hand,
And knawis nowthir cours nor tyd,
Bot presumpteous in pryd,

custumar: lessee of burgh customs and dues
tinklar: tinker
trucour: (rogue)
but by whim
drechour: ? loafer
truphane: ? pilferer
dirk: dark
tratlar: chatterer
trumpour: deceiver
bot for lour:

42

Practing no thing expert,
In cunnyng, cumpas, nor kert,
A skeg, a scornar, a skald,
A balestrod and a bald,
An unthrifty dapill man,
A rebald, a ruffian,
A murderer of leil men,
A revischer of wemen;
And two lerit men thame by,
Schir Ockir and Ser Symony,
Yit mony in a grit rout
For lak of rowme stud about.

skeg: termagant   skald: scold   balestrod: procuress
bald: bawd   ockir: usurer

15 From *Golagros and Gawane* (*c.* 1470)

THAI passit in thare pilgramage, the proudest in pall,
  The prince provit in prese, that prise wes and deir;
Syne war thai war of ane wane, wrocht with ane wal,
Reirdit on ane riche roche, beside ane riveir,
With doubill dykis be-dene drawin our all;
Micht nane thame note with invy, nor nygh thame to neir.
The land wes likand in large and lufsum to call;
Propir schene schane the son, seymly and seir.

pall: rich cloth   prese: battle   prise: praiseworthy   war
thai war: were they aware   wane: dwelling   be-dene:
together   our all: all round nygh: approach   likand: pleasant
in large: in extent   lufsum to call: worthy to be called lovely
seymly and seir: seemly, like himself

The king stude vesiand the wall, maist vailyeand to se:
On that river he saw
Cumly towris to knaw;
The roy rekinnit on raw
Thretty and thre.

Apone that riche river, randonit full evin,
The side-wallis war set, sad to the see;
Schippis saland thame by, sexty and sevyn,
To send, quhen thame self list, in seir cuntre,
That al thai that ar wrocht undir the hie hevin
Micht nocht warne thame at wil to ische nor entre.
Than carpit the cumly king, with ane lowd stevin:
'Yone is the seymliast sicht that ever couth I se.
Gif thair be ony keyne knycht that can tell it,
Quha is lord of yone land,
Lusty and likand,
Or quham of is he haldand,
Fayne wald I wit.'

Than schir Spynagrose with speche spak to the king:
'Yone lord haldis of nane leid, that yone land aw,
Bot ever-lesting but legiance, to his leving,
As his eldaris has done, enduring his daw.'
'Hevinly God!' said the heynd, 'how happynis this thing?
Herd thair euer ony sage sa selcouth ane saw!

vesiand: viewing   vailyeand: noble   randonit full evin: which
ran swiftly full level with its banks   sad to: strong towards   seir:
many a   warne: prevent   ische: go out   carpit: said   stevin:
voice   keyne: brave   quham of: of whom   leid: man
aw: possesses   bot: but   but: without   to his
leving: in his lifetime   enduring: during   daw: day
heynd: courteous one   selcouth ane saw: unusual a speech

44

ANONYMOUS

Sal never myne hart be in saill na in liking,
Bot gif I loissing my life, or be laid law,
Be the pilgramage compleit I pas for saull prow,
Bot dede be my destenyng,
He sall at my agane cumyng
Mak homage and oblissing,
I mak myne avow!'

saill: happiness   bot gif: unless   loissing: losing   or: first
compleit (be): let be completed   pas: perform   for saull
prow: for the good of my soul   bot: unless   dede: death
oblissing: submission

16   From *Rauf Coilyear* (? *c.* 1480)

THE Coilyear, gudlie in feir, tuke him be the hand,
  And put him befoir him, as ressoun had bene;
Quhen thay come to the dure, the King begouth to stand,
To put the Coilyear in befoir, maid him to mene.
He said: 'Thou art uncourtes, that sall I warrand.'
He tyt the King be the nek, twa part in tene;
'Gif thou at bidding suld be boun or obeysand,
And gif thou of Courtasie couth, thou hes foryet it clene;
Now is anis,' said the Coilyear, ' kynd aucht to creip,
    Sen ellis thou art unknawin,
    To mak me Lord of my awin;
    Sa mot I thrive, I am thrawin,
      Begin we to threip.'

feir: company   dure: door   begouth: began   maid him
to mene: acted as if he meant   tyt: seized   tene: anger   boun:
prompt   couth: knew   now is anis ... begin we to threip:
now that's one mistake you have made; however, you must creep before
you walk. Besides, you are a stranger here, and you do not know how to
make me lord of my own. Bless me! I am getting angry, and we are already
beginning to fall out

Than benwart thay yeid, quhair brandis was bricht,
To ane bricht byrnand fyre as the Carll bad;
He callit on Gyliane, his wyfe, thair Supper to dicht.
'Of the best that thair is, help that we had,

  . . . .

  . . . .

Efter ane evill day to have ane mirrie nicht,
For sa troublit with stormis was I never stad;
Of ilk airt of the Eist sa laithly it laid,
  Yit was I mekle willar than,
  Quhen I met with this man.'
  Of sic taillis thay began,
    Quhill the supper was graid.

Sone was the Supper dicht, and the fyre bet,
And thay had weschin, I wis, the worthiest was thair:
'Tak my wyfe be the hand, in feir, withoutin let,
And gang begin the buird,' said the Coilyear.
'That war unsemand, forsuith, and thy self unset;'
The King profferit him to gang, and maid ane strange fair.
'Now is twyse,' said the Carll, 'me think thou hes foryet.'
He leit gyrd to the King, withoutin ony mair,
And hit him under the eir with his richt hand,
  Quhill he stakkerit thair with all
  Half the breid of the hall;
  He faind never of ane fall,
    Quhill he the eird fand.

benwart: inside yeid: went dicht: prepare help that we had: serve what we hold stad: pressed airt: quarter mekle: much willar: more bewildered than: then graid: prepared bet: mended weschin: washed worthiest: best of everything unset: not seated fair: fuss foryet: forgotten leit gyrd: hit out breid: breadth faind: stopped quhill: till

He start up stoutly agane, uneis micht he stand,
For anger of that outray that he had thair tane.
He callit on Gyliane his wyfe: 'Ga, tak him be the hand,
And gang agane to the buird, quhair ye suld air have gane.'
'Schir, thou art unskilfull, and that sall I warrand,
Thou byrd to have nurtour aneuch, and thou hes nane;
Thou hes walkit, I wis, in mony wyld land,
The mair vertew thou suld have, to keip the fra blame;
Thou suld be courtes of kynd, and ane cunnand Courteir.
    Thocht that I simpill be,
    Do as I bid the,
    The hous is myne, pardie,
      And all that is heir.'

The King said to him self: 'This is an evill lyfe,
Yit was I never in my lyfe thus gait leird;
And I have oft tymes bene quhair gude hes bene ryfe,
That maist couth of courtasie in this Cristin eird.
Is nane sa gude as leif of, and mak na mair stryfe,
For I am stonischit at this straik, that hes me thus steird.'
In feir fairlie he foundis, with the gude wyfe,
Quhair the Coilyear bad, sa braithlie he beird.
Quhen he had done his bidding, as him gude thocht,
    Doun he sat the King neir,
    And maid him glaid and gude cheir,
    And said: 'Ye ar welcum heir,
      Be him that me bocht.'

uneis: hardly   buird: table   byrd: shouldst   nurtour:
good manners   leird (thus gait): taught (in this way)   eird:
earth   is nane . . . leif of: the best thing to do is leave off   foundis:
goes   braithlie: violently   beird: roared

BLIN HARY

From *THE WALLACE* (c. 1460)

17

[*Schir William Wallace*]

WALLACE statur off gretnes, and off hycht,
    Was jugyt thus, be discretioun off rycht,
That saw him bath dissembill and in weid;
IX quartaris large he was in lenth indeid;
Thryd part lenth in schuldrys braid was he,
Rycht sembly, strang, and lusty for to se;
Hys lymmys gret, with stalwart paiss and sound,
Hys browys hard, his armes gret and round;
His handis maid rycht lik till a pawmer,
Off manlik mak, with naless gret and cler;
Proportionyt lang and fayr was his vesage;
Rycht sad off spech, and abill in curage;
Braid breyst and heych, with sturdy crag and gret;
His lyppys round, his noys was squar and tret;
Bowand bron haryt, on browis and breis lycht,
Cler aspre eyn, lik dyamondis brycht.
Undyr the chin, on the left syd, was seyn,
Be hurt, a wain; his colour was sangweyn.
Woundis he had in mony divers place,
Bot fair and weill kepyt was his face.
Off ryches he kepyt no propyr thing;
Gaiff as he wan, lik Alexander the king.

---

dissembill: unclothed	quartaris: quarter-ells	paiss: weight
pawmer: palm-tree	cler: bright	sad: serious	crag: neck
tret: long and well-proportioned	bowand: pliant	bron: brown
breis: eyebrows	aspre: keen	wain: scar

In tym off pes, mek as a maid was he;
Quhar wer approchyt the rycht Ector was he.
To Scottis men a gret credens he gaiff;
Bot knawin enemys thai couth him nocht disayff.

mek: meek

18   *[Lament for the Graham]*

QUHEN thai him fand, and gud Wallace him saw,
    He lychtyt doun, and hynt him fra thaim aw
In armys up; behaldand his paill face,
He kyssyt him, and cryt full oft; 'Allace!
My best brothir in warld that evir I had!
My a fald freynd quhen I was hardest stad!
My hop, my heill, thou was in maist honour!
My faith, my help, strenthiast in stour!
In thee was wit, fredom, and hardines;
In thee was treuth, manheid, and nobilnes;
In thee was rewll, in thee was governans;
In thee was vertu with outyn varians;
In thee lawte, in thee was gret largnas;
In thee gentrice, in thee was stedfastnas.
Thou was gret caus off wynnyng off Scotland;
Thocht I began, and tuk the wer on hand.
I vow to God, that has the warld in wauld,
Thy dede sall be to Sotheroun full der sauld.
Martyr thou art for Scotlandis rycht and me;
I sall thee venge, or ellis tharfor to de.'

hynt: took hold of   a fald: single-hearted   stour: fight
rewll: good principle   varians: variance   lawte: loyalty
largnas: liberality   wauld: control   der: dear

ROBERT HENRYSON

c. 1420–c. 1490

19   *The Testament of Cresseid*

ANE doolie sessoun to ane cairfull dyte
  Suld correspond, and be equivalent.
Richt sa it wes quhen I began to wryte
This tragedie, the wedder richt fervent,
Quhen Aries, in middis of the Lent,
Schouris of haill can fra the north discend,
That scantlie fra the cauld I micht defend.

Yit nevertheles within myne oratur
I stude, quhen Titan had his bemis bricht
Withdrawin doun, and sylit under cure
And fair Venus, the bewtie of the nicht,
Uprais, and set unto the west full richt
Hir goldin face in oppositioun
Of God Phebus direct discending doun.

Throw out the glas hir bemis brast sa fair
That I micht se on everie syde me by
The Northin wind had purifyit the Air
And sched the mistie cloudis fra the sky,
The froist freisit, the blastis bitterly
Fra Pole Artick come quhisling loud and schill,
And causit me remufe aganis my will.

---

doolie: doleful   fervent: severe   oratur: oratory   sylit:
hidden   cure: cover   brast: burst   schill: shrill

For I traistit that Venus, luifis Quene,
To quhome sum tyme I hecht obedience,
My faidit hart of lufe scho wald mak grene,
And therupon with humbill reverence,
I thocht to pray hir hie Magnificence;
Bot for greit cald as than I lattit was,
And in my Chalmer to the fyre can pas.

Thocht lufe be hait, yit in ane man of age
It kendillis nocht sa sone as in youtheid,
Of quhome the blude is flowing in ane rage,
And in the auld the curage doif and deid,
Of quhilk the fyre outward is best remeid;
To help be Phisike quhair that nature faillit
I am expert, for baith I have assailit.

I mend the fyre and beikit me about,
Than tuik ane drink my spreitis to comfort,
And armit me weill fra the cauld thairout:
To cut the winter nicht and mak it schort,
I tuik ane Quair, and left all uther sport,
Writtin be worthie Chaucer glorious,
Of fair Creisseid, and worthie Troylus.

And thair I fand, efter that Diomeid
Ressavit had that Lady bricht of hew,
How Troilus neir out of wit abraid,
And weipit soir with visage paill of hew;
For quhilk wanhope his teiris can renew
Quhill Esperus rejoisit him agane,
Thus quhyle in Joy he levit, quhyle in pane.

sum tyme: formerly   hecht: promised   lattit: prevented
hait: hot   doif: deaf   assaillit: tried   beikit: warmed
quair: book   abraid: started   wanhope: despair   quhill:
till   quhyle: sometimes

51

Of hir behest he had greit comforting,
Traisting to Troy that scho suld mak retour,
Quhilk he desyrit maist of eirdly thing
Forquhy scho was his only Paramour;
Bot quhen he saw passit baith day and hour
Of hir ganecome, than sorrow can oppres
His wofull hart in cair and hevines.

Of his distres me neidis nocht reheirs,
For worthie Chauceir in the samin buik
In gudelie termis and in Joly veirs
Compylit hes his cairis, quha will luik.
To brek my sleip ane uther quair I tuik,
In quhilk I fand the fatall destenie
Of fair Cresseid, that endit wretchitlie.

Quha wait gif all that Chauceir wrait was trew?
Nor I wait nocht gif this narratioun
Be authoreist, or fenyeit of the new
Be sum Poeit, throw his Inventioun,
Maid to report the Lamentatioun
And wofull end of this lustie Creisseid,
And quhat distres scho thoillit, and quhat deid.

Quhen Diomeid had all his appetyte,
And mair, fulfillit of this fair Ladie,
Upon ane uther he set his haill delyte
And send to hir ane Lybell of repudie,
And hir excludit fra his companie.
Than desolait scho walkit up and doun,
And sum men sayis into the Court commoun.

forquhy: because   ganecome: return   wait: knows
fenyeit . . . new: newly invented   thoillit: suffered

O fair Creisseid, the flour and A per se
Of Troy and Grece, how was thou fortunait!
To change in filth all thy Feminitie,
And be with fleschlie lust sa maculait,
And go amang the Greikis air and lait
Sa giglotlike, takand thy foull plesance!
I have pietie thou suld fall sic mischance.

Yit nevertheless quhat ever men deme or say
In scornefull langage of thy brukkilnes,
I sall excuse, als far furth as I may,
Thy womanheid, thy wisdome and fairnes:
The quhilk Fortoun hes put to sic distres
As hir pleisit, and nathing throw the gilt
Of the, throw wickit langage to be spilt.

This fair Lady, in this wyse destitute
Of all comfort and consolatioun,
Richt privelie, but fellowschip, on fute
Disagysit passit far out of the toun
Ane myle or twa, unto ane Mansioun
Beildit full gay, quhair hir father Calchas
Quhilk than amang the Greikis dwelland was.

Quhen he hir saw, the caus he can Inquyre
Of hir cumming; scho said, siching full soir:
'Fra Diomeid had gottin his desyre
He wox werie, and wald of me no moir.'
Quod Calchas, 'douchter, weip thou not thairfoir;
Peraventure all cummis for the best;
Welcum to me, thou art full deir ane Gest.'

A per se: A by itself, first of all, Ampersand   fortunait: ordained
maculait: stained   air: early   deme: censur   giglotlike:
wantonly   brukkilnes: frailty   but: without   disagysit:
disguised   beildit: built for shelter   siching: sighing
fra: after   gest: guest

This auld Calchas, efter the Law was tho,
Wes keiper of the Tempill as ane Preist,
In quhilk Venus and hir Sone Cupido
War honourit, and his Chalmer was thame neist,
To quhilk Cresseid with baill aneuch in breist
Usit to pas, hir prayeris for to say.
Quhill at the last, upon ane Solempne day,

As custome was, the pepill far and neir
Befoir the none, unto the Tempill went,
With Sacrifice, devoit in thair maneir:
Bot still Cresseid, hevie in hir Intent,
Into the Kirk wald not hir self present,
For giving of the pepill ony deming
Of hir expuls fra Diomeid the King:

Bot past into ane secreit Orature
Quhair scho micht weip hir wofull desteny;
Behind hir bak scho cloisit fast the dure
And on hir kneis bair fell doun in hy.
Upon Venus and Cupide angerly
Scho cryit out, and said on this same wyse,
'Allace that ever I maid you Sacrifice.

'Ye gave me anis ane devine responsaill
That I suld be the flour of luif in Troy,
Now am I maid ane unworthie outwaill,
And all in cair translatit is my Joy;
Quha sall me gyde? quha sall me now convoy
Sen I fra Diomeid and Nobill Troylus
Am clene excludit, as abject odious?

tho: then   neist: next   baill aneuch: trouble enough
devoit: devout   for giving: lest she should give   hy: haste
responsaill: answer to prayer   outwaill: outcast   abject: cast-off

54

'O fals Cupide, is nane to wyte bot thow,
And thy Mother, of lufe the blind Goddes!
Ye causit me alwayis understand and trow
The seid of lufe was sawin in my face,
And ay grew grene throw your supplie and grace.
Bot now allace that seid with froist is slane,
And I fra luifferis left and all forlane.'

Quhen this was said, doun in ane extasie,
Ravischit in spreit, intill ane dreame scho fell,
And be apperance hard, quhair scho did ly,
Cupide the King ringand ane silver bell,
Quhilk men micht heir fra hevin unto hell;
At quhais sound befoir Cupide appeiris
The seven Planetis discending fra thair Spheiris,

Quhilk hes power of all thing generabill
To reull and steir be thair greit Influence,
Wedder and wind, and coursis variabill:
And first of all Saturne gave his sentence,
Quhilk gave to Cupide litill reverence,
Bot, as ane busteous Churle on his maneir,
Come crabitlie with auster luik and cheir,

His face fronsit, his lyre was lyke the Leid,
His teith chatterit, and cheverit with the Chin,
His Ene drowpit, how sonkin in his heid,
Out of his Nois the Meldrop fast can rin,
With lippis bla and cheikis leine and thin;
The Iceschoklis that fra his hair doun hang
Was wonder greit, and as ane speir als lang.

wyte: blame   supplie: support   hard: heard   generabill:
that can be generated   busteous: blustering   fronsit: wrinkled
lyre: complexion   cheverit: shivered   how: hollow   nois:
nose   meldrop: mucus-drop   bla: livid   iceschoklis: icicles

Atouir his belt his lyart lokkis lay
Felterit unfair, ouirfret with Froistis hoir;
His garmound and his gyis full gay of gray,
His widderit weid fra him the wind out woir;
Ane busteous bow within his hand he boir;
Under his girdill ane flasche of felloun flanis,
Fedderit with Ice, and heidit with hailstanis.

Than Juppiter, richt fair and amiabill,
God of the Starnis in the Firmament,
And Nureis to all thing generabill,
Fra his Father Saturne far different,
With burelie face, and browis bricht and brent,
Upon his heid ane Garland, wonder gay,
Of flouris fair, as it had bene in May.

His voice was cleir, as Cristall wer his Ene,
As goldin wyre sa glitterand was his hair;
His garmound and his gyis full gay of grene,
With golden listis gilt on everie gair;
Ane burelie brand about his midill bair;
In his richt hand he had ane groundin speir,
Of his Father the wraith fra us to weir.

Nixt efter him come Mars, the God of Ire,
Of strife, debait, and all dissensioun,
To chide and fecht, als feirs as ony fyre;
In hard Harnes, hewmound and Habirgeoun,
And on his hanche ane roustie fell Fachioun;
And in his hand he had ane roustie sword;
Wrything his face with mony angrie word,

atouir: about   lyart: hoary   felterit: matted   ouirfret:
laced over   gyis: attire   gay of gray: (a cliché)   weid:
clothing   flasche: sheaf   felloun: cruel   flanis: arrows
fedderit: feathered   burelie: goodly   brent: smooth   listis: edges
gair: strip   groundin: sharpened   weir: ward   hewmound: helmet
habirgeoun: mail coat   roustie: rusty   fachioun: short sword

Schaikand his sword, befoir Cupide he come
With reid visage, and grislie glowrand Ene;
And at this mouth ane bullar stude of fome
Lyke to ane Bair quhetting his Tuskis kene,
Richt Tuitlyeour lyke, but temperance in tene;
Ane horne he blew, with mony bosteous brag,
Quhilk all this warld with weir hes maid to wag.

Than fair Phebus, Lanterne & Lamp of licht
Of man and beist, baith frute and flourisching,
Tender Nureis, and banischer of nicht,
And of the warld causing, be his moving
And Influence, lyfe in all eirdlie thing,
Without comfort of quhome, of force to nocht
Must all ga die that in this warld is wrocht.

As King Royall he raid upon his Chair
The quhilk Phaeton gydit sum tyme upricht;
The brichtnes of his face quhen it was bair
Nane micht behald for peirsing of his sicht.
This goldin Cart with fyrie bemis bricht
Four yokkit steidis full different of hew,
But bait or tyring, throw the Spheiris drew.

The first was soyr, with Mane als reid as Rois,
Callit Eoye into the Orient;
The secund steid to Name hecht Ethios,
Quhitlie and paill, and sum deill ascendent;
The thrid Peros, richt hait and richt fervent:
The feird was blak, callit Philologie
Quhilk rollis Phebus doun into the sey.

glowrand: glaring   bullar: mass of bubbles   bair: boar
tuitlyeour lyke: brawler-like, quarrelsome   tene: anger   bosteous:
rough   weir: war   but bait: without pause   soyr: sorrel
Eoye . . .: Eöus, belonging to the dawn   hecht Ethios: called Aethon
sum deill: somewhat

Venus was thair present that goddes gay,
Hir Sonnis querrell for to defend and mak
Hir awin complaint, cled in ane nyce array,
The ane half grene, the uther half Sabill black;
Quhyte hair as gold kemmit and sched abak;
Bot in hir face semit greit variance,
Quhyles perfyte treuth, and quhyles Inconstance.

Under smyling scho was dissimulait,
Provocative, with blenkis Amorous,
And suddanely changit and alterait,
Angrie as ony Serpent vennemous
Richt pungitive, with wordis odious.
Thus variant scho was, quha list tak keip,
With ane Eye lauch, and with the uther weip,

In taikning that all fleschelie Paramour
Quhilk Venus hes in reull and governance,
Is sum tyme sweit, sum tyme bitter and sour
Richt unstabill, and full of variance,
Mingit with cairful Joy and fals plesance,
Now hait, now cauld, now blyith, now full of wo,
Now grene as leif, now widderit and ago.

With buik in hand than come Mercurius,
Richt Eloquent, and full of Rethorie,
With polite termis and delicious,
With pen and Ink to report al reddie,
Setting sangis and singand merilie:
His Hude was reid, heklit atouir his Croun,
Lyke to ane Poeit of the auld fassoun.

blenkis: glances	pungitive: pungent	keip: heed
taikning: tokening	mingit: mingled	ago: gone	sangis:
songs (to music)	heklit: fringed	fassoun: fashion (cf. Chaucer's
portrait)		

Boxis he bair with fine Electuairis,
And sugerit Syropis for digestioun,
Spycis belangand to the Pothecairis,
With mony hailsum sweit Confectioun,
Doctour in Phisick cled in ane Skarlot goun,
And furrit weill, as sic ane aucht to be,
Honest and gude, and not ane word culd le.

Nixt efter him come Lady Cynthia,
The last of all, and swiftest in hir Spheir,
Of colour blak, buskit with hornis twa,
And in the nicht scho listis best appeir.
Haw as the Leid, of colour nathing cleir;
For all hir licht scho borrowis at hir brother
Titan, for of hir self scho hes nane uther.

Hir gyse was gray, and ful of spottis blak,
And on hir breist ane Churle paintit full evin,
Beirand ane bunche of Thornis on his bak,
Quhilk for his thift micht clim na nar the hevin.
Thus quhen thay gadderit war, thir Goddes sevin,
Mercurius thay cheisit with ane assent
To be foirspeikar in the Parliament.

Quha had bene thair, and liken for to heir
His facound toung, and termis exquisite,
Of Rethorick the prettick he micht leir,
In breif Sermone ane pregnant sentence **wryte:**
Befoir Cupide veiling his Cap alyte,
Speiris the caus of that vocatioun,
And he anone schew his Intentioun.

buskit: adorned   haw: wan   nar: nearer   cheisit:
chose   facound: eloquent   prettick: practice   leir: learn
alyte: a little   speiris: asks   schew: show

'Lo!' (quod Cupide), 'quha will blaspheme the name
Of his awin God, outher in word or deid,
To all Goddis he dois baith lak and schame,
And suld have bitter panis to his meid.
I say this by yone wretchit Cresseid,
The quilk throw me was sum tyme flour of lufe,
Me and my Mother starklie can reprufe.

'Saying of hir greit Infelicitie
I was the caus, and my Mother Venus,
Ane blind Goddes, hir cald, that micht not se,
With sclander and defame Injurious;
Thus hir leving unclene and Lecherous
Scho wald returne on me and my Mother,
To quhome I schew my grace abone all uther.

'And sen ye ar all sevin deificait,
Participant of devyne sapience,
This greit Injurie done to our hie estait
Me think with pane we suld mak recompence;
Was never to Goddes done sic violence.
Asweill for yow, as for myself I say;
Thairfoir ga help to revenge I yow pray.'

Mercurius to Cupide gave answeir
And said: 'Schir King my counsall is that ye
Refer yow to the hiest planeit heir,
And tak to him the lawest of degre,
The pane of Cresseid for to modifie;
As god Saturne, with him tak Cynthia.'
'I am content' (quod he) 'to tak thay twa.'

lak: reproach   sen: since   modifie: determine

60

Than thus proceidit Saturne and the Mone,
Quhen thay the mater rypelie had degest,
For the dispyte to Cupide scho had done,
And to Venus oppin and manifest,
In all hir lyfe with pane to be opprest,
And torment sair, with seiknes Incurabill,
And to all lovers be abhominabill.

This duleful sentence Saturne tuik on hand,
And passit doun quhair cairfull Cresseid lay,
And on hir heid he laid ane frostie wand;
Than lawfullie on this wyse can he say:
'Thy greit fairnes and all thy bewtie gay,
Thy wantoun blude, and eik thy goldin Hair,
Heir I exclude fra the for evermair.

'I change thy mirth into Melancholy,
Quhilk is the Mother of all pensivenes;
Thy Moisture and thy heit in cald and dry;
Thyne Insolence, thy play and wantones
To greit diseis; thy Pomp and thy riches
In mortall neid; and greit penuritie
Thou suffer sall, and as ane beggar die.'

O cruell Saturne! fraward and angrie,
Hard is thy dome, and to malitious;
On fair Cresseid quhy hes thou na mercie,
Quhilk was sa sweit, gentill and amorous?
Withdraw thy sentence and be gracious
As thou was never; so schawis thow thy deid,
Ane wraikfull sentence gevin on fair Cresseid.

lawfullie: in accordance with the judgement   wraikfull:
revengeful

Than Cynthia, quhen Saturne past away,
Out of hir sait discendit doun belyve,
And red ane bill on Cresseid quhair scho lay,
Contening this sentence diffinityve:
'Fra heit of bodie I the now depryve,
And to thy seiknes sal be na recure,
Bot in dolour thy dayis to Indure.

'Thy Cristall Ene minglit with blude I mak,
Thy voice sa cleir, unplesand hoir and hace,
Thy lustie lyre ouirspred with spottis blak,
And lumpis haw appeirand in thy face.
Quhair thou cumis, Ilk man sal fle the place.
This sall thou go begging fra hous to hous
With Cop and Clapper lyke ane Lazarous.'

This doolie dreame, this uglye visioun
Brocht to ane end, Cresseid fra it awoik,
And all that Court and convocatioun
Vanischit away, than rais scho up and tuik
Ane poleist glas, and hir schaddow culd luik:
And quhen scho saw hir face sa deformait
Gif scho in hart was wa aneuch God wait.

Weiping full sair, 'Lo quhat it is '(quod sche)
'With fraward langage for to mufe and steir
Our craibit Goddis, and sa is sene on me!
My blaspheming now have I bocht full deir.
All eirdlie Joy and mirth I set areir.
Allace this day, allace this wofull tyde,
Quhen I began with my Goddis for to Chyde.'

belyve: quickly   hoir: old (hoar)   hace: harsh   lyre: skin
lazarous: leper   wa aneuch: woeful enough   wait: knows
areir: behind

Be this was said ane Chyld come fra the Hall
To warne Cresseid the Supper was reddy,
First knokkit at the dure, and syne culd call:
'Madame your Father biddis yow cum in hy.
He hes mervell sa lang on grouf ye ly,
And sayis your prayers bene to lang sum deill:
The goddis wait all your Intent full weill.'

Quod scho: 'Fair Chyld ga to my Father deir,
And pray him cum to speik with me anone.'
And sa he did, and said: 'douchter quhat cheir?'
'Allace' (quod scho), 'Father my mirth is gone.'
'How sa' (quod he); and scho can all expone
As I have tauld, the vengeance and the wraik
For hir trespas, Cupide on hir culd tak.

He luikit on hir uglye Lipper face,
The quhilk before was quhyte as Lillie flour,
Wringand his handis oftymes he said allace
That he had levit to se that wofull hour,
For he knew weill that thair was na succour
To hir seiknes, and that dowblit his pane.
Thus was thair cair aneuch betuix thame twane.

Quhen thay togidder murnit had full lang,
Quod Cresseid: 'Father, I wald not be kend.
Thairfoir in secreit wyse ye let me gang
Into yone Hospitall at the tounis end.
And thidder sum meit for Cheritie me send
To leif upon, for all mirth in this eird
Is fra me gane, sic is my wickit weird.'

hy: haste   grouf: grovelling   wraik: punishment   kend: known   eird: earth   weird: fate

Than in ane Mantill and ane bawer Hat,
With Cop and Clapper wonder prively,
He opnit ane secreit yet, and out thair at
Convoyit hir, that na man suld espy,
Into ane Village half ane myle thairby,
Delyverit hir in at the Spittaill hous,
And daylie sent hir part of his Almous.

Sum knew her weill, & sum had na knawledge
Of hir becaus scho was sa deformait,
With bylis blak ouirspred in hir visage,
And hir fair colour faidit and alterait.
Yit thay presumit for her hie regrait
And still murning, scho was of Nobill kin:
With better will thairfoir they tuik hir in.

The day passit, and Phebus went to rest,
The Cloudis blak ouirquhelmit all the sky.
God wait gif Cresseid was ane sorrowfull Gest,
Seing that uncouth fair and Harbery:
But meit or drink scho dressit hir to ly
In ane dark Corner of the Hous allone.
And on this wyse weiping, scho maid her mone:

The Complaint of Cresseid

'O sop of sorrow, sonkin into cair:
O Cative Creisseid, for now and ever mair,
Gane is thy Joy and all thy mirth in Eird,
Of all blyithnes now art thou blaiknit bair.

bawer: beaver   yet: gate   spittaill hous: hospital   almous:
alms   bylis: boils   regrait: grief   fair: fare   harbery:
lodging   sonkin: sunk   cative: wretched   blaiknit:
blackened

Thair is na Salve may saif the of thy sair,
Fell is thy Fortoun, wickit is thy weird:
Thy blys is baneist, and thy baill on breird;
Under the Eirth, God gif I gravin wer,
Quhair nane of Grece nor yit of Troy micht heird.

'Quhair is thy Chalmer wantounlie besene?
With burely bed and bankouris browderit bene,
Spycis and Wyne to thy Collatioun,
The Cowpis all of gold and silver schene:
The sweit Meitis, servit in plaittis clene,
With Saipheron sals of ane gud sessoun:
Thy gay garmentis with mony gudely Goun,
Thy plesand Lawn pinnit with goldin prene:
All is areir, thy greit Royall Renoun.

'Quhair is thy garding with thir greissis gay?
And fresche flowris, quhilk the Quene Floray
Had paintit plesandly in everie pane,
Quhair thou was wont full merilye in May
To walk and tak the dew be it was day
And heir the Merle and Mawis mony ane,
With Ladyis fair in Carrolling to gane,
And se the Royall Rinkis in thair array,
In garmentis gay garnischit on everie grane.

'Thy greit triumphand fame and hie honour,
Quhair thou was callit of Eirdlye wichtis Flour,

---

baill on breird: woe burgeoning   heird: hear it   wantounlie:
gaily   besene: furnished   burely: pleasant   bankouris:
tapestries   browderit: embroidered   bene: well
saipheron: saffron   sals: sauce   sessoun: seasoning
prene: pin   pane: flower-bed   carrolling: circular dances with song
rinkis: personages   grane: colour

All is decayit, thy weird is welterit so.
Thy hie estait is turnit in darknes dour.
This Lipper Ludge tak for thy burelie Bour.
And for thy Bed tak now ane bunche of stro;
For waillit Wyne, and Meitis thou had tho,
Tak mowlit Breid, Peirrie and Ceder sour:
Bot Cop and Clapper, now is all ago.

'My cleir voice, and courtlie carrolling,
Quhair I was wont with Ladyis for to sing,
Is rawk as Ruik, full hiddeous hoir and hace;
My plesand port all utheris precelling:
Of lustines I was hald maist conding.
Now is deformit the Figour of my face;
To luik on it, na Leid now lyking hes:
Sowpit in syte, I say with sair siching,
Ludgeit amang the Lipper Leid allace.

'O Ladyis fair of Troy and Grece, attend
My miserie, quhilk nane may comprehend,
My frivoll Fortoun, my Infelicitie,
My greit mischeif quhilk na man can amend.
Be war in tyme, approchis neir the end,
And in your mynd ane mirrour mak of me:
As I am now, peradventure that ye
For all your micht may cum to that same end,
Or ellis war, gif ony war may be.

welterit: turned	dour: enduring	ludge: lodging
waillit: choice	tho: then	mowlit: mouldy	peirrie: perry
(pear cider)	ceder: cider	rawk: hoarse	ruik: rook
hace: hoarse	precelling: excelling	conding: worthy	leid:
man (or people)	sowpit: soaked	syte: grief	lipper leid:
leper folk	war: worse	gif: if	

'Nocht is your fairnes bot ane faiding flour,
Nocht is your famous laud and hie honour
Bot wind Inflat in uther mennis eiris.
Your roising reid to rotting sall retour:
Exempill mak of me in your Memour,
Quhilk of sic thingis wofull witnes beiris,
All Welth in Eird, away as Wind it weiris.
Be war thairfoir, approchis neir the hour:
Fortoun is fikkill, quhen scho beginnis & steiris.'

Thus chydand with hir drerie destenye,
Weiping, scho woik the nicht fra end to end,
Bot all in vane; hir dule, hir cairfull cry
Micht not remeid, nor yit hir murning mend.
Ane Lipper Lady rais and till hir wend,
And said: 'quhy spurnis thow aganis the Wall,
To sla thy self, and mend nathing at all?

'Sen thy weiping dowbillis bot thy wo,
I counsall the mak vertew of ane neid.
To leir to clap thy Clapper to and fro,
And leir efter the Law of Lipper Leid.'
Thair was na buit, bot furth with thame scho yeid,
Fra place to place, quhill cauld and hounger sair
Compellit hir to be ane rank beggair.

That samin tyme of Troy the Garnisoun,
Quhilk had to chiftane worthie Troylus,
Throw Jeopardie of Weir had strikken doun
Knichtis of Grece in number mervellous;
With greit tryumphe and Laude victorious
Agane to Troy richt Royallie they raid
The way quhair Cresseid with the Lipper baid.

roising: rose	steiris: stirs	dule: sorrow	remeid: remedy
wend: went	dowbillis: doubles	buit: help	yeid: went
baid: dwelt			

Seeing that companie thai come all with ane stevin;
Thay gaif ane cry and schuik coppis gude speid,
Said 'worthie Lordis for goddis lufe of Hevin,
To us Lipper part of your Almous deid.'
Than to thair cry Nobill Troylus tuik heid,
Having pietie, neir by the place can pas,
Quhair Cresseid sat, not witting quhat scho was.

Than upon him scho kest up baith hir Ene,
And with ane blenk it come into his thocht,
That he sumtime hir face befoir had sene.
Bot scho was in sic plye he knew hir nocht;
Yit than hir luik into his mynd it brocht
The sweit visage and amorous blenking
Of fair Cresseid sumtyme his awin darling.

Na wonder was, suppois in mynd that he
Tuik hir figure sa sone, and lo now quhy?
The Idole of ane thing, in cace may be
Sa deip Imprentit in the fantasy
That it deludis the wittis outwardly,
And sa appeiris in forme and lyke estait,
Within the mynd as it was figurait.

Ane spark of lufe than till his hart culd spring
And kendlit all his bodie in ane fyre.
With hait Fewir ane sweit and trimbling
Him tuik, quhill he was reddie to expyre.
To beir his Scheild, his Breist began to tyre;
Within ane quhyle he changit mony hew,
And nevertheless not ane ane uther knew.

stevin (ane): one voice   blenk: glance   plye: plight
suppois . . . that: although   tuik hir figure: had a mental picture
of her   cace (in): perhaps

For Knichtlie pietie and memoriall
Of fair Cresseid, ane Gyrdill can he tak,
Ane Purs of gold, and mony gay Jowall,
And in the Skirt of Cresseid doun can swak;
Than raid away, and not ane word he spak,
Pensive in hart, quhill he come to the Toun,
And for greit care oft syis almaist fell doun.

The lipper folk to Cresseid than can draw,
To se the equall distributioun
Of the Almous, bot quhen the gold thay saw,
Ilk ane to uther prevelie can roun,
And said: 'Yone Lord hes mair affectioun,
How ever it be, unto yone Lazarous
Than to us all, we knaw be his Almous.'

'Quhat Lord is yone' (quod scho), 'have ye na feill,
Hes done to us so greit humanitie?'
'Yes' (quod a Lipper man), 'I knaw him weill,
Schir Troylus it is, gentill and fre:'
Quhen Cresseid understude that it was he,
Stiffer than steill, thair stert ane bitter stound
Throwout hir hart, and fell doun to the ground.

Quhen scho ouircome, with siching sair & sad,
With mony cairfull cry and cald ochane:
'Now is my breist with stormie stoundis stad,
Wrappit in wo, ane wretch full will of wane.'
Than swounit scho oft or scho culd refrane,
And ever in hir swouning cryit scho thus:
'O fals Cresseid and trew Knicht Troylus.

swak (can): flung   oft syis: often   roun: whisper
feill: knowledge   stound: pang   stad: bestead   full
will of wane: uncertain of purpose

'Thy lufe, thy lawtie, and thy gentilnes,
I countit small in my prosperitie,
Sa elevait I was in wantones,
And clam upon the fickill quheill sa hie:
All Faith and Lufe I promissit to the,
Was in the self fickill and frivolous:
O fals Cresseid, and trew Knicht Troilus.

'For lufe of me thou keipt gude continence,
Honest and chaist in conversatioun.
Of all wemen protectour and defence
Thou was, and helpit thair opinioun.
My mynd in fleschelie foull affectioun
Was Inclynit to Lustis Lecherous:
Fy fals Cresseid, O trew Knicht Troylus.

'Lovers be war and tak gude heid about
Quhome that ye lufe, for quhome ye suffer paine.
I lat yow wit, thair is richt few thairout
Quhome ye may traist to have trew lufe agane.
Preif quhen ye will, your labour is in vaine.
Thairfoir, I reid, ye tak thame as ye find,
For thay ar sad as Widdercock in Wind,

'Because I knaw the greit unstabilnes
Brukkill as glas, into my self I say,
Traisting in uther als greit unfaithfulnes,
Als unconstant, and als untrew of fay.
Thocht sum be trew, I wait richt few ar thay,
Quha findis treuth lat him his Lady ruse:
Nane but my self as now I will accuse.'

lawtie: loyalty	quheill: wheel (of fortune)	the self: myself
opinioun: good fame	thairout: existing	preif: test
sad: sober	widdercock: weathercock	brukkill: brittle
fay: faith	ruse: praise	

Quhen this was said, with Paper scho sat doun,
And on this maneir maid hir Testament.
'Heir I beteiche my Corps and Carioun
With Wormis and with Taidis to be rent.
My Cop and Clapper and myne Ornament,
And all my gold the Lipper folk sall have,
Quhen I am deid, to burie me in grave.

'This Royal Ring, set with this Rubie reid,
Quhilk Troylus in drowrie to me send,
To him agane I leif it quhen I am deid,
To mak my cairfull deid unto him kend:
Thus I conclude schortlie and mak ane end,
My Spreit I leif to Diane quhair scho dwellis,
To walk with hir in waist Woddis and Wellis.

'O Diomeid, thou hes baith Broche and Belt,
Quhilk Troylus gave me in takning
Of his trew lufe,' and with that word scho swelt,
And sone ane Lipper man tuik of the Ring,
Syne buryit hir withouttin tarying:
To Troylus furthwith the Ring he bair,
And of Cresseid the deith he can declair.

Quhen he had hard hir greit infirmitie,
Hir Legacie and Lamentatioun,
And how scho endit in sic povertie,
He swelt for wo, and fell doun in ane swoun,
For greit sorrow his hart to brist was boun:
Siching full sadlie, said: 'I can no moir,
Scho was untrew, and wo is me thairfoir.'

beteiche: bequeath   taidis: toads   drowrie: troth   kend:
known   wellis: marshes   swelt: expired   boun: ready

71

Sum said he maid ane Tomb of Merbell gray,
And wrait hir name and superscriptioun,
And laid it on hir grave quhair that scho lay,
In goldin Letteris, conteining this ressoun:
'Lo, fair Ladyis, Crisseid, of Troyis toun,
Sumtyme countit the flour of Womanheid,
Under this stane lait Lipper lyis deid.'

Now, worthie Wemen, in this Ballet schort,
Made for your worschip and Instructioun,
Of Cheritie, I monische and exhort,
Ming not your lufe with fals deceptioun.
Beir in your mynd this schort conclusioun
Of fair Cresseid, as I have said befoir.
Sen scho is deid, I speik of hir no moir.

Finis.

monische: admonish   ming: mingle

20   *The Preiching of the Swallow*

THE hie prudence, and wirking mervelous,
The profound wit off God omnipotent,
Is sa perfyte, and sa Ingenious,
Excellent ffar all mannis argument;
For quhy to him all thing is ay present,
Rycht as it is, or ony tyme sall be,
Befoir the sicht off his Divinitie.

excellent: excelling   for quhy: because   or: before

Thairfoir our Saull with Sensualitie
So fetterit is in presoun Corporall,
We may not cleirlie understand nor se
God as he is, nor thingis Celestiall:
Our mirk and deidlie corps materiale
Blindis the Spirituall operatioun,
Lyke as ane man wer bundin in presoun.

In Metaphisik Aristotell sayis
That mannis Saull is lyke ane Bakkis Ee,
Quhilk lurkis still als lang as licht off day is,
And in the gloming cummis furth to fle;
Hir Ene ar waik, the Sone scho may not se:
Sa is our Saull with fantasie opprest,
To knaw the thingis in nature manifest.

For God is in his power Infinite,
And mannis Saull is febill and over small,
Off understanding waik and unperfite,
To comprehend him that contenis all.
Nane suld presume, be ressoun naturall,
To seirche the secreitis off the Trinitie,
Bot trow fermelie, and lat all ressoun be.

Yit nevertheles we may haif knawlegeing
Off God almychtie, be his Creatouris,
That he is gude, ffair, wyis and bening;
Exempill tak be thir Jolie flouris,
Rycht sweit off smell, and plesant off colouris,
Sum grene, sum blew, sum purpour, quhyte, and reid,
Thus distribute be gift off his Godheid.

mirk: dark   bakkis: bat's   gloming: twilight   trow:
believe

The firmament payntit with sternis cleir,
From eist to west rolland in cirkill round,
And everilk Planet in his proper Spheir,
In moving makand Harmonie and sound;
The fyre, the Air, the watter, and the ground—
Till understand it is aneuch, I wis,
That God in all his werkis wittie is.

Luke weill the fische that swimmis in the se;
Luke weill in eirth all kynd off bestiall;
The foulis ffair, sa forcelie thay fle,
Scheddand the air with pennis grit and small;
Syne luke to man, that he maid last off all,
Lyke to his Image and his similitude:
Be thir we knaw, that God is ffair and gude.

All Creature he maid ffor the behufe
Off man, and to his supportatioun
In to this eirth, baith under and abufe,
In number, wecht, and dew proportioun;
The difference off tyme, and ilk seasoun,
Concorddand till our opurtunitie,
As daylie by experience we may se.

The Somer with his Jolie mantill off grene,
With flouris fair furrit on everilk fent,
Quhilk Flora Goddes, off the flouris Quene,
Hes to that Lord as ffor his seasoun sent,
And Phebus with his goldin bemis gent
Hes purfellit and payntit plesandly,
With heit and moysture stilland ffrom the sky.

sternis: stars	cleir: shining	till: to	bestiall: beasts
forcelie: strongly	furrit: furred		fent: vent (in mantle)
gent: beautiful	purfellit: decorated		stilland: distilling

Syne Harvest hait, quhen Ceres that Goddes
Hir barnis benit hes with abundance;
And Bachus, God off wyne, renewit hes
The tume Pyipis in Italie and France,
With wynis wicht, and liquour off plesance;
And Copia temporis to fill hir horne,
That never wes full of quheit nor uther corne.

Syne wynter wan, quhen Austerne Eolus,
God off the wynd, with blastis boreall,
The grene garment off Somer glorious
Hes all to rent and revin in pecis small;
Than flouris fair faidit with froist man fall,
And birdis blyith changit thair noitis sweit
In styll murning, neir slane with snaw and sleit.

Thir dalis deip with dubbis drounit is,
Baith hill and holt heillit with frostis hair;
And bewis bene laifit bair off blis,
Be wickit windis off the winter wair.
All wyld beistis than ffrom the bentis bair
Drawis ffor dreid unto thair dennis deip,
Coucheand ffor cauld in coifis thame to keip.

Syne cummis Ver, quhen winter is away,
The Secretar off Somer with his Sell,
Quhen Columbie up keikis throw the clay,
Quhilk fleit wes befoir with froistes fell.
The Mavis and the Merle beginnis to mell;

barnis: barns	benit: filled	tume: empty	pyipis: barrels
wicht: strong	quheit: wheat	revin: torn	man: must
dubbis: puddles	holt: wood	heillit: hidden	hair: hoar
bewis: boughs	bair: bare	wair: wild	bentis: grasses
coifis: hollows (coves)		sell: seal (of office)	columbie: the
columbine flower	keikis: peeps	fleit wes: was withered	mavis
and merle: thrush and blackbird		mell: mate	

The Lark on loft, with uther birdis haill,
Than drawis furth ffra derne, over doun and daill.

That samin seasoun, in to ane soft morning,
Rycht blyth that bitter blastis wer ago,
Unto the wod, to se the flouris spring,
And heir the Mavis sing and birdis mo,
I passit ffurth, syne lukit to and ffro,
To se the Soill that wes richt sessonabill,
Sappie, and to resave all seidis abill.

Moving thusgait, grit myrth I tuke in mynd,
Off lauboraris to se the besines,
Sum makand dyke, and sum the pleuch can wynd,
Sum sawand seidis fast ffrome place to place,
The Harrowis hoppand in the saweris trace:
It wes grit Joy to him that luifit corne,
To se thame laubour, baith at evin and morne.

And as I baid under ane bank full bene,
In hart gritlie rejosit off that sicht,
Unto ane hedge, under ane Hawthorne grene,
Off small birdis thair come ane ferlie flicht,
And doun belyif can on the leifis licht,
On everilk syde about me quhair I stude,
Rycht mervellous, ane mekill multitude.

Amang the quhilks ane Swallow loud couth cry,
On that Hawthorne hie in the croip sittand:

haill: altogether   derne: hiding   samin: same   wynd:
guide (the plough)   ferlie: sudden (probably, here)   belyif:
straightway   can . . . licht: did alight   mekill: great
croip: top of a tree

'O ye Birdis on bewis, heir me by,
Ye sall weill knaw, and wyislie understand,
Quhair danger is, or perrell appeirand;
It is grit wisedome to provyde befoir,
It to deuoyd, ffor dreid it hurt yow moir.'

'Schir Swallow' (quod the Lark agane), and leuch,
'Quhat haif ye sene that causis yow to dreid?'
'Se ye yone Churll' (quod scho) 'beyond yone pleuch,
Fast sawand hemp, and gude linget seid?
Yone lint will grow in lytill tyme in deid,
And thairoff will yone Churll his Nettis mak,
Under the quhilk he thinkis us to tak.

'Thairfoir I reid we pas quhen he is gone,
At evin, and with our naillis scharp and small
Out off the eirth scraip we yone seid anone,
And eit it up; ffor, giff it growis, we sall
Have cause to weip heirefter ane and all:
Se we remeid thairfoir ffurth with Instante,
Nam leuius lædit quicquid prævidimus ante.

'For Clerkis sayis it is nocht sufficient
To considder that is befoir thyne Ee;
Bot prudence is ane inwart Argument,
That garris ane man prouyde and foirse
Quhat gude, quhat evill is liklie ffor to be,
Off euerilk thing behald the fynall end,
And swa ffra perrell the better him defend.'

The Lark, lauchand, the Swallow thus couth scorne,
And said, scho fischit lang befoir the Net;

---

ffor dreid: for fear, in case   linget seid: linseed   *nam leuius*
. . . : For whatever we have foreseen hurts us more lightly.

'The barne is eith to busk that is unborne;
All growis nocht that in the ground is set;
The nek to stoup, quhen it the straik sall get,
Is sone aneuch; deith on the fayest fall.'—
Thus scornit thay the Swallow ane and all.

Despysing thus hir helthsum document,
The foullis ferlie tuke thair flicht anone;
Sum with ane bir thay braidit over the bent,
And sum agane ar to the grene wod gone.
Upon the land quhair I wes left allone,
I tuke my club, and hamewart couth I carie,
Swa ferliand, as I had sene ane farie.

Thus passit furth quhill June, that Jolie tyde,
And seidis that wer sawin off beforne
Wer growin hie, that Hairis mycht thame hyde,
And als the Quailye craikand in the corne;
I movit furth, betwix midday and morne,
Unto the hedge under the Hawthorne grene,
Quhair I befoir the said birdis had sene.

And as I stude, be aventure and cace,
The samin birdis as I haif said yow air,
I hoip, because it wes thair hanting place,
Mair off succour, or yit mair solitair,
Thay lychtit doun: and, quhen thay lychtit wair,
The Swallow swyth put furth ane pietuous pyme,
Said, 'wo is him can not bewar in tyme.

barne: child   eith: easy   busk: dress   fayest: most
fated (fey)   document: warning   ferlie: quickly   bir:
whirr   braidit: started quickly   carie: proceed   swa ferliand,
as: as wondering as if   farie: vision   sawin: sown   quailye:
corncrake(s)   craikand: croaking   be aventure and cace: by
chance   said yow air: mentioned to you before   swyth: soon
pyme: cry

ROBERT HENRYSON

'O, blind birdis! and full off negligence,
Unmyndfull of your awin prosperitie,
Lift up your sicht, and tak gude advertence;
Luke to the Lint that growis on yone le;
Yone is the thing I bad forsuith that we,
Quhill it wes seid, suld rute furth off the eird;
Now is it Lint, now is it hie on breird.

'Go yit, quhill it is tender and small,
And pull it up; let it na mair Incres;
My flesche growis, my bodie quaikis all,
Thinkand on it I may not sleip in peis.'
Thay cryit all, and bad the Swallow ceis,
And said, 'yone Lint heirefter will do gude,
For Linget is to lytill birdis fude.

'We think, quhen that yone Lint bollis ar ryip,
To mak us Feist, and fill us off the seid,
Magre yone Churll, and on it sing and pyip.'
'Weill' (quod the Swallow), 'freindes hardilie beid;
Do as ye will, bot certane sair I dreid,
Heirefter ye sall find als sour, as sweit,
Quhen ye ar speldit on yone Carlis speit.

'The awner off yone lint ane fouler is,
Richt cautelous and full off subteltie;
His pray full sendill tymis will he mis,
Bot giff we birdis all the warrer be;
Full mony off our kin he hes gart de,
And thocht it bot ane sport to spill thair blude:
God keip me ffra him, and the halie Rude.'

eird: earth   on breird: burgeoning   growis: shudders
bollis: pods   magre: (malgré) in spite of   hardilie: by all
means   beid: be it so   speldit: skewered, spread-eagled
speit: spit   awner: owner   cautelous: treacherous
sendill tymis: seldom   bot giff: unless   warrer: more wary

79

Thir small birdis haveand bot lytill thocht
Off perrell that micht fall be aventure,
The counsell off the Swallow set at nocht,
Bot tuke thair flicht, and furth togidder fure;
Sum to the wode, sum markit to the mure.
I tuke my staff, quhen this wes said and done,
And walkit hame, ffor it drew neir the none.

The Lint ryipit, the Carll pullit the Lyne,
Rippillit the bollis, and in beitis set,
It steipit in the burne, and dryit syne,
And with ane bittill knokkit it, and bet,
Syne swingillit it weill, and hekkillit in the flet;
His wyfe it span, and twynit it in to threid,
Of quhilk the Fowlar Nettis maid in deid.

The wynter come, the wickit wind can blaw,
The woddis grene were wallowit with the weit,
Baith firth and fell with froistys were maid faw,
Slonkis and slaik maid slidderie with the sleit ;
The foulis ffair ffor falt thay ffell off feit;
On bewis bair it wes na bute to byde,
Bot hyit unto housis thame to hyde.

Sum in the barn, sum in the stak off corne
Thair lugeing tuke, and maid thair residence;
The Fowlar saw, and grit aithis hes sworne,
Thay suld be tane trewlie ffor thair expence.
His Nettis hes he set with diligence,

fure: set out   markit: made (for)   mure: moor   rippillit:
removed the seeds   beitis: bundles   steipit: steeped
bittill: club   swingillit: scutched   hekkillit: combed, carded
flet: inner part of a house   faw: bright   slonkis, slaik: mires
slidderie: slippery   ffor falt thay ffell off feit: for lack (of food) they
actually fell   tane: taken

And in the snaw he schulit hes ane plane,
And heillit it all ouer with calf agane.

Thir small birdis seand the calff wes glaid;
Trowand it had bene corne, thay lychtit doun;
Bot of the Nettis na presume thay had,
Nor of the Fowlaris fals Intentioun;
To scraip, and seik thair meit thay maid thame boun.
The Swallow on ane lytill branche neir by,
Dreiddand for gyle, thus loud on thame couth cry:

'In to that calf scraip quhill your naillis bleid,
Thair is na corne, ye laubour all in vane;
Trow ye yone Churll for pietie will yow feid?
Na, na, he hes it heir layit for ane trane;
Remove, I reid, or ellis ye will be slane;
His Nettis he hes set full prively,
Reddie to draw; in tyme be war ffor thy.'

Grit fule is he that puttis in dangeir
His lyfe, his honour, ffor ane thing off nocht;
Grit fule is he, that will not glaidlie heir
Counsall in tyme, quhill it availl him nocht;
Grit fule is he, that hes na thing in thocht
Bot thing present, and efter quhat may fall,
Nor off the end hes na memoriall.

Thir small birdis ffor hunger famischit neir,
Full besie scraipand ffor to seik thair fude,
The counsall off the Swallow wald not heir,
Suppois thair laubour did thame lytill gude.

schulit: shovelled   plane: hollow space   heillit: covered
calf(f): chaff   maid thame boun: prepared themselves   trane:
snare   ffor thy: of this

Quhen scho thair fulische hartis understude,
Sa Indurate, up in ane tre scho flew;
With that this Churll over thame his Nettis drew.

Allace! it wes grit hart sair for to se
That bludie Bowcheour beit thay birdis doun,
And ffor till heir, quhen thay wist weill to de,
Thair cairfull sang and lamentatioun:
Sum with ane staf he straik to eirth on swoun:
Off sum the heid he straik, off sum he brak the crag,
Sum half on lyfe he stoppit in his bag.

And quhen the Swallow saw that thay wer deid,
'Lo' (quod scho), 'thus it happinnis mony syis
On thame that will not tak counsall nor reid
Off Prudent men, or Clerkis that ar wyis;
This grit perrell I tauld thame mair than thryis;
Now ar thay deid, and wo is me thairfoir!'
Scho tuke hir flicht, bot I hir saw no moir.

Moralitas

Lo, worthie folk, Esope, that Nobill clerk,
Ane Poet worthie to be Lawreate,
Quhen that he waikit from mair autentik werk,
With uther ma, this foirsaid Fabill wrate,
Quhilk at this tyme may weill be applicate
To guid morall edificatioun,
Haifand ane sentence, according to ressoun.

This Carll and bond of gentrice spoliate,
Sawand this calf, thir small birdis to sla,
It is the Feind, quhilk fra the Angelike state

crag: neck   stoppit: enclosed   syis: times   autentik:
important, proper   bond: husbandman   of gentrice spoliate:
entirely devoid of compassion

Exylit is, as fals Apostata:
Quhilk day and nycht weryis not for to ga
Sawand poysoun in mony wickit thocht
In mannis Saull, quhilk Christ full deir hes bocht.

And quhen the saull, as seid in to the eird,
Gevis consent unto delectioun,
The wickit thocht beginnis for to breird
In deidlie sin, quhilk is dampnatioun;
Ressoun is blindit with affectioun,
And carnall lust grouis full grene and gay,
Throw consuetude hantit from day to day.

Proceding furth be use and consuetude,
The sin ryipis, and schame is set on syde;
The Feynd plettis his Nettis scharp and rude,
And under plesance previlie dois hyde;
Syne on the feild he sawis calf full wyde,
Quhilk is bot tume and verray vanitie
Of fleschlie lust, and vaine prosperitie.

Thir hungrie birdis wretchis we may call,
As scraipand in this warldis vane plesance,
Greddie to gadder gudis temporall,
Quhilk as the calf ar tume without substance,
Lytill of availl, and full of variance,
Lyke to the mow befoir the face of wind
Quhiskis away and makis wretchis blind.

This Swallow, quhilk eschaipit is the snair,
The halie Preichour weill may signifie,
Exhortand folk to walk and ay be wair
Fra Nettis of our wickit enemie,

consuetude: habit   hantit: accustomed   tume: empty
mow: heap (of chaff)

Quha sleipis not, bot ever is reddie,
Quhen wretchis in this warld calf dois scraip,
To draw his Net, that thay may not eschaip.

Allace! quhat cair, quhat weiping is and wo,
Quhen Saull and bodie departit ar in twane!
The bodie to the wormis Keitching go,
The Saull to Fyre, to everlestand pane,
Quhat helpis than this calf, thir gudis vane,
Quhen thow art put in Luceferis bag,
And brocht to hell, and hangit be the crag?

Thir hid Nettis for to persave and se,
This sarie calf wyislie to understand,
Best is bewar in maist prosperite,
For in this warld thair is na thing lestand;
Is na man wait how lang his stait will stand,
His lyfe will lest, nor how that he sall end
Efter his deith, nor quhidder he sall wend.

Pray we thairfoir, quhill we ar in this lyfe,
For four thingis: the first, fra sin remufe;
The secund is fra all weir and stryfe;
The thrid is perfite cheritie and lufe;
The feird thing is, and maist for oure behufe,
That is in blis with Angellis to be fallow.
And thus endis the preiching of the Swallow.

Finis

keitching: kitchen   everlestand: everlasting   fallow:
companion

84

21 *The Taill of the Foxe, that begylit the Wolf,*
   in the schadow of the Mone

IN elderis dayis, as Esope can declair,
   Thair wes ane Husband, quhilk had ane pleuch to steir.
His use wes ay in morning to ryse air;
Sa happinnit him in streiking tyme off yeir
Airlie in the morning to follow ffurth his feir,
Unto the pleuch, bot his gadman and he;
His stottis he straucht with 'Benedicite'.

The Caller cryit: 'how, haik, upon hicht;
Hald draucht, my dowis;' syne broddit thame ffull sair.
The Oxin wes unusit, young and licht,
And ffor fersnes thay couth the fur fforfair.
The Husband than woxe angrie as ane hair,
Syne cryit, and caist his Patill and grit stanis:
'The Wolff' (quod he) 'mot have yow all at anis.'

Bot yit the Wolff wes neirar nor he wend,
For in ane busk he lay, and Lowrence baith,
In ane Rouch Rone, wes at the furris end,
And hard the hecht; than Lowrence leuch full raith:
'To tak yone bud' (quod he) it wer na skaith.'

streiking tyme: ploughing time   feir: companion (the driver)
gadman: goad-man, who, on foot, drove the team, while the other steered
stottis: oxen   straucht: urged on   caller: the driver   haik:
go   hicht: height   hald draucht: keep on pulling   dowis:
doves (dous, dears)   broddit: goaded   licht: ill-tempered
fur: furrow   couth ... fforfair: did spoil   patill: pattle, a stick for
clearing the coulter of stalks, etc.   wend: thought   busk: bush
Lowrence: the fox   rouch: rough   rone: thicket   furris:
furrow's   hecht: promise   raith: soon   bud: bid, offer
skaith: damage

'Weill' (quod the Wolff), 'I hecht the be my hand;
Yone Carllis word, as he wer King, sall stand.'

The Oxin waxit mair reullie at the last;
Syne efter thay lousit, ffra that it worthit weill lait;
The Husband hamewart with his cattell past.
Than sone the Wolff come hirpilland in his gait,
Befoir the Oxin, and schupe to mak debait.
The Husband saw him, and worthit sumdeill agast,
And bakwart with his beistis wald haif past.

The Wolff said, 'quhether dryvis thou this Pray?
I chalenge it, ffor nane off thame ar thyne.'
The man thairoff wes in ane felloun fray,
And soberlie to the Wolff answerit syne:
'Schir, be my Saull, thir oxin ar all myne;
Thairfoir I studdie quhy ye suld stop me,
Sen that I faltit never to you, trewlie.'

The Wolff said, 'Carle, gaif thou not me this drift
Airlie, quhen thou wes eirrand on yone bank?
And is thair oucht (sayis thou) frear than gift?
This tarying wyll tyne the all thy thank;
Far better is frelie ffor to giff ane plank
Nor be compellit on force to giff ane mart.
Fy on the fredome that cummis not with hart!'

'Schir' (quod the husband), 'ane man may say in greif,
And syne ganesay, fra he avise and se:
I hecht to steill, am I thairfoir ane theif?'

reullie: orderly   lousit: unyoked   ffra that: because
worthit weill lait: was growing very late   hirpilland: limping
gait: way   schupe: began   sumdeill: somewhat   felloun:
terrible   fray: fright   studdie: wonder   gaif: gave
drift: team   eirrand: ploughing   tyne: lose   plank: plack,
copper coin   mart: fat ox   fredome: freedom, generosity

86

'God forbid, Schir, all hechtis suld haldin be!
Gaif I my hand or oblissing' (quod he)
'Or have ye witnes, or writ ffor to schaw?
Schir, reif me not, but go and seik the Law!'

'Carll' (quod the Wolff), 'ane Lord, and he be leill,
That schrinkis for schame, or doutis to be repruvit,
His saw is ay als sikker as his Seill.
Fy on the Leid that is not leill and lufit!
Thy argument is fals, and eik contrufit,
For it is said in Proverb: "But lawte
All uther vertewis ar nocht worth ane fle."'

'Schir,' said the husband, 'remember of this thing:
Ane leill man is not tane at halff ane taill.
I may say, and ganesay, I am na King:
Quhair is your witnes that hard I hecht thame haill?'
Than said the Wolff, 'thairfoir it sall nocht faill;
Lowrence' (quod he), 'cum hidder of that Schaw,
And say na thing bot as thow hard and saw.'

Lowrence come lourand, for he lufit never licht,
And sone appeirit befoir thame in that place:
The man leuch na thing, quhen he saw that sicht.
'Lowrence' (quod the Wolff), 'Thow man declair this cace,
Quhairof we sall schaw the suith in schort space;
I callit on the leill witnes for to beir:
Quhat hard thow that this man hecht me lang eir?'

'Schir' (said the Tod), 'I can not hastelie
Swa sone as now gif sentence finall;

oblissing: obligation	reif: steal	saw: word	sikker:
sure	seill: seal	leid: man	leill: honest	taill:
account	lourand: skulking	na thing: not at all	

87

Bot wald ye baith submit yow heir to me,
To stand at my decreit perpetuall,
To pleis baith I suld preif, gif it may fall.'
'Weill' (quod the Wolff), 'I am content for me:'
The man said, 'swa am I, how ever it be.'

Than schew thay furth thair allegeance but fabill,
And baith proponit thair pley to him compleit.
(Quod Lowrence): 'now I am ane Juge amycabill:
Ye sall be sworne to stand at my decreit,
Quhether heirefter ye think it soure or sweit.'
The Wolff braid furth his fute, the man his hand,
And on the Toddis Taill sworne thay ar to stand.

Than tuke the Tod the man furth till ane syde,
And said him, 'friend, thow art in blunder brocht;
The Wolff will not forgif the ane Oxe hyde,
Yit wald my self fane help the, and I mocht;
Bot I am laith to hurt my conscience ocht.
Tyne nocht thy querrell in thy awin defence;
This will not throw but grit coist and expence.

'Seis thow not Buddis beiris Bernis throw,
And giftis garris crukit materis hald ffull evin?
Sumtymis ane hen haldis ane man in ane Kow.
All ar not halie that heifis thair handis to hevin.'
'Schir' (said the man), 'ye sall have sex or sevin,
Richt off the fattest hennis off all the floik:
I compt not all the laif, leif me the Coik.'

---

decreit: decree   preif: try   braid: stretched   ane syde:
aside   and I mocht: if I might   buddis: bids, bribes
beiris: carry   bernis: men   throw: through   garris: make
kow: cow   laif: rest   coik: cock

'I am ane Juge' (quod Lowrence than), and leuch;
'Thair is na Buddis suld beir me by the rycht;
I may tak hennis and Caponis weill aneuch,
For God is gane to sleip; as ffor this nycht,
Sic small thingis ar not sene in to his sicht;
Thir hennis' (quod he) 'sall mak thy querrell sure,
With emptie hand na man suld Halkis lure.'

Concordit thus, than Lowrence tuke his leiff,
And to the Wolff he went in to ane ling;
Syne prevelie he plukkit him be the sleiff:
'Is this in ernist' (quod he) 'ye ask sic thing?
Na, be my Saull, I trow it be in heithing.'
Than saith the Wolff, 'Lowrence, quhy sayis thow sa?
Thow hard the hecht thy self that he couth ma.'

'The hecht' (quod he) 'yone man maid at the pleuch,
Is that the cause quhy ye the cattell craif?'
Halff in to heithing (said Lowrence than), and leuch;
'Schir, be the Rude, unroikit now ye raif;
The Devill ane stirk taill thairfoir sall ye haif;
Wald I tak it upon my conscience
To do sa pure ane man as yone offence?

'Yit haif I communit with the Carll' (quod he);
'We ar concordit upon this cunnand:
Quyte off all clamis, swa ye will mak him fre,
Ye sall ane Cabok have in to your hand,
That sic ane sall not be in all this land;
For it is Somer Cheis, baith fresche and ffair,
He sayis it weyis ane stane, and sumdeill mair.'

querrell: legal case	halkis: hawks	ling: patch of heather
heithing: mockery	couth ma: did make	unroikit: unbalanced
pure: poor	cunnand: covenant, understanding	quyte: quit
cabok: cheese		

'Is that thy counsell' (quod the Wolff), 'I do,
That yone Carll ffor ane Cabok suld be fre?'
'Ye, be my Saull, and I wer sworne yow to,
Ye suld nane uther counsell have for me;
For gang ye to the maist extremitie,
It will not wyn yow worth ane widderit neip;
Schir, trow ye not, I have ane Saull to keip?'

'Weill' (quod the Wolff), 'it is aganis my will
That yone Carll for ane Cabok suld ga quhyte.'
'Schir' (quod the Tod), 'ye tak it in nane evill,
For, be my Saull, your self had all the wyte.'
'Than' (said the Wolff) 'I bid na mair to flyte,
Bot I wald se yone Cabok off sic pryis.'
'Schir' (said the Tod), 'he tauld me quhar it lyis.'

Than hand in hand thay held unto ane hill;
The Husband till his hous hes tane the way,
For he wes fane; he schaipit ffrom thair ill,
And on his feit woke the dure quhill day.
Now will we turne vnto the uther tway.
Throw woddis waist thir Freikis on fute can fair,
Fra busk to busk, quhill neir midnycht and mair.

Lowrence wes ever remembring upon wrinkis
And subtelteis the Wolff for to begyle;
That he had hecht ane Caboik, he forthinkis,
Yit at the last he findis furth ane wyle,
Than at him selff softlie couth he smyle.
The Wolff sayis, 'Lowrence, thow playis bellie blind;
We seik all nycht, bot na thing can we find.'

widderit: withered	neip: turnip	wyte: blame	flyte:
wrangle, altercate	fane: eager, glad		schaipit: escaped
woke the dure: guarded the door		quhill: till	freikis: 'people'
wrinkis: tricks	wyle: trick	bellie blind: blind man's buff	

'Schir' (said the Tod), 'we ar at it almaist;
Soft yow ane lytill, and ye sall se it sone.'
Than to ane Manure place thay hyit in haist:
The nicht wes lycht, and pennyfull the Mone.
Than till ane draw well thir Senyeours past but hone,
Quhair that twa bukkettis severall suithlie hang;
As ane come up, ane uther doun wald gang.

The schadow of the Mone schone in the well.
'Schir' (said Lowrence), 'anis ye sall find me leill;
Now se ye not the Caboik weill your sell,
Quhyte as ane Neip, and round als as ane seill?
He hang it yonder, that na man suld it steill:
Schir, traist ye weill, yone Caboik ye se hing
Micht be ane present to ony Lord or King.'

'Na' (quod the Wolff) 'mycht I yone Caboik haif
On the dry land, as I it yonder se,
I wald quitclame the Carll of all the laif;
His dart Oxin I compt thame not ane fle;
Yone wer mair meit for sic ane man as me.
Lowrence' (quod he), 'leip in the bukket sone,
And I sall hald the ane, quhill thow have done.'

Lowrence gird doun baith sone and subtellie;
The uther baid abufe, and held the flaill.
'It is sa mekill' (quod Lowrence) 'it maisteris me,
On all my tais it hes not left ane naill;
Ye man mak help upwart, and it haill.
Leip in the uther bukket haistelie,
And cum sone doun, and make me sum supple.'

soft yow: be patient   manure place: manor house   hyit:
hurried   pennyfull: full and round   thir: these   but hone:
without delay   suithlie: all ready   schadow: reflection
seill: seal   dart: draught   gird: went   baid: stayed
flaill: beam   tais: toes   supple: help

Than lychtlie in the bukket lap the loun;
His wecht but weir the uther end gart ryis;
The Tod come hailland up, the Wolf yeid doun;
Than angerlie the Wolff upon him cryis:
'I cummand thus dounwart, quhy thow upwart hyis?'
'Schir' (quod the Foxe), 'thus fairis it off Fortoun:
As ane cummis up, scho quheillis ane uther doun!'

Than to the ground sone yeid the Wolff in haist;
The Tod lap on land, als blyith as ony bell,
And left the Wolff in watter to the waist.
Quha haillit him out, I wait not, off the well,
Heir endis the Text; thair is na mair to tell.
Yit men may find ane gude moralitie
In this sentence, thocht it ane Fabill be.

Moralitas

This Wolff I likkin to ane wickit man,
Quhilk dois the pure oppres in everie place,
And pykis at thame all querrellis that he can,
Be Rigour, reif, and uther wickitnes.
The Foxe the Feind I call in to this cais,
Actand ilk man to ryn unrychteous rinkis,
Thinkand thairthrow to lok him in his linkis.

The Husband may be callit ane godlie man,
With quhome the Feynd falt findes (as Clerkis reids),
Besie to tempt him with all wayis that he can.
The hennis ar warkis that fra ferme faith proceidis:
Quhair sic sproutis spreidis, the evill spreit thair not speids,
Bot wendis unto the wickit man agane;
That he hes tint his travell is full unfane.

; but weir: without doubt   quheillis: wheels   yeid: went
pykis: picks   actand: actuating   ryn . . . rinkis: perform . . .
deeds   thairthrow: thereby   ferme: firm   sproutis: good
seed   travell: work   unfane: frustrated

The wodds waist, quhairin wes the Wolff wyld,
Ar wickit riches, quhilk all men gaipis to get;
Quha traistis in sic Trusterie ar oft begyld;
For Mammon may be callit the Devillis Net,
Quhilk Sathanas for all sinfull hes set.
With proud plesour quha settis his traist thairin,
But speciall grace, lychtlie can not outwin.

The Cabok may be callit Covetyce,
Quhilk blomis braid in mony mannis Ee;
Wa worth the well of that wickit vyce!
For it is all bot fraud and fantasie,
Dryvand ilk man to leip in the buttrie
That dounwart drawis unto the pane of hell.—
Christ keip all Christianis from that wickit well!

Finis

trusterie: securities   lychtlie: easily   wa worth . . . !: evil to . . . !
buttrie: larder (? bucket)

[? JOHN REID OF STOBO

? c. 1430–1505]

22   Prologue to *The Thre Prestis of Peblis*

IN Peblis town sum tyme, as I heard tell,
   The formest day of Februare befell
Thrie Preists went unto collatioun
Into ane privie place of the said toun,

Quhair that thay sat richt soft and unfutesair:
Thay luifit not na rangald nor repair.
And gif I sall the suith reckin and say,
I traist it was upon Sanct Bryds day,
Quhair that thay sat ful easilie and soft,
With monie lowd lauchter upon loft.
And wit ye weil thir thrie thay maid gude cheir—
To them thair was na dainteis than too deir—
With thrie fed capons on a speit with creische,
With monie uther sindrie dyvers meis;
And them to serve thay had nocht bot a boy;
Fra cumpanie thay keipit them sa coy;
Thay lufit nocht with ladry nor with lown
Nor with trumpours to travel throw the town,
Bot with themself quhat thay wald tel or crak,
Umquhyle sadlie, umquhyle jangle and jak.

Thus sat thir thrie besyde ane felloun fyre
Quhil thair capons war roistit lim and lyre.
Befoir them was sone set a Roundel bricht;
And with ane clene claith fynelie dicht
It was owirset, and on it breid was laid.
The eldest than began the grace and said,
And blissit the breid with *Benedicete*,
With *Dominus, Amen*, sa mot I the.
And be thay had drunken about a quarte
Than spak ane thus that Maister was in Arte,
And to his name than callit Johne was he,
And said, 'Sen we ar heir Preists thrie,
Syne wantis nocht, be him that maid the Mone
Til us me think ane tail sould cum in tune.'

na: neither	rangald: disturbance	repair: company
creische: dripping	meis: meats	ladry: idle lads	lown:
lazy people	trumpours: cheats	felloun: fierce	lim and
lyre: bone and flesh	roundel: table	sa mot I the: so may I thrive

Than spak ane other hecht Maister Archebald:
'Now be the hiest Hevin,' quod he, 'I hald
To tel ane tail me think I sould not tyre,
To hald my fute out of this felloun fyre.'
Than spak the thrid to name hecht Sir Williame:
'To grit clargie I can not count nor clame,
Nor yit I am not travellit, as ar ye,
In monie sundrie Land beyond the See;
Thairfoir me think it nouther shame nor sin
Ane of yow twa the first tail to begin.'
'Heir I protest,' than spak maister Archebald;
'Ane travellit Clerk suppois I be cald,
Presumpteouslie I think not to presume,
As I that was never travellit bot to Rome,
To tel ane tail; bot eirar, I suppone,
The first tail tald mot be Maister Johne;
For he hath bene in monie uncouth Land:
In Portingale and in Ciuile the grand,—
In fyve kinrikis of Spane al hes he bene,
In foure christin and ane heathin I wene,—
In Rome, Flanders, and in Venice toun,
And uther Lands sundrie up and doun;
And for that he spak first of ane tail,
Thairfoir to begin he sould not fail.'
Than speiks Maister Johne, 'Now be the Rude,
Me to begin ane tail sen ye conclude,
And I deny than had I sair offendit:
The thing begun, the soner it is endit.'

    hecht: called   eirar: rather   Ciuile: Seville

[? JOHN] CLERK

? before 1500

Fane wald I luve

FANE wald I luve, bot quhair about?
   Thair is so mony luvaris thairout
That thair is left no place to me;
Quhairof I hovit now in dout,
Gif I sould luve or lat it be.

Sa mony ar, thair ladeis treitis
With triumphand amoures balleitis,
And dois thair bewteis pryis so he,
That I find not bot daft consaitis
To say of luve. Bot lat it be.

Sum thinkis his lady lustiest;
Sum haldis his lady for the best;
Sum sayis his luve is A *per se;*
Bot sum forsuth ar so opprest
With luve, wer bettir lat it be.

Sum for his ladyis luve lyis seik,
Suppois scho comptis it not a leik,
And sum droupis doun as he wold die;
Sum strykis doun a threid-bair cheik
For luve, war bettir lat it be.

Sum luvis lang and lyis behind;
Sum luvis and freindschip can not fynd;
Sum festnit is and ma not fle;
Sum led is lyk the belly blynd
With luve, wer bettir lat it be.

   hovit: remained   treitis: entreat

Thocht luve be grene in gud curage,
And be difficill till assuage,
The end of it is miserie.
Misgovernit youth makis gowsty age.
Forbeir ye not, and lat it be.

Bot quha perfytly wald imprent,
Sould fynd his luve moist permanent;
Luve God, thy prince, and freind, all thre;
Treit weill thyself and stand content,
And latt all uthir luvaris be.

gowsty: dreary, empty   bot quha ... imprent: but he who would
make the most lasting impression   moist: most

MERSAR

? *c.* 1500

24   *Allace! so Sobir is the Micht*

ALLACE! so sobir is the micht
Of wemen for to mak debait
In contrair menis subtell slicht,
Quhilk ar fulfillit with dissait;
With tressone so intoxicait
Ar mennis mouthis at all houris,
Quhome in to trest no woman wait.
Sic perrell lyis in paramouris.

wait: knows

Sum sweris that he luvis so weill
That he will de without remeid,
Bot gife that he hir freindschip feill
That garris him sic langour leid;
And thocht he haif no doubt of speid,
Yit will he sich and schaw grit schouris,
As he wald sterfe in to that steid.
Sic perrell lyis in paramouris.

Athis to sweir and giftis to hecht
Moir than he hes thretty fold,
And for hir honour for to fecht
Quhill that his blude be cumin cold;
Bot fra scho to his willis yòld,
Adew, fairweill thir somer flouris;
All grows in glas that semit gold.
Sic perrell lyis in paramouris.

Than turnis he his saill annone
And passis to ane uthir port.
Thocht scho be nevir so wobegone,
Hir cairis cauld ar his confort.
Heirfoir I pray in termys schort,
Chryst keip thir birdis bricht in bowris
Fra fals luvaris and thair resort.
Sic perrell lyis in paramouris.

speid: success	sterfe: die	steid: place	athis: oaths
hecht: promise	fra: from the time that		yold: yield
grows in: turns into			

WALTER KENNEDY

? 1460–? 1508

25   *Honour with Age*

A T matyne houre in midis of the nicht,
　Walknit of sleip I saw besyd me sone
Ane aigit man semit sextie yeiris of sicht
This sentence sett and song it in gud tone:
'Omnipotent and eterne God in trone,
To be content and lufe the I haif caus
That my licht youtheid is opprest and done;
Honor with age to every vertew drawis.

'Grene youth, to aige thou mon obey and bow;
Thy foly lustis lestis skant ane May;
That than wes witt, is naturall foly now,
As warldly witt, honor, riches or fresche array;
Deffy the devill; dreid God and domisday,
For all salbe accusit as thou knawis;
Blissit be God my yutheid is away;
Honor with aige to every vertew drawis.

'O bittir youith that semis delitious;
O haly aige that sumtyme semit soure;
O restles youth hie, hait, and vicious;
O honest aige fulfillit with honoure;
O frawart youth, frutles and fedand flour,
Contrair to conscience baith to God and lawis,
Off all vanegloir the lamp and the mirroure;
Honor with aige till every vertew drawis.

in trone: enthroned   youtheid: youth   mon: must   fedand
flour: fading flower

'This warld is sett for to dissaive us evin;
Pryd is the nett and covece is the trane;
For na reward except the joy of hevin
Wald I be yung in to this warld agane;
The schip of faith tempestous wind and rane
Dryvis in the see of Lollerdry that blawis:
My youth is gane and I am glaid and fane;
Honor with aige till every vertew drawis.

'Law, luve and lawtie gravin law thay ly;
Dissimulance hes borrowit conscience clayis;
Aithis, writ, walx nor seilis ar not set by;
Flattery is fosterit baith with freindis and fayis;
The sone to bruike it that his fader hais
Wald se him deid, Sathanas sic seid sawis;
Youtheid adew, ane of my mortall fais;
Honor with aige till every vertew drawis.'

ffinis q kennedy

evin: completely   covece: covetousness   trane: snare
fane: pleased   clayis: clothes   bruike it that: possess what
seid: seed

WILLIAM DUNBAR

? 1456–? 1513

26   *To a Ladye*

SWEIT rois of vertew and of gentilnes,
    Delytsum lyllie of everie lustynes,
    Richest in bontie and in bewtie cleir,
    And everie vertew that is held most deir,
Except onlie that ye ar mercyles.

In to your garthe this day I did persew,
Thair saw I flowris that fresche wer of hew;
  Baith quhyte and reid moist lusty wer to seyne,
  And halsum herbis upone stalkis grene;
Yit leif nor flour fynd could I nane of rew.

I dout that Merche, with his caild blastis keyne,
Hes slane this gentill herbe that I of mene,
  Quhois petewous deithe dois to my hart sic pane
  That I wald mak to plant his rute agane.
So confortand his levis unto me bene.

garthe: garden

27 *Meditatioun in Wyntir*

IN to thir dirk and drublie dayis,
 Quhone sabill all the hevin arrayis
  With mystie vapouris, cluddis, and skyis,
  Nature all curage me denyis
Off sangis, ballattis, and of playis.

Quhone that the nycht dois lenthin houris,
With wind, with haill, and havy schouris,
  My dule spreit dois lurk for schoir,
  My hairt for languor dois forloir
For laik of symmer with his flouris.

I walk, I turne, sleip may I nocht,
I vexit am with havie thocht;
  This warld all ouir I cast about,
  And ay the mair I am in dout,
The mair that I remeid have socht.

dirk: dark   drublie: dank, dismal   dule: depressed   spreit:
spirit   schoir; apprehension   forloir: weaken   remeid:
remedy, salvation

I am assayit on everie syde:
Dispair sayis ay, 'In tyme provyde
  And get sum thing quhairon to leif,
  Or with grit trouble and mischief
Thow sall in to this court abyd.'

Than Patience sayis, 'Be not agast:
Hald Hoip and Treuthe within the fast,
  And lat Fortoun wirk furthe hir rage,
  Quhome that no rasoun may assuage,
Quhill that hir glas be run and past.'

And Prudence in my eir sayis ay,
'Quhy wald thow hald that will away?
  Or craif that thow may have no space,
  Thow tending to ane uther place,
A journay going everie day?'

And than sayis Age, 'My freind, cum neir,
And be not strange, I the requeir:
  Cum, brodir, by the hand me tak,
  Remember thow hes compt to mak
Off all thi tyme thow spendit heir.'

Syne Deid castis upe his yettis wyd,
Saying, 'Thir oppin sall the abyd;
  Albeid that thow wer never sa stout,
  Undir this lyntall sall thow lowt:
Thair is nane uther way besyde.'

leif: live   compt: count, account   yettis: gates   lowt: stoop

For feir of this all day I drowp;
No gold in kist, nor wyne in cowp,
  No ladeis bewtie, nor luiffis blys,
  May lat me to remember this,
How glaid that ever I dyne or sowp.

Yit, quhone the nycht begynnis to schort,
It dois my spreit sum pairt confort,
  Off thocht oppressit with the schowris.
  Cum, lustie symmer! with thi flowris,
That I may leif in sum disport.

lat: prevent

28   *Lament for the Makaris*

Quhen He Wes Sek

I THAT in heill wes and gladnes,
  Am trublit now with gret seiknes,
And feblit with infermite;
  Timor mortis conturbat me.

Our plesance heir is all vane glory,
This fals warld is bot transitory,
The flesche is brukle, the Fend is sle;
  Timor mortis conturbat me.

The stait of man dois change and vary,
Now sound, now seik, now blith, now sary,
Now dansand mery, now like to dee;
  Timor mortis conturbat me.

makaris: poets, creators   heill: health   brukle: brittle, frail
sle: subtle

No stait in erd heir standis sickir;
As with the wynd wavis the wickir,
Wavis this warldis vanite;
   Timor mortis conturbat me.

On to the ded gois all Estatis,
Princis, Prelotis, and Potestatis,
Baith riche and pur of al degre;
   Timor mortis conturbat me.

He takis the knychtis in to feild,
Anarmit under helme and scheild;
Victour he is at all mellie;
   Timor mortis conturbat me.

That strang unmercifull tyrand
Takis, on the moderis breist sowkand,
The bab full of benignite;
   Timor mortis conturbat me.

He takis the campion in the stour,
The capitane closit in the tour,
The lady in bour full of bewte;
   Timor mortis conturbat me.

He sparis no lord for his piscence;
Na clerk for his intelligence;
His awfull strak may no man fle;
   Timor mortis conturbat me.

Art-magicianis and astrologgis,
Rethoris, logicianis, and theologgis,
Thame helpis no conclusionis sle;
   Timor mortis conturbat me.

       sickir: certain   piscence: puissance

In medicyne the most practicianis,
Lechis, surrigianis, and phisicianis,
Thame self fra ded may not supple;
   Timor mortis conturbat me.

I se that makaris amang the laif
Playis heir ther pageant, syne gois to graif;
Sparit is nocht ther faculte;
   Timor mortis conturbat me.

He hes done petuously devour,
The noble Chaucer, of makaris flour,
The Monk of Bery, and Gower, all thre;
   Timor mortis conturbat me.

The gude Syr Hew of Eglintoun,
And eik Heryot, and Wyntoun,
He hes tane out of this cuntre;
   Timor mortis conturbat me.

That scorpion fell hes done infek
Maister Johne Clerk, and James Afflek,
Fra balat making and tragidie;
   Timor mortis conturbat me.

Holland and Barbour he hes berevit;
Allace! that he nocht with us levit
Schir Mungo Lokert of the Le;
   Timor mortis conturbat me.

Clerk of Tranent eik he hes tane,
That maid the Anteris of Gawane;
Schir Gilbert Hay endit hes he;
   Timor mortis conturbat me.

               laif: rest, remainder

He hes Blind Hary and Sandy Traill
Slaine with his schour of mortall haill,
Quhilk Patrik Johnestoun myght nocht fle;
   Timor mortis conturbat me.

He hes reft Merseir his endite,
That did in luf so lifly write,
So schort, so quyk, of sentence hie;
   Timor mortis conturbat me.

He hes tane Roull of Aberdene,
And gentill Roull of Corstorphin;
Two bettir fallowis did no man se;
   Timor mortis conturbat me.

In Dumfermelyne he hes done roune
With Maister Robert Henrisoun;
Schir Johne the Ros enbrast hes he;
   Timor mortis conturbat me.

And he hes now tane, last of aw,
Gud gentill Stobo and Quintyne Schaw,
Of quham all wichtis hes pete:
   Timor mortis conturbat me.

Gud Maister Walter Kennedy
In poynt of dede lyis veraly,
Gret reuth it wer that so suld be;
   Timor mortis conturbat me.

Sen he hes all my brether tane,
He will nocht lat me lif alane,
On forse I man his nyxt pray be;
   Timor mortis conturbat me.

endite: poem, writings   done roune: whispered, talked

Sen for the deid remeid is none,
Best is that we for dede dispone,
Eftir our deid that lif may we;
Timor mortis conturbat me.

dispone: prepare

29 *On the Resurrection of Christ*

DONE is a battell on the dragon blak,
  Our campioun Chryst confountet hes his force;
The yettis of hell ar brokin with a crak,
The signe triumphall rasit is of the croce
The divillis trymmillis with hiddous voce,
The saulis ar borrowit and to the blis can go,
Chryst with his blud our ransonis dois indoce:
Surrexit Dominus de sepulchro.

Dungin is the deidly dragon Lucifer,
The crewall serpent with the mortall stang;
The auld kene tegir with his teith on char,
Quhilk in a wait hes lyne for us so long,
Thinking to grip us in his clows strang;
The mercifull Lord wald nocht that it were so,
He maid him for to felye of that fang:
Surrexit Dominus de sepulchro.

yettis: gates   voce: voice   indoce: endorse   dungin:
struck down, overcome   stang: sting   tegir: tiger   on char:
snarling   felye: fail   fang: plunder

He for our saik that sufferit to be slane,
And lyk a lamb in sacrifice wes dicht,
Is lyk a lyone rissin up agane,
And as gyane raxit him on hicht;
Sprungin is Aurora radius and bricht,
On loft is gone the glorius Appollo,
The blisfull day depairtit fro the nycht:
Surrexit Dominus de sepulchro.

The grit victour agane is rissin on hicht,
That for our querrell to the deth wes woundit;
The sone that wox all paill now schynis bricht,
And dirknes clerit, our fayth is now refoundit;
The knell of mercy fra the hevin is soundit,
The Cristin ar deliverit of thair wo,
The Jowis and thair errour ar confoundit:
Surrexit Dominus de sepulchro.

The fo is chasit, the battell is done ceis,
The presone brokin, the jevellouris fleit and flemit;
The weir is gon, confermit is the peis,
The fetteris lowsit and the dungeoun temit,
The ransoun maid, the presoneris redemit;
The feild is win, ourcumin is the fo,
Dispulit of the tresur that he yemit:
Surrexit Dominus de sepulchro.

---

dicht: prepared   gyane: giant   raxit: reached, raised
querrell: cause   jevellouris: jailers   fleit and flemit: put to flight
and banished   weir: war   lowsit: loosened   temit: emptied
yemit: held, intended to keep

Ane Ballat of Our Lady

HALE, sterne superne! Hale, in eterne,
   In Godis sicht to schyne!
Lucerne in derne for to discerne
   Be glory and grace devyne;
Hodiern, modern, sempitern,
   Angelicall regyne!
Our tern inferne for to dispern
   Helpe, rialest rosyne.
     Ave Maria, gracia plena!
   Haile, fresche floure femynyne!
Yerne us, guberne, virgin matern,
   Of reuth baith rute and ryne.

Haile, yhyng, benyng, fresche flurising!
   Haile, Alphais habitakle!
Thy dyng ofspring maid us to syng
   Befor his tabernakle;
All thing maling we doune thring,
   Be sicht of his signakle;
Quhilk king us bring unto his ryng,
   Fro dethis dirk umbrakle.
     Ave Maria, gracia plena!
   Haile, moder and maide but makle!
Bricht syng, gladyng our languissing,
   Be micht of thi mirakle.

Haile, bricht be sicht in hevyn on hicht!
   Haile, day sterne orientale!

sterne: star   superne: supreme   in derne: in darkness   hodiern:
daily, diurnal   regyne: queen—*regina*   tern: trouble   dispern:
disperse   yerne: succour   habitakle: dwelling-place   dyng:
worthy   maling: malign   thring: hurl, press down
signakle: sign (of cross)   umbrakle: shade   makle: spot   syng:
sign

Our licht most richt, in clud of nycht,
　Our dirknes for to scale:
Hale, wicht in ficht, puttar to flicht
　Of fendis in battale!
Haile, plicht but sicht! Hale, mekle of mycht!
　Haile, glorius Virgin, haile!
　　Ave Maria, gracia plena!
　Haile, gentill nychttingale!
Way stricht, cler dicht, to wilsome wicht,
　That irke bene in travale.

Hale, qwene serene! Hale, most amene!
　Haile, hevinlie hie emprys!
Haile, schene unseyne with carnale eyne!
　Haile, ros of paradys!
Haile, clene, bedene, ay till conteyne!
　Haile, fair fresche flour delyce!
Haile, grene daseyne! Haile, fro the splene,
　Of Jhesu genetrice!
　　Ave Maria, gracia plena!
　Thow baire the prince of prys;
Our teyne to meyne, and ga betweyne
　As humile oratrice.

Haile, more decore than of before,
　And swetar be sic sevyne,
Our glore forlore for to restore,
　Sen thow art qwene of hevyn!
Memore of sore, stern in Aurore,
　Lovit with angellis stevyne;

plicht: sheet anchor　　　irke: exhausted, worn　　　amene: pleasant
schene: beauty　　　bedene: altogether　　　daseyne: daisy　　　splene:
heart　　　teyne: misery　　　meyne: relieve, cure　　　forlore: lost
lovit: praised　　　stevyne: vocal sound, praise

Implore, adore, thow indeflore,
  To mak our oddis evyne.
    Ave Maria, gracia plena!
  With lovingis lowde ellevyn.
Quhill store and hore my youth devore,
  Thy name I sall ay nevyne.

Empryce of prys, imperatrice,
  Brycht polist precious stane;
Victrice of vyce, hie genetrice
  Of Jhesu, lord soverayne:
Our wys pavys fra enemys,
  Agane the feyndis trayne;
Oratrice, mediatrice, salvatrice,
  To God gret suffragane!
    Ave Maria, gracia plena!
  Haile, sterne meridiane!
Spyce, flour delice of paradys,
  That baire the gloryus grayne.

Imperiall wall, place palestrall,
  Of peirles pulcritud;
Tryumphale hall, hie trone regall
  Of Godis celsitud;
Hospitall riall, the lord of all
  Thy closet did include;
Bricht ball cristall, ros virginall,
  Fulfillit of angell fude.
    Ave Maria, gracia plena!
  Thy birth has with his blude
Fra fall mortall, originall,
  Us raunsound on the rude.

ellevyn: elevated, exalted	store: trouble	hore: age	nevyne:
name pavys: shield	celsitud: greatness, excellence		

31   *Remonstrance to the King*

SCHIR, ye have mony servitouris
And officiaris of dyvers curis;
Kirkmen, courtmen, and craftismen fyne;
Doctouris in jure, and medicyne;
Divinouris, rethoris, and philosophouris,
Astrologis, artistis, and oratouris;
Men of armes, and vailyeand knychtis,
And mony uther gudlie wichtis;
Musicianis, menstralis, and mirrie singaris:
Chevalouris, cawandaris, and flingaris;
Cunyouris, carvouris, and carpentaris,
Beildaris of barkis and ballingaris;
Masounis lyand upon the land,
And schipwrichtis hewand upone the strand;
Glasing wrichtis, goldsmythis, and lapidaris,
Pryntouris, payntouris, and potingaris;
And all of thair craft cunning,
And all at anis lawboring;
Quhilk pleisand ar and honorable,
And to your hienes profitable,
And richt convenient for to be
With your hie regale majestie;
Deserving of your grace most ding
Bayth thank, rewarde, and cherissing.

And thocht that I, amang the laif,
Unworthy be ane place to have,
Or in thair nummer to be tald,
Alas lang in mynd my wark sall hald,
Als haill in everie circumstance,

curis: cares   cawandaris: ?   flingaris: dancers   cunyouris: coiners   ballingaris: ships   potingaris: apothecaries   ding: worthy

In forme, in mater, and substance,
But wering, or consumptioun,
Roust, canker, or corruptioun,
As ony of thair werkis all,
Suppois that my rewarde be small.

  Bot ye sa gracious ar and meik,
That on your hienes followis eik
Ane uthir sort, more miserabill,
Thocht thai be nocht sa profitable:
Fenyeouris, fleichouris, and flatteraris;
Cryaris, craikaris, and clatteraris;
Soukaris, groukaris, gledaris, gunnaris;
Monsouris of France, gud clarat-cunnaris;
Innopportoun askaris of Yrland kynd;
And meit revaris, lyk out of mynd;
Scaffaris, and scamleris in the nuke,
And hall huntaris of draik and duik;
Thrimlaris and thristaris, as thay war woid,
Kokenis, and kennis na man of gude;
Schulderaris, and schowaris, that hes no schame,
And to no cunning that can clame;
And can non uthir craft nor curis
Bot to mak thrang, Schir, in your duris,
And rusche in quhair thay counsale heir,
And will at na man nurtir leyr:
In quintiscence, eik, ingynouris joly,
That far can multiplie in folie;
Fantastik fulis, bayth fals and gredy,
Off toung untrew, and hand evill deidie:

fleichouris: fawners   craikaris: boasters   clatteraris: gossips
groukaris: ?   gledaris: ?   revaris: stealers   scaffaris: beggars
scamleris: spongers   thrimlaris: jostlers   thristaris: thrusters
kokenis: rogues   schulderaris and schowaris: shoulderers and
shovers   can: know, have skill in   thrang: crowd   duris:
doors   leyr: learn

Few dar, of all this last additioun,
Cum in tolbuyth without remissioun.

   And thocht this nobill cunning sort,
Quhom of befoir I did report,
Rewardit be, it war bot ressoun,
Thairat suld no man mak enchessoun:
Bot quhen the uther fulis nyce,
That feistit at Cokelbeis gryce,
Ar all rewardit, and nocht I,
Than on this fals world I cry, Fy!
My hart neir bristis than for teyne,
Quhilk may nocht suffer nor sustene
So grit abusioun for to se,
Daylie in court befoir myn E!

   And yit more panence wald I have,
Had I rewarde amang the laif,
It wald me sumthing satisfie,
And les of my malancolie,
And gar me mony falt ouerse,
That now is brayd befoir myn E:
My mind so fer is set to flyt,
That of nocht ellis I can endyt;
For owther man my hart to breik,
Or with my pen I man me wreik;
And sen the tane most nedis be,
In to malancolie to de,
Or lat the vennim ische all out,
Be war, anone, for it will spout,
Gif that the tryackill cum nocht tyt
To swage the swalme of my dispyt!

---

enchessoun: blame   Cokelbeis gryce: refers to poem *Cockelbie's
Sow*   teyne: anger, despairing rage   flyt: scold, vilify   endyt:
write   wreik: avenge   tryackill: medicine   swalme:
swelling

32

The Petition of the Gray Horse, Auld Dunbar

NOW lufferis cummis with larges lowd,
  Quhy sould not palfrayis thane be prowd,
Quhen gillettis wil be schomd and schroud,
That ridden ar baith with lord and lawd?
    Schir, lat it nevir in toun be tald,
    That I suld be ane Youllis yald!

Quhen I was young and into ply,
And wald cast gammaldis to the sky,
I had beine bocht in realmes by,
Had I consentit to be sauld.
    Schir, lett it nevir in toun be tauld,
    That I suld be ane Youllis yald!

With gentill hors quhen I wald knyp,
Thane is thair laid on me ane quhip,
To colleveris than man I skip,
That scabbit ar, hes cruik and cald.
    Schir, lett it nevir in toun be tald,
    That I suld be ane Youllis yald!

Thocht in the stall I be not clappit,
As cursouris that in silk beine trappit,
With ane new hous I wald be happit,
Aganis this Crysthinmes for the cald.
    Schir, lett it nevir in toun be tald,
    That I suld be ane Yuillis yald!

---

lufferis: lovers,? liveries   gillettis: mares   schomd and schroud:
combed and brushed   lawd: low-born   Youllis yald: an old horse
turned out undressed at Christmas   ply: condition   gammaldis:
gambols   knyp: nibble   colleveris: coalheavers

Suppois I war ane ald yaid aver,
Schott furth our clewch to squische the clever,
And hed the strenthis off all Strenever,
I wald at Youll be housit and stald,
   Schir, lat it never in toune be tald,
   That I suld be ane Yuillis yald!

I am ane auld hors, as ye knaw,
That ever in duill dois drug and draw;
Great court hors puttis me fra the staw,
To fang the fog be firthe and fald.
   Schir, lat it never in toune be tald,
   That I suld be ane Yuillis yald!

I heff run lang furth in the feild
On pastouris that ar plane and peld;
I mycht be now tein in for eild,
My bekis ar spruning he and bald.
   Schir, lat it never in toun be tald,
   That I suld be ane Yuillis yald!

My maine is turned in to quhyt,
And thair off ye heff all the wyt!
Quhen uthair hors hed brane to byt
I gat bot gris, grype giff I wald.
   Schir, lat it never in towne be tald,
   That I suld be ane Yuillis yald!

I was never dautit in to stabell,
My lyff hes bein so miserabell,

---

ald yaid aver: old done nag   clewch: cliff   clever: clover
And hed . . . : whole line obscure   duill: sadness   drug: drudge
fang: endure   peld: stripped bare   bekis: tusks   wyt:
blame   brane: bran   gris: grass   dautit: petted

My hyd to offer I am abell,
For evill schoud strae that I reiv wald.
    Schir, lat it never in towne be tald,
    That I suld be ane Yuillis yald!

And yett, suppois my thrift be thyne,
Gif that I die your aucht within,
Lat nevir the soutteris have my skin,
With uglie gumes to be gnawin.
    Schir, lat it nevir in toun be tald,
    That I suld be ane Yuillis yald!

The court hes done my curage cuill,
And maid me ane forriddin muill;
Yett, to weir trapperis at the Yuill,
I wald be spurrit at everie spald.
    Schir, lat it nevir in toun be tald,
    That I suld be ane Yuillis yald!

Respontio Regis

Efter our wrettingis, thesaurer,
Tak in this gray hors, Auld Dumbar,
Quhilk in my aucht with service trew
In lyart changeit is in hew.
Gar hows him now aganis this Yuill,
And busk him lyk ane bischopis muill,
For with my hand I have indost
To pay quhatevir his trappouris cost.

---

schoud: cleaned   strae: straw   reiv: rob   aucht: possession
soutteris: shoemakers   gnawin: shoemakers chewed the leather to
soften it   spald: joint   lyart: hoary   gar: compel

33 *To the Merchantis of Edinburgh*

QUHY will ye, merchantis of renoun,
  Lat Edinburgh, your nobill toun,
For laik of reformatioun
The commone proffeitt tyine and fame?
  Think ye not schame,
That onie uther regioun
Sall with dishonour hurt your name!

May nane pas throw your principall gaittis
For stink of haddockis and of scattis,
For cryis of carlingis and debaittis,
For fensum flyttingis of defame:
  Think ye not schame,
Befoir strangeris of all estaittis
That sic dishonour hurt your name!

Your stinkand Style, that standis dirk,
Haldis the lycht fra your parroche kirk;
Your foirstairis makis your housis mirk,
Lyk na cuntray bot heir at hame:
  Think ye not schame,
Sa litill polesie to wirk
In hurt and sklander of your name!

At your hie Croce, quhar gold and silk
Sould be, thair is bot crudis and milk;
And at your Trone bot cokill and wilk,
Pansches, pudingis of Jok and Jame:
  Think ye not schame,
Sen as the world sayis that ilk
In hurt and sclander of your name!

tyine: lose   carlingis: old women   fensum flyttingis: offensive
denunciations   stinkand Style: the Stynkand Style was a tenement of
shops and such   parroche kirk: i.e. kirk of St. Giles   pansches: tripe

Your commone menstrallis hes no tone
Bot 'Now the day dawis,' and 'Into Joun';
Cunningar men man serve Sanct Cloun,
And nevir to uther craftis clame:
   Think ye not schame,
To hald sic mowaris on the moyne,
In hurt and sclander of your name!

Tailyouris, soutteris, and craftis vyll,
The fairest of your streitis dois fyll;
And merchandis at the Stinkand Styll
Ar hamperit in ane hony came:
   Think ye not schame,
That ye have nether witt nor wyll
To win yourselff ane bettir name!

Your burgh of beggeris is ane nest,
To schout thai swentyouris will not rest;
All honest folk they do molest,
Sa piteuslie thai cry and rame:
   Think ye not schame,
That for the poore hes nothing drest,
In hurt and sclander of your name!

Your proffeit daylie dois incres,
Your godlie workis les and les;
Through streittis nane may mak progres
For cry of cruikit, blind, and lame:
   Think ye not schame,
That ye sic substance dois posses,
And will nocht win ane bettir name!

tone: tune	mowaris: jokers	soutteris: shoemakers
came: comb	swentyouris: rogues	rame: clamour

Sen for the Court and the Sessioun,
The great repair of this regioun
Is in your burgh, thairfoir be boun
To mend all faultis that ar to blame,
   And eschew schame;
Gif thai pas to ane uther toun
Ye will decay, and your great name!

Thairfoir strangeris and leigis treit,
Tak not ouer meikle for thair meit,
And gar your merchandis be discreit,
That na extortiounes be, proclame
   All fraud and schame:
Keip ordour, and poore nighbouris beit,
That ye may gett ane bettir name!

Singular proffeit so dois yow blind,
The common proffeit gois behind:
I pray that Lord remeid to fynd,
That deit into Jerusalem,
   And gar yow schame!
That sum tyme ressoun may yow bind,
For to [   ] yow guid name.

boun: ready   treit: draw   meikle: much   gar: compel
proclame: denounce   beit: supply   remeid: salvation, help

34   *The Goldyn Targe*

R YGHT as the stern of day begouth to schyne,
  Quhen gone to bed war Vesper and Lucyne,
I raise and by a rosere did me rest;
Up sprang the goldyn candill matutyne,

stern: star   rosere: rose-garden

With clere depurit bemes cristallyne,
  Glading the mery foulis in thair nest;
  Or Phebus was in purpur cape revest
Up raise the lark, the hevyns menstrale fyne
  In May, in till a morow myrthfullest.

Full angellike thir birdis sang thair houris
Within thair courtyns grene, in to thair bouris
  Apparalit quhite and red wyth blomes suete;
Anamalit was the felde wyth all colouris,
The perly droppis schake in silvir schouris,
  Quhill all in balme did branch and levis flete;
  To part fra Phebus did Aurora grete,
Hir cristall teris I saw hyng on the flouris,
  Quhilk he for lufe all drank up wyth his hete.

For mirth of May, wyth skippis and wyth hoppis,
The birdis sang upon the tender croppis,
  With curiouse note, as Venus chapell clerkis:
The rosis yong, new spreding of thair knopis,
War powderit brycht with hevinly beriall droppis,
  Throu bemes rede birnyng as ruby sperkis;
  The skyes rang for schoutyng of the larkis,
The purpur hevyn, our scailit in silvir sloppis,
  Ourgilt the treis, branchis, lef, and barkis.

Doune throu the ryce a ryvir ran wyth stremys,
So lustily agayn thai lykand lemys,
  That all the lake as lamp did leme of licht,
Quhilk schadowit all about wyth twynkling glemis;

flete: float   croppis: shoots   knopis: buds   beriall: beryl
our scailit in silver sloppis: mackerel-clouded   ryce: grove
lemys: rays

That bewis bathit war in secund bemys
   Throu the reflex of Phebus visage brycht;
   On every syde the hegies raise on hicht,
The bank was grene, the bruke was full of bremys,
   The stanneris clere as stern in frosty nycht.

The cristall air, the sapher firmament,
The ruby skyes of the orient,
   Kest beriall bemes on emerant bewis grene;
The rosy garth depaynt and redolent,
With purpur, azure, gold, and goulis gent
   Arayed was, by dame Flora the quene,
   So nobily, that joy was for to sene;
The roch agayn the rivir resplendent
   As low enlumynit all the leves schene.

Quhat throu the mery foulys armony,
And throu the ryveris soune rycht ran me by,
   On Florais mantill I slepit as I lay,
Quhare sone in to my dremes fantasy
I saw approch, agayn the orient sky,
   A saill, als quhite as blossum upon spray,
   Wyth merse of gold, brycht as the stern of day,
Quhilk tendit to the land full lustily,
   As falcoune swift desyrouse of hir pray.

And hard on burd unto the blomyt medis,
Amang the grene rispis and the redis,
   Arrivit sche, quhar fro anone thare landis
Ane hundreth ladyes, lusty in to wedis,

---

bremys: bream   stanneris: gravel   garth: garden   goulis
gent: beautiful red   roch: rock   low: flame   merse: mast-button
rispis: sedges

Als fresch as flouris that in May up spredis,
   In kirtillis grene, withoutyn kell or bandis:
   Thair brycht hairis hang gletering on the strandis
In tressis clere, wyppit wyth goldyn thredis;
   With pappis quhite, and mydlis small as wandis.

Discrive I wald, bot quho coud wele endyte
How all the feldis wyth thai lilies quhite
   Depaynt war brycht, quhilk to the hevyn did glete:
Noucht thou, Omer, als fair as thou coud wryte,
For all thine ornate stilis so perfyte;
   Nor yit thou, Tullius, quhois lippis suete
   Off rethorike did in to termes flete:
Your aureate tongis both bene all to lyte,
   For to compile that paradise complete.

Thare saw I Nature and Venus, quene and quene,
The fresch Aurora, and lady Flora schene,
   Juno, Appollo, and Proserpyna,
Dyane the goddesse chaste of woddis grene,
My lady Cleo, that help of makaris bene,
   Thetes, Pallas, and prudent Minerva,
   Fair feynit Fortune, and lemand Lucina,
Thir mychti quenis in crounis mycht be sene,
   Wyth bemys blith, bricht as Lucifera.

There saw I May, of myrthfull monethis quene,
Betuix Aprile and June, her sistir schene,
   Within the gardyng walking up and doun,
Quham of the foulis gladdith al bedene;
Scho was full tender in hir yeris grene.
   Thare saw I Nature present hir a goune

kell: head-dress   glete: glitter   schene: beautiful   bedene:
at once

Rich to behald and nobil of renoune,
Off eviry hew under the hevin that bene
  Depaynt, and broud be gude proporcioun.

Full lustily thir ladyes all in fere
Enterit within this park of most plesere,
  Quhare that I lay our helit wyth levis ronk;
The mery foulis, blisfullest of chere,
Salust Nature, me thoucht, on thair manere,
  And eviry blome on branch, and eke on bonk,
  Opnyt and spred thair balmy levis donk,
Full low enclynyng to thair Quene so clere,
  Quham of thair nobill norising thay thonk.

Syne to dame Flora, on the samyn wyse,
Thay saluse, and thay thank a thousand syse;
  And to dame Venus, lufis mychti quene,
Thay sang ballettis in lufe, as was the gyse,
With amourouse notis lusty to devise,
  As thay that had lufe in thair hertis grene;
  Thair hony throtis, opnyt fro the splene,
With werblis suete did perse the hevinly skyes,
  Quhill loud resownyt the firmament serene.

Ane othir court thare saw I consequent,
Cupide the king, wyth bow in hand ybent,
  And dredefull arowis grundyn scharp and square;
Thare saw I Mars, the god armypotent,
Aufull and sterne, strong and corpolent;
  Thare saw I crabbit Saturn ald and haire,
  His luke was lyke for to perturb the aire;
Thare was Mercurius, wise and eloquent,
  Of rethorike that fand the flouris faire;

fere: company	our helit: covered over	bonk: bank
saluse: saluted	syse: times	gyse: custom	splene: heart
quhill: until		

Thare was the god of gardingis, Priapus;
Thare was the god of wildernes, Phanus;
   And Janus, god of entree delytable;
Thare was the god of fludis, Neptunus;
Thare was the god of wyndis, Eolus,
   With variand luke, rycht lyke a lord unstable;
   Thare was Bacus the gladder of the table;
Thare was Pluto, the elrich incubus,
   In cloke of grene, his court usit no sable.

And eviry one of thir, in grene arayit,
On harp or lute full merily thai playit,
   And sang ballettis with michty notis clere:
Ladyes to dance full sobirly assayit,
Endlang the lusty ryvir so thai mayit,
   Thair observance rycht hevynly was to here;
   Than crap I throu the levis, and drew nere,
Quhare that I was rycht sudaynly affrayit,
   All throu a luke, quhilk I have boucht full dere.

And schortly for to speke, be lufis quene
I was aspyit, scho bad hir archearis kene
   Go me arrest; and thay no time delayit;
Than ladyes fair lete fall thair mantillis grene,
With bowis big in tressit hairis schene,
   All sudaynly thay had a felde arayit;
   And yit rycht gretly was I noucht affrayit,
The party was so plesand for to sene,
   A wonder lusty bikkir me assayit.

And first of all, with bow in hand ybent,
Come dame Beautee, rycht as scho wald me schent;

elrich: supernatural   thir: these   bikkir: commotion, attack
schent: destroyed

Syne folowit all hir dameselis yfere,
With mony diverse aufull instrument,
Unto the pres, Fair Having wyth hir went,
   Fyne Portrature, Plesance, and lusty Chere.
   Than come Resoun, with schelde of gold so clere,
In plate and maille, as Mars armypotent,
   Defendit me that nobil chevallere.

Syne tender Youth come wyth hir virgyns ying,
Grene Innocence, and schamefull Abaising,
   And quaking Drede, wyth humble Obedience;
The Goldyn Targe harmyt thay no thing;
Curage in thame was noucht begonne to spring;
   Full sore thay dred to done a violence:
   Suete Womanhede I saw cum in presence,
Of artilye a warld sche did in bring,
   Servit wyth ladyes full of reverence.

Sche led wyth hir Nurture and Lawlynes,
Contenence, Pacience, Gude Fame, and Stedfastnes,
   Discrecioun, Gentrise, and Considerance,
Levefell Company, and Honest Besynes,
Benigne Luke, Mylde Chere, and Sobirnes:
   All thir bure ganyeis to do me grevance;
   But Resoun bure the Targe wyth sik constance,
Thair scharp assayes mycht do no dures
   To me, for all thair aufull ordynance.

Unto the pres persewit Hie Degree,
Hir folowit ay Estate, and Dignitee,
   Comparisoun, Honour, and Noble Array,
Will, Wantonnes, Renoun, and Libertee,
Richesse, Fredome, and eke Nobilitee:

        ganyeis: darts   dures: injuries

Wit ye thay did thair baner hye display;
A cloud of arowis as hayle schour lousit thay.
And schot, quhill wastit was thair artilye,
Syne went abak reboytit of thair pray.

Quhen Venus had persavit this rebute,
Dissymilance scho bad go mak persute,
At all powere to perse the Goldyn Targe;
And scho, that was of doubilnes the rute,
Askit hir choise of archeris in refute.
Venus the best bad hir go wale at large;
Scho tuke Presence, plicht ankers of the barge,
And Fair Callyng, that wele a flayn coud schute,
And Cherising for to complete hir charge.

Dame Hamelynes scho tuke in company,
That hardy was and hende in archery,
And broucht dame Beautee to the felde agayn;
With all the choise of Venus chevalry
Thay come and bikkerit unabaisitly:
The schour of arowis rappit on as rayn;
Perilouse Presence, that mony syre has slayne,
The bataill broucht on bordour hard us by,
The salt was all the sarar suth to sayn.

Thik was the schote of grundyn dartis kene;
Bot Resoun, with the Scheld of Gold so schene,
Warly defendit quho so evir assayit;
The aufull stoure he manly did sustene,
Quhill Presence kest a pulder in his ene,
And than as drunkyn man he all forvayit:

reboytit: repulsed   refute: defence, protection   wale: choose
plicht ankers: sheet anchors   flayn: arrow   hende: skilled
bikkerit unabaisitly: attacked unceasingly   salt: assualt   sarar: fiercer
pulder: powder   forvayit: went astray

127

Quhen he was blynd, the fule wyth hym thay playit,
And banyst hym amang the bewis grene;
   That sory sicht me sudaynly affrayit.

Than was I woundit to the deth wele nere,
And yoldyn as a wofull prisonnere
   To lady Beautee, in a moment space;
Me thoucht scho semyt lustiar of chere,
Efter that Resoun tynt had his eyne clere,
   Than of before, and lufliare of face:
   Quhy was thou blyndit, Resoun? quhi, allace!
And gert ane hell my paradise appere,
   And mercy seme, quhare that I fand no grace.

Dissymulance was besy me to sile,
And Fair Calling did oft apon me smyle,
   And Cherising me fed wyth wordis fair;
New Acquyntance enbracit me a quhile,
And favouryt me, quhill men mycht go a myle,
   Syne tuk hir leve, I saw hir nevir mare:
   Than saw I Dangere toward me repair,
I coud eschew hir presence be no wyle.
   On syde scho lukit wyth ane fremyt fare,

And at the last departing coud hir dresse,
And me delyverit unto Hevynesse
   For to remayne, and scho in cure me tuke.
Be this the Lord of Wyndis, wyth wodenes,
God Eolus, his bugil blew I gesse,
   That with the blast the levis all to-schuke;
   And sudaynly, in the space of a luke,
All was hyne went, thare was bot wildernes,
   Thare was no more bot birdis, bank, and bruke.

yoldyn: yielded   tynt: lost   gert: compelled   sile:
corrupt   fremyt fare: strange expression   hyne: hence

In twynkling of ane eye to schip thai went,
And swyth up saile unto the top thai stent,
    And with swift course atour the flude thay frak;
Thay fyrit gunnis wyth powder violent,
Till that the reke raise to the firmament,
    The rochis all resownyt wyth the rak,
    For rede it semyt that the raynbow brak;
Wyth spirit affrayde apon my fete I sprent
    Amang the clewis, so carefull was the crak.

And as I did awake of my sueving,
The joyfull birdis merily did syng
    For myrth of Phebus tendir bemes schene;
Suete war the vapouris, soft the morowing,
Halesum the vale, depaynt wyth flouris ying;
    The air attemperit, sobir, and amene;
    In quhite and rede was all the felde besene,
Throu Naturis nobil fresch anamalyng,
    In mirthfull May, of eviry moneth Quene.

O reverend Chaucere, rose of rethoris all,
As in oure tong ane flour imperiall,
    That raise in Britane evir, quho redis rycht,
Thou beris of makaris the tryumph riall;
Thy fresch anamalit termes celicall
    This mater coud illumynit have full brycht:
    Was thou noucht of oure Inglisch all the lycht,
Surmounting eviry tong terrestriall,
    Alls fer as Mayis morow dois mydnycht?

swyth: swiftly   stent: stretch   frak: rush   reke: smoke
rochis: rocks   rak: crack, detonation   rede: fear
sprent: sprang   clewis: cliffs   sueving: dream   celicall:
heavenly

O morall Gower, and Ludgate laureate,
Your sugurit lippis and tongis aureate,
   Bene to oure eris cause of grete delyte;
Your angel mouthis most mellifluate
Oure rude language has clere illumynate,
   And faire ourgilt oure speche, that imperfyte
   Stude, or your goldyn pennis schupe to wryte;
This Ile before was bare and desolate
   Off rethorike or lusty fresch endyte.

Thou lytill Quair, be evir obedient,
Humble, subject, and symple of entent,
   Before the face of eviry connyng wicht:
I knaw quhat thou of rethorike hes spent;
Off all hir lusty rosis redolent
   Is none in to thy gerland sett on hicht;
   Eschame thar of, and draw the out of sicht.
Rude is thy wede, disteynit, bare, and rent,
   Wele aucht thou be aferit of the licht.

> schupe: began   disteynit: stained

35   The Tretis of the Tua Mariit Wemen and the Wedo

APON the Midsummer evin, mirriest of nichtis,
  I muvit furth allane, neir as midnicht wes past,
Besyd ane gudlie grein garth, full of gay flouris,
Hegeit, of ane huge hicht, with hawthorne treis;
Quhairon ane bird, on ane bransche, so birst out hir notis
That never ane blythfullar bird was on the beuche harde:

> garth: garden   harde: heard

WILLIAM DUNBAR

Quhat throw the sugarat sound of hir sang glaid,
And throw the savour sanative of the sueit flouris,
I drew in derne to the dyk to dirkin efter mirthis;
The dew donkit the daill and dynnit the feulis.

   I hard, under ane holyn hevinlie grein hewit,
Ane hie speiche, at my hand, with hautand wourdis;
With that in haist to the hege so hard I inthrang
That I was heildit with hawthorne and with heynd leveis:
Throw pykis of the plet thorne I presandlie luikit,
Gif ony persoun wald approche within that plesand garding.

   I saw thre gay ladeis sit in ane grene arbeir,
All grathit in to garlandis of fresche gudlie flouris;
So glitterit as the gold wer thair glorius gilt tressis,
Quhill all the gressis did gleme of the glaid hewis;
Kemmit was thair cleir hair, and curiouslie sched
Attour thair schulderis doun schyre, schyning full bricht;
With curches, cassin thair abone, of kirsp cleir and thin:
Thair mantillis grein war as the gress that grew in May sessoun,
Fetrit with thair quhyt fingaris about thair fair sydis:
Off ferliful fyne favour war thair faceis meik,
All full of flurist fairheid, as flouris in June;
Quhyt, seimlie, and soft, as the sweit lillies
New upspred upon spray, as new spynist rose;
Arrayit ryallie about with mony rich vardour,
That nature full nobillie annamalit with flouris
Off alkin hewis under hevin, that ony heynd knew,
Fragrant, all full of fresche odour fynest of smell.
Ane cumlie tabil coverit wes befoir tha cleir ladeis,
With ryalle cowpis apon rawis full of ryche wynis.

in derne: in secret   dirkin: eavesdrop   donkit: moistened
feulis: birds   inthrang: pressed in   heildit: hidden   heynd:
sheltering   grathit: attired   curiouslie: carefully   schyre: fell
sheerly   curches: kerchiefs   kirsp: light, diaphanous fabric
ferliful: wonderful   new spynist: new-blown   heynd: person
cleir: beautiful, peerless   cowpis: cups

And of thir fair wlonkes, tua weddit war with lordis,
Ane wes ane wedow, I wis, wantoun of laitis.
And, as thai talk at the tabill of many taill sindry,
Thay wauchtit at the wicht wyne and waris out wourdis;
And syne thai spak more spedelie, and sparit no matiris.

Bewrie, said the Wedo, ye woddit wemen ying,
Quhat mirth ye fand in maryage, sen ye war menis wyffis;
Reveill gif ye rewit that rakles conditioun?
Or gif that ever ye luffit leyd upone lyf mair
Nor thame that ye your fayth hes festinit for ever?
Or gif ye think, had ye chois, that ye wald cheis better?
Think ye it nocht ane blist band that bindis so fast,
That none undo it a deill may bot the deith ane?

Than spak ane lusty belyf with lustie effeiris;
It, that ye call the blist band that bindis so fast,
Is bair of blis, and bailfull, and greit barrat wirkis.
Ye speir, had I fre chois, gif I wald cheis better?
Chenyeis ay ar to eschew; and changeis ar sueit:
Sic cursit chance till eschew, had I my chois anis,
Out of the chenyeis of ane churle I chaip suld for evir.
God gif matrimony were made to mell for ane yeir!
It war bot merrens to be mair, bot gif our myndis pleisit:
It is agane the law of luf, of kynd, and of nature,
Togiddir hairtis to strene, that stryveis with uther:
Birdis hes ane better law na bernis be meikill,
That ilk yeir, with new joy, joyis ane maik,
And fangis thame ane fresche feyr, unfulyeit, and constant,

wlonkes: beauties	laitis: manners, habits	wauchtit: drank
waris: dealt, spent	bewrie: reveal, confess	rakles: reckless
leyd: man, lover	band: bond	belyf: at once	barrat:
trouble	chaip: escape	mell: mate	merrens: wretchedness
bernis: men, mankind	meikill: much	maik: mate
fangis: takes, seizes	unfulyeit: unspoiled

And lattis thair fulyeit feiris flie quhair thai pleis.
Cryst gif sic ane consuetude war in this kith haldin!
Than weill war us wemen that evir we war fre;
We suld have feiris as fresche to fang quhen us likit,
And gif all larbaris thair leveis, quhen thai lak curage.
My self suld be full semlie in silkis arrayit,
Gymp, jolie, and gent, richt joyus, and gentryce.
I suld at fairis be found new faceis to se;
At playis, and at preichingis, and pilgrimages greit,
To schaw my renone, royaly, quhair preis was of folk,
To manifest my makdome to multitude of pepill,
And blaw my bewtie on breid, quhair bernis war mony;
That I micht cheis, and be chosin, and change quhen me lykit.
Than suld I waill ane full weill, our all the wyd realme,
That suld my womanheid weild the lang winter nicht;
And when I gottin had ane grome, ganest of uther,
Yaip, and ying, in the yok ane yeir for to draw;
Fra I had preveit his pitht the first plesand moneth,
Than suld I cast me to keik in kirk, and in markat,
And all the cuntre about, kyngis court, and uther,
Quhair I ane galland micht get aganis the nixt yeir,
For to perfurneis furth the werk quhen failyeit the tother;
A forky fure, ay furthwart, and forsy in draucht,
Nother febill, nor fant, nor fulyeit in labour,
But als fresche of his forme as flouris in May;
For all the fruit suld I fang, thocht he the flour burgeoun.

I have ane wallidrag, ane worme, ane auld wobat carle,
A waistit wolroun, na worth bot wourdis to clatter;
Ane bumbart, ane dron bee, ane bag full of flewme,

larbaris: impotent lovers   gymp: neat   gent: beautiful
gentryce: ladylike   preis: crowds   on breid: abroad   waill:
choose   ganest: superior   yaip: ardent   forky fure:
man of stamina   forsy: strong   wallidrag: weakling   wobat:
caterpillar   wolroun: boar   bumbart: drone

Ane skabbit skarth, ane scorpioun, ane scutarde behind;
To see him scart his awin skyn grit scunner I think.
Quhen kisses me that carybald, than kyndillis all my sorow;
As birs of ane brym bair, his berd is als stiff,
Bot soft and soupill as the silk is his sary lume;
He may weill to the syn assent, bot sakles is his deidis.
With goreis his tua grym ene ar gladderrit all about,
And gorgeit lyk twa gutaris that war with glar stoppit;
Bot quhen that glowrand gaist grippis me about,
Than think I hiddowus Mahowne hes me in armes;
Thair ma na sanyne me save fra that auld Sathane;
For, thocht I croce me al cleine, fra the croun doun,
He will my corse all beclip, and clap me to his breist.
Quhen schaiffyne is that ald schalk with a scharp rasour,
He schowis one me his schevill mouth and schedis my lippis;
And with his hard hurcheone skyn sa heklis he my chekis,
That as a glemand gleyd glowis my chaftis;
I schrenk for the scharp stound, bot schout dar I nought,
For schore of that auld schrew, schame him betide!
The luf blenkis of that bogill, fra his blerde ene,
As Belzebub had on me blent, abasit my spreit;
And quhen the smy one me smyrkis with his smake smolet,
He fepillis like a farcy aver that flyrit one a gillot.

   Quhen that the sound of his saw sinkis in my eris,
Than ay renewis my noy, or he be neir cumand:

---

skarth: cormorant   scutarde: beshitten   skart: scratch
scunner: revulsion   carybald: cannibal   birs: hairs   brym:
fierce   bair: boar   sary lume: sorry tool   sakles: innocent
goreis: matter   gladderrit: encrusted   glar: mud, filth   glowrand:
gaping   sanyne: signing with the cross   schaiffyne: shaven   schalk:
churl   schevill: wry, twisted   glemand gleyd: glowing ember
chaftis: cheeks   schore: fear   bogill: spectre   blent: glanced,
leered   smy: wretch   smake smolet: ? wretched, ? grimace
fepillis: fidgets   farcy aver: diseased old horse   flyrit: leered
gillot: mare   saw: speech   noy: annoyance

Quhen I heir nemmyt his name, than mak I nyne crocis,
To keip me fra the cummerans of that carll mangit,
That full of eldnyng is and anger and all evill thewis.
I dar nought luke to my luf for that lene gib,
He is sa full of jelusy and engyne fals;
Ever ymagynyng in mynd materis of evill,
Compasand and castand casis a thousand
How he sall tak me, with a trawe, at trist of ane othir:
I dar nought keik to the knaip that the cop fillis,
For eldnyng of that ald schrew that ever one evill thynkis;
For he is waistit and worne fra Venus werkis,
And may nought beit worth a bene in bed of my mystirs.
He trowis that young folk I yerne yeild, for he gane is,
Bot I may yuke all this yer, or his yerd help.

Ay quhen that caribald carll wald clyme one my wambe,
Than am I dangerus and daine and dour of my will;
Yit leit I never that larbar my leggis ga betueene,
To fyle my flesche, na fumyll me, without a fee gret;
And thoght his pene purly me payis in bed,
His purse pays richely in recompense efter:
For, or he clym on my corse, that carybald forlane,
I have conditioun of a curche of kersp allther fynest,
A goun of engranyt claith, right gaily furrit,
A ring with a ryall stane, or other riche jowell,
Or rest of his rousty raid, thoght he wer rede wod:
For all the buddis of Johne Blunt, quhen he abone clymis,
Me think the baid deir aboucht, sa bawch ar his werkis;
And thus I sell him solace, thoght I it sour think:
Fra sic a syre, God yow saif, my sueit sisteris deir!

cummerans: encumbrance   carll mangit: old dotard   eldnyng:
jealousy   gib: tom-cat   engyne: imagination, intelligence
trawe: trick   knaip: knave, boy   mystirs: needs   for:
because   yuke: itch   daine: haughty   dour: unrelenting
rousty raid: spiritless ride   rede wod: stark mad   buddis: bribes
Johne Blunt: proverbial personage   baid: ?reward   bawch: worthless

Quhen that the semely had said her sentence to end,
Than all thai leuch apon loft with latis full mery,
And raucht the cop round about full of riche wynis,
And ralyeit lang, or thai wald rest, with ryatus speche.

The wedo to the tothir wlonk warpit ther wordis;
Now, fair sister, fallis yow but fenyeing to tell,
Sen man ferst with matrimony yow menskit in kirk,
How haif ye farne be your faith? confese us the treuth:
That band to blise, or to ban, quhilk yow best thinkis?
Or how ye like lif to leid in to leill spousage?
And syne my self ye exeme one the samyn wise,
And I sall say furth the south, dissymyland no word.

The plesand said, I protest, the treuth gif I schaw,
That of your toungis ye be traist. The tothir twa grantit;
With that sprang up hir spreit be a span hechar.
To speik, quoth scho, I sall nought spar; ther is no spy neir:
I sall a ragment reveil fra rute of my hert,
A roust that is sa rankild quhill risis my stomak;
Now sall the byle all out brist, that beild has so lang;
For it to beir one my brist wes berdin our hevy:
I sall the venome devoid with a vent large,
And me assuage of the swalme, that suellit wes gret.

My husband wes a hur maister, the hugeast in erd,
Tharfor I hait him with my hert, sa help me our Lord!
He is a young man ryght yaip, bot nought in youth flouris;
For he is fadit full far and feblit of strenth:
He wes as flurising fresche within this few yeris,

---

semely: charmer   leuch: laughed   raucht: reached   warpit: uttered   ther: these   menskit: honoured   leill: loyal
exeme: examine   south: truth   hechar: higher   ragment: catalogue   roust: complaint   quhill: until   beild: suppurated
swalme: swelling   hur: whore   erd: earth

Bot he is falyeid full far and fulyeid in labour;
He has bene lychour so lang quhill lost is his natur,
His lume is waxit larbar, and lyis in to swonne:
Wes never sugeorne wer set na one that snaill tyrit,
For efter vii oulkis rest, it will nought rap anys;
He has bene waistit apone wemen, or he me wif chesit,
And in adultre, in my tyme, I haif him tane oft:
And yit he is als brankand with bonet one syde,
And blenkand to the brichtest that in the burgh duellis,
Alse curtly of his clething and kemmyng of his hair,
As he that is mare valyeand in Venus chalmer;
He semys to be sumthing worth, that syphyr in bour,
He lukis as he wald luffit be, thocht he be litill of valour;
He dois as dotit dog that damys on all bussis,
And liftis his leg apone loft, thoght he nought list pische;
He has a luke without lust and lif without curage;
He has a forme without force and fessoun but vertu,
And fair wordis but effect, all fruster of dedis;
He is for ladyis in luf a right lusty schadow,
Bot in to derne, at the deid, he salbe drup fundin;
He ralis, and makis repet with ryatus wordis,
Ay rusing him of his radis and rageing in chalmer;
Bot God wait quhat I think quhen he so thra spekis,
And how it settis him so syde to sege of sic materis.
Bot gif him self, of sum evin, myght ane say amang thaim,
Bot he nought ane is, bot nane of naturis possessories.

    Scho that has ane auld man nought all is begylit;
He is at Venus werkis na war na he semys:
I wend I josit a gem, and I haif geit gottin;

swonne: limp, swoon   sugeorne: ? journey   oulkis: weeks
rap: beat   brankand: swaggering   blenkand: winking
damys: pisses   fessoun: manner, style   fruster: useless   drup:
droop   rusing: boasting   thra: boldly   syde: at large
sege: talk   wend: thought   josit: enjoyed   geit: jet

He had the glemyng of gold, and wes bot glase fundin.
Thought men be ferse, wele I fynd, fra falye ther curage,
Thar is bot eldnyng or anger ther hertis within.
Ye speik of berdis one bewch: of blise may thai sing,
That, one Sanct Valentynis day, ar vacandis ilk yer;
Hed I that plesand prevelege to part quhen me likit,
To change, and ay to cheise agane, than, chastite, adew!
Than suld I haif a fresch feir to fang in myn armes:
To hold a freke, quhill he faynt, may foly be calit.

  Apone sic materis I mus, at mydnyght, full oft,
And murnys so in my mynd I murdris my selfin;
Than ly I walkand for wa, and walteris about,
Wariand oft my wekit kyn, that me away cast
To sic a craudoune but curage, that knyt my cler bewte,
And ther so mony kene knyghtis this kenrik within:
Than think I on a semelyar, the suth for to tell,
Na is our syre be sic sevin; with that I sych oft:
Than he ful tenderly dois turne to me his tume person,
And with a yoldin yerd dois yolk me in armys,
And sais, 'My soverane sueit thing, quhy sleip ye no betir?
Me think ther haldis yow a hete, as ye sum harme alyt.'
Quoth I, 'My hony, hald abak, and handill me nought sair;
A hache is happinit hastely at my hert rut.'
With that I seme for to swoune, thought I na swerf tak;
And thus beswik I that swane with my sueit wordis:
I cast on him a crabit E, quhen cleir day is cummyn,
And lettis it is a luf blenk, quhen he about glemys,
I turne it in a tender luke, that I in tene warit,
And him behaldis hamely with hertly smyling.

  I wald a tender peronall, that myght na put thole,

---

freke: man	wariand: cursing	craudoune: coward	knyt:
joined	kenrik: kingdom	na: than	tume: empty	yoldin: soft
hete: ? fever	hache: ache	swerf: faint	beswik: cheat
lettis: pretends	peronall: young girl	put: thrust	thole: endure

That hatit men with hard geir for hurting of flesch,
Had my gud man to hir gest; for I dar God suer,
Scho suld not stert for his straik a stray breid of erd.
And syne, I wald that ilk band, that ye so blist call,
Had bund him so to that bryght, quhill his bak werkit;
And I wer in a beid broght with berne that me likit,
I trow that bird of my blis suld a bourd want.

Onone, quhen this amyable had endit hir speche,
Loudly lauchand the laif allowit hir mekle:
Thir gay Wiffis maid game amang the grene leiffis;
Thai drank and did away dule under derne bewis;
Thai swapit of the sueit wyne, thai swanquhit of hewis,
Bot all the pertlyar in plane thai put out ther vocis.
Than said the Weido, I wis ther is no way othir;
Now tydis me for to talk; my taill it is nixt:
God my spreit now inspir and my speche quykkin,
And send me sentence to say, substantious and noble;
Sa that my preching may pers your perverst hertis,
And mak yow mekar to men in maneris and conditiounis.
    I schaw yow, sisteris in schrift, I wes a schrew evir,
Bot I wes schene in my schrowd, and schew me innocent;
And thought I dour wes, and dane, dispitous, and bald,
I wes dissymblit suttelly in a sanctis liknes:
I semyt sober, and sueit, and sempill without fraud,
Bot I couth sexty dissaif that suttillar wer haldin.
    Unto my lesson ye lyth, and leir at me wit,
Gif you nought list be forleit with losingeris untrew:
Be constant in your governance, and counterfeit gud maneris,

geir: goods	bryght: beauty	bourd: joke	dule: sorrow
thai swanquhit: those swanwhite		pertlyar: livelier	plane:
complaint	schene: beautiful	schrowd: dress	bald: bold
lyth: listen	losingeris: deceivers		

Thought ye as tygris be terne, be tretable in luf,
And be as turtoris in your talk, thought ye haif talis brukill;
Be dragonis baith and dowis ay in double forme,
And quhen it nedis yow, onone, note baith ther strenthis;
Be amyable with humble face, as angellis apperand,
And with a terrebill tail be stangand as edderis;
Be of your luke like innocentis, thoght ye haif evill myndis;
Be courtly ay in clething and costly arrayit,
That hurtis yow nought worth a hen; yowr husband pays for all.

    Twa husbandis haif I had, thai held me baith deir,
Thought I dispytit thaim agane, thai spyit it na thing:
Ane wes ane hair hogeart, that hostit out flewme;
I hatit him like a hund, thought I it hid preve:
With kissing and with clapping I gert the carll fone;
Weil couth I keyth his cruke bak, and kemm his cowit noddill,
And with a bukky in my cheik bo on him behind,
And with a bek gang about and bler his ald E,
And with a kynd contynance kys his crynd chekis;
In to my mynd makand mokis at that mad fader,
Trowand me with trew lufe to treit him so fair.
This cought I do without dule and na dises tak,
Bot ay be mery in my mynd and myrthfull of cher.

    I had a lufsummar leid my lust for to slokyn,
That couth be secrete and sure and ay saif my honour,
And sew bot at certayne tymes and in sicir placis;
Ay when the ald did me anger, with akword wordis,
Apon the galland for to goif it gladit me agane.
I had sic wit that for wo weipit I litill,
Bot leit the sueit ay the sour to gud sesone bring.

terne: fierce   turtoris: turtle-doves   brukill: frail   dowis:
doves   hair hogeart: ?hoary huckster   hostit: coughed
fone: silly   keyth: ?   kemm, etc.: comb his cropped pate
bukky in my cheik: tongue in cheek   bo: make a face   crynd:
withered, shrunken   cought: could   leid: lover   slokyn:
slake   sew: sue   goif: gaze

Quhen that the chuf wald me chid, with girnand chaftis,
I wald him chuk, cheik and chyn, and cheris him so mekill,
That his cheif chymys he had chevist to my sone,
Suppose the churll wes gane chaist, or the child wes gottin:
As wis woman ay I wrought and not as wod fule,
For mar with wylis I wan na wichtnes of handis.

    Syne maryit I a marchand, myghti of gudis:
He was a man of myd eld and of mene statur;
Bot we na fallowis wer in frendschip or blud,
In fredome, na furth bering, na fairnes of persoune,
Quhilk ay the fule did foryhet, for febilnes of knawlege,
Bot I sa oft thought him on, quhill angrit his hert,
And quhilum I put furth my voce and Pedder him callit:
I wald ryght tuichandly talk be I wes tuyse maryit,
For endit wes my innocence with my ald husband:
I wes apperand to be pert within perfit eild;
Sa sais the curat of our kirk, that knew me full ying:
He is our famous to be fals, that fair worthy prelot;
I salbe laith to lat him le, quhill I may luke furth.
I gert the buthman obey, ther wes no bute ellis;
He maid me ryght hie reverens, fra he my rycht knew:
For, thocht I say it my self, the severance wes mekle
Betuix his bastard blude and my birth noble.
That page wes never of sic price for to presome anys
Unto my persone to be peir, had pete nought grantit.
Bot mercy in to womanheid is a mekle vertu,
For never bot in a gentill hert is generit ony ruth.
I held ay grene in to his mynd that I of grace tuk him,
And for he couth ken him self I curtasly him lerit:

He durst not sit anys my summondis, for, or the second charge,
He wes ay redy for to ryn, so rad he wes for blame.
Bot ay my will wes the war of womanly natur;
The mair he loutit for my luf, the les of him I rakit;
And eik, this is a ferly thing, or I him faith gaif,
I had sic favour to that freke, and feid syne for ever.

    Quhen I the cure had all clene and him ourcummyn haill,
I crew abone that craudone, as cok that wer victour;
Quhen I him saw subject and sett at myn bydding,
Than I him lichtlyit as a lowne and lathit his maneris.
Than woxe I sa unmerciable to martir him I thought,
For as a best I broddit him to all boyis laubour:
I wald haif ridden him to Rome with raip in his heid,
Wer not ruffill of my renoune and rumour of pepill.
And yit hatrent I hid within my hert all;
Bot quhilis it hepit so huge, quhill it behud out:
Yit tuk I nevir the wosp clene out of my wyde throte,
Quhill I ought wantit of my will or quhat I wald desir.
Bot quhen I severit had that syre of substance in erd,
And gottin his biggingis to my barne, and hie burrow landis,
Than with a stew stert out the stoppell of my hals,
That he all stunyst throu the stound, as of a stele wappin.
Than wald I, efter lang, first sa fane haif bene wrokin,
That I to flyte wes als fers as a fell dragoun.
I had for flattering of that fule fenyeit so lang,
Mi evidentis of heritagis or thai wer all selit,
My breist, that wes gret beild, bowdyn wes sa huge,
That neir my baret out brist or the band makin.
Bot quhen my billis and my bauchles wes all braid selit,

rad: afraid	loutit: stooped	ferly: wonderful	feid: enmity
lichtlyit: slighted	lowne: boy, fool		broddit: prodded
raip: rope	ruffill: ruffling, bruising		wosp: straw stopper
oucht: anything		biggingis: buildings	
barne: child	hals: throat	stunyst: astonished, stunned	wrokin: avenged
bowdyn: swollen	bauchles: documents		

142

I wald na langar beir on bridill, bot braid up my heid;
Thar myght na molet mak me moy, na hald my mouth in:
I gert the renyeis rak and rif into sondir;
I maid that wif carll to werk all womenis werkis,
And laid all manly materis and mensk in this eird.
Than said I to my cumaris in counsall about,
'Se how I cabeld yone cout with a kene brydill!
The cappill, that the crelis kest in the caf mydding,
Sa curtasly the cart drawis, and kennis na plungeing,
He is nought skeich, na yit sker, na scippis nought one syd':
And thus the scorne and the scaith scapit he nothir.

   He wes no glaidsum gest for a gay lady,
Tharfor I gat him a game that ganyt him bettir;
He wes a gret goldit man and of gudis riche;
I leit him be my lumbart to lous me all misteris,
And he wes fane for to fang fra me that fair office,
And thoght my favoris to fynd through his feill giftis.
He grathit me in a gay silk and gudly arrayis,
In gownis of engranyt claith and gret goldin chenyeis,
In ringis ryally set with riche ruby stonis,
Quhill hely raise my renoune amang the rude peple.
Bot I full craftely did keip thai courtly wedis,
Quhill eftir dede of that drupe, that dotht nought in chalmir:
Thought he of all my clathis maid cost and expense,
Ane othir sall the worschip haif, that weildis me eftir;
And thoght I likit him bot litill, yit for luf of otheris,
I wald me prunya plesandly in precius wedis,
That luffaris myght apone me luke and ying lusty gallandis,
That I held more in daynte and derer be ful mekill

molet: bridle bit   moy: tame   rak: crack   mensk:
honour, manhood   cumaris: neighbours   cabeld: haltered
cout: colt   cappill: horse   caf: chaff   skeich: shy
sker: frightened   scaith: harm   lumbart: banker (Lombard)
feill: many   hely: highly   prunya: preen   wedis: clothes

Ne him that dressit me so dink: full dotit wes his heyd.
Quhen he wes heryit out of hand to hie up my honoris,
And payntit me as pako, proudest of fedderis,
I him miskennyt, be Crist, and cukkald him maid;
I him forleit as a lad and lathlyit him mekle:
I thoght my self a papingay and him a plukit herle;
All thus enforsit he his fa and fortifyit in strenth,
And maid a stalwart staff to strik him selfe doune.

  Bot of ane bowrd in to bed I sall yow breif yit:
Quhen he ane hail year was hanyt, and him behuffit rage,
And I wes laith to be loppin with sic a lob avoir,
Alse lang as he wes on loft, I lukit on him never,
Na leit never enter in my thoght that he my thing persit,
Bot ay in mynd ane other man ymagynit that I haid;
Or ellis had I never mery bene at that myrthles raid.
Quhen I that grome geldit had of gudis and of natur,
Me thought him gracelese one to goif, sa me God help.
Quhen he had warit all one me his welth and his substance,
Me thoght his wit wes all went away with the laif;
And so I did him despise, I spittit quhen I saw
That super spendit evill spreit, spulyeit of all vertu.
For, weill ye wait, wiffis, that he that wantis riches
And valyeandnes in Venus play, is ful vile haldin:
Full fruster is his fresch array and fairnes of persoune,
All is bot frutlese his effeir and falyeis at the upwith.

  I buskit up my barnis like baronis sonnis,
And maid bot fulis of the fry of his first wif.
I banyst fra my boundis his brethir ilkane;
His frendis as my fais I held at feid evir;
Be this, ye belief may, I luffit nought him self,
For never I likit a leid that langit till his blude:

And yit thir wisemen, thai wait that all wiffis evill
Ar kend with ther conditionis and knawin with the samin.

  Deid is now that dyvour and dollin in erd:
With him deit all my dule and my drery thoghtis;
Now done is my dolly nyght, my day is upsprungin,
Adew dolour, adew! my daynte now begynis:
Now am I a wedow, I wise and weill am at ese;
I weip as I were woful, but wel is me for ever;
I busk as I wer bailfull, bot blith is my hert;
My mouth it makis murnyng, and my mynd lauchis;
My clokis thai ar caerfull in colour of sabill,
Bot courtly and ryght curyus my corse is ther undir:
I drup with a ded luke in my dule habit,
As with manis daill I had done for dayis of my lif.

  Quhen that I go to the kirk, cled in cair weid,
As foxe in a lambis fleise fenye I my cheir;
Than lay I furght my bright buke one breid one my kne,
With mony lusty letter ellummynit with gold;
And drawis my clok forthwart our my face quhit,
That I may spy, unaspyit, a space me beside:
Full oft I blenk by my buke, and blynis of devotioun,
To se quhat berne is best brand or bredest in schulderis,
Or forgeit is maist forcely to furnyse a bancat
In Venus chalmer, valyeandly, withoutin vane ruse:
And, as the new mone all pale, oppressit with change,
Kythis quhilis her cleir face through cluddis of sable,
So keik I through my clokis, and castis kynd lukis
To knychtis, and to cleirkis, and cortly personis.

  Quhen frendis of my husbandis behaldis me one fer,
I haif a watter spunge for wa, within my wyde clokis,

dyvour: bankrupt	dollin: delved	dolly: woeful	curyus:
cared for	daill: dealings	cair weid: mourning clothes	
blynis: ceases	brand: brawned, muscled	kythis: reveals	
cluddis: clouds	one fer: afar		

Than wring I it full wylely and wetis my chekis,
With that watteris myn ene and welteris doun teris.
Than say thai all, that sittis about, 'Se ye nought, allace!
Yone lustlese led so lelely scho luffit hir husband:
Yone is a pete to enprent in a princis hert,
That sic a perle of plesance suld yone pane dre!'
I sane me as I war ane sanct, and semys ane angell;
At langage of lichory I leit as I war crabit:
I sich, without sair hert or seiknes in body;
According to my sable weid I mon haif sad maneris,
Or thai will se all the suth; for certis, we wemen
We set us all fra the syght to syle men of treuth:
We dule for na evill deid, sa it be derne haldin.

  Wise wemen has wayis and wonderfull gydingis
With gret engyne to bejaip ther jolyus husbandis;
And quyetly, with sic craft, convoyis our materis
That, under Crist, no creatur kennis of our doingis.
Bot folk a cury may miscuke, that knawledge wantis,
And has na colouris for to cover thair awne kindly fautis;
As dois thir damysellis, for derne dotit lufe,
That dogonis haldis in dainte and delis with thaim so lang,
Quhill all the cuntre knaw ther kyndnes and faith:
Faith has a fair name, bot falsheid faris bettir:
Fy one hir that can nought feyne her fame for to saif!
Yit am I wise in sic werk and wes all my tyme;
Thoght I want wit in warldlynes, I wylis haif in luf,
As ony happy woman has that is of hie blude:
Hutit be the halok las a hunder yeir of eild!

  I have ane secrete servand, rycht sobir of his toung,
That me supportis of sic nedis, quhen I a syne mak:
Thoght he be sympill to the sicht, he has a tong sickir;

lustlese led: unhappy person   dre: injure   crabit: offended
syle: mislead   miscuke: miscook   dogonis: worthless fellows
halok: foolish

Full mony semelyar sege wer service dois mak:
Thought I haif cair, under cloke, the cleir day quhill nyght,
Yit haif I solace, under serk, quhill the sone ryse.

Yit am I haldin a haly wif our all the haill schyre,
I am sa peteouse to the pur, quhen ther is personis mony.
In passing of pilgrymage I pride me full mekle,
Mair for the prese of peple na ony perdoun wynyng.

Bot yit me think the best bourd, quhen baronis and knychtis,
And othir bachilleris, blith blumyng in youth,
And all my luffaris lele, my lugeing persewis,
And fyllis me wyne wantonly with weilfair and joy:
Sum rownis; and sum ralyeis; and sum redis ballatis;
Sum raiffis furght rudly with riatus speche;
Sum plenis, and sum prayis; sum prasis mi bewte;
Sum kissis me; sum clappis me; sum kyndnes me proferis;
Sum kerffis to me curtasli; sum me the cop giffis;
Sum stalwardly steppis ben, with a stout curage,
And a stif standand thing staiffis in my neiff;
And mony blenkis ben our, that but full fer sittis,
That mai, for the thik thrang, nought thrif as thai wald.
Bot, with my fair calling, I comfort thaim all:
For he that sittis me nixt, I nip on his finger;
I serf him on the tothir syde on the samin fasson;
And he that behind me sittis, I hard on him lene;
And him befor, with my fut fast on his I stramp;
And to the bernis far but sueit blenkis I cast:
To every man in speciall speke I sum wordis
So wisly and so womanly, quhill warmys ther hertis.

Thar is no liffand leid so law of degre
That sall me luf unluffit, I am so loik hertit;
And gif his lust so be lent into my lyre quhit,

serk: shirt	rownis: whispers	furght: forth	kerffis: bows
neiff: fist	ben: inside	thrang: crowd	but: outside
loik: warm, luke			

That he be lost or with me lig, his lif sall nocht danger.
I am so mercifull in mynd, and menys all wichtis,
My sely saull salbe saif, quhen sa bot all jugis.
Ladyis leir thir lessonis and be no lassis fundin:
This is the legeand of my lif, thought Latyne it be nane.

Quhen endit had her ornat speche, this eloquent wedow,
Lowd thai lewch all the laif, and loffit hir mekle;
And said thai suld exampill tak of her soverane teching,
And wirk efter hir wordis, that woman wes so prudent.
Than culit thai thair mouthis with confortable drinkis;
And carpit full cummerlik with cop going round.

Thus draif thai our that deir nyght with danceis full noble,
Quhill that the day did up daw, and dew donkit flouris;
The morow myld wes and meik, the mavis did sing,
And all remuffit the myst, and the meid smellit;
Silver schouris doune schuke as the schene cristall,
And berdis schoutit in schaw with thair schill notis;
The goldin glitterand gleme so gladit ther hertis,
Thai maid a glorius gle amang the grene bewis.
The soft sowch of the swyr and soune of the stremys,
The sueit savour of the sward and singing of foulis,
Myght confort ony creatur of the kyn of Adam,
And kindill agane his curage, thocht it wer cald sloknyt.

Than rais thir ryall roisis, in ther riche wedis,
And rakit hame to ther rest through the rise blumys;
And I all prevely past to a plesand arber,
And with my pen did report thair pastance most mery.

Ye auditoris most honorable, that eris has gevin
Oneto this uncouth aventur, quhilk airly me happinnit;
Of thir thre wantoun wiffis, that I haif writtin heir,
Quhilk wald ye waill to your wif, gif ye suld wed one?

lig: lie   loffit: praised   carpit: chatted   cummerlik: like gossips
mavis: thrush   schaw: grove   swyr: ? breeze   rise: brushwood

36   *The Dance of the Sevin Deidly Synnis*

OFF Februar the fyiftene nycht,
    Full lang befoir the dayis lycht,
I lay in till a trance;
And then I saw baith hevin and hell:
Me thocht, amangis the feyndis fell,
Mahoun gart cry ane dance
Off schrewis that wer nevir schrevin,
Aganis the feist of Fasternis evin
To mak thair observance;
He bad gallandis ga graith a gyis,
And kast up gamountis in the skyis,
That last came out of France.

'Lat se,' quod he, 'Now quha begynnis;'
With that the fowll Sevin Deidly Synnis
Begowth to leip at anis.
And first of all in dance wes Pryd,
With hair wyld bak and bonet on syd,
Lyk to mak waistie wanis;
And round abowt him, as a quheill,
Hang all in rumpillis to the heill
His kethat for the nanis:
Mony prowd trumpour with him trippit,
Throw skaldand fyre ay as thay skippit
Thay gyrnd with hiddous granis.

Heilie harlottis on hawtane wyis
Come in with mony sindrie gyis,

Mahoun: Mahomet, i.e. the devil   graithe a gyis: prepare a play
gamountis: gambols, dances   waistie wanis: desolate houses   kethat:
cloak   trumpour: deceiver   gyrnd: grimaced.   granis:
groans   gyis: disguises

Bot yit luche nevir Mahoun,
Quhill preistis come in with bair schevin nekkis,
Than all the feyndis lewche and maid gekkis,
Blak Belly and Bawsy Brown.

Than Yre come in with sturt and stryfe;
His hand wes ay upoun his knyfe,
He brandeist lyk a beir:
Bostaris, braggaris, and barganeris,
Eftir him passit in to pairis,
All bodin in feir of weir;
In jakkis, and stryppis and bonettis of steill,
Thair leggis wer chenyeit to the heill,
Frawart wes thair affeir:
Sum upoun udir with brandis beft,
Sum jaggit uthiris to the heft,
With knyvis that scherp cowd scheir.

Nixt in the dance followit Invy,
Fild full of feid and fellony,
Hid malyce and dispyte;
For pryvie hatrent that tratour trymlit.
Him followit mony freik dissymlit,
With fenyeit wirdis quhyte;
And flattereris in to menis facis;
And bakbyttaris in secreit places,
To ley that had delyte;
And rownaris of fals lesingis;
Allace! that courtis of noble kingis
Of thame can nevir be quyte.

---

gekkis: mocking faces   beir: ? bear   weir: war   affeir:
address   beft: struck   feid: feud   hatrent: hatred
freik: men   lesingis: lies

Nixt him in dans come Cuvatyce,
Rute of all evill and grund of vyce,
That nevir cowd be content;
Catyvis, wrechis, and ockeraris,
Hud-pykis, hurdaris, and gadderaris,
All with that warlo went:
Out of thair throttis thay schot on udder
Hett moltin gold, me thocht a fudder,
As fyreflawcht maist fervent;
Ay as thay tomit thame of schot,
Feyndis fild thame new up to the thrott
With gold of allkin prent.

Syne Sweirnes, at the secound bidding,
Come lyk a sow out of a midding,
Full slepy wes his grunyie:
Mony sweir bumbard belly huddroun,
Mony slute daw and slepy duddroun,
Him servit ay with sounyie;
He drew thame furth in till a chenyie,
And Belliall, with a brydill renyie,
Evir lascht thame on the lunyie:
In dance thay war so slaw of feit,
Thay gaif thame in the fyre a heit,
And maid thame quicker of counyie.

Than Lichery, that lathly cors,
Come berand lyk a bagit hors,

ockeraris: usurers   hud-pykis: misers   hurdaris: hoarders
a fudder: a great amount, a lot   fyreflawcht: lightning   tomit:
emptied   sweirness: sloth   grunyie: muzzle   bumbard
belly huddroun: drone-bellied sluggard   slute daw: sluttish slattern
duddroun: sloven   sounyie: care (Fr. *soigner*)   lunyie: loin
counyie: ? coining   bagit hors: stallion

And Ydilnes did him leid;
Thair wes with him ane ugly sort,
And mony stynkand fowll tramort,
That had in syn bene deid.
Quhen thay wer entrit in the dance,
Thay wer full strenge of countenance,
Lyk turkas birnand reid;
All led thay uthir by the tersis,
Suppois thay fyllit with thair ersis,
It mycht be na remeid.

Than the fowll monstir Glutteny,
Off wame unsasiable and gredy,
To dance he did him dres:
Him followit mony fowll drunckart,
With can and collep, cop and quart,
In surffet and excess;
Full mony a waistles wallydrag,
With wamis unweildable, did furth wag,
In creische that did incres;
'Drynk!' ay thay cryit, with mony a gaip,
The feyndis gaif thame hait leid to laip,
Thair lovery wes na les.

Na menstrallis playit to thame but dowt,
For glemen thair wer haldin owt,
Be day and eik by nicht;
Except a menstrall that slew a man,
Swa till his heretage he wan,
And entirt be breif of richt.

---

tramort: dead body, corpse   turkas: pincers   tersis: penises
fyllit: defiled   remeid: help   wallydrag: weakling   creische:
fat   hait leid to laip: hot lead to lap   lovery: livery, allowance

Than cryd Mahoun for a Heleand padyane;
Syne ran a feynd to feche Makfadyane,
Far northwart in a nuke;
Be he the correnoch had done schout,
Erschemen so gadderit him abowt,
In Hell grit rowme thay tuke.
Thae tarmegantis, with tag and tatter,
Full lowd in Ersche begowth to clatter,
And rowp lyk revin and ruke:
The Devill sa devit wes with thair yell,
That in the depest pot of hell
He smorit thame with smuke.

correnoch: dirge   Ersche: Gaelic   rowp: croak   revin:
raven   devit: deafened   smorit: smothered

37   *The Testament of Mr. Andro Kennedy*

I, MAISTER Andro Kennedy,
    Curro quando sum vocatus,
Gottin with sum incuby,
    Or with sum freir *infatuatus*;
In faith I can nought tell redly,
    Unde aut ubi fui natus,
Bot in treuth I trow trewly,
    Quod sum dyabolus incarnatus.

Cum nichill sit certius morte,
    We mon all de, quhen we haif done,
Nescimus quando vel qua sorte,
    Na blind Allane wait of the mone,

na blind . . . etc.: than blind Allan knew of the moon

153

Ego pacior in pectore,
    This night I myght nocht sleip a wink;
Licet eger in corpore,
    Yit wald my mouth be wet with drink.

Nunc condo testamentum meum,
    I leiff my saull for evermare,
Per omnipotentem Deum,
    In to my lordis wyne cellar;
Semper ibi ad remanendum,
    Quhill domisday without dissever,
Bonum vinum ad bibendum,
    With sueit Cuthbert that luffit me nevir.

Ipse est dulcis ad amandum,
    He wald oft ban me in his breith,
Det michi modo ad potandum,
    And I forgif him laith and wraith:
Quia in cellario cum cervisia,
    I had lever lye baith air and lait,
Nudus solus in camesia,
    Na in my Lordis bed of stait.

A barell bung ay at my bosum,
    Of warldis gud I bad na mair;
Corpus meum ebriosum,
    I leif on to the toune of Air;
In a draf mydding for ever and ay
    Ut ibi sepeliri queam,
Quhar drink and draff may ilka day
    Be cassyne *super faciem meam:*

I leif my hert that never wes sicir,
    Sed semper variabile,
That never mair wald flow or flicir,
    Consorti meo Iacobe:
Thought I wald bynd it with a wicir,
    Verum Deum renui;
Bot and I hecht to teme a bicker,
    Hoc pactum semper tenui.

Syne leif I the best aucht I bocht,
    Quod est Latinum propter caupe,
To hede of kyn, bot I wait nought
    Quis est ille, than I schrew my scawpe:
I callit my Lord my heid, but hiddill,
    Sed nulli alii hoc dixerunt,
We weir as sib as seve and riddill,
    In una silva que creverunt.

Omnia mea solacia,
    Thay wer bot lesingis all and ane,
Cum omni fraude et fallacia
    I leif the maistter of Sanct Antane;
Willelmo Gray, sine gratia,
    Myne awne deir cusing, as I wene,
Qui nunquam fabricat mendacia,
    Bot quhen the holyne growis grene.

My fenyening and my fals wynyng
    Relinquo falsis fratribus;
For that is Goddis awne bidding,
    Dispersit, dedit pauperibus.

sicir: steady, sure   teme: empty   aucht: possession   scawpe: scalp
but hiddill: without secrecy   as sib: as closely akin   lesingis:
lies   cusing: cousin, relative   holyne: holly   fenyening: feigning

For menis saulis thay say thai sing,
Mencientes pro muneribus;
Now God gif thaim ane evill ending,
Pro suis pravis operibus.

To lok Fule, my foly fre
Lego post corpus sepultum;
In faith I am mair fule than he,
Licet ostendit bonum vultum:
Of corne and catall, gold and fe,
Ipse habet valde multum,
And yit he bleris my lordis E
Fingendo eum fore stultum.

To Master Johne Clerk syne,
Do et lego intime,
Goddis malisone and myne;
Ipse est causa mortis mee.
War I a dog and he a swyne,
Multi mirantur super me,
Bot I suld ger that lurdane quhryne,
Scribendo dentes sine de.

Residuum omnium bonorum
For to dispone my Lord sall haif,
Cum tutela puerorum,
Ade, Kytte, and all the laif.
In faith I will na langar raif.
Pro sepultura ordino
On the new gys, sa God me saif,
Non sicut more solito.

---

lurdane: sluggard   quhryne: ? run, ? whine   dispone:
dispose   gys: manner, fashion

In die mee sepulture
  I will nane haif bot our awne gyng,
Et duos rusticos de rure
  Berand a barell on a styng;
Drynkand and playand cop out, evin,
  Sicut egomet solebam;
Singand and gretand with hie stevin,
  Potum meum cum fletu miscebam.

I will na preistis for me sing,
  Dies illa, Dies ire;
Na yit na bellis for me ring,
  Sicut semper solet fieri;
Bot a bag pipe to play a spryng,
  Et enum ail wosp ante me;
In stayd of baneris for to bring
  Quatuor lagenas cervisie,
Within the graif to set sic thing,
  In modum crucis juxta me,
To fle the fendis, than hardely sing
  De terra plasmasti me.

gyng: gang	styng: pole	gretand: weeping	stevin:
clamour	ail wosp: inn sign		

GAVIN DOUGLAS

c. 1475–1522

From *THE AENEID*

The Prologue to Book VII

AS bryght Phebus, scheyn soverane hevynnys e,
The opposit held of hys chymmys hie,
Cleir schynand bemys, and goldyn symmyris hew,
In laton cullour alteryng haill of new,
Kythyng no syng of heyt be hys vissage,
So neir approchit he his wyntir stage;
Reddy he was to entyr the thrid morn
In clowdy skyis undre Capricorn;
All thocht he be the hart and lamp of hevyn,
Forfeblit wolx hys lemand gylty levyn,
Throu the declynyng of hys large round speir.
The frosty regioun ryngis of the yer,
The tyme and sesson bittir, cald and paill,
The schort days that clerkis clepe brumaill,
Quhen brym blastis of the northyn art
Ourquhelmyt had Neptunus in his cart,
And all to schaik the levis of the treis,
The rageand storm ourweltrand wally seys.
Ryveris ran reid on spait with watir browne,
And burnys hurlys all thar bankis downe,

scheyn: shining, beautiful   e: eye   chymmys: chief dwelling,
(astrol.) mansion   laton: brass   kythyng: showing   syng:
sign   lemand gylty levyn: gleaming gilded light   speir: sphere
brumaill: wintry   brym: fierce   ourquhelmyt: overwhelmed
ourweltrand: overriding   wally: swelling

And landbrist rumland rudely with sik beir,
So lowd ne rumyst wild lyoun or ber;
Fludis monstreis, sik as meirswyne or quhalis,
Fro the tempest law in the deip devalis.
Mars occident, retrograde in his speir,
Provocand stryfe, regnyt as lord that yer;
Rany Oryon with his stormy face
Bewavit oft the schipman by hys race;
Frawart Saturn, chill of complexioun,
Throu quhais aspect darth and infectioun
Beyn causyt oft, and mortal pestilens,
Went progressyve the greis of his ascens;
And lusty Hebe, Junoys douchtir gay,
Stude spulyeit of hir office and array.
The soyl ysowpit into watir wak,
The firmament ourcast with rokis blak,
The grond fadyt, and fawch wolx all the feildis,
Montane toppis slekit with snaw ourheildis;
On raggit rolkis of hard harsk quhyn stane
With frosyn frontis cauld clynty clewis schane.
Bewte was lost, and barrand schew the landis,
With frostis hair ourfret the feldis standis.
Seir bittir bubbis and the schowris snell
Semyt on the sward a symylitude of hell,
Reducyng to our mynd, in every sted,
Gousty schaddois of eild and grisly ded.

landbrist: surf   beir: rasping noise   rumyst: roared, rumbled
meirswyne: dolphins or porpoises   quhalis: whales   law: low
devalis: dive down   bewavit: stirred up   greis: degrees
wak: watery   rokis: clouds   fawch: pale brown or
yellow   ourheildis: covered over   rolkis: rocks   quhyn
stane: whinstone   clynty clewis schane: stony gorges sparkled
hair: hoary   ourfret: overlaced, embroidered   seir: one after
another   bubbis: squalls   snell: biting   sted: place
gousty: dismal

Thik drumly skuggis dyrknyt so the hevyn,
Dym skyis oft furth warpit feirfull levyn,
Flaggis of fire, and mony felloun flaw,
Scharpe soppys of sleit and of the snypand snaw.
The dolly dichis war all donk and wait,
The law valle flodderit all with spait,
The plane stretis and every hie way
Full of floschis, dubbis, myre and clay.
Laggerit leyis wallowit farnys schew,
Browne muris kythit thar wysnyt mossy hew,
Bank, bra and boddum blanchit wolx and bar.
For gurl weddir growit bestis hair.
The wynd maid waif the red wed on the dyke,
Bedowyn in donkis deip was every sike.
Our craggis and the front of rochis seir
Hang gret ische schouchlis lang as ony speir.
The grond stud barrant, widderit, dosk or gray,
Herbis, flowris and gersis wallowyt away.
Woddis, forrestis, with nakyt bewis blowt,
Stude stripyt of thar weid in every howt.
So bustuusly Boreas his bugill blew,
The deyr full dern doun in the dalis drew;
Smale byrdis, flokkand throu thik ronys thrang,
In chyrmyng and with cheping changit thar sang,

---

skuggis: shadows   dyrknyt: darkened   warpit: threw out
levyn: lightning   felloun: fierce   flaw: blast   soppys:
little clouds   snypand: cutting   dolly: dismal   spait: flood
stretis: streets   floschis: marshes   dubbis: puddles   laggerit:
bemired   muris: moors   kythit: showed   gurl: stormy
bedowyn: soaked   donkis: marshes   sike: stream   our:
over   seir: several   ische schouchlis: icicles   dosk: dark
gersis: grasses   wallowyt: withered   blowt: bare   howt: wood
bustuusly: roughly, boisterously   dern: secretly   ronys:
thickets

Sekand hidlis and hyrnys thame to hyde
Fra feirfull thuddis of the tempestuus tyde;
The watir lynnys rowtis, and every lynd
Quhislit and brayt of the swouchand wynd.
Puyr lauboraris and bissy husband men
Went wait and wery draglit in the fen.
The silly scheip and thar litil hyrd gromys
Lurkis undre le of bankis, woddis and bromys;
And other dantit grettar bestiall,
Within thar stabillis sesyt into stall,
Sik as mulis, horssis, oxin and ky,
Fed tuskyt barys and fat swyne in sty,
Sustenyt war by mannys governance
On hervist and on symmeris purvyance.
Wyde quhar with fors so Eolus schowtis schill
In this congelit sesson scharp and chill,
The callour ayr, penetratyve and puyr,
Dasyng the blude in every creatur,
Maid seik warm stovis and beyn fyris hoyt,
In dowbill garmont cled and wily coyt,
With mychty drink and metis confortyve,
Agane the stern wyntir forto stryve.
Repatyrrit weil, and by the chymnay bekyt,
At evin be tyme downe a bed I me strekyt,
Warpit my hed, kest on clathis thrynfald,
Fortil expell the peralus persand cald;
I crosyt me, syne bownyt forto sleip,
Quhar, lemand throu the glas, I dyd tak kepe

---

hidlis, hyrnys: hiding-places   rowtis: roar   lynd: linden tree
swouchand: whistling   bromys: the broom plant   dantit:
domesticated   sesyt: tied   barys: boars   schill: shrill
callour: fresh   wily coyt: under-coat   repatyrrit: fed
bekyt: warmed   warpit: wrapped   bownyt: prepared
lemand: gleaming

Latonya, the lang irksum nyght,
Hir subtell blenkis sched and watry lycht,
Full hie up quhirlyt in hir regioun,
Till Phebus ryght in oppositioun,
Into the Crab hir proper mansioun draw,
Haldand the hight all thocht the son went law.
Hornyt Hebowd, quhilk we clepe the nycht owle,
Within hir cavern hard I schowt and yowle,
Laithly of form, with crukyt camscho beke,
Ugsum to heir was hir wild elrich screke;
The wild geis claking eik by nyghtis tyde
Atour the cite fleand hard I glyde.
On slummyr I slaid full sad, and slepit sound
Quhil the oriyont upwart gan rebound.
Phebus crownyt byrd, the nyghtis orlager,
Clapping his weyngis thrys had crawin cleir;
Approching neir the greking of the day,
Within my bed I walkynnyt quhar I lay;
So fast declynys Synthea the moyn,
And kays keklis on the ruyf aboyn;
Palamedes byrdis crowpyng in the sky,
Fleand on randon, schapyn like ane Y,
And as a trumpat rang thar vocis soun,
Quhois cryis bene pronosticatioun
Of wyndy blastis and ventositeis;
Fast by my chalmyr, in heich wysnyt treis,
The soir gled quhislis lowd with mony a pew:
Quhar by the day was dawyn weil I knew,

---

camscho: crooked   hard: heard   orlager: time-keeper (cock)
greking: breaking (crack) of dawn   kays: jackdaws   Palamedes
byrdis: cranes   crowpyng: crying harshly   randon (on): in
formation   schapyn: shaped   ventositeis: blasts of gale   soir:
sorrel-coloured   gled: kite

Bad beit the fyre and the candill alyght,
Syne blissyt me, and in my wedis dyght,
A schot wyndo onschet a litill on char,
Persavyt the mornyng bla, wan and har,
With clowdy gum and rak ourquhelmyt the ayr,
The sulye stythly, hasart, rouch and hair,
Branchis bratlyng, and blaknyt schew the brays
With hirstis harsk of waggand wyndill strays,
The dew droppis congelit on stibbil and rynd,
And scharp hailstanys mortfundeit of kynd
Hoppand on the thak and on the causay by.
The schot I closit, and drew inwart in hy,
Chyvirrand for cald, the sesson was so snell,
Schupe with hayt flambe to fleym the fresyng fell.
And, as I bownyt me to the fyre me by,
Baith up and down the hows I dyd aspy,
And seand Virgill on a lettron stand,
To write onone I hynt a pen in hand,
Fortil perform the poet grave and sad,
Quham sa fer furth or than begun I had,
And wolx ennoyt sum deill in my hart
Thar restit oncompletit sa gret a part.
And to my self I said: 'In gud effect
Thou mon draw furth, the yok lyis on thy nek.'

bad beit . . .: had the fire mended   schot wyndo: window that
may be opened or shut   onschet: opened   on char: ajar
bla: whitish-blue   har: frosty, hoary   gum: fog   rak: mist
sulye: soil   stythly: stiff (i.e. frozen)   hasart: grey
bratlyng: rattling   blaknyt: blackened   brays: hills   hirstis:
hillsides   wyndill strays: dry grass-stalks   rynd: hoar frost
mortfundeit: benumbed   causay: causeway   hy: haste   snell:
biting   schupe: tried   fleym: drive out   fell: fierce
bownyt: hastened   hows: house   lettron: lectern
hynt: took   fortil: in order to   sum deill: somewhat

Within my mynde compasyng thocht I so,
Na thing is done quhil ocht remanys ado;
For byssynes, quhilk occurrit on cace,
Ourvolvyt I this volume, lay a space;
And, thocht I wery was, me list not tyre,
Full laith to leif our wark swa in the myre,
Or yit to stynt for bitter storm or rane.
Heir I assayt to yok our pleuch agane,
And, as I couth, with afald diligens,
This nixt buke following of profond sentens
Has thus begun in the chil wyntir cald,
Quhen frostis doith ourfret baith firth and fald.

compasyng: examining   on cace: as it happened   ourvolvyt:
laid aside   afald: single-minded   firth and fald: everywhere
(wood and field)

39   *The Prologue to Book XIII*

Heir begynnys the Proloug of the Threttene
and last Buk of Eneados ekit to Virgill
be Mapheus Vegius

TOWART the evyn, amyd the symmyris heit,
   Quhen in the Crab Appollo held hys sete,
Duryng the joyus moneth tyme of June,
As gone neir was the day and supper doyn,
I walkyt furth abowt the feildis tyte,
Quhilkis tho replenyst stud full of delyte,
With herbys, cornys, catal, and frute treis,
Plente of stoir, byrdis and byssy beys,

tyte: soon   tho: then   stoir: domestic animals

GAVIN DOUGLAS

In amerant medis fleand est and west,
Eftir laubour to tak the nychtis rest.
And as I lukit on the lift me by,
All byrnand red gan walxin the evyn sky:
The son enfyrit haill, as to my sight,
Quhirlit about hys ball with bemys brycht,
Declynand fast towart the north in deid,
And fyry Phegon, his dun nychtis steid,
Dowkit hys hed sa deip in fludis gray
That Phebus rollis doun undir hell away;
And Esperus in the west with bemys brycht
Upspryngis, as forrydar of the nycht.
Amyd the hawchis, and every lusty vaill,
The recent dew begynnys doun to scaill,
To meys the byrnyng quhar the son had schyne,
Quhilk tho was to the neddir warld declyne:
At every pilis poynt and cornys croppis
The techrys stude, as lemand beryall droppis,
And on the hailsum herbis, cleyn but wedis,
Lyke cristal knoppis or smal silver bedis.
The lyght begouth to quynchyng owt and faill,
The day to dyrkyn, declyne and devaill;
The gummys rysis, doun fallis the donk rym,
Baith heir and thar scuggis and schaddois dym.
Upgois the bak with hir pelit ledderyn flycht,
The lark discendis from the skyis hycht,
Syngand hir complyng sang, efter hir gys,
To tak hir rest, at matyn hour to rys.

amerant: emerald-green   lift: sky   dowkit: immersed
hawchis: meadows   scaill: pour   meys: assuage   pilis:
grass-blades   techrys: water-drops   beryall: like the beryl
cleyn but: free from   knoppis: knobs, buds   quynchyng: die out
devaill: fall   gummys: mists   scuggis: shadows   bak: bat
pelit: bald, plucked of hair (the bat's wing)   complyng: compline
gys: manner

165

Owt our the swyre swymmys the soppis of myst,
The nycht furthspred hir cloke with sabill lyst,
That all the bewte of the fructuus feld
Was with the erthis umbrage cleyn ourheld;
Baith man and beste, fyrth, flude and woddis wild
Involvyt in tha schaddois warryn syld.
Still war the fowlis fleis in the air,
All stoir and catall seysit in thar lair,
And every thing, quharso thame lykis best,
Bownys to tak the hailsum nychtis rest
Eftir the days laubour and the heyt.
Clos warryn all and at thar soft quyet,
But sterage or removing, he or sche,
Owder best, byrd, fysch, fowle, by land or sey.
And schortlie, every thing that doith repar
In firth or feild, flude, forest, erth or ayr,
Or in the scroggis, or the buskis ronk,
Lakis, marrasis, or thir pulys donk,
Astabillit lyggis still to slepe, and restis;
Be the smaill byrdis syttand on thar nestis,
The litill mygeis, and the vrusum fleys,
Laboryus emmotis, and the bissy beys;
Als weill the wild as the taym bestiall,
And every othir thingis gret and small,
Owtak the mery nychtgaill, Philomeyn,
That on the thorn sat syngand fra the spleyn;
Quhais myrthfull notis langyng fortil heir,
Ontill a garth undir a greyn lawrer
I walk onon, and in a sege down sat,
Now musyng apon this and now on that.

swyre: valley   lyst: hem   ourheld: covered over   syld:
hidden   scroggis: brushwood   buskis: bushes   ronk: rank (adj.)
mygeis: gnats   vrusum: error for *unrusum*, ? restless   owtak: except
fortil: to   garth: garden   lawrer: laurel   sege: seat

I se the poill, and eik the Ursis brycht,
And hornyt Lucyn castand bot dym lycht,
Becaus the symmyr skyis schayn sa cleir;
Goldyn Venus, the maistres of the yeir,
And gentill Jove, with hir participate,
Thar bewtuus bemys sched in blyth estait:
That schortly, thar as I was lenyt doun,
For nychtis silens, and this byrdis soun,
On sleip I slaid, quhar sone I saw appeir
Ane agit man, and said: 'Quhat dois thou heir
Undyr my tre, and willyst me na gude?'
Me thocht I lurkit up under my hude
To spy this ald, that was als stern of spech
As he had beyn ane medicyner or lech;
And weill persavit that hys weid was strange,
Tharto so ald, that it had not beyn change,
Be my consait, fully that fourty yeir,
For it was threidbair into placis seir;
Syde was this habyt, round, and closyng meit,
That strekit to the grund doun our his feit;
And on his hed of lawrer tre a crown,
Lyke to sum poet of the ald fasson.
Me thocht I said to hym with reverens:
'Fader, gif I have done you ony offens,
I sall amend, gif it lyis in my mycht:
Bot suythfastly, gyf I have perfyte sycht,
Onto my doym, I, saw you nevir ayr,
Fayn wald wyt quhen, on quhat wys, or quhar,
Aganyst you trespassit ocht have I.'
'Weill,' quod the tother, 'wald thou mercy cry

poill: pole star   lurkit: peered   lech: physician   consait:
fancy   seir: several   syde: large   doym: judgement
ayr: before   tother: other

167

And mak amendis, I sal remyt this falt;
Bot, other ways, that sete salbe full salt.
Knawis thou not Mapheus Vegius, the poet,
That onto Virgillis lusty bukis sweit
The thretteyn buke ekit Eneadan?
I am the sammyn, and of the na thyng fayn,
That hes the tother twelf into thy tong
Translait of new, thai may be red and song
Our Albyon ile into your vulgar leid;
Bot to my buke yit lyst the tak na heid.'
'Mastir,' I said, 'I heir weill quhat yhe say,
And in this cace of perdon I you pray,
Not that I have you ony thing offendit,
Bot rathir that I have my tyme mysspendit,
So lang on Virgillis volume forto stair,
And laid on syde full mony grave mater,
That, wald I now write in that trety mor,
Quhat suld folk deym bot all my tyme forlor?
Als, syndry haldis, fader, trastis me,
Your buke ekit but ony necessite,
As to the text accordyng never a deill,
Mair than langis to the cart the fift quheill.
Thus, sen yhe beyn a Cristyn man, at large
Lay na sik thing, I pray you, to my charge;
It may suffys Virgill is at ane end.
I wait the story of Jherom is to you kend,
Quhou he was dung and beft intill hys sleip,
For he to gentilis bukis gaif sik keip.

---

sete: seat, predicament   salbe: shall be   salt: salt, uncomfortable
ekit: added   the: thee   fayn: fond   lyst the tak: desire you to
take   trety: treatise   syndry: sundry people   haldis: consider
trastis: believe   langis: belongs   quheill: wheel   dung:
struck   beft: beaten   keip: attention

Full scharp repreif to sum is write, ye wist,
In this sentens of the haly Psalmyst:
"Thai ar corruppit and maid abhominabill
In thar studeyng thyngis onprofitabill":
Thus sair me dredis I sal thoill a heit,
For the grave study I have so long forleit.'
'Ya, smy,' quod he, 'wald thou eschape me swa?
In faith we sall nocht thus part or we ga!
Quhou think we he essonyeis hym to astart,
As all for consciens and devoit hart,
Fenyeand hym Jherom forto contyrfeit,
Quhar as he lyggis bedovyn, lo, in sweit!
I lat the wyt I am nane hethyn wight,
And gif thou has afortyme gayn onrycht,
Followand sa lang Virgill, a gentile clerk,
Quhy schrynkis thou with my schort Cristyn wark?
For thocht it be bot poetry we say,
My buke and Virgillis morall beyn, bath tway:
Len me a fourteyn nycht, how evir it be,
Or, be the faderis sawle me gat,' quod he,
'Thou salt deir by that evir thou Virgill knew.'
And, with that word, doun of the sete me drew,
Syne to me with hys club he maid a braid,
And twenty rowtis apon my riggyng laid,
Quhill, 'Deo, Deo, mercy,' dyd I cry,
And, be my rycht hand strekit up inhy,
Hecht to translait his buke, in honour of God
And hys Apostolis twelf, in the numbir od.
He, glaid tharof, me by the hand uptuke,
Syne went away, and I for feir awoik,

---

heit: heating   forleit: neglected   smy: rogue   essonyeis:
excuses   lyggis: lies   bedovyn: plunged   braid: threatening flourish   rowtis: blows   riggyng: back   inhy: in
haste   hecht: promised

And blent abowt to the north est weill far,
Saw gentill Jubar schynand, the day star,
And Chiron, clepit the syng of Sagittary,
That walkis the symmyrris nycht, to bed gan cary.
Yondyr doun dwynys the evyn sky away,
And upspryngis the brycht dawyng of day
Intill ane other place nocht far in sundir
That tobehald was plesans, and half wondir.
Furth quynchyng gan the starris, on be on,
That now is left bot Lucifer allon.
And forthirmor to blason this new day,
Quha mycht discryve the byrdis blisfull bay?
Belyve on weyng the bissy lark upsprang,
To salus the blyth morrow with hir sang;
Sone our the feildis schynys the lycht cleir,
Welcum to pilgrym baith and lauborer;
Tyte on hys hynys gaif the greif a cry,
'Awaik on fut, go till our husbandry.'
And the hyrd callis furth apon hys page,
'Do dryve the catall to thar pasturage.'
The hynys wife clepis up Katheryn and Gill;
'Ya, dame,' said thai, 'God wait, with a gude will.'
The dewy greyn, pulderit with daseis gay,
Schew on the sward a cullour dapill gray;
The mysty vapouris spryngand up full sweit,
Maist confortabill to glaid all manis spreit;
Tharto, thir byrdis syngis in the schawys,
As menstralis playng 'The joly day now dawys.'
Than thocht I thus: I will my cunnand kepe,
I will not be a daw, I will not slepe,

blent: looked   syng: sign   discryve: describe   belyve:
immediately   tyte: soon   hynys: farm labourers   greif: farm
manager, foreman   clepis: calls   pulderit: sprinkled
cunnand: covenant, understanding

I will compleit my promys schortly, thus
Maid to the poet master Mapheus,
And mak upwark heirof, and cloys our buke,
That I may syne bot on grave materis luke:
For, thocht hys stile be nocht to Virgill lyke,
Full weill I wayt my text sall mony like,
Sen eftir ane my tung is and my pen,
Quhilk may suffys as for our vulgar men.
Quha evir in Latyn hes the bruyt or glor,
I speke na wers than I have doyn befor:
Lat clerkis ken the poetis different,
And men onletterit to my wark tak tent;
Quhilk, as twiching this thretteynt buke infeir,
Begynnys thus, as furthwith followis heir.

Explicit prologus in decimumtertium librum Eneados

sen eftir . . . my pen: my speech and writing are the same, i.e. both Scots
bruyt: fame   tak tent: pay attention   infeir: together

[? WILLIAM] STEWART
? 1481–? 1550

40   *Thir Lenterne Dayis ar Luvely Lang*

THIR Lenterne dayis ar luvely lang,
   And I will murne ne mair,
Nor for no mirthles may me mang
That will not for me cair.

may: maid   me mang: agitate myself

I wil be glaid and latt hir gang
With falsat in hir fair.
I fynd ane freschar feir to fang,
Baith of hyd, hew and hair.

The wintter nycht is lang but weir;
I may murne gif I will.
Scho will not murne for me, that cleir;
Thairfoir I wil be still.
O King of Luve that is so cleir,
I me acquyt you till.
Sa scho fra me and I fra hir,
And not bot it be skill.

O Lord of Luve, how lykis the
My lemmen's laitis unleill?
Scho luvis ane uthir bettir than me;
I haif caus to appeill.
I pray to him that deit on tre,
That for us all thold baill,
Mot send my lemmane twa or thre,
Sen scho can not be leill.

Uthir hes hir hairt. Sowld scho haif myne,
Trewly that war grit wrang.
Quhen thay haif play, gif I haif pyne,
On gallowis mot I hang,

---

falsat: falsehood   fair: appearance   feir: companion   fang:
take hold of   but weir: without doubt   gif: if   cleir: beauty
bot . . . skill: without . . . good reason   lemmen: lover   laitis:
tricks   unleill: faithless   thold: endured   baill: suffering

Or for hir luve gif I declyne.
Thocht scho ewill nevir so lang,
Quhen I think on hir foirheid fyne,
Than mon I sing ane sang.

Of all the houris of the nycht
I can not tell you ane;
So murne I for my lady bricht
Fro sleip haif me ourtane.
Fro scho be past out of my sicht
The casting of ane stane,
I haif no langour, be this licht;
I love God of his lane.

Allace that evir fader me gat,
Or moder me wend in clais,
Gif I sowld for ane woman's saik
My lyfe thus leid in lais.
For ye saw nevir so fair a caik
Of meill that millar mais,
Bot yit ane man wald get the maik.
As gud luve cumis as gais.

thocht: thought	ewill: evil, ill	ourtane: overtaken
of his lane: alone	wend: wound, wrapped	leid in lais: spend
in singing songs of complaint	mais: made	maik: equal, mate

ANONYMOUS

? c. 1500

41

Four May Poems

I

QUHEN Flora had ourfret the firth
  In May, of every moneth quene,
Quhen merle and mavis singis with mirth,
Sweit melling in the schawis schene,
Quhen all luvaris rejosit bene,
And most desyrus of thair pray,
I hard a lusty luvar mene,
'I luve, bot I dar nocht assay.

Strang ar the panis I daylie prufe,
Bot yit with pacience I sustene,
I am so fetterit with the lufe
Onlie of my lady schene,
Quhilk for hir bewty mycht be quene,
Natour so craftely alwey
Hes done depaint that sweit serene:
Quhome I luf, I dar nocht assay.

Scho is so brycht of hyd and hew,
I lufe bot hir allone, I wene;
Is non hir luf that may eschew
That blenkis of that dulce amene,

---

ourfret: adorned   firth: wood   merle: blackbird   mavis.
thrush   melling: mingling   schawis: groves   schene:
beautiful   mene: moan   hyd: skin   blenkis: looks, glances
amene: pleasant

So cumly cleir at hir twa ene,
That scho ma luvaris dois effrey
Than evir of Grice did fair Helene;
Quhom I luve, I dar nocht assay.'

II

NOW in this mirthfull tyme of May
My dullit spreit for to rejos,
I sall with sobir mynd assay
Gif I can ocht in metir glos,
Syn all the poyntis of my purpois
In secreit wyis sal be asselyeit,
How in my garth thair growis a rois,
Wes fresche and fair, and now is felyeit.

All winttir throcht this ros wes reid,
And now in May it changis hew;
Thairfoir I trow that it be deid,
And als the stak that it on grew.
Suld I for plesour plant a new?
Na!—that I vow to God in plane:
Said it fair-weill, all flouris adew,
Bot gif that rois revert agane,

For of all plesans to my sycht
That grew on grund, it beris the gre.
My hairt wes on that day and nycht,
It wes so plesand for to se.
Now thair is nowdir erb nor tre
Sall grow within my garding mair,
Quhill I get wit quhat gart it de,
This foirsaid flour that wes so fair.

ma: more   effrey: affright   asselyeit: attempted
felyeit: withered   in plane: clearly   beris the gre: bears off the
prize   quhill: until   gart: made

III

O LUSTY May with Flora quene,
  The balmy dropis from Phebus schene
Preluciand bemes befoir the day.
Be that Diana growis grene
Throwch glaidnes of this lusty May.

Than Esperus that is so bricht
Till wofull hairtis castis his lycht
With bankis that blumes on every bray,
And schuris ar sched furth of thair sicht
Thruch glaidnes of this lusty May.

Birdis on bewis of every birth
Rejosing nottis makand thair mirth
Rycht plesandly upoun the spray
With flurissingis our field and firth
Thruch glaidnes of this lusty May.

All luvaris that ar in cair,
To thair ladeis thay do repair
In fresch mornyngis befoir the day,
And ar in mirth ay mair and mair
Thruch glaidnes of this lusty May.

IV

B E glaid, al ye that luvaris bene,
  For now hes May depaynt with grene
The hillis, valis and the medis,
And flouris lustely upspreidis.

---

be that: by means of that   bray: hillside   ´bewis: boughs
of every birth: of all kinds   our field and firth: everywhere (field
and wood)

176

Awalk out of your sluggairdy
To heir the birdis melody,
Quhois suggourit nottis, loud and cleir,
Is now ane parradice to heir.
Go, walk upoun sum rever fair;
Go, tak the fresch and holsum air;
Go, luk upoun the flurist fell;
Go, feill the herbis plesand smell,
Quhilk will your comfort gar incres,
And all avoyd your havines.
The new-cled purpour hevin aspy;
Behald the lark now in the sky;
With besy wyng scho clymis on hicht
For grit joy of the dayis licht.
Behald the verdour fresch of hew,
Powdderit with grene, quhyt and blew,
Quhairwith dame Flora in this May
Dois richely all the feild array,
And how Aurora with visage pale
Inbalmes with hir cristall hale
The grene and tendir pylis ying
Of every gres that dois upspryng,
And with hir beriall droppis bricht
Makis the gresys gleme of licht.
Luk on the saufir firmament,
And on the annammellit orient.
Luke, or Phebus put up his heid,
As he dois rais his baneris reid,
He dois the eist so bricht attyre
That all semis birnyng in a fyre,

suggourit: sweet   rever: river-bank   flurist fell: flowery hilltop
gar: cause to   avoyd: disperse   purpour: purple   quhyt:
white   pylis: blades of grass   beriall: like the beryl   saufir:
sapphire   annammellit: coloured as by enamel   or: before

Quhilk comfort dois to everything,
Man, bird, beist and flurissing.
Quhairfar, luvaris, be glaid and lycht,
For schort is your havy nycht,
And lenthit is your myrry day.
Thairfoir ye welcum new this May.
And, birdis, do your haill plesance,
With merry song and observance,
This May to welcum at your mycht,
At fresch Phebus uprysing bricht.
And all ye flouris that dois spreid,
Lay furth your levis upoun breid,
And welcum May with benyng cheir,
The quene of every moneth cleir.
And everry man thank in his mynd
The God of Natur and of Kynd,
Quhilk ordanit all for our behufe
The erd undir, the air abufe,
Bird, beist, flour, tyme, day and nycht,
The planeitis for to gif us licht.

quhilk: which   upoun breid: abroad   benyng: benign   cheir:
spirit   kynd: nature

SIR DAVID LINDSAY

? 1490–? 1555

From *THE DREME*

42

Of the Realme of Scotland

QUHEN that I had oversene this Regioun,
  The quhilk, of nature, is boith gude and fair,
I did propone ane lytill questioun,
Beseikand hir the sam for to declare.
Quhat is the cause our boundis bene so bair?
Quod I: or quhate dois mufe our Miserie?
Or quhareof dois proceid our povertie?

For, throw the supporte of your hie prudence,
Off Scotland I persave the properteis,
And, als, considderis, be experience,
Off this countre the gret commoditeis.
First, the haboundance of fyschis in our seis,
And fructual montanis for our bestiall;
And, for our cornis, mony lusty vaill;

The ryche Ryueris, plesand and proffitabyll;
The lustie loochis, with fysche of sindry kyndis;
Hountyng, halkyng, for nobyllis convenabyll;
Forrestis full of Da, Ra, Hartis, and Hyndis;
The fresche fontanis, quhose holesum cristel strandis
Refreschis so the fair fluriste grene medis:
So laik we no thyng that to nature nedis.

---

propone: ask, propose   loochis: lochs   da: doe   ra: roe

Off euery mettell we have the ryche Mynis,
Baith Gold, Sylver, and stonis precious.
Howbeit we want the Spyces and the Wynis,
Or uther strange fructis delycious,
We have als gude, and more neidfull for us.
Meit, drynk, fyre, clathis, thar mycht be gart abound,
Quhilkis als is nocht in al the Mapamound;

More fairer peple, nor of gretar ingyne,
Nor of more strenth gret dedis tyll indure.
Quharefor, I pray yow that ye wald defyne
The principall cause quharefor we ar so pure;
For I marvell gretlie, I yow assure,
Considderand the peple and the ground,
That Ryches suld nocht in this realme redound.

My Sonne, scho said, be my discretioun,
I sall mak answeir, as I understand.
I say to the, under confessioun,
The falt is nocht, I dar weill tak on hand,
Nother in to the peple nor the land.
As for the land, it lakis na uther thing
Bot laubour and the pepyllis governyng.

Than quharein lyis our Inprosperitie?
Quod I. I pray yow hartfullie, Madame,
Ye wald declare to me the veritie;
Or quho sall beir of our barrat the blame?
For, be my treuth, to se I thynk gret schame
So plesand peple, and so fair ane land,
And so few verteous dedis tane on hand.

gart: caused to   mapamound: map of the world   ingyne:
ingenuity   barrat: trouble   tane: taken

Quod scho: I sall, efter my Jugement,
Declare sum causis, in to generall,
And, in to termes schorte, schaw myne intent,
And, syne, transcend more in to speciall.
So, this is myne conclusion fynall:
Wantyng of Justice, polycie, and peace,
Ar cause of thir unhappynes, allace,

It is deficill Ryches tyll incres,
Quhare Polycie makith no residence,
And Policey may never have entres,
Bot quhare that Justice dois delygence
To puneis quhare thare may be found offence.
Justice may nocht have Dominatioun,
Bot quhare Peace makis habitatioun.

43   *The Compleynt of the
        Comoun Weill of Scotland*

AND, thus as we wer talking to and fro,
    We saw a boustius berne cum ouir the bent,
But hors, on fute, als fast as he mycht go,
Quhose rayment wes all raggit, revin, & rent,
With visage leyne, as he had fastit lent:
And fordwart fast his wayis he did advance,
With ane rycht malancolious countynance,

boustius: robust   berne: man   but: without   revin: torn

181

With scrip on hip, and pyikstaff in his hand,
As he had purposit to passe fra hame.
Quod I: gude man, I wald faine understand,
Geve that ye plesit, to wyt quhat wer your name.
Quod he: my Sonne, of that I think gret schame;
Bot, sen thow wald of my name have ane feill,
Forsuith, thay call me Ihone the Comoun Weill.

Schir Commoun Weill, quho hes yow so disgysit?
Quod I: or quhat makis yow so miserabyll?
I have marvell to se yow so supprysit,
The quhilk that I have sene so honorabyll.
To all the warld ye have bene proffitabyll,
And weill honorit in everilk Natioun:
How happinnis, now, your tribulatioun?

Allace, quod he, thow seis how it dois stand
With me, and quhow I am disherisit
Off all my grace, and mon pas of Scotland,
And go, afore quhare I was cherisit.
Remane I heir, I am bot perysit.
For thare is few to me that takis tent,
That garris me go so raggit, revin, and rent.

My tender friendis ar all put to the flycht;
For polecey is fled agane in France.
My Syster, Justice, almaist haith tynt hir sycht,
That scho can nocht hald evinly the ballance.
Plane wrang is plane capitane of Ordinance,
The quhilk debarris Laute and reassoun,
And small remeid is found for oppin treassoun.

geve: if   feill: information   disgysit: disguised   mon pas
of: must leave   takis tent: pays attention   polecey: good government   tynt: lost   laute: loyalty

In to the south, allace, I was neir slane:
Over all the land I culd fynd no releiff;
Almoist betwix the Mers and Lowmabane
I culde nocht knaw ane leill man be ane theif.
To schaw thare reif, thift, murthour, and mischeif,
And vecious workis, it wald infect the air:
And, als, langsum to me for tyll declair.

In to the Hieland I could fynd no remeid,
Bot suddantlie I was put to exile.
Tha sweir swyngeoris thay tuke of me non heid,
Nor amangs thame lat me remane ane quhyle.
Als, in the oute Ylis, and in Argyle,
Unthrift, sweirnes, falset, povertie, and stryfe
Pat polacey in dainger of hir lyfe.

In the Law land I come to seik refuge,
And purposit thare to mak my residence.
Bot singulare proffect gart me soune disluge,
And did me gret injuris and offence,
And said to me: swyith, harlote, hy the hence;
And in this countre se thow tak no curis,
So lang as my auctoritie induris.

And now I may mak no langer debait;
Nor I wate nocht quhome to I suld me mene;
For I have socht throw all the Spirituall stait,
Quhilkis tuke na compt for to heir me complene.
Thare officiaries, thay held me at disdane;
For Symonie, he rewlis up all that rowte;
And Covatyce, that Carle, gart bar me oute.

Mers and Lowmabane: north-east to south-west   reif: stealing
sweir: unwilling   swyngeoris: parasites   Law land: Lowlands
singulare proffect: individual profit   swyith: quick, ready   curis:
care(s)   mene: complain   rewlis . . . rowte: rules over that crowd

Pryde haith chaist far frome thame humilitie;
Devotioun is fled unto the freris;
Sensuale plesour hes baneist Chaistitie;
Lordis of Religioun, thay go lyke Seculeris,
Taking more compt in tellyng thare deneris
Nor thay do of thare constitutioun,
Thus ar thay blyndit be ambitioun.

Oure gentyll men ar all degenerate;
Liberalitie and Lawte, boith, ar loste;
And Cowardyce with Lordis is laureate;
And knychtlie curage turnit in brag and boste;
The Civele weir misgydis everilk oist.
Thare is nocht ellis bot ilk man for hym self,
That garris me go, thus baneist lyke ane elf.

Tharefor, adew; I may no langer tarye.
Fair weill, quod I, and with sanct Ihone to borrow.
Bot, wyt ye weill, my hart was wounder sarye,
Quhen Comoun Weill so sopit was in sorrow.
Yit, efter the nycht cumis the glaid morrow;
Quharefor, I pray yow, schaw me, in certane,
Quhen that ye purpose for to cum agane.

That questioun, it sall be sone desydit,
Quod he: thare sall na Scot have confortyng
Off me, tyll that I see the countre gydit
Be wysedome of ane gude auld prudent kyng,
Quhilk sall delyte hym maist, abone all thyng,
To put Justice tyll exicutioun,
And on strang tratouris mak puneisioun.

tellyng thare deneris: counting their coppers   oist: army
borrow (to): as surety   sopit: sunk

Als yit to the I say ane uther thyng:
I se, rycht weill, that proverbe is full trew,
Wo to the realme that hes ouir young ane king.
With that, he turnit his bak, and said adew.
Ouer firth and fell rycht fast fra me he flew,
Quhose departyng to me was displesand.
With that, Remembrance tuk me be the hand,

And sone, me thocht, scho brocht me to the roche,
And to the cove quhare I began to sleip.
With that, ane schip did spedalye approche,
Full plesandlie saling apone the deip,
And syne did slake hir salis, and gan to creip
Towart the land, anent quhare that I lay:
Bot, wyt ye weill, I gat ane fellown fraye.

All hir Cannounis sche leit craik of at onis:
Down schuke the stremaris frome the topcastell;
Thay sparit nocht the poulder, nor the stonis;
Thay schot thare boltis, & doun thar ankeris fell;
The Marenaris, thay did so youte and yell,
That haistalie I stert out of my dreme,
Half in ane fray, and spedalie past hame,

And lychtlie dynit, with lyste and appityte,
Syne efter, past in tyll ane Oritore,
And tuke my pen, and thare began to wryte
All the visioun that I have schawin afore.
Schir, of my dreme as now thou gettis no more,
Bot I beseik God for to send the grace
To rewle thy realme in unitie and peace.

ouir: too   firth and fell: wood and hill, everywhere   anent:
towards   fellown: terrible   fraye: fright   youte: shout
lychtlie: cheerfully   lyste: pleasure

From *THE HISTORIE OF SQUYER WILLIAM MELDRUM*

44   *Squire Meldrum at Carrickfergus*

FOR he was wounder amiabill
    And in all deidis honorabill,
And ay his honour did avance
In Ingland first and syne in France.
And thair his manheid did assaill
Under the Kingis greit Admirall,
Quhen the greit Navie of Scotland
Passit to the sey aganis Ingland.
And as thay passit be Ireland Coist
The Admirall gart land his Oist,
And set Craigfergus into Fyre,
And saifit nouther Barne nor Byre.
It was greit pietie for to heir
Of the pepill the bailfull cheir,
And how the Land folk wer spuilyeit;
Fair wemen underfute wer fuilyeit.
Bot this young Squyer bauld and wicht
Savit all wemen quhair he micht,
All Preistis and Freiris he did save.
Till at the last he did persave
Behind ane Garding amiabill
Ane womanis voce richt lamentabill,
And on that voce he followit fast
Till he did see hir at the last
Spuilyeit, nakit as scho was borne.
Twa men of weir wer hir beforne,
Quhilk wer richt cruell men and kene,
Partand the spuilyie thame betwene.

oist: host   spuilyeit: despoiled   fuilyeit: defiled

Ane fairer woman nor scho wes
He had not sene in onie place.
Befoir him on hir kneis scho fell,
Sayand, for him that heryit Hell,
Help me, sweit Sir, I am ane Mayd.
Than softlie to the men he said,
I pray yow give againe hir sark
And tak to yow all uther wark.
Hir Kirtill was of Scarlot reid,
Of gold ane garland of hir heid
Decorit with Enamelyne,
Belt and Brochis of silver fyne.
Of yallow Taftais wes hir sark,
Begaryit all with browderit wark
Richt craftelie with gold and silk.
Than said the Ladie quhyte as milk,
Except my sark no thing I crave;
Let thame go hence, with all the lave.
Quod thay to hir, be Sanct Fillane,
Of this ye get nathing agane.
Than said the Squyer courteslie,
Gude Freindis I pray yow hartfullie,
Gif ye be worthie Men of Weir
Restoir to hir agane hir Geir;
Or, be greit God that all hes wrocht,
That spuilyie salbe full deir bocht.
Quod thay to him, we the defy,
And drew thair swordis haistely
And straik at him with sa greit Ire
That from his Harnes flew the fyre:

begaryit: ornamented   lave: rest   quod: said   salbe: shall be

With duntis sa darflie on him dang
That he was never in sic ane thrang.
Bot he him manfullie defendit,
And with ane bolt on thame he bendit
And hat the ane upon the heid
That to the ground he fell doun deid:
For to the teith he did him cleif,
Lat him ly thair with ane mischeif.
Than with the uther, hand for hand,
He beit him with his birneist brand:
The uther was baith stout and strang,
And on the Squyer darflie dang.
And than the Squyer wrocht greit wonder,
Ay till his sword did shaik in sunder.
Than drew he furth ane sharp dagair,
And did him cleik be the Collair,
And evin in at the collerbane
At the first straik he hes him slane:
He founderit fordward to the ground.
Yit was the Squyer haill and sound:
For quhy, he was sa weill enarmit,
He did escaip fra thame unharmit.
And quhen he saw thay wer baith slane
He to that Ladie past agane
Quhair scho stude nakit on the bent,
And said, tak your abulyement;
And scho him thankit full humillie,
And put hir claithis on spedilie.
Than kissit he that Ladie fair,
And tuik his leif at hir but mair.
Be that the Taburne and Trumpet blew,
And everie man to shipburd drew.

duntis: blows   darflie: boldly   dang: struck   in . . . thrang: so
hard-pressed

That Ladie was dolent in hart,
From tyme scho saw he wald depart
That hir relevit from hir harmes,
And hint the Squyer in hir armes
And said, will ye byde in this Land,
I sall yow tak to my Husband.
Thocht I be cassin now in cair
I am (quod scho) my Fatheris Air,
The quhilk may spend, of pennies round,
Of yeirlie Rent ane thowsand Pound:
With that hartlie scho did him kis.
Ar ye (quod scho) content of this?
Of that (quod he) I wald be fane,
Gif I micht in this Realme remane.
Bot I mon first pas into France;
Sa quhen I cum agane, perchance,
And efter that the Peice be made,
To marie yow I will be glaid:
Fair weill, I may no longer tarie;
I pray God keip yow, and sweit sanct Marie.
Than gaif scho him ane Lufe taking,
Ane riche Rubie set in ane Ring.
I am (quod scho) at your command,
With yow to pas into Scotland.
I thank yow hartfullie (quod he)
Ye ar ouir young to saill the See,
And speciallie with Men of weir.
Of that (quod scho) tak ye na feir,
I sall me cleith in mennis clais
And ga with yow quhair euir ye pleis.
Suld I not lufe him Paramour
That saifit my Lyfe and my honour?

hint: took   cassin: thrown by chance   taking: token

Ladie, I say yow in certane
Ye sall have lufe for lufe agane
Trewlie, unto my Lyfis end:
Fairweill, to God I yow commend.
With that, into his Boit he past,
And to the ship he rowit fast.

From *THE MONARCHE*

45   *After the Flood*

QUHEN Noye had maid his Sacrifyce,
    Thankand God of his Benifyce,
He standand on mont Armanye,
Quhare he the countre mycht espye,
Ye may beleve his hart was sore,
Seyng the erth, quhilk wes affore
The Flude so plesand and perfyte,
Quhilk to behald wes gret delyte,
That now was barren maid and bair,
Afore quhilk fructuous was and fair.
The plesand treis beryng fructis
Wer lyand revin up be the rutis.
The holsum herbis and fragrant flouris
Had tynt boith vertew and cullouris.
The feildis grene and fluryst meidis
Wer spulyeit of thare plesand weidis.
The erth, quhilk first wes so fair formit,
Wes, be that furious flude, deformit.

seyng: seeing   revin: torn   tynt: lost

190

Quhare umquhyle wer the plesand planis,
Wer holkit Glennis and hie montanis.
Frome clattryng cragis, gret and gray,
The erth was weschin quyte away.

    Bot Noye had gretast displesouris,
    Behauldand the dede Creatouris,
Quhilk wes ane sycht rycht Lamentabyll.
Men, Wemen, Beistis Innumerabyll,
Seyng thame ly upone the landis,
And sum wer fleityng on the strandis.
Quhalis and Monstouris of the seis
Stickit on stobbis, amang the treis,
And, quhen the Flude was decressand,
Thay wer left welteryng on the land.
Affore the Flude duryng that space,
The sey wes all in to ane place.
Rycht so the erth, as bene desydit,
In syndrie partis wes nocht devydit,
As bene Europe and Asia
Devydit ar frome Africa.
Ye se, now, divers Famous Ilis
Stand frome the mane land mony mylis:
All thir gret Ilis, I understand,
War, than, equall with the ferme land.
Thare wes none sey Mediterrane,
Bot onely the gret Occiane,
Quhilk did nocht spred sic bulryng strandis
As it dois, now, ouirthort the landis.
Than, be the ragyng of that flude,
The erth of vertew wes denude,

umquhyle: formerly   holkit: hollow   weschin: washed
quhalis: whales   stobbis: stumps   welteryng: rolling   bulryng: roaring (with the waves)   ouirthort: across   vertew: fertility, fruitfulness

The quhilk afore wes to be prysit,
Quhose bewtie than wes dissagysit.
Than wes the Maledictioun knawin
Quhilk wes be God tyll Adam schawin.
I reid quhow Clerkis dois conclude,
Induryng that moste furious flude.
With quhilk the erth wes so supprest,
The wynd blew furth of the southwest.
As may be sene, be experience,
Quhow, throw the watteris violence,
The heych montanis, in every art,
Ar bair forgane the southwest part,
As the Montanis of Parraneis,
The Alpis, and Rochis in the seis,
Rycht so, the Rochis, gret and gray,
Quhilk standis into Norroway,
The heychast hyllis, in every art,
And in Scotland, for the moste part.
Throuch weltryng of that furious flude,
The Cragis of erth war maid denude:
Travellyng men may consydder best
The montanis bair nyxt the southwest.

dissagysit: disguised   induryng: during   art: direction
forgane: in front of Parraneis: Pyrenees   heychast: highest

SIR RICHARD MAITLAND

1496–1586

Solace in Age

THOCHT that this warld be verie strange,
  And thevis hes done my rowmes range,
    And teymd my fald,
Yit wald I leif and byd ane change,
    Thocht I be ald.

Now me to spulyie sum not spairis;
To tak my geir no captane cairis,
    Thai ar so bald;
Yit tyme may cum may mend my sairis,
    Thocht I be ald.

Sum now be force of men of weir
My hous my landis and my geir
    Fra me thai hald;
Yit as I may sall mak gud cheir,
    Thocht I be ald.

Sa weill is kend my innocence,
That I will not for none offence
    Flyt lyke ane skald,
Bot thank God and tak patience,
    For I am ald.

For eild and my infirmite,
Warme claythis ar bettir for me
    To keip fra cald
Nor in dame Venus chamber be,
    Now being ald.

rowmes: possessions   range: harm   teymd: emptied   fald:
and   geir: possessions   sairis: sores   flyt: scold (vb.)
skald: scold (n.)

Off Venus play past is the heit,
For I may not the mistiris beit
    Off Meg nor Mald;
For ane young las I am not meit,
    I am sa ald.

The fairast wenche in all this toun,
Thocht I hir had in hir best gown
    Rycht braiflie braild,
Withe hir I mycht not play the loun,
    I am so ald.

My wyff sum tyme wald telis trow,
And mony lesingis weill allow
    War of me tald;
Scho will not eyndill on me now,
    And I sa ald.

My hors my harnes and my speir,
And all uther my hoisting geir
    Now may be sald;
I am not habill for the weir,
    I am so ald.

Quhone young men cumis fra the grene,
At the futball playing had bene,
    With brokin spald,
I thank my God I want my ene,
    And am so ald.

mistiris: needs   beit: satisfy   braild: arrayed   telis trow:
believe tales   lesingis: lies   eyndill: be jealous   hoisting:
army   spald: collar-bone

Thocht I be sweir to ryd or gang,
Thair is sum thing I wantit lang
  Fane have I wald
And thame puneist that did me wrang,
  Thocht I be ald.

      quod R maitland of lethingtoun

   sweir: unwilling

[?] JAMES V

1513–1542

47   *Christ's Kirk on the Green*

WAS never in Scotland hard nor sene
  Sic dansing nor deray,
Nother in Falkland on the grene,
Nor Peblis to the play,
As was of wowaris as I wene
At Chrystis kirk on ane day.
Thair come our Kittie wesching clene
In hir new kirtill of gray,
  Full gay,
At Chrystis kirk on the grene.

To dance the damisallis thame dicht,
And lassis licht of laittis;
Thair gluvis war of the raffell richt;
Thair schone war of the straitis:

 deray: disturbance   Peblis: Peebles   wowaris: suitors
dicht: got ready   laittis: manners   raffell: roe-skin   of the
straitis: of Moroccan leather

Thair kirtillis war off the lincum licht
Weill prest with mony plaitis.
Thay war so nyce quhen men tham nicht
Thay squeild lyk ony gaitis,
Ful loud
At Chrystis kirk on the grene.

Sche scornit Jok and scrippit at him,
And morgeound him with mokkis;
He wald have luffit hir; sche wald nocht lat him,
For all his yallow lokkis;
He cherist hir; scho bad ga chat him,
Sche comptit him nocht tua clokkis;
Sa schamfullie ane schort goun sat him,
His lymmis was lyk twa rokkis,
Sche said
At Chrystis kirk on the grene.

Off all thir madinis myld as meid,
Was nane sa gymp as Gillie;
As ony rose hir rude was reid,
Hir lyre was lyk the lillie;
Bot yallow yallow was hir heid,
And sche of luif so sillie,
Thocht all hir kin suld have bein deid,
Sche wald have bot sweit Willie,
Allane,
At Chrystis kirk on the grein.

lincum: Lincoln green   nicht: neared   gaitis: goats
scrippit: scoffed   morgeound: grimaced at   chat him: 'hang'
himself   clokkis: beetles   lymmis: limbs   rokkis: distaffs
gymp: slender   rude: cheek   lyre: skin, complexion

Stevin come steppand in with stendis,
No renk mycht him arrest;
Platfut he bobbit up with bendis,
For Mald he maid requeist;
He lap quhill he lay on his lendis,
Bot rysand he was prest
Quhill he hostit at bayth the endis
In honour of the feist
That day
At Chrystis kirk on the grein.

Thome Lutar was thair menstrale meit;
O Lord, gif he culd lance!
He playit so schill and sang so sweit
Quhill Towsie tuik ane trance;
All auld lycht futtis he did forleyt
And counterfutit France;
He him avysit as man discreit
And up the moreis dance
Scho tuik
At Chrystis kirk on the grein.

Than Robene Roy begouth to revell,
And Dowie to him druggit;
'Lat be!' quod Johke, and callit him gavell,
And be the taill him tuggit;
He turnit and cleikit to the cavell,
Bot Lord than gif thai luggit!

stendis: strides   renk: man   platfut: Flatfoot (name of
clown, and of dance he did)   bendis: leaps   hostit: 'coughed'
lance: spring   quhill: till   forleyt: forsake   counterfutit
France: counterfeited a French dance   druggit: dragged   gavell:
rascal   cleikit to: hooked on to   cavell: low fellow

Thai partit thair play thane with ane nevell
Men wait gif hair wes ruggit
Betwene thame
At Chrystis kirk on the grein.

Ane bend ane bow, sic sturt couth steir him;
Grit scayth war to have scard him;
He chesit ane flaine as did affeir him;
The tother said dirdum dardum;
Throw bayth the cheikis he thocht to cheir him,
Or throw the chaftis have charde him
Bot be ane myle it come nocht neir him.
I can nocht say quhat mard him
Thair
At Chrystis kirk on the grein.

With that ane freynd of his cryit, fy!
And up ane arow drew,
He forgeit it so ferslye
The bow in flenders flew;
Sa was the will of God, trow I;
For had the tre bene trew,
Men said that kend his archerie
That he had slane anew
That day
At Chrystis kirk on the grein.

Ane haistie hensour callit Harie,
Quhilk wes ane archer heynd,
Tit up ane takill but ony tarye,
That turment so him teynd;

nevell: blow   ruggit: tugged   sturt: rage   scard: scared
flaine: arrow   chaftis: jaws   charde: pierced   forgeit:
bent   flenders: splinters   hensour: young fellow   heynd:
skilful   tit: pulled   takill: weapon   teynd: vexed

[?] JAMES V

I wait nocht quhidder his hand cud varie,
Or gif the man was his freynd,
Bot he chapit throw the michtis of Marie
As man that na evill meynd
That tyme
At Chrystis kirk on the grein.

Than Lowrie as ane lyoun lap,
And sone ane flane culd fedder;
He hecht to pers him at the pape,
Thairon to wed ane wedder;
He hit him on the wambe ane wap,
And it bust lyk ane bledder;
Bot lo! as fortoun was and hap,
His doublat was of ledder
And sauft him
At Chrystis kirk on the grein.

The baff so boustuousle abasit him,
To the erd he duschit doun;
The tother for dreid he preissit him
And fled out of the toun;
The wyffis come furth and up thay paisit him
And fand lyff in the loun
And with thre routis thay raisit him
And coverit him of swoune
Agane
At Chrystis kirk on the grein.

chapit: escaped   hecht: promised   wed: bet, wager
wedder: wether, castrated ram   wambe: belly   preissit: pressed
paisit him: lifted him to his feet   routis: shouts   coverit:
recovered

199

Ane yaip young man that stude him neist
Lousit of ane schot with ire;
He etlit the berne evin in the breist,
The bout flew our the byre;
Ane cryit that he had slane ane preist
Ane myle beyond ane myre;
Than bow and bag fra him he caist,
And fled als fers as fyre
Of flint
At Chrystis kirk on the grein.

With forkis and flalis thay leit grit flappis,
And flang togither with friggis
With bougaris of barnis thai birst blew cappis,
Quhill thay of bernis maid briggis;
The rerde rais rudlie with the rappis,
Quhen rungis was layd on riggis;
The wyffis come furth with cryis and clappis
'Lo quhair my lyking liggis,'
Quod scho
At Chrystis kirk on the grein.

Thay girnit and leit gird with granis;
Ilk gossop uther grevit;
Sum straikit stingis, sum gadderit stanis,
Sum fled and weill eschewit;

yaip: keen	lousit: let go	etlit: aimed at	berne: man
bout: bolt	friggis: stout fellows	bougaris: rafters	cappis:
? bonnets	bernis: men	briggis: bridges	rerde: din
rungis: cudgels	riggis: backs	lyking: sweetheart	liggis:
lies	girnit: wept	leit gird: begun to nag	granis:
groans	stingis: poles		

[?] JAMES V

The menstrale wan within ane wanis;
That day full weill he previt,
For he come hame with unbrisde banis,
Quhair fechtaris war mischevit
For ever
At Chrystis kirk on the grein.

Heich Hunchoun with ane hissill rys
To red can throw thame rummill;
He mudlit thame doun lyk ony myse;
He wes na baty bummill.
Thocht he wes wicht he wes nocht wys,
With sic Jatouris to geummill.
For fra his thoume thay dang ane sklys
Quhill he cryit barlaw fummill
Ouris
At Chrystis kirk on the grein.

Quhen that he saw his blude so reid,
To fle micht no man lat him;
He wend it had bene for ald feid,
The far sarar it sat him;
He gart his feit defend his heid;
He thocht thay cryit have at him,
Quhill he was past out of all pleid—
He suld be swyft that gat him
Throw speid
At Chrystis kirk on the grein.

wanis: dwelling(s)   hissill rys: hazel-branch   red: separate
(v.)   rummill (can): did rush   mudlit: struck   baty
bummill: backward softie   Jatouris: tatlers   geummill: meddle
sklys: slice   barlaw fummill ouris: parley, truce (cf. barley, as the
children say today), pax! enough!   feid: feud   sarar: sorer
sat: oppressed   pleid: dispute

The toun soutar in breif was boudin;
His wyf hang in his waist;
His body was in blude all browdin;
He granit lyk ony gaist;
Hir glitterand hairis that war full goldin,
So hard in luif him laist
That for hir saik he wes unyoldin
Sevin myle quhen he wes chaist
And mair
At Chrystis kirk on the grein.

The millar was of manlie mak;
To meit him was na mowis;
Thair durst na ten cum him to tak
So nobbit he thair nowis.
The buschement haill about him brak
And bickert him with bowis,
Syn tratourlie behind his bak
Ane hewit him on the howis
Behind
At Chrystis kirk on the grein.

Twa that was herdismen of the herde
Ran upone uther lyk rammis;
Thair forsy freikis richt uneffeird
Bet on with barow trammis;
Bot quhair thair gobbis war bayth ungird,
Thai gat upon the gammis,
Quhill bludie barkit was thair berd,
As thay had worreit lambis

soutar: shoemaker   breif: rage   boudin: swollen   browdin:
decorated   luif: love   laist: held   unyoldin: unyielded
mowis: joke   nobbit: knocked   nowis: heads   buschement:
ambush   bickert: assaulted   howis: houghs   freikis: men
trammis: shafts   gobbis: mouths   ungird: unguarded   gammis:
mouths   barkit: clotted

Most lyk
At Chrystis kirk on the grein.

The wyffis cast up ane hidduous yell,
Quhen all the youngkeiris yokkit;
Als fers as ony fyr flauchtis fell
Freikis to the feild thai flokit;
Thay cavellis with clubbis culd uther quell,
Quhill blude at breistis out bokkit;
So rudlie rang the Commoun bell
Quhill all the steipill rokkit
For rerde
At Chrystis kirk on the grein.

Quhen thai had beirit lyk batit bullis,
And brane wode brynt in balis,
Thai wox als mait as ony mulis,
That maggit war with malis,
For fantnes thay forfochin fulis
Fell doun lyk flauchter falis;
Fresche men com hame and halit the dulis,
And dang thame doun in dalis
Bedene
At Chrystis kirk on the grein.

Quhen all wes done, Dic with ane ax
Come furth to fell ane futher;
Quod he, 'Quhair ar yon hangit smaikis
Richt now that hurt my brother?'

yokkit: set to   fyr flauchtis: lightning   cavellis: fellows
bokkit: spurted   beirit: bellowed   brane wode brynt: ? brushwood burnt   balis: ? bonfires   mait: exhausted
maggit: heaped   malis: packloads   forfochin:
tired out   flauchter falis: large thin pieces of turf   halit the dulis:
? won the match   dalis: heaps   bedene: quickly   futher:
load   smaikis: wretches

His wyf bad him gang hame gud glaikis
And swa did Meg his mother,
He turnit and gaif thame bath thair paikis,
For he durst stryk na uther,
Men said
At Chrystis kirk on the grene.

finis.

gud glaikis: scornful deception   paikis: blows

ANONYMOUS

Reigns of James V and Mary I

48   *O Maistres Myn*

O MAISTRES myn, till you I me commend;
   All haill, my hairt sen that ye haif in cure;
For, but your grace, my lyfe is neir the end;
Now lat me nocht in danger me endure;
Off lyiflyk lufe suppois I be sure,
Quhay wat na god may me sum succur send?
Than for your lufe quhy wald ye I forfure?
O maistres myn till you I me commend.

The wynttir nycht ane hour I may nocht sleip
For thocht of you bot tumland to and fro.
Me think ye ar in to my armys, sweit,
And quhen I walkyn, ye ar so far me fro.

till: to   in cure: in your care   quhay wat: who knows
forfure: perish(ed)

Allace, allace, than walkynnis my wo;
Than wary I the tyme that I you kend;
War nocht gud hoip, my hairt wald birst in two.
O maistres myn, till you I me commend.

Sen ye ar ane that hes my hairt al haill,
Without fenyeing I may it nocht genstand;
Ye ar the bontie blis of all my baill;
Bayth lyfe and deth standis in to your hand.
Sen that I am sair bunding in your band,
That nycht or day I wait nocht quhair to wend,
Let me anis say that I your freindschip fand.
O maistres myn, till you I me commend.

walkynnis: wakens   wary: curse   hoip: hope   wait:
know   quhair: where   fand: found

49   *Baith Gud and Fair and Womanlie*

BAITH gud and fair and womanlie,
Debonair, steidfast, wyis and trew,
Courtas, hummill and lawlie,
And grundit weill in all vertew,
To quhois service I sall persew
Wirchep without villony,
And evir annone I sal be trew,
Baith gud and fair and womanlie.

Honour for evir unto that fre
That Natur formit hes so fair.
In wirchep of hir fresche bewtie
To Luvis court I will repair

grundit: founded   fre: lady

To serve and lufe without dispair,
Forthy I wait hir most wirthy
For to be callit our allquhair
Baith gud and fair and womanlie.

Sen that I gif my hairt hir to,
Quhy wyt I hir of my murnyng?
Thocht I be wo, quhat wyt hes scho?
Quhat wald I moir of my sweit thing
That wait nocht of my womenting?
Quhen I hir se, confort am I;
Hir fair effeir and fresch having
Is gud and fair and womanlie.

Thing in this warld that I best luf,
My verry hairt and conforting,
To quhois service I sall persew,
Quhill deid mak our depairting:
Faythfull, constant and bening
I sal be quhill the lyfe is in me,
And luf hir best attour all thing,
Baith gud and fair and womanlie.

our allquhair: everywhere   quhy wyt I hir of: why do I blame
her for   thocht: though   womenting: lamenting   effeir:
appearance   having: demeanour   bening: benign   attour:
above

50 *The Well of Vertew and Flour of Womanheid*

THE well of vertew and flour of womanheid,
And patrone unto patiens,
Lady of lawty baith in word and deid,
Rycht sobir sweit, full meik of eloquens,
Bayth gud and fair, to your magnificens
I me commend, as I haif done befoir,
My sempill hairt for now and evir moir.

For evir moir I sall you service mak,
Syne of befoir in to my mynd I maid,
Sen first I knew your ladischip but lak,
Bewty, youth of womanheid ye had,
Withouttin rest my hairt cowth nocht evad;
Thus am I youris, and evir sensyne hes bene,
Commandit be your gudly twa fair ene.

Your twa fair ene makis me oft syis to sing;
Your twa fair ene makis me to syche also;
Your twa fair ene makis me grit conforting;
Your twa fair ene is wycht of all my wo;
Your twa fair ene, may no man keip thame fro
Withouttin rest that gettis a sycht of thame;
This of all vertew were ye now the name.

Ye beir the name of gentilnes of blud;
Ye beir the name that mony for you deis;
Ye beir the name ye ar bayth fair and gud;
Ye beir the name that faris than you seis;
Ye beir the name Fortoun and ye aggreis;
Ye beir the name of landis of lenth and breid,
The well of vertew and flour of womanheid.

lawty: loyalty   sempill: simple, dedicated   but lak: without
fault, blamelessly   oft syis: oft times   faris than: ?   seis:
see into

51 *Off Womanheid Ane Flour Delice*

THE bewty of hir amorus ene,
  Quhen I behald my lady bricht,
Dois pers my Hairt with dairtis kene,
I am so reft be luvis micht;
Rest man I nocht day nor nycht,
My hairt is so in hir service,
Quhilk is the verry lantrene lycht,
Off womanheid ane flour delice.

Scho is the preclair portratour
Fulfillit with all lustines,
Of puchritud the fair figour,
The mirrour eik of all meiknes,
The verry stapill of steidfastnes,
Off flurist fame the strang pavice;
Scho is the gem of gentilnes,
Off womanheid ane flour delice.

Now sen I am hir servitoure
And flurist in my yeiris grene,
I trest I do to lang indure
That will nocht schaw my karis kene;
This to my lady will I mene
That I so lufe without fantice;
She is my soverene and serene,
Off womanheid the flour delice.

man: must   preclair: illustrious   portratour: image   pavice:
shield, defence   mene: utter   fantice: vain show

52 *My Hairt is Heich Aboif*

MY hairt is heich aboif, my body is full of blis,
For I am sett in lufe als weill as I wald wis.
I lufe my lady pure and scho luvis me agane;
I am hir serviture, scho is my soverane;
Scho is my verry harte, I am hir howp and heill;
Scho is my joy inwart, I am hir luvar leill;
I am hir bound and thrall, scho is at my command;
I am perpetuall hir man both fute and hand.
The thing that may hir pleis, my body sall fulfill;
Quhatevir hir diseis, it dois my body ill.
My bird, my bony ane, my tendir bab venust,
My lufe, my lyfe allane, my liking and my lust,
We interchange our hairtis in utheris armis soft;
Spreitles we twa depairtis, usand our luvis oft.
We murne quhen licht day dawis; we plene the nycht is schort;
We curs the cok that crawis that hinderis our disport.
I glowffin up agast quhen I hir mys on nycht,
And in my oxster fast I find the bowster richt.
Than langour on me lyis, lyk Morpheus, the mair,
Quhilk causis me uprys and to my sweit repair,
And than is all the sorrow furth of remembrance,
That evir I had a forrow in luvis observance.
Thus nevir I do rest, so lusty a lyfe I leid
Quhen that I list to test the well of womanheid.
Luvaris in pane, I pray God send you sic remeid
As I haif nycht and day, you to defend frome deid.
Thairfoir be evir trew unto your ladeis fre,
And thay will on you rew, as mine hes done one me.

---

venust: charming   plene: complain   glowffin: glare   oxster:
armpit   bowster: bolster   a forrow: before   rew: have
pity

53 From *The Bankis of Helicon*

DECLAIR, ye bankis of Helicon,
        Pernassus hillis and daillis ilkon,
And fontaine Caballein,
Gif onye of your Muses all,
Or Nymphes may be peregall
Unto my ladye schein;
Or of the ladyis that did lave
Thair bodyis by your brim,
So seimlie war or sa suave,
So bewtifull or trim.
            Contempill
            Exempill
Tak be hir proper port
            Gif onye
            So bonye
Amang you did resort.

No, no, forsuith, wes never none
That with this perfyte paragon
In beawtie micht compair.
The Muses wald have gevin the grie
To hir, as to the A *per se*
And peirles perle preclair,
Thinking with admiratioun
Hir persone so perfyite,
Nature in hir creatioun
To forme hir tuik delyite.
            Confes then
            Expres then,

ilkon: each one   peregall: equal   contempill: contemplate
grie: superiority, prize   preclair: illustrious

Your Nymphes and all thair trace,
For bewtie,
Of dewtie
Sould yeild and give hir place.

54 *Fairweill*

ALLACE depairting, grund of wo,
Thou art of everilk joy ane end!
How suld I pairte my lady fro?
How suld I tak my leif to wend?
Sen fals Fortoun is nocht my frend,
Bot evir castis me to keill,
Now sen I most no langir lend,
I tak my leif aganis my will.

Fairweill, fairweill, my weilfair may;
Fairweill, fegour most fresche of hew;
Fairweill, the saiffar of assay;
Fairweill, the hart of quhyt and blew;
Fairweill, baith kynd, curtas and trew;
Fairweill, woman withowttin ill;
Fairweill, the cumliest that evir I knew.
I tak my leif aganis my will.

Fairweill, my rycht fair lady deir;
Fairweill, most wys and womanlie;
Fairweill, my lufe fro yeir to yeir;
Fairweill, thow beriall blycht of blie;

keill (to): on my back   lend: abide   fegour: figure   saiffar:
sapphire   beriall: like the beryl   blycht: dazzling   blie:
colour

211

Fairweill, leill lady liberall and fre;
Fairweill, that may me saif and spill;
Howevir I fair, go fair weill ye;
I tak my leif aganis my will.

Fairweill fra me, my gudly grace;
Fairweill, the well of wirdines;
Fairweill, my confort in everilk place;
Fairweill, the hoip of steidfastnes;
Fairweill, the rut of my distres;
Fairweill, the luffar trew and still;
Fairweill, the nureis of gentilnes;
I tak my leif aganis my will.

saif and spill: save (or) destroy   wirdines: worthiness

55   *Remeidis of Luve*

SO prayis me as ye think caus quhy,
And lufe me as you lykis best;
As pleisis you, so plesit am I;
Gif nocht I fynd, of nocht I traist.

Gif ye be trew, I wil be just;
Gif ye be fals, flattery is fre
All tymes and houris, evin as ye lust,
For me till use als weill as ye.

Gif ye do mok, I will bot play;
Gif ye do lawch, I will nocht weip.
Evin as ye list, think, do or say;
Sic law ye mak, sic law I keip.

prayis: praise

Schaw fathfull lufe, lufe sall ye haif;
Schaw dowbilnes, I sall you quyt.
Ye can nocht use, nor no ways craif,
Bot evin that same is my delyt.

Bot gif ye wald be trew and plane,
Ye wald me pleis and best content;
And gif ye will nocht so remane,
As I haif said, so am I lent.

Avys you as ye think to do,
And use me as ye list to fynd.
Quhat neidis lang talking thairto?
For as I am, ye knaw my mynd.

Be war thairfoir and tak gud heid
Quhat is the sentens of this bill,
For and ye beir me ocht at feid,
I sall you hald ay at evill will.

Thairfoir be trew but vairians,
And I salbe as of befoir.
Uthirwayis generis discrepans.
Content yow. This ye get no moir.

lent: absent, withdrawn   feid: enmity

56   *Thair is nocht ane Winche*

THAIR is nocht ane winche that I se
    Sall win ane vantage of me.
Be scho fals, I sal be sle,

          winche: wench   sle: sly

213

And say to dispyt hir;
Be scho trew, I will confyd;
Will scho remane, I sall abyd;
Will scho slip, I will bot slyd,
And so sall I quyt hir.

Be scho constant and trew,
I sall evir hir persew;
Be scho fals, than adew,
No langer I tary;
Be scho fathfull in mynd,
I sal be to hir inclynd;
Be scho strange and unkynd,
I gif hir to fary.

Be scho haltand and he,
Rycht so sall scho fynd me;
Be scho lawly and fre.
The suth I sall say hir;
Be scho secreit and wyis,
I sall await on hir servyis;
Will scho glaik and go nyis,
I leif hir to play hir.

And I magyn my mailis,
I sall feid hir with caillis;
Thocht my sawis haif no seillis,
I sall leir hir to fan;
Be scho wylie as ane tod,
Quhen scho winkis, I sall nod.
Scho sall nocht begyle me, be God,
For ocht that scho can.

fary: confusion, hell   haltand: haughty   he: high   glaik:
trifle   and: if   magyn: heap up   mailis: burdens, loads,
tributes   feid: feed   caillis: cabbages   sawis: words, decrees
seillis: seals   fan: submit (fawn)   tod: fox

From *THE GUDE AND GODLIE BALLATIS*

Till Christ

57

TILL Christ, quhome I am haldin for to lufe,
 I gif my thirlit hart in governance.
How suld I lufe, and fra his treuth remufe,
Full wo war me, that drerie disseverance.
Is na remeid, saif onlie esperance:
For weill, for wo, for boist, or yit for schoir,
Quhair I am set, I sall lufe ever moir.

And sen I moste depart, on neid I sall
Be till him trew, with hart, and that I hecht,
And sen that I becummin am his thrall,
With body him serve, with mind & all my micht:
He is the ture of my remembrance rycht,
The verray crop, quhome of I confort tak;
Quhy suld I not do service for his saik?

Quhome suld I serve bot him, that did me save?
Quhome suld I dout bot him, that dantis deide?
Quhome suld I lufe bot him, attour the laif?
Of all my wo he is the haill remeid;
How suld I fle, and can not find na feid?
Quhome suld I lufe but him, that hes my hart?
How suld we twin that na man can depart?

This umbeset I am on evrie syde,
And quhat to do I can not weill devise:
My flesche biddis fle, my spreit biddis me byde;

haldin: compelled   thirlit: bound   boist: boasting   schoir:
threatening   hecht: promise   dantis: subdues   attour the
laif: above the rest   feid: strife   twin: separate   depart:
separate   umbeset: beset about

Quhen cair cumis, than confort on me cryis,
Hope says get up, than langour on me lyis.
My panis biddis my wofull hart repent,
Bot never mair thairto will I consent.

Depart him fra, my hart will never consent,
It biddis me byde, and I sall never fle:
For be I takin, slaine, or yit schent,
For sic ane King it is na schame to die.
Gif thair be grace in to this eird for me
It is committit, from the heven abufe,
Till Christ, quhome I am haldin for to lufe.

58

Go, hart

GO, hart, unto the lampe of lycht,
Go, hart, do service and honour,
Go, hart and serve him day and nycht,
Go, hart, unto thy Saviour.

Go, hart, to thy onlie remeid
Descending from the hevinlie tour:
The to deliver from pyne, and deide,
Go, hart, unto thy Saviour.

Go, hart, but dissimulatioun,
To Christ, that tuke our vylde nature,
For the to suffer passioun,
Go, hart, unto thy Saviour.

Go, hart, rycht humill and meik,
Go, hart, as leill and trew serviture,
To him that heill is for all seik,
Go, hart, unto thy Saviour.

leill: loyal   heill: health

216

Go, hart, with trew and haill intent,
To Christ thy help and haill succour,
The to redeme he was all rent,
  Go, hart, unto thy Saviour.

To Christ, that rais from deith to live,
Go, hart, unto my latter hour,
Quhais greit mercy can nane discrive,
  Go, hart, unto thy Saviour.

discrive: describe

59 *The Reid in the Loch Sayis*

THOCHT raging stormes movis us to schaik,
  And wind makis waters us ouerflow,
We yeild thairto bot dois not brek,
And in the calme bent up we grow.

So baneist men, thocht princes raige,
And prisoners be not disparit,
Abyde the calm quhill that it suaige;
For tyme sic caussis hes reparit.

baneist: banished   disparit: desperate

60 *The Bewteis of the Fute-Ball*

BRISSIT brawnis and brokin banis,
  Stryf, discorde and waistie wanis,
Cruikit in eild, syn halt withall—
Thir are the bewteis of the fute-ball.

brissit: burst   waistie wanis: ruined homes

217

61   *Quhy Sowld Nocht Allane Honorit Be?*

QUHEN he wes yung, and cled in grene,
   Haifand his air about his ene,
Baith men and wemen did him mene,
Quhen he grew on yon hillis he—
Quhy sowld nocht Allane honorit be?

His foster faider fure of the toun,
To vissy Allane he maid him boun;
He saw him lyane, allace! in swoun,
For falt of help, and lyk to de—
Quhy sowld nocht Allane honorit be?

Thay saw his heid begin to ryfe;
Syne for ane nureiss thay send belyfe,
Quha brocht with hir fyfty and fyve
Of men of war full prevely—
Quhy sowld nocht Allane honorit be?

Thay ruschit furth lyk hellis rukis,
And every ane of thame had hukis;
They cawcht him schortly in thair clukis,
Syne band him in ane creddill of tre—
Quhy sowld nocht Allane honorit be?

Thay brocht him inwart in the land,
Syne every freynd maid him his band,
Quhill they micht owdir gang or stand,
Nevir ane fute fra him to fle—
Quhy sowld nocht Allane honorit be?

haifand: having   air: hair   ene: eyes   mene: esteem
fure: went out   vissy: inspect   boun: ready   ryfe: burst
open   belyfe: quickly   creddill of tre: wooden cradle

The grittest cowart in this land,
Fra he with Allane entir in band,
Thocht he may nowdir gang nor stand,
Yit fowrty sall nocht gar him fle—
Quhy sowld nocht Allane honorit be?

Schir Allanis hewmond is ane cop,
With ane sege feddir in his top:
Fra hand till hand so dois he hop,
Quhill sum may nowdir speik nor se—
Quhy sowld nocht Allane honorit be?

In Yule, quhen ilk man singis his carrell
Gude Allane lyis in to ane barrell;
Quhen he is thair, he dowtis no parrell
To cum on him be land or se—
Quhy sowld nocht Allane honorit be?

Yit wes thair nevir sa gay a gallane,
Fra he meit with our maistir Ser Allane,
Bot gif he hald him by the hallane,
Bakwart on the flure fallis he—
Quhy sowld nocht Allane honorit be?

My maistir Allane grew so stark,
Quhill he maid mony cunning clerk,
Upoun thair faiss he settis his mark,
A blud reid noiss besyd thair E—
Quhy sowld nocht Allane honorit be?

fra: provided that   thocht: though   gar: make
hewmond: helmet   cop: cup   dowtis: fears   parrell: peril
bot gif: unless   hald . . . hallane: hold on to the partition

My maistir Allane I may sair curs,
He levis no mony in my purs,
At his command I mon deburs
Moir nor the twa pairt of my fe;—
Quhy sowld nocht Allane honorit be?

And last, of Allane to conclude;
He is bening, courtas and gude,
And servis us of our daly fude,
And that with liberalitie;—
Quhy sowld nocht Allane honorit be?

Finis quod allane matsonis suddartis

bening: benign

ALEXANDER SCOTT

? c. 1520–c. 1590

62

Of May

MAY is the moneth maist amene,
For thame in Venus service bene,
To recreat thair havy hartis;
May caussis curage frome the splene,
And every thing in May revartis.

In May the plesant spray upspringis;
In May the mirthfull maveiss singis;
And now in May to madynnis fawis
With tymmer wechtis to trip in ringis,
And to play upcoill with the bawis.

amene: pleasant   revartis: revives   fawis: falls   tymmer
wechtis: a sort of tambourines   upcoill: 'toss up', a ball game

In May gois gallandis bring in symmer,
And trymly occupyis thair tymmer
  With 'Hunts up,' every morning plaid;
In May gois gentill wemen gymmer,
  In gardynnis grene thair grumis to glaid.

In May quhen men yeid everich one,
With Robene Hoid and Littill Johne,
  To bring in bowis and birkin bobbynis;
Now all sic game is fastlingis gone
  Bot gif it be amangis clovin Robbynis.

Abbotis by rewll, and Lordis but ressone,
Sic senyeouris tymis ourweill this sessone;
  Upoun thair vyce war lang to waik,
Quhais falsatt, fibilnes, and tressone,
  Hes rung thryis oure this zodiak.

In May begynnis the golk to gaill;
In May drawis deir to doun and daill;
  In May men mellis with famyny,
And ladeis meitis thair luvaris laill,
  Quhen Phebus is in Gemyny.

Butter, new cheis, and beir in May,
Condamis, cokkillis, curdis and quhay,
  Lapstaris, lempettis, mussillis in schellis,
Grene leikis and all sic, men may say,
  Suppois sum of thame sourly smellis.

tymmer: time   gymmer: neater dressed   yeid: went   birkin
bobbynis: seed-pods of birch   by: but, without (cf. Abbot of Un-
reason)   sic: such   senyeouris: lords   ourweill: abound
this sessone: nowadays (there are plenty of such lords)   war lang
to waik: it would take too long to wait   quhais: whose   hes . . .
zodiak: have shown themselves three times this year   golk: cuckoo
gaill: sing   mellis: mate   famyny: women   laill: loyal
beir: beer   condamis: ?(corruption of 'connyngs') rabbits   lapstaris:
lobsters

In May grit men within thair boundis
Sum halkis the walteris, sum with houndis
　　The hairis owtthrowch the forrestis cachis;
Syne efter thame thair ladeis foundis,
　　To sent the rynnyng of the rachis.

In May frank archeris will affix
In place to meit, syne marrowis mix,
　　To schute at buttis, at bankis and brais;
Sum at the reveris, sum at the prikkis,
　　Sum laich and to beneth the clais.

In May sowld men of amouris go
To serf thair ladeis, and no mo,
　　Sen thair releis in ladeis lyis;
For sum may cum in favouris so,
　　To kiss his loif on Buchone wyis.

In May gois dammosalis and dammis
In gardyngis grene to play lyk lammis;
　　Sum at the bairis they brace lyk billeis;
Sum rynis at barlabreikis lyk rammis,
　　Sum round abowt the standand pilleis.

In May gois madynis till Lareit,
And hes thair mynyonis on the streit
　　To horss thame quhair the gait is ruch:
Sum at Inchebukling bray thay meit,
　　Sum in the middis of Mussilburch.

halkis: fish (verb)　　foundis: go　　rachis: hounds　　marrowis:
friends (equals)　　reveris: roving targets　　prikkis: fixed targets
laich: low　　to: down　　clais: clothes　　Buchone: Buchan
bairis: the game of 'Prisoners'　　brace: embrace　　billeis: lovers
barlabreikis: game of 'tig'　　pilleis: pillars　　Lareit: Loretto (near
Musselburgh)　　mynyonis: lovers (Fr. mignon)　　horss: carry
gait: road　　Mussilburch: Musselburgh

So May and all thir monethis thre
Ar hett and dry in thair degre;
 Heirfoir, ye wantoun men in yowth,
For helth of body now haif e
 Nocht oft till mell with thankless mowth.

Sen every pastyme is at plesure,
I counsale yow to mel with mesure,
 And namely now, May, June, & Julij,
Delyt nocht lang in luvaris lesure,
 Bot weit your lippis & labor hully.

e: an eye, a care mell: mate thankless mowth: *pudenda*
muliebria lippis: desires hully: moderately

63   *Quha is perfyte*

Q UHA is perfyte
  To put in wryt
The inwart murnyng & mischance,
  Or to indyte
  The grit delyte
Of lustie lufis obschervance,
  Bot he that may certane
  Patiently suffir pane,
  To wyn his soverane
    In recompance.

  Albeid I knaw
  Of luvis law
The plesour & the panis smart,
  Yit I stand aw
  For to furthschaw
The quyet secreitis of my harte;

223

For it may fortoun raith,
To do hir body skaith,
Quhilk wait that of thame baith
    I am expert.

Scho wait my wo
That is ago—
Scho wait my weilfair and remeid—
Scho wait also
I lufe no mo
Bot hir—the well of womanheid;
Scho wait withouttin faill
I am hir luvar laill;
Scho hes my hairt alhaill
    Till I be deid.

That bird of bliss
In bewty is
In erd the only A *per se*,
Quhais mowth to kiss
Is worth, I wiss,
The warld full of gold to me;
Is nocht in erd I cure,
Bot pleiss my lady pure,
Syne be hir scherviture
    Unto I de.

Scho is my lufe;
At hir behufe

raith: anger   skaith: harm   wait: knows   ago: gone
remeid: remedy   alhaill: completely   A *per se*: A by itself,
first of all   cure: care for   scherviture: servitor

My hairt is subject, bound & thrall;
　　For scho dois moif
　　My hairt aboif,
To se hir proper persoun small.
　　Sen scho is wrocht at will,
　　That natur may fulfill,
　　Glaidly I gif hir till
　　　　Body and all.

　　Thair is nocht wie
　　Can estimie
My sorrow and my sichingis sair;
　　For I am so
　　Done fathfullie
In favouris with my lady fair.
　　That baith our hairtis ar ane,
　　Luknyt in luvis chene,
And evirilk greif is gane
　　　　For evir mair.

moif: move   hir till: to her   luknyt: locked   chene: chain

64   *Up, Helsum Hairt*

UP, helsum hairt! thy rutis rais, and lowp;
　　Exalt and clym within my breist in staige;
Art thou nocht wantoun, haill, & in gud howp,
　　Fermit in grace and free of all thirlaige,
　　Bathing in bliss, and sett in hie curaige?
Braisit in joy, no falt may the affray,
　　Having thy ladeis hart as heretaige
In blenche ferme for ane sallat every May:

*helsum: joyful   lowp: leap   in staige: aloft   howp: hope
fermit: established   thirlaige: bondage   braisit: enveloped
falt: lack   blenche ferme: free tenure   sallat: salad, a slight
service*

812131   225   I

So neidis thou nocht now sussy, sytt, nor sorrow,
Sen thou art sure of sollace evin & morrow.

Thou, Cupeid, rewardit me with thiss;
   I am thy awin trew liege without tressone;
Thair levis no man in moir eisse, welth, and bliss;
   I knaw no siching, sadnes, nor yit soun,
    Walking, thocht, langour, lamentatioun,
Dolor, dispair, weiping, nor jelosye;
   My breist is voyd and purgit of pussoun;
I feill no pane, I haif no purgatorye,
   Bot peirles, perfytt, paradisall plesour,
    With mirry hairt and mirthfulnes but mesoure.

My lady, lord, thou gaif me for to hird,
   Within myne armes I nureiss on the nycht;
Kissing, I say, my bab, my tendir bird,
   Sweit maistres, lady luffe, & lusty wicht,
    Steir, rewll, and gyder of my senssis richt.
My voice surmontis the sapheir cludis hie,
   Thanking grit God of that tressour & micht.
I coft hir deir, bot scho fer derrer me,
   Quhilk hasard honor, fame, in aventeur,
    Committing clene hir corse to me in cure.

In oxsteris cloiss we kiss, and cossis hairtis,
   Brynt in desyre of amouris play and sport;
Meittand oure lustis, spreitles we twa depairtis.
   Prolong with lasar, lord, I the exort,

Sic tyme that we may boith tak our confort,
First for to sleip, syne walk withowt espyis.
I blame the cok, I plene the nicht is schort;
Away I went, my wache the cuschett cryis,
Wissing all luvaris leill to haif sic chance,
That thay may haif us in remembrance.

espyis: witnesses   went: go   cuschett: cushat dove   leill: loyal

65   *Returne The, Hairt*

RETURNE the, hairt, hamewart agane,
    And byd quhair thou was wont to be;
Thou art ane fule to suffer pane
    For luve of hir that luvis not the.
    My hairt, lat be sic fantesie;
Luve nane bot as thay mak the causs;
    And lat hir seik ane hairt for the,
For feind a crum of the scho fawis.

To quhat effect sowld thow be thrall
    But thank, sen thou hes thy fre will?
My hairt, be not sa bestiall,
    Bot knaw quho dois the guid or ill;
    Remane with me and tary still,
And se quha playis best thair pawis,
    And lat fillok ga fling hir fill,
For feind a crum of the scho fawis.

the: thee   byd: stay   mak the causs: give you reason
feind a crum: not a bit   fawis: cares   but thank: without thanks   bestiall: stupid   thair pawis: their own part
fillok: wanton girl

Thocht scho be fair I will not fenyie;
　Scho is the kind of uthiris ma;
For quhy thair is a fellone menyie,
　That semis gud, and ar not sa.
　My hairt, tak nowdir pane nor wa,
For Meg, for Meriory, or yit Mawis,
　Bot be thou glaid and latt hir ga,
For feind a crum of the scho fawis.

Becaus I find scho tuik in ill,
　At hir departing thou mak na cair;
Bot all begyld, go quhair scho will,
　Beschrew the hairt that mane makis mair.
　My hert, be mirry lait and air,
This is the fynall end and clauss,
　And latt hir fallow ane filly fair,
For feind a crum of the scho fawis.

<table>
<tr><td>fenyie: feign</td><td>kind: lover</td><td>uthiris ma: many others</td></tr>
<tr><td>fellone: great</td><td>menyie: many</td><td>wa: woe</td><td>tuik in ill:</td></tr>
<tr><td>took it badly</td><td>mane: moan　air: early</td><td>filly fair: foolish dandy</td></tr>
</table>

66　　　　　　*To Luve Unluvit*

TO luve unluvit it is ane pane;
　For scho that is my soverane,
　Sum wantoun man so he hes set hir,
That I can get no lufe agane,
　Bot brekis my hairt, & nocht the bettir.

Quhen that I went with that sweit may,
To dance, to sing, to sport and pley,
　And oft tymes in my armis plet hir;
I do now murne both nycht & day,
　And brekis my hart, & nocht the bettir.

　　　　　may: maid　　plet: embraced

Quhair I wes wont to se hir go
Rycht trymly passand to and fro,
  With cumly smylis quhen that I met hir;
And now I leif in pane & wo,
  And brekis my hairt, and nocht the bettir.

Quhattane ane glaikit fule am I
To slay myself with malancoly,
  Sen weill I ken I may nocht get hir!
Or quhat suld be the caus, and quhy,
  To brek my hairt, and nocht the bettir?

My hairt, sen thou may nocht hir pleiss,
Adew, as gude lufe cumis as gaiss,
  Go chuss ane udir and forget hir;
God gif him dolour and diseiss,
  That brekis thair hairt and nocht the bettir.

Finis q. Scott, Quhen **His** Wyfe Left Him.

glaikit: silly

67   *A Rondel of Luve*

L O! quhat it is to lufe,
    Lerne ye, that list to prufe,
Be me, I say, that no wayis may
    The grund of greif remufe,
Bot still decay, both nycht and day:
    Lo! quhat it is to lufe.

ALEXANDER SCOTT

Lufe is ane fervent fyre,
Kendillit without desyre:
Schort plesour, lang displesour;
Repentence is the hyre;
Ane pure tressour without mesour:
Lufe is ane fervent fyre.

To lufe and to be wyiss,
To rege with gud advyiss,
Now thus, now than, so gois the game,
Incertane is the dyiss:
Thair is no man, I say, that can
Both lufe and to be wyiss.

Fle alwayis frome the snair;
Lerne at me to be ware;
It is ane pane and dowbill trane
Of endless wo and cair;
For to refrane that denger plane,
Fle alwayis frome the snair.

advyiss: deliberation   dyiss: dice

JOHN ROLLAND

? c. 1530–c. 1580

68   Epilogue to his Book, *The Sevin Seages*

IN haist ga hy thee to sum hoill,
And hyde thee, be not callit ane buik;
Ga, cowme thee owir all clene with coill,
Sone smeir thee owir with smiddie smuik,

cowme: begrime

230

Or scour pottis to sum creischie Cuik:
Or in sum kitching turne the speit:
Amang Ladeis thou dar not luik,
For thay will on thee with thair feit;
For men of gude thou art not meit:
Thay will thee hald of small availl:
Quhat restis thair than bot yald thy Spreit,
Or to tryit Tinklaris tell thy taill?
Thy roustie ryme amang thame raill;
For honest folk, few will set by thee,
And I sweir by the Rude of Craill,
Tuitching my part, heir I deny thee.
My counsall is, that thou gar cry thee
Amang Cowclinkis and commoun hures;
All gude wemen, thay may defy thee;
Of all thy crakis thay tak na cures.
But fond Fillokis up in the Mures,
Quha first you reddis, Sym Skynnar hang thame;
Se on them thou wirk all Injures;
Pas on, and fend thy self amang thame.

Quod Rolland in Dalkeith.

creischie: greasy   yald: yield   tinklaris: tinkers   cowclinkis:
whores   crakis: boasts   tak na cures: take no heed   fond fillokis:
foolish girls

HENRY STEWART
(LORD DARNLEY)
1545-1567

69   *To the Queen*

BE governour baith guid and gratious;
  Be leill and luifand to thy liegis all;
Be large of fredome and no thing desyrous;
Be just to pure for ony thing may fall;
Be ferme of faith and constant as ane wall;
Be reddye evir to stanche evill and discord;
Be cheretabill, and sickerlye thou sall
Be bowsum ay to knaw thy God and Lord.

Be nocht to proud of wardlie guidis heir;
Be weill bethocht thai will remane na tyde;
Be sicker als that thou man die but weir;
Be war thairwith the tyme will no man byde;
Be vertewus and set all vyce on syde;
Be patient, lawlie and misericord;
Be rewlit so quhairevir thou go or byde;
Be bowsum ay to knaw thy God and Lord.

Be weill avysit of quhome thow counsale tais;
Be sewer of thame that thai be leill and trew;
Bethink the als quhidder thai be freindis, or fais.
Be to thy saull, thair sawis or thou persew:
Be nevir our hastye to wirk and syne to rew;
Be nocht thair freind that makis the fals record;
Be reddye evir all guid workis to renew;
Be bowsum ay to knaw thy God and Lord.

pure: the poor folk   sickerlye: surely   bowsum: tractable
guidis: goods   sicker: sure   man: must   weir: doubt
sawis: words   wirk: act

HENRY STEWART (LORD DARNLEY)

Be traist and conquese thy awin heretage
Be ennemyes of auld now occupyit;
Be strenth and force thou sobir thai man swage
Be law of God—thair may no man deny it;
Be nocht as lantern in mirknes unspyit;
Be thou in rycht thi landis suld be restored,
Be wirschop so thy name beis magnefeit;
Be bowsum ay to knaw thy God and Lord.

Be to rebellis strong as lyoun eik;
Be ferce to follow thame quhairevir thai found;
Be to thy liegemen bayth soft and meik;
Be thair succour and help thame haill and sound;
Be knaw thy cure and caus quhy thow was cround;
Be besye evir that justice be nocht smord;
Be blyith in hart; thir wordis oft expound;
Be bowsum ay to knaw thy God and Lord.

swage: assuage   eik: each, any   smord: smothered

70   *Gife Langour—*

GIFE langour makis men licht,
  Or dolour thame decoir,
In erth thair is no wicht
May me compair in gloir.
Gif cairfull thochtis restoir
My havy hairt frome sorrow,
I am for evirmoir
In joy both evin and morrow.

gife, gif: if   licht: cheerful   decoir: adorn   gloir: glory

233

Gif plesour be to pance,
I playnt me nocht opprest;
Or absence micht avance,
My hairt is haill possest.
Gif want of quiet rest
From cairis micht me convoy,
My mind is nocht mollest,
Bot evirmoir in joy.

Thocht that I pance in pane
In passing to and fro,
I laubor all in vane;
For so hes mony mo
That hes nocht servit so
In suting of thair sueit.
The nar the fyre I go,
The grittar is my heit.

The turtour for hir maik
Mair dule may nocht indure
Nor I do for hir saik,
Evin hir quha hes in cure
My hart, quhilk sal be sure
In service to the deid
Unto that lady pure,
The well of womanheid.

Schaw schedull to that sueit,
My pairt so permanent,
That no mirth quhill we meit
Sall cause me be content;

pance: think   suting: pursuing   sueit: sweet   nar: nearer
turtour: turtle dove   maik: mate   dule: sorrow   schedull:
bill, statement

Bot still my hairt lament
In sorrowfull siching soir
Till tyme scho be present.
Fairweill. I say no moir.

siching: sighing

CAPTAIN ALEXANDER MONTGOMERIE

? 1545–? 1610

71 *To Henry Constable and Henry Keir*

ADEW, my King, court, cuntrey, and my kin:
Adew, swete Duke, whose father held me deir:
Adew, companiones, Constable and Keir:
Thrie trewar hairts, I trow, sall never twin.
If byganes to revolve I suld begin,
My tragedie wald cost you mony a teir
To heir how hardly I am handlit heir,
Considring once the honour I wes in.
Sirs, ye haif sene me griter with his Grace,
And with your umquhyle Maister, to, and myne,
Quha thoght the Poet somtyme worth his place,
Suppose ye sie they shot him out sensyne.
Sen wryt, nor wax, nor word is not a word,
I must perforce ga seik my fathers sword.

umquhyle: former   sen: since

72 *To R. Hudson*

MY best belovit brother of the band,
I grein to sie the silly smiddy smeik.
This is no lyfe that I live upaland
On raw rid herring reistit in the reik,
Syn I am subject somtyme to be seik,
And daylie deing of my auld diseis.
Eit bread, ill aill, and all things are ane eik;
This barme and blaidry buists up all my bees.
Ye knaw ill guyding genders mony gees,
And specially in poets. For example,
Ye can pen out twa cuple, and ye pleis;
Yourself and I, old Scot and Robert Semple.
Quhen we ar dead, that all our dayis bot daffis,
Let Christan Lyndesay wryt our epitaphis.

band: James VI's Castalian band of poets   grein: long   smiddy:
poetic forge   reistit: dried, cured   eit: oatmeal   ane eik:
the same kind   barme and blaidry: nonsense   buists up: shuts up
bees: fancy   guyding: guiding   gees: vexations   daffis: play
the fool

73 *To his Maistres*

SO swete a kis yistrene fra thee I reft,
In bowing down thy body on the bed,
That evin my lyfe within thy lippis I left;
Sensyne from thee my spirits wald never shed;
To folow thee it from my body fled,
And left my corps als cold as ony kie.
Bot when the danger of my death I dred,
To seik my spreit I sent my harte to thee;
Bot it wes so inamored with thyn ee,

yistrene: last night   kie: key

With thee it myndit likwyse to remane:
So thou hes keepit captive all the thrie,
More glaid to byde then to returne agane.
Except thy breath thare places had suppleit,
Even in thyn armes, thair doutles had I deit.

74
A Description of Tyme

TAK tyme in tym, or tym will not be tane;
 Thairfor tak tent how thou this tyme suld tak:
Sho hes no hold, to hold hir by, bot ane;
A toppe befor, bot beld behind hir bak.
Let thou hir slippe, or slipperly grow slak,
Thou gettis no grippe agane fra sho be gane.
If thou wald speid, remember what I spak;
Tak tyme in tyme, or tym will not be tane.

For I haif hard in adagies of auld,
That tyme dois waist and weir all things away;
Then trow the taill that trew men oft hes tauld—
A turne in tyme is ay worth other tway.
Siklyk, I haif hard oft-tymis suith men say,
That negligence yit nevir furtherit nane;
Als, seindle tymis luck folowes long delayis.
Tak tyme in tyme, or tyme will not be tane.

tak tent: take care   toppe: forelock   beld: bald   slipperly:
sleepily   seindle tymis: seldom

75 *The Solsequium*

LYK as the dum
  Solsequium,
With cair ouercum,
And sorow, when the sun goes out of sight,
  Hings doun his head,
  And droups as dead,
  And will not spread,
Bot louks his leavis throu langour of the nicht,
  Till folish Phaeton ryse,
    With whip in hand,
  To cleir the cristall skyis,
    And light the land:
  Birds in thair bour
  Luiks for that hour,
And to thair prince ane glaid good-morow givis;
  Fra thyn, that flour
  List not to lour,
Bot laughis on Phoebus lousing out his leivis:

  So fairis with me,
  Except I be
  Whair I may se
My lamp of licht, my Lady and my Love.
  Fra scho depairts,
  Ten thousand dairts,
  In syndrie airts,
Thirlis throu my hevy hart, but rest or rove;

solsequium: sunflower   louks: locks up   list not: cease not
to lour: to lure   thirlis: pierces   rove: repose

My countenance declairs
　　My inward grief;
Good hope almaist dispairs
　　To find relief.
I die—I dwyn—
Play does me pyn—
I loth on eviry thing I look—alace!
　　Till Titan myne
　　Upon me shyne,
That I revive throu favour of hir face.

　　Fra she appeir
　　Into hir spheir,
　　Begins to cleir
The dawing of my long desyrit day:
　　Then Curage cryis
　　On Hope to ryse,
　　Fra he espyis
My noysome nicht of absence worne away.
　　No wo, when I awalk,
　　　May me impesh;
　　Bot, on my staitly stalk,
　　　I florish fresh.
　　I spring—I sprout—
　　My leivis ly out—
My colour changes in ane hartsum hew.
　　No more I lout,
　　Bot stands up stout,
As glade of hir, for whom I only grew.

　　O happie day!
　　Go not away.
　　Apollo! stay

dwyn: dwindle　　　impesh: prevent　　　lout: bow down

239

Thy chair from going doun into the west:
    Of me thou mak
    Thy zodiak,
    That I may tak
My plesur, to behold whom I love best.
    Thy presence me restores
      To lyf from death;
    Thy absence also shores
      To cut my breath.
    I wish, in vane,
    Thee to remane,
Sen *primum mobile* sayis alwayis nay;
    At leist thy wane
    Turn soon agane.
Fareweill, with patience perforce, till day.

      chair: chariot   shores: threatens

76   *The Night is Neir Gone*

H AY! now the day dawis;
   The jolie Cok crawis;
Now shroudis the shawis,
    Throw Natur anone.
The thissell-cok cryis
On lovers wha lyis.
Now skaillis the skyis:
    The nicht is neir gone.

The feildis owerflowis
With gowans that growis,
Quhair lilies lyk low is,
    Als rid as the rone.

  shawis: groves   thissell-cok: mistle-thrush cock   skaillis:
clears, empties   gowans: large wild daisies   low: flame
rone: rowan

The turtill that trew is,
With nots that renewis,
Hir pairtie persewis:
    The night is neir gone.

Now Hairtis with Hyndis,
Conforme to thair kyndis,
Hie tursis thair tyndis,
    On grund whair they grone.
Now Hurchonis, with Hairis,
Ay passis in pairis;
Quhilk deuly declaris
    The night is neir gone.

The sesone excellis
Thrugh sweetnes that smellis;
Now Cupid compellis
    Our hairtis echone
On Venus wha waikis,
To muse on our maikis,
Syn sing, for thair saikis:—
    The night is neir gone.

All curageous knichtis
Aganis the day dichtis
The breist plate that bright is,
    To feght with thair fone.
The stoned steed stampis
Throw curage and crampis,
Syn on the land lampis:
    The night is neir gone.

pairtie: partner	tursis: toss	tyndis: antler-branches
grone: groan	hurchonis: hedgehogs	dichtis: make ready
crampis: ? uprears, ? bucks	lampis: gallops	

The freikis on feildis
That wight wapins weildis
With shyning bright shieldis
　As Titan in trone:
Stiff speiris in reistis,
Ower cursoris cristis,
Ar brok on thair breistis:
　The night is neir gone.

So hard ar thair hittis,
Some sweyis, some sittis,
And some perforce flittis
　On grund whill they grone.
Syn groomis that gay is,
On blonkis that brayis,
With swordis assayis:
　The night is neir gone.

freikis: soldiers　　　cristis: crests, plumes　　　blonkis: white horses

JOHN STEWART OF BALDYNNEIS
? 1550–? 1605

77　　　　*To his Darrest Freind*

IN signe of favor stedfast still
　With suir guidwill　Thois lyns I send;
Ye most amend　Quhair as I spill
This litill bill　In meitir pend
Unto the end　It salbe kend
That I pretend　With constant part
In Joy and smart　For to defend
Your grand commend　With luifing hart.

spill: spoil

My luifing hart dois weill aggrie
With you to bie   Quhair evir I go;
In weill and wo   It conforts me
The freindschip frie   Betwix us two.
But fleing fro   Thair is no mo
Quhom I luif so   With firm effect.
As ye derect   Gif I say no,
Even as your fo   Than me reject.

Lyk as the recent rubie rois
Is maist formois   Of flouris fair,
So but compair   Quhill lyf I lois
Ye ar my chois   For vertew rair.
Thus I declair,   And mair and mair
Sall on you spair   Quhat in me lyis.
As ye devyis   Both lait and air
To eise your cair   My will applyis.

As Adamant dois yrne alluir,
So in your cuir   I do remaine
Without disdaine,   Subdewit suir,
Ay till induir,   Unto you plaine.
I am in pain   Gif ye refraine
To quyt againe   My thocht synceir,
Quhilk is inteir,   Thocht verse be vaine,
With bruisit braine   Composit heir.

formois: beautiful   adamant: lodestone, diamond

ALEXANDER HUME

? 1557–1609

78   *Of the Day Estivall*

O PERFITE light, quhilk schaid away,
    The darkenes from the light,
And set a ruler ou'r the day,
    Ane uther ou'r the night,

    Thy glorie when the day foorth flies,
    Mair vively dois appeare,
Nor at midday unto our eyes,
    The shining Sun is cleare.

    The schaddow of the earth anon,
    Remooves and drawes by,
Sine in the East, when it is gon,
    Appeares a clearer sky.

    Quhilk Sunne perceaves the little larks,
    The lapwing and the snyp,
And tunes their sangs like natures clarks,
    Ou'r midow, mure, and stryp.

    Bot everie bais'd nocturnall beast,
    Na langer may abide,
They hy away baith maist and least,
    Them selves in howis to hide.

stryp: rill   bais'd: abased   hy: hurry   howis: holes

They dread the day fra thay it see,
And from the sight of men,
To saits, and covers fast they flee,
As Lyons to their den.

Oure Hemisphere is poleist clein,
And lightened more and more,
While everie thing be clearely sein,
Quhilk seemed dim before.

Except the glistering astres bright,
Which all the night were cleere,
Offusked with a greater light,
Na langer dois appeare.

The golden globe incontinent,
Sets up his shining head,
And ou'r the earth and firmament,
Displayes his beims abroad.

For joy the birds with boulden throts,
Agains his visage shein,
Takes up their kindelie musicke nots,
In woods and gardens grein.

Up braids the carefull husbandman,
His cornes, and vines to see,
And everie tymous artisan,
In buith worke busilie.

The pastor quits the slouthfull sleepe,
And passis forth with speede,
His little camow-nosed sheepe,
And rowtting kie to feede.

boulden: swollen   camow-nosed: flat-nosed   rowtting: lowing

The passenger from perrels sure,
Gangs gladly foorth the way:
Breife, everie living creature,
Takes comfort of the day,

The subtile mottie rayons light,
At rifts thay are in wonne;
The glansing phains, and vitre bright,
Resplends against the sunne.

The dew upon the tender crops,
Lyke pearles white and round,
Or like to melted silver drops,
Refreshes all the ground.

The mystie rocke, the clouds of raine,
From tops of mountaines skails,
Cleare are the highest hils and plaine,
The vapors takes the vails.

Begaried is the saphire pend,
With spraings of skarlet hew,
And preciously from end till end,
Damasked white and blew.

The ample heaven of fabrik sure,
In cleannes dois surpas,
The chrystall and the silver pure,
Or clearest poleist glas.

mottie: full of motes   rifts: cracks   in wonne: got in   phains:
vanes   vitre: window-pane   skails: clears away   begaried:
adorned   pend: vault   spraings: streaks

The time sa tranquill is and still,
That na where sall ye find,
Saife on ane high, and barren hill,
Ane aire of peeping wind.

All trees and simples great and small,
That balmie leife do beir,
Nor thay were painted on a wall,
Na mair they move or steir.

Calme is the deepe, and purpour se,
Yee, smuther nor the sand,
The wals that woltring wont to be,
Are stable like the land.

Sa silent is the cessile air,
That every cry and call,
The hils, and dails, and forrest fair,
Againe repeates tham all.

The rivers fresh, the callor streames,
Ou'r rockes can softlie rin,
The water cleare like chrystall seames,
And makes a pleasant din.

The fields, and earthly superfice,
With verdure greene is spread,
And naturallie but artifice,
In partie coulors cled.

The flurishes and fragrant flowres,
Throw Phoebus fostring heit,
Refresht with dew and silver showres,
Casts up ane odor sweit.

simples: medicinal herbs   purpour: purple   smuther: smoother
wals: waves   woltring: rolling   cessile: yielding   callor: fresh
flurishes: blossom

The clogged busie humming beis,
That never thinks to drowne,
On flowers and flourishes of treis,
Collects their liquor browne.

The Sunne maist like a speedie post,
With ardent course ascends,
The beautie of the heavenly host,
Up to our zenith tends.

Nocht guided be na Phaeton,
Nor trained in a chyre,
Bot be the high and haly On,
Quhilk dois all where impire.

The burning beims downe from his face,
Sa fervently can beat:
That man and beast now seekes a place
To save them fra the heat.

The brethles flocks drawes to the shade,
And frechure of their fald,
The startling nolt as they were made,
Runnes to the rivers cald.

The heards beneath some leaffie trie,
Amids the flowers they lie,
The stabill ships upon the sey,
Tends up their sails to drie.

The hart, the hynd, and fallow deare,
Are tapisht at their rest,
The foules and birdes that made the beir,
Prepares their prettie nest.

clogged: loaded   chyre: chariot   nolt: cattle   made: mad
tapisht: crouching   beir: noise

The rayons dures descending downe,
All kindlis in a gleid,
In cittie nor in borroughstowne,
May nane set foorth their heid.

Back from the blew paymented whun,
And from ilk plaister wall:
The hote reflexing of the sun,
Inflams the aire and all.

The labourers that timellie raise
All wearie faint and weake:
For heate downe to their houses gais,
Noone-meate and sleepe to take.

The callowr wine in cave is sought,
Mens brothing breists to cule:
The water cald and cleare is brought,
And sallets steipt in ule.

Sume plucks the honie plowm and peare,
The cherrie and the pesche,
Sume likes the reamand London beare,
The bodie to refresh.

Forth of their skepps some raging bees,
Lyes out and will not cast,
Some uther swarmes hyves on the trees,
In knots togidder fast.

gleid: flame   borroughstowne: town   paymented: made into
pavement   whun: whinstone   brothing: steaming   ule: oil
reamand: spilling over   skepps: hives

The corbeis, and the kekling kais,
May scarce the heate abide,
Halks prunyeis on the sunnie brais,
And wedders back, and side.

With gilted eyes and open wings,
The cock his courage shawes,
With claps of joy his breast he dings,
And twentie times he crawes.

The dow with whistling wings sa blew,
The winds can fast collect,
Hir pourpour pennes turnes mony hew,
Against the sunne direct.

Now noone is went, gaine is mid-day,
The heat dois slake at last,
The sunne descends downe west away,
Fra three of clock be past.

A little cule of braithing wind,
Now softly can arise,
The warks throw heate that lay behind
Now men may enterprise.

Furth fairis the flocks to seeke their fude,
On everie hill and plaine,
Ilk labourer as he thinks gude,
Steppes to his turne againe.

The rayons of the Sunne we see,
Diminish in their strength,
The schad of everie towre and tree,
Extended is in length.

corbeis: crows   kais: jackdaws   halks: hawks   prunyeis:
preen   dow: pigeon

Great is the calme for everie quhair,
The wind is sitten downe,
The reik thrawes right up in the air,
From everie towre and towne.

Their firdoning the bony birds,
In banks they do begin,
With pipes of reides the jolie hirds,
Halds up the mirrie din.

The Maveis and the Philomeen,
The Stirling whissilles lowd,
The Cuschetts on the branches green,
Full quietly they crowd.

The gloming comes, the day is spent,
The Sun goes out of sight,
And painted is the occident,
With pourpour sanguine bright.

The Skarlet nor the golden threid,
Who would their beawtie trie,
Are nathing like the colour reid,
And beautie of the sky.

Our West Horizon circuler,
Fra time the Sunne be set,
Is all with rubies (as it wer)
Or Rosis reid ou'rfret.

What pleasour were to walke and see,
Endlang a river cleare,
The perfite forme of everie tree,
Within the deepe appeare?

firdoning: piping   stirling: starling   crowd: coo   gloming:
twilight   ou'rfret: embroidered

The Salmon out of cruifs and creils
Up hailed into skowts,
The bels, and circles on the weills,
Throw lowpping of the trouts.

O: then it were a seemely thing,
While all is still and calme,
The praise of God to play and sing,
With cornet and with shalme.

Bot now the hirds with mony schout,
Cals uther be their name,
Ga, Billie, turne our gude about,
Now time is to go hame.

With bellie fow the beastes belive,
Are turned fra the corne,
Quhilk soberly they hameward drive,
With pipe and lilting horne.

Throw all the land great is the gild,
Of rustik folks that crie,
Of bleiting sheepe fra they be fild,
Of calves and rowting ky.

All labourers drawes hame at even,
And can till uther say,
Thankes to the gracious God of Heaven,
Quhilk send this summer day.

cruifs and creils: osier traps   skowts: cobles   weills: pools
gude: stock   gild: clamour

MARK ALEXANDER BOYD

1563–1601

Sonet

FRA banc to banc, fra wod to wod, I rin
  Ourhailit with my feble fantasie,
Lyc til a leif that fallis from a trie
Or til a reid ourblawin with the wind.
Twa gods gyds me: the ane of tham is blind,
Ye, and a bairn brocht up in vanitie;
The nixt a wyf ingenrit of the se,
And lichter nor a dauphin with hir fin.

Unhappie is the man for evirmaire
That teils the sand and sawis in the aire;
Bot twyse unhappier is he, I lairn,
That feidis in his hairt a mad desyre,
And follows on a woman throw the fyre,
Led be a blind and teichit be a bairn.

ourhailit: overcome   bairn: child   teils: tills

JAMES VI

1566–1625

80   *Admonition to Montgomerie*

*An admonition to the Master poet (Montgomerie) to be warr of great
bragging hereafter, lest he not onlie slander himselfe; bot also the
whole professours of the art:*

GIVE patient eare to sumething I man saye,
Beloved Sanders, maistre of our art.
The mouse did helpe the lion on a daye;
So I protest ye take it in good part,
My admonition cumming from a hart
That wishes well to you and all your craft,
Who woulde be sorie for to see you smart,
Thogh other poets trowes ye be gone daft.

A friend is aye best knowen in tyme of neede,
Which is the cause that gars me take such caire
Now for your state, since there is cause indeed;
For all the poets leaves you standing baire:
Olde crucked Robert makes of you the haire,
And elfegett Polward helpes the smitthie smuike;
He comptes you done, and houpes but anie mair
His tyme about, to winne the chimnay nuike.

Bot as the good chirurgian oft does use—
I meane to rype the wounde before he heal'd;
Appardone me, I thinke it no excuse,
Suppose I tell the cause why they have rail'd;

man: must   gars: makes   elfegett: 'changeling'   rype:
clean out

And sine considder whither ye have fail'd,
Or what hath caus'd them this waye to backbite you:
Into that craft they never yett prevail'd,
Albeit of late they houpe for to outflite you.

For ye was cracking crouslie of your broune,
If Robert lie not, all the other night,
That there was anie like him in this toune;
Upon the grounde ye wolde not lett it light,
He was so firie speedie, yaulde and wight;
For to be shorte, he was an A *per se*.
Bot yett beleeve ye saw an other sight
Or all was done (or Robins rithme does lie).

Thus cracked ye and bragged but replie
Or answer made by anie present then,
As Dares did, when as he did ou'rhie
Æneas court nor coulde not finde a man
That matche him durst; the stirke for him that wann
Which ordain'd was, he craved at Ænes hand
And saide 'Since there is none that does or can
Be matche to me, what longer shall I stand?

Delaye no more, bot give me the rewarde
Preordinate for them that victor war.'
Thus Dares ended, bot Æneas stairde
The campe about; 'Since there is none that darr,'
Æneas said, 'bot all seemes verrie skarr
T'essaye yone man, gar bring the bullock soone.'
Thus as he bade, they broght the bullocke narr
Which hade his hornes ou'rgilded all abone.

sine: then   cracking: boasting   broune: brown horse
yaulde: alert   wight: strong   A *per se*: A by itself, best of all
ou'rhie: go all over   stirke: bullock   skarr: scared   abone:
over

Amongs the armie which were witnes thair,
And not but wonder harde yone Dares boaste,
Entellus raise, a man of stature mair
Nor Dares was, and saide 'Cheefe of our hoaste,
I now repent my former youthe is loste;
Bot since I see he shames your armie so,
Have at him then, it shall be on his coste,
As I beleeve, if Jove be not my foe.'

The circumstances of this bargane keene
I will remitt to Virgils ornate stile;
Bot well I watt Entellus soone was seene
By all to winne: So cracked ye a while,
That none might neere you scarcelie by a mile,
Till your Entellus harde you at the last.
The daye was sett, bot ye begoode to smile
For scorne, and thought to winne by running fast.

The wavering worde did spredd abroade belive
Of all your crackes and bargane that was made;
Eache one with other bussillie did strive
Who should be soonest at that solemne rade,
That they might judge which of the horse shoulde leade;
Ye saide there woulde no question be of that
Besides, ye saide, ye caired not all there feade:
Brecke as they woulde, the race it should no latt.

That night ye ceas'd and went to bed, bot grien'd
Yett fast for day, and thocht the night to lang:
At last Diana doune her heade reclin'd
Into the sea, then Lucifer up sprang,

begoode: began	belive: immediately	rade: riding contest
feade: feud	brecke: get off the mark	no latt: not hinder
grien'd: longed		

Auroras poste, whome she did send amang
The gettie cloudes for to foretell ane houre
Before she staye her teares, which Ovide sang
Was for her love which turned into a floure.

Fra Lucifer hade thus his message done,
The rubie virgin came for to forspeeke
Apollos cumming in his glistring throne,
Who suddainlie therafter cleare did keeke
Out through his cart, where Eöüs was eke
With other three which Phaëton hade drawen
About the earthe till he became so seeke
As he fell doune where Neptune fand him fawen.

Bot to conclude, the houre appointed came:
Ye made yow readie for to rinne the race:
Ye bracke togither, and ranne out the same,
As Robin sayes, it hade bene fil'd your face.
It chanc'd ye were forerunne a prettie space,
A mile or more, that keeped it so cleene.
When all was done, ye hade so evill a grace
Ye stoll awaye and durst no more be seene.

gettie: jet-black   bene: well   fil'd: dirtied

SIR WILLIAM ALEXANDER
(EARL OF STIRLING)

1567–1640

From *AURORA*

81

Sonnet 25

CLEARE moving cristall, pure as the Sunne beames,
   Which had the honor for to be the glasse,
Of the most daintie beautie ever was;
And with her shadow did inrich thy streames,
Thy treasures now cannot be bought for monie,
Whil'st she dranke thee, thou drank'st thy fill of love,
And of those roses didst the sweetnes prove,
From which the Bees of love do gather honie:
Th'ambrosian liquor that he fils above,
Whom th'Eagle ravish'd from th'inferior round,
It is not like this Nectar (though renown'd)
Which thou didst tast, whil'st she her lips did move:
   But yet beware lest burning with desires,
   That all thy waters cannot quench thy fires.

shadow: reflection

Sonnet 26

ILE give thee leave my love, in beauties field
   To reare red colours whiles, and bend thine eyes;
Those that are bashfull still, I quite despise
Such simple soules are too soone mov'd to yeeld:

whiles: sometimes

Let majestie arm'd in thy count'nance sit,
As that which will no injurie receive;
And Ile not hate thee, whiles although thou have
A sparke of pride, so it be rul'd by wit.
This is to chastitie a powerfull guard,
Whil'st haughtie thoughts all servile things eschue,
That sparke hath power the passions to subdue,
And would of glorie chalenge a reward:
    But do not fall in love with thine owne selfe;
    Narcissus earst was lost on such a shelfe.

earst: formerly

SIR ROBERT AYTOUN

1569–1638

83   *Upone Tabacco*

FORSAKEN of all comforts but these two,
   My faggott and my Pipe, I sitt and Muse
On all my crosses, and almost accuse
The heavens for dealing with me as they doe.
Then hope steps in and with a smyling brow
Such chearfull expectations doth infuse
As makes me thinke ere long I cannot chuse
But be some Grandie, whatsoever I'm now.
But haveing spent my pype, I then perceive
That hopes and dreames are Couzens, both deceive.
Then make I this conclusion in my minde,
Its all one thing, both tends unto one Scope
To live upon Tobacco and on hope,
The ones but smoake, the other is but winde.

WILLIAM FOWLER

1560–1612

84

In Orknay

UPON the utmost corners of the warld,
    and on the borders of this massive round,
quhaire fates and fortoune hes me harld,
I doe deplore my greiffs upon this ground;
and seing roring seis from roks rebound
by ebbs and streames of contrair routing tyds,
and phebus chariot in their wawes ly dround,
quha equallye now night and day divyds,
I cal to mynde the storms my thoughts abyde,
which ever wax and never dois decress,
for nights of dole dayes joys ay ever hyds,
and in their vayle doith al my weill suppress:
so this I see, quhaire ever I remove,
I change bot sees, bot can not chainge my love.

      harld: drawn   dole: woe

WILLIAM DRUMMOND

1585–1649

85

Sonet to Sleepe

SLEEPE, *Silence*' Child, sweet Father of soft Rest,
    Prince, whose Approach Peace to all Mortals brings,
Indifferent Host to Shepheards and to Kings,
Sole Comforter of Minds with Griefe opprest;

Loe, by thy charming Rod all breathing things
Lie slumbring, with forgetfulnesse possest,
And yet o're me to spred thy drowsie Wings
Thou spares, (alas) who cannot be thy Guest.
Since I am thine, O come, but with that Face
To inward Light which thou art wont to show,
With fained Solace ease a true felt Woe,
Or if, *deafe God* thou doe denie that Grace,
    Come as thou wilt, and what thou wilt bequeath—
I long to kisse the *Image of my Death*.

ANONYMOUS
(ATTRIBUTED TO DRUMMOND)

86

[From *Polemo-Middinia*]

NYMPHAE quae colitis highissima monta *Fifaea*,
    Seu vos *Pittenwema* tenant seu *Crelia* crofta,
Sive *Anstraea* domus, ubi nat haddocus in undis,
Codlineusque ingens, et fleuca et sketta pererrant
Per costam, et scopulis lobster mony-footus in udis
Creepat, et in mediis ludit whitenius undis;
Et vos skipperii, soliti qui per mare breddum
Valde procul lanchare foris, iterumque redire,
Linquite scellatas bottas shippasque picatas,
Whistlantesque simul fechtam memorate bloodaeam,
Fechtam terribilem, quam marvellaverit omnis
Banda Deum, et Nympharum Cockelshelleatarum,
Maia ubi sheepifeda atque ubi solgoosifera *Bassa*
Suellant in pelago, cum Solboottatus *Edenum*
Postabat radiis madidis et shouribus atris.

Quo viso, ad fechtae noisam cecidere volucres
Ad terram cecidere grues, plish plashque dedere
Sol-goosi in pelago prope littora *Bruntiliana;*
Sea-sutor obstupuit, summique in margine saxi
Scartavit praelustre caput, wingasque flapavit;
Quodque magis, alte volitans heronius ipse
Ingeminans clig clag shyttavit in undis.
Namque in principio (storiam tellabimus omnem)
Muckrellium ingentem turbam *Vitarva* per agros
Nebernae marchare fecit, et dixit ad illos:
Ite hodie armati greppis, dryvate caballos
Crofta per et agros *Nebernae,* transque fenestras:
Quid si forte ipsa *Neberna* venerit extra,
Warrantabo omnes, et vos bene defendebo.
Hic aderant *Geordie Akinhedius* et little *Johnus*
Et *Jamie Richaeus* et stout *Michael Hendersonus*
Qui jolly tryppas ante alios dansare solebat,
Et bobbare bene, et lassas kissare bonaeas;
Duncan Oliphantus valde stalvartus, et ejus
Filius eldestus joly boyus, atque *Oldmoudus*
Qui pleugham longo gaddo dryvare solebat,
Et *Rob Gib* wantonus homo, atque *Oliver Hutchin*
Et plouky-fac'd *Wattie Strang,* atque inkne'd *Alshinder
    Atkin,*
Et *Willie Dick* heavi-arstus homo, pigerrimus omnium,
Valde lethus pugnare, sed hunc Corn-greivus heros
Nout-headdum vocavit, et illum forcit ad arma.

JAMES GRAHAM
(MARQUIS OF MONTROSE)
1612–1650

His Metrical Vow

(*On the death of Charles I*)

GREAT, Good and Just, could I but rate
My Grief to Thy too Rigid Fate!
I'd weep the World in such a Strain,
As it would once deluge again:
But since Thy loud-tongu'd Blood demands Supplies,
More from *Briareus* Hands, than *Argus* Eyes,
I'll tune Thy Elegies to Trumpet-sounds,
And write Thy Epitaph in Blood and Wounds!

88

His Metrical Prayer

(*On the eve of his own execution*)

LET them bestow on ev'ry Airth a Limb;
Open all my Veins, that I may swim
To Thee my Saviour, in that Crimson Lake;
Then place my pur-boil'd Head upon a Stake;
Scatter my Ashes, throw them in the Air:
Lord (since Thou know'st where all these Atoms are)
I'm hopeful, once Thou'lt recollect my Dust,
And confident Thou'lt raise me with the Just.

89   From *Montrose to his Mistress*

MY dear and only Love, I pray
    This noble World of thee,
Be govern'd by no other Sway
    But purest Monarchie.
For if Confusion have a Part,
    Which vertuous Souls abhore,
And hold a Synod in thy Heart,
    I'll never love thee more.

Like *Alexander* I will reign,
    And I will reign alone,
My Thoughts shall evermore disdain
    A Rival on my Throne.
He either fears his Fate too much,
    Or his Deserts are small,
That puts it not unto the Touch,
    To win or lose it all.

BALLADS

90   From *Oterborne*

YT fell abowght the Lamasse tyde,
    Whan husbondes wynnes ther haye,
The dowghtye Dowglasse bowynd hym to ryde,
    In Ynglond to take a praye.

wynnes: harvest

The yerlle of Fyffe, wythowghten stryffe,
   He bowynd hym over Sulway;
The grete wolde ever to-gether ryde;
   That raysse they may rewe for aye.

Over Hoppertope hyll they cam in,
   And so down by Rodclyffe crage;
Vpon Grene Lynton they lyghted dowyn,
   Styrande many a stage.

And boldely brente Northomberlond,
   And haryed many a towyn;
They dyd owr Ynglyssh men grete wrange,
   To batell that were not bowyn.

Than spake a berne vpon the bent,
   Of comforte that was not colde,
And sayd, We haue brente Northomberlond,
   We haue all welth in holde.

Now we haue haryed all Bamborowe schyre
   All the welth in the worlde haue wee,
I rede we ryde to Newe Castell,
   So styll and stalworthlye.

Vpon the morowe, when it was day,
   The standerds schone full bryght;
To the Newe Castell the(y) toke the waye,
   And thether they cam full ryght.

Syr Henry Perssy laye at the New Castell,
   I tell yow wythowtten drede;
He had byn a march-man all hys dayes,
   And kepte Barwyke vpon Twede.

To the Newe Castell when they cam,
   The Skottes they cryde on hyght.
'Syr Hary Perssy, and thou byste within,
   Com to the fylde, and fyght.

'For we haue brente Northomberlonde,
   Thy erytage good and ryght,
And syne my logeyng I haue take
   Wyth my brande dubbyd many a knyght.'

91   *The Fause Knicht upon the Road*

'O WHARE are ye gaun?'
    Quo the fause knicht upon the road:
'I'm gaun to the scule,'
   Quo the wee boy, and still he stude.

'What is that upon your back?'
   Quo the fause knicht upon the road:
'Atweel, it is my bukes,'
   Quo the wee boy, and still he stude.

'What's that ye've got in your arm?'
'Atweel it is my peit.'

'Wha's aucht they sheep?'
'They are mine and my mither's.'

'How monie o them are mine?'
'A' they that hae blue tails.'

gaun: going   peit: lunch-piece   wha's aucht they sheep?:
who owns those sheep?   A' they: all those

'I wiss ye were on yon tree:'
'And a gude ladder under me.'

'And the ladder for to break:'
'And you for to fa down.'

'I wiss ye were in yon sie:'
'And a gude bottom under me.'

'And the bottom for to break:'
'And ye to be drowned.'

92 *The Twa Sisters*

THERE was twa sisters in a bowr,
  Binnorie, O Binnorie.
There was twa sisters in a bowr,
  By the bonnie milldams o Binnorie.
There was twa sisters in a bowr,
  Binnorie, O Binnorie.
There cam a knight to be their wooer,
  By the bonnie milldams o Binnorie.

He courted the eldest wi glove an ring,
But he lovd the youngest above a' thing.

He courted the eldest wi brotch an knife,
But lovd the youngest as his life.

The eldest she was vexed sair,
An much envi'd her sister fair.

Into her bowr she could not rest,
Wi grief an spite she almos brast.

Upon a morning fair an clear,
She cried upon her sister dear:

'O sister, come to yon sea stran,
An see our father's ships come to lan.'

She's taen her by the milk-white han,
An led her down to yon sea stran.

The younges(t) stood upon a stane,
The eldest came an threw her in.

She tooke her by the middle sma,
An dashd her bonny back to the jaw.

'O sister, sister, tak my han,
An Ise mack you heir to a' my lan.

'O sister, sister, tak my middle,
An yes get my goud and my gouden girdle.

'O sister, sister, save my life
An I swear Ise never be nae man's wife.'

'Foul fa the han that I should tacke,
It twin'd me an my wardles make.

'Your cherry cheeks an yallow hair
Gars me gae maiden for evermair.'

gouden: golden   wardles make: world's mate

268

Sometimes she sank, an sometimes she swam,
Till she came down yon bonny milldam.

O out it came the miller's son,
An saw the fair maid swimmin in.

'O father, father, draw your dam,
Here's either a mermaid or a swan.'

The miller quickly drew the dam,
An there he found a drownd woman.

You coudna see her yellow hair
For gold and pearle that were so rare.

You coudna see her middle sma
For gouden girdle that was sae braw.

You coudna see her fingers white,
For gouden rings that was sae gryte.

An by there came a harper fine,
That harped to the king at dine.

When he did look that lady upon,
He sighd and made a heavy moan.

He's taen three locks o her yellow hair,
An wi them strung his harp sae fair.

The first tune he did play and sing,
Was, 'Farewell to my father the king.'

braw: brave   gryte: great

The nextin tune that he played syne,
Was, 'Farewell to my mother the queen.'

The lasten tune that he playd then,
Was, 'Wae to my sister, fair Ellen.'

93 *Lord Randal*

'O WHERE ha you been, Lord Randal,
    my son?
And where ha you been, my handsome
    young man?'
'I ha been at the greenwood; mother,
    mak my bed soon,
For I'm wearied wi hunting, and fain
    wad lie down.'

'An wha met ye there, Lord Randal,
    my son?
An wha met you there, my handsome
    young man?'
'O I met wi my true-love; mother,
    mak my bed soon,
For I'm wearied wi huntin, an fain
    wad lie down.'

'And what did she give you, Lord Randal,
    my son?
And what did she give you, my handsome
    young man?'

'Eels fried in a pan; mother,
  mak my bed soon,
For I'm wearied wi huntin, and fain
  wad lie down.'

'And wha gat your leavins, Lord Randal,
  my son?
And wha gat your leavins, my handsom
  young man?'
'My hawks and my hounds; mother,
  mak my bed soon,
For I'm wearied wi hunting, and fain
  wad lie down.'

'And what becam of them, Lord Randal,
  my son?
And what becam of them, my handsome
  young man?'
'They stretched their legs out an died;
  mother, mak my bed soon,
For I'm wearied wi huntin, and fain wad
  lie down.'

'O I fear you are poisoned, Lord Randal,
  my son!'
I fear you are poisoned, my handsome
  young man!'
'O yes, I am poisoned; mother,
  mak my bed soon,
For I'm sick at the heart, and I fain
  wad lie down.'

'What d'ye leave to your mother, Lord
    Randal, my son?
What d'ye leave to your mother, my
    handsome young man?'
'Four and twenty milk kye; mother,
    mak my bed soon,
For I'm sick at the heart, and I fain
    wad lie down.'

'What d'ye leave to your sister, Lord
    Randal, my son?
What d'ye leave to your sister, my
    handsome young man?'
'My gold and my silver; mother,
    mak my bed soon,
For I'm sick at the heart, and I fain
    wad lie down.'

'What d'ye leave to your brother, Lord
    Randal, my son?
What d'ye leave to your brother, my
    handsome young man?'
'My houses and my lands; mother, mak
    my bed soon,
For I'm sick at the heart, and I fain
    wad lie down.'

'What d'ye leave to your true-love,
    Lord Randal, my son?
What d'ye leave to your true-love, my
    handsome young man?'
'I leave her hell and fire; mother, mak
    my bed soon,
For I'm sick at the heart, and I fain
    wad lie down.'

kye: cows

Edward

'WHY dois your brand sae drap wi bluid,
        Edward, Edward,
Why dois your brand sae drap wi bluid,
  And why sae sad gang yee O?'
'O I hae killed my hauke sae guid,
        Mither, mither,
O I hae killed my hauke sae guid,
  And I had nae mair bot hee O.'

'Your haukis bluid was nevir sae reid,
        Edward, Edward,
Your haukis bluid was nevir sae reid,
  My deir son I tell thee O.'
'O I hae killed my reid-roan steid,
        Mither, mither,
O I hae killed my reid-roan steid,
  That erst was sae fair and frie O.'

'Your steid was auld, and ye hae gat mair,
        Edward, Edward,
Your steid was auld, and ye hae gat mair,
  Sum other dule ye drie O.'
'O I hae killed my fadir deir,
        Mither, mither,
O I hae killed my fadir deir,
  Alas, and wae is mee O!'

'And whatten penance wul ye drie for that,
        Edward, Edward?
And whatten penance will ye drie for that?
  My deir son, now tell me O.'

'Ile set my feit in yonder boat,
   Mither, mither,
Ile set my feit in yonder boat,
 And Ile fare ovir the sea O.'

'And what wul ye doe wi your towirs and your ha,
   Edward, Edward?
And what wul ye doe wi your towirs and your ha,
 That were sae fair to see O?'
'Ile let thame stand tul they doun fa,
   Mither, mither,
Ile let thame stand tul they doun fa,
 For here nevir mair maun I bee O.'

'And what wul ye leive to your bairns and your wife,
   Edward, Edward?
And what wul ye leive to your bairns and your wife,
 When ye gang ovir the sea O?'
'The warldis room, late them beg thrae life,
   Mither, mither,
The warldis room, late them beg thrae life,
 For thame nevir mair wul I see O.'

'And what wul ye leive to your ain mither deir,
   Edward, Edward?
And what wul ye leive to your ain mither deir?
 My deir son, now tell me O.'
'The curse of hell frae me sall ye beir,
   Mither, mither,
The curse of hell frae me sall ye beir,
 Sic counseils ye gave to me O.'

95   *The Twa Corbies*

A S I was walking all alane,
   I heard twa corbies making a mane;
The tane unto the t'other say,
'Where sall we gang and dine to-day?'

'In behint yon auld fail dyke,
I wot there lies a new slain knight;
And naebody kens that he lies there,
But his hawk, his hound, and lady fair.

'His hound is to the hunting gane,
His hawk to fetch the wild-fowl hame,
His lady's ta'en another mate,
So we may mak our dinner sweet.

'Ye'll sit on his white hause-bane,
And I'll pike out his bonny blue een;
Wi ae lock o his gowden hair
We'll theek our nest when it grows bare.

'Mony a one for him makes mane,
But nane sall ken where he is gane;
Oer his white banes, when they are bare,
The wind sall blaw for evermair.'

mane: moan   fail dyke: wall of turf   hause-bane: neck-bone
theek: thatch

Tam Lin

96

O I FORBID you, maidens a',
   That wear gowd on your hair,
To come or gae by Carterhaugh,
   For young Tam Lin is there.

There's nane that gaes by Carterhaugh
   But they leave him a wad,
Either their rings, or green mantles,
   Or else their maidenhead.

Janet has kilted her green kirtle
   A little aboon her knee,
And she has broded her yellow hair
   A little aboon her bree,
And she's awa to Carterhaugh,
   As fast as she can hie.

When she came to Carterhaugh
   Tam Lin was at the well,
And there she fand his steed standing,
   But away was himsel.

She had na pu'd a double rose,
   A rose but only twa,
Till up then started young Tam Lin,
   Says, Lady, thou's pu nae mae.

Why pu's thou the rose, Janet,
   And why breaks thou the wand?
Or why comes thou to Carterhaugh
   Withoutten my command?

gowd: gold gae: go broded: braided bree: brow
fand: found

'Carterhaugh, it is my ain,
  My daddie gave it me;
I'll come and gang by Carterhaugh,
  And ask nae leave at thee.'

          .   .   .   .   .   .

Janet has kilted her green kirtle
  A little aboon her knee,
And she has snooded her yellow hair
  A little aboon her bree,
And she is to her father's ha,
  As fast as she can hie.

Four and twenty ladies fair
  Were playing at the ba,
And out then cam the fair Janet,
  Ance the flower amang them a'.

Four and twenty ladies fair
  Were playing at the chess,
And out then cam the fair Janet,
  As green as onie glass.

Out then spak an auld grey knight,
  Lay oer the castle wa,
And says, Alas, fair Janet, for thee
  But we'll be blamed a'.

'Haud your tongue, ye auld fac'd knight,
  Some ill death may ye die!
Father my bairn on whom I will,
  I'll father nane on thee.'

                ba: ball

277

Out then spak her father dear,
   And he spak meek and mild;
'And ever alas, sweet Janet,' he says,
   'I think thou gaes wi child.'

'If that I gae wi child, father,
   Mysel maun bear the blame;
There's neer a laird about your ha
   Shall get the bairn's name.

'If my love were an earthly knight,
   As he's an elfin grey,
I wad na gie my ain true-love
   For nae lord that ye hae.

'The steed that my true-love rides on
   Is lighter than the wind;
Wi siller he is shod before,
   Wi burning gowd behind.'

Janet has kilted her green kirtle
   A little aboon her knee,
And she has snooded her yellow hair
   A little aboon her bree,
And she's awa to Carterhaugh,
   As fast as she can hie.

When she cam to Carterhaugh,
   Tam Lin was at the well,
And there she fand his steed standing,
   But away was himsel.

ha: hall

278

She had na pu'd a double rose,
  A rose but only twa,
Till up then started young Tam Lin,
  Says, Lady, thou pu's nae mae.

Why pu's thou the rose Janet,
  Amang the groves sae green,
And a' to kill the bonie babe
  That we gat us between?

'O tell me, tell me, Tam Lin,' she says,
  'For's sake that died on tree,
If eer ye was in holy chapel,
  Or christendom did see?'

'Roxbrugh he was my grandfather,
  Took me with him to bide,
And ance it fell upon a day
  That wae did me betide.

'And ance it fell upon a day,
  A cauld day and a snell,
When we were frae the hunting come,
  That frae my horse I fell;
The Queen o Fairies she caught me,
  In yon green hill to dwell.

'And pleasant is the fairy land,
  But, an eerie tale to tell,
Ay at the end of seven years
  We pay a tiend to hell;
I am sae fair and fu o flesh,
  I'm feard it be mysel.

ance: once   snell: biting

'But the night is Halloween, lady,
　　The morn is Hallowday;
Then win me, win me, an ye will,
　　For weel I wat ye may.

'Just at the mirk and midnight hour
　　The fairy folk will ride,
And they that wad their true-love win,
　　At Miles Cross they maun bide.'

'But how shall I thee ken, Tam Lin,
　　Or how my true-love know,
Amang sae mony unco knights
　　The like I never saw?'

'O first let pass the black, lady,
　　And syne let pass the brown,
But quickly run to the milk-white steed,
　　Pu ye his rider down.

'For I'll ride on the milk-white steed,
　　And ay nearest the town;
Because I was an earthly knight
　　They gie me that renown.

'My right hand will be glovd, lady,
　　My left hand will be bare,
Cockt up shall my bonnet be,
　　And kaimd down shall my hair,
And thae's the takens I gie thee,
　　Nae doubt I will be there.

unco: strange　　　　thae's the takens: those are the tokens

'They'll turn me in your arms, lady,
   Into an esk and adder;
But hold me fast, and fear me not,
   I am your bairn's father.

'They'll turn me to a bear sae grim,
   And then a lion bold;
But hold me fast, and fear me not,
   As ye shall love your child.

'Again they'll turn me in your arms
   To a red het gaud of airn;
But hold me fast, and fear me not,
   I'll do to you nae harm.

'And last they'll turn me in your arms
   Into the burning gleed;
Then throw me into well water,
   O throw me in wi speed.

'And then I'll be your ain true-love,
   I'll turn a naked knight;
Then cover me wi your green mantle,
   And cover me out o sight.'

Gloomy, gloomy was the night,
   And eerie was the way,
As fair Jenny in her green mantle
   To Miles Cross she did gae.

About the middle o the night
   She heard the bridles ring;
This lady was as glad at that
   As any earthly thing.

esk: newt   gaud: bar   gleed: faggot

First she let the black pass by,
   And syne she let the brown;
But quickly she ran to the milk-white steed,
   And pu'd the rider down.

Sae weel she minded what he did say,
   And young Tam Lin did win;
Syne covered him wi her green mantle,
   As blythe's a bird in spring.

Out then spak the Queen o Fairies.
   Out of a bush o broom:
'Them that has gotten young Tam Lin
   Has gotten a stately groom.'

Out then spak the Queen o Fairies,
   And an angry woman was she:
'Shame betide her ill-far'd face,
   And an ill death may she die,
For she's taen awa the boniest knight
   In a' my companie.

'But had I kend, Tam Lin,' she says,
   'What now this night I see,
I wad hae taen out thy twa grey een,
   And put in twa een o tree.'

97   *Sir Patrick Spens*

THE king sits in Dumferling toune,
   Drinking the blude-reid wine:
'O whar will I get guid sailor,
   To sail this schip of mine?'

Up and spak an eldern knicht,
  Sat at the kings richt kne:
'Sir Patrick Spence is the best sailor
  That sails upon the se.'

The king has written a braid letter,
  And signd it wi his hand,
And sent it to Sir Patrick Spence,
  Was walking on the sand.

The first line that Sir Patrick red,
  A loud lauch lauched he;
The next line that Sir Patrick red,
  The teir blinded his ee.

'O wha is this has don this deid,
  This ill deid don to me,
To send me out this time o' the yeir,
  To sail upon the se!

'Mak hast, mak haste, my mirry men all,
  Our guid schip sails the morne:'
'O say na sae, my master deir,
  For I feir a deadlie storme.

'Late late yestreen I saw the new moone,
  Wi the auld moone in hir arme,
And I feir, I feir, my deir master,
  That we will cum to harme.'

braid: informal

O our Scots nobles wer richt laith
   To weet their cork-heild schoone;
Bot lang owre a' the play wer playd,
   Thair hats they swam aboone.

O lang, lang may their ladies sit,
   Wi thair fans into their hand,
Or eir they se Sir Patrick Spence
   Cum sailing to the land.

O lang, lang may the ladies stand,
   Wi thair gold kems in their hair,
Waiting for thair ain deir lords,
   For they'll se thame na mair.

Haf owre, haf owre to Aberdour,
   It's fiftie fadom deip,
And thair lies guid Sir Patrick Spence,
   Wi the Scots lords at his feit.

aboone: above kems: combs

98   *Clerk Saunders*

CLERK Saunders and may Margaret
   Walked ower yon garden green;
And sad and heavy was the love
   That fell thir twa between.

'A bed, a bed,' Clerk Saunders said,
   A bed for you and me!'
'Fye na, fye na,' said may Margaret,
   'Till anes we married be.

may: maid thir twa: these two anes: once

'For in may come my seven bauld brothers,
  Wi' torches burning bright;
They'll say—"We hae but ae sister,
  And behold she's wi' a knight!" '

'Then take the sword frae my scabbard,
  And slowly lift the pin;
And you may swear, and safe your aith,
  Ye never let Clerk Saunders in.

'And take a napkin in your hand,
  And tie up baith your bonny een;
And you may swear, and safe your aith,
  Ye saw me na since late yestreen.'

It was about the midnight hour,
  When they asleep were laid,
When in and came her seven brothers,
  Wi' torches burning red.

When in and came her seven brothers,
  Wi' torches burning bright;
They said, 'We hae but ae sister,
  And behold her lying with a knight!'

Then out and spake the first o' them,
  'I bear the sword shall gar him die!'
And out and spake the second o' them,
  'His father has nae mair than he!'

And out and spake the third o' them,
  'I wot that they are lovers dear!'
And out and spake the fourth o' them,
  'They hae been in love this mony a year!'

  aith: oath gar him: force him

Then out and spake the fifth o' them,
   'It were great sin true love to twain!'
And out and spake the sixth o' them,
   'It were shame to slay a sleeping man!'

Then up and gat the seventh o' them,
   And never a word spake he;
But he has striped his bright brown brand
   Out through Clerk Saunders' fair bodye.

Clerk Saunders he started, and Margaret she turned
   Into his arms as asleep she lay;
And sad and silent was the night
   That was atween thir twae.

And they lay still and sleeped sound,
   Until the day began to daw;
And kindly to him she did say,
   'It is time, true-love, you were awa'.'

But he lay still, and sleeped sound,
   Albeit the sun began to sheen;
She looked atween her and the wa',
   And dull and drowsie were his een.

Then in and came her father dear,
   Said—'Let a' your mourning be;
I'll carry the dead corpse to the clay,
   And I'll come back and comfort thee.'

'Comfort weel your seven sons;
   For comforted will I never be:
I ween 'twas neither knave nor loon
   Was in the bower last night wi' me.'

    twain: part   thir twae: these two

The clinking bell gaed through the town,
  To carry the dead corse to the clay;
And Clerk Saunders stood at may Margaret's window,
  I wot, an hour before the day.

'Are ye sleeping, Margaret?' he says,
  'Or are ye waking presentlie?
Give me my faith and troth again,
  I wot, true love, I gied to thee.'

'Your faith and troth ye sall never get,
  Nor our true love sall never twin,
Until ye come within my bower,
  And kiss me cheik and chin.'

'My mouth it is full cold, Margaret,
  It has the smell now of the ground;
And if I kiss thy comely mouth,
  Thy days of life will not be lang.

'O cocks are crowing a merry midnight,
  I wot the wild fowls are boding day;
Give me my faith and troth again,
  And let me fare me on my way.'

'Thy faith and troth thou sall na get,
  And our true love sall never twin,
Until ye tell what comes of women,
  I wot, who die in strong traivelling?'

'Their beds are made in the heavens high,
  Down at the foot of our good Lord's knee,
Weel set about wi' gillyflowers;
  I wot sweet company for to see.

traivelling: labour

287

'O cocks are crowing a merry midnight,
 I wot the wild fowl are boding day;
The psalms of heaven will soon be sung,
 And I, ere now, will be missed away.'

Then she has ta'en a crystal wand,
 And she has stroken her troth thereon,
She has given it him out at her shot-window,
 Wi' mony a sad sigh, and heavy groan.

'I thank ye, Marg'ret; I thank ye, Marg'ret;
 And aye I thank ye heartilie;
Gin ever the dead come for the quick,
 Be sure, Marg'ret, I'll come for thee.'

It's hosen and shoon, and gown alone,
 She climbed the wall, and followed him,
Until she came to the green forest,
 And there she lost the sight o' him.

'Is there ony room at your head, Saunders,
 Is there ony room at your feet?
Or ony room at your side, Saunders,
 Where fain, fain, I wad sleep?'

'There's nae room at my head, Marg'ret,
 There's nae room at my feet;
My bed it is full lowly now:
 Amang the hungry worms I sleep.

'Cauld mould is my covering now,
 But and my winding-sheet;
The dew it falls nae sooner down,
 Than my resting-place is weet.

'But plait a wand o' bonnie birk,
  And lay it on my breast;
And shed a tear upon my grave,
  And wish my saul gude rest.

'And fair Marg'ret, and rare Marg'ret,
  And Marg'ret o' veritie,
Gin ere ye love another man,
  Ne'er love him as ye did me.'

Then up and crew the milk-white cock
  And up and crew the gray,
Her lover vanish'd in the air
  And she gaed weeping away.

gaed: went

99   *The Wife of Usher's Well*

THERE lived a wife at Usher's Well,
  And a wealthy wife was she;
She had three stout and stalwart sons,
  And sent them oer the sea.

They hadna been a week from her,
  A week but barely ane,
Whan word came to the carline wife
  That her three sons were gane.

They hadna been a week from her,
  A week but barely three,
Whan word came to the carlin wife
  That her sons she'd never see.

'I wish the wind may never cease,
  Nor fashes in the flood,
Till my three sons come hame to me,
  In earthly flesh and blood.'

It fell about the Martinmass,
  When nights are lang and mirk,
The carlin wife's three sons came hame,
  And their hats were o the birk.

It neither grew in syke nor ditch,
  Nor yet in ony sheugh;
But at the gates o Paradise,
  That birk grew fair eneugh.

   .   .   .   .   .   .

'Blow up the fire, my maidens,
  Bring water from the well;
For a' my house shall feast this night,
  Since my three sons are well.'

And she has made to them a bed,
  She's made it large and wide,
And she's taen her mantle her about,
  Sat down at the bed-side.

   .   .   .   .   .   .

Up then crew the red, red cock,
  And up and crew the gray;
The eldest to the youngest said,
  'T is time we were away.

birk: birch   syke: grove   sheugh: dell

The cock he hadna crawd but once,
　　And clappd his wings at a',
When the youngest to the eldest said,
　　'Brother, we must awa.

'The cock doth craw, the day doth daw,
　　The channerin worm doth chide;
Gin we be mist out o our place,
　　A sair pain we maun bide.

'Fare ye weel, my mother dear!
　　Fareweel to barn and byre!
And fare ye weel, the bonny lass
　　That kindles my mother's fire!'

　　　　channerin: plaintive　　　　sair: sore

100　　　　　　*Archie of Cafield*

A S I was walking mine alane,
　　　It was by the dawing o the day,
I heard twa brothers make their maine,
　　And I listned well what they did say.

The eldest to the youngest said,
　　'O dear brother, how can this be!
There was three brethren of us born,
　　And one of us is condemnd to die.'

'O chuse ye out a hundred men,
　　A hundred men in Christ(e)ndie,
And we'll away to Dumfries town,
　　And set our billie Archie free.'

　　　　　　maine: moan

291

'A hundred men you cannot get,
　　Nor yet sixteen in Christendie;
For some of them will us betray,
　　And other some will work for fee.

'But chuse ye out eleven men,
　　And we ourselves thirteen will be,
And we'ill away to Dumfries town,
　　And borrow bony billie Archie.'

There was horsing, horsing in haste,
　　And there was marching upon the lee,
Untill they came to the Murraywhat,
　　And they lighted a' right speedylie.

'A smith, a smith!' Dickie he crys,
　　'A smith, a smith, right speedily,
To turn back the cakers of our horses feet!
　　For it is forward we woud be.'

There was a horsing, horsing in haste,
　　There was marching on the lee,
Untill they came to Dumfries port,
　　And there they lighted right manfulie.

'There six of us will hold the horse,
　　And other five watchmen will be;
But who is the man among you a'
　　Will go to the Tollbooth door wi me?'

O up then spake Jokie Hall
　　(Fra the laigh of Tiviotdale was he),
'If it should cost my life this very night,
　　I'll ga to the Tollbooth door wi thee.'

　　　　cakers: shoes　　　laigh: low

'O sleepst thou, wakest thow, Archie laddie?
   O sleepst thou, wakest thow, dear billie?'
'I sleep but saft, I waken oft,
   For the morn's the day that I man die.'

'Be o good cheer now, Archie lad,
   Be o good cheer now, dear billie;
Work thow within and I without,
   And the morn thou's dine at Cafield wi me.'

'O work, O work?' Archie he cries,
   'O work, O work? ther's na working for me;
For ther's fifteen stane o Spanish iron,
   And it lys fow sair on my body.'

O Jokie Hall stept to the door,
   And he bended it back upon his knee,
And he made the bolts that the door hang on
   Jump to the wa right wantonlie.

He took the prisoner on his back,
   And down the Tollbooth stairs came he;
Out then spak Dickie and said,
   Let some o the weight fa on me;
'O shame a ma!' co Jokie Ha,
   For he's no the weight of a poor flee.'

The grey mare stands at the door,
   And I wat neer a foot stirt she,
Till they laid the links out oer her neck,
   And her girth was the gowd-twist to be.

fow sair: full sore

And they came down thro Dumfries town,
   And O but they came bonily!
Untill they came to Lochmaben port,
   And they leugh a' the night manfullie.

There was horsing, horsing in haste,
   And there was marching on the lee,
Untill they came to the Murraywhat,
   And they lighted a' right speedilie.

'A smith, a smith!' Dickie he cries,
   'A smith, a smith, right speedlie,
To file aff the shackles fra my dear brother!
   For it is forward we wad be.'

They had not filtt a shakle of iron,
   A shakle of iron but barely three,
Till out then spake young Simon brave,
   'Ye do na see what I do see.'

'Lo yonder comes Liewtenant Gordon,
   And a hundred men in his company:
'O wo is me!' then Archie cries,
   'For I'm the prisoner, and I must die.'

O there was horsing, horsing in haste,
   And there was marching upon the lee,
Untill they came to Annan side,
   And it was flowing like the sea.

'I have a colt, and he's four years old,
   And he can amble like the wind,
But when he comes to the belly deep,
   He lays himself down on the ground.'

      leugh: laughed   filtt: filed

'But I have a mare, and they call her Meg,
     And she's the best in Christendie;
Set ye the prisoner me behind;
     Ther'll na man die but he that's fae!'

Now they did swim that wan water,
     And O but they swam bonilie!
Untill they came to the other side,
     And they wrang their cloathes right drunk(i)lie.

'Come through, come through, Lieutenant Gordon!
     Come through, and drink some wine wi me!
For ther's a ale-house neer hard by,
     And it shall not cost thee one penny.'

'Throw me my irons, Dickie!' he cries,
     'For I wat they cost me right dear;'
'O shame a ma!' cries Jokie Ha,
     'For they'll be good shoon to my gray mare.'

'Surely thy minnie has been some witch,
     Or thy dad some warlock has been;
Else thow had never attempted such,
     Or to the bottom thow had gone.

'Throw me my irons, Dickie!' he cries,
     'For I wot they cost me dear enough;'
'O shame a ma!' cries Jokie Ha,
     'They'll be good shakles to my plough.'

'Come through, come through, Liewtenant Gordon!
     Come throw, and drink some wine wi me!
For yesterday I was your prisoner,
     But now the night I am set free.'

101   *The Bonny Earl o' Murray*

(Version still sung in Scotland, as heard by editors.)

YE hielands and ye lawlands,
    O whaur hae ye been?
They hae slain the Earl o Moray
And laid him on the green.

He was a braw callant
    And he rid at the ring,
And the bonnie Earl o Moray,
    He micht hae been a king.

O lang will his ladie look
    Owre the Castle Doune,
Ere she see the Earl o Moray
    Come soondan throu the toun.

Nou wae be tae ye, Huntly,
    And wharfore did ye sae?
I bad ye bring him wi ye,
    But forbad ye him to slay.

He was a braw callant,
    And he playd at the gluve,
And the bonnie Earl o Moray,
    He wes the queen's true-love.

O lang will his ladie look, etc.

braw callant: brave young man   soondan: sounding   wae:
woe   sae: so

Son David[1]

O WHAT'S the blood that's on your sword,
　　My son David, ho son David,
What's the blood it's on your sword—
　　Come promise, tell me true.
O that's the blood of my grey meir,
　　Hy lady mother, ho lady mother,
That's the blood of my grey meir,
　　Because it wadnae rule by me.

O but that blood it is ower clear,
　　My son David, ho son David,
That blood it is ower clear—
　　Come promise tell me true.
O but that's the blood of my grey hound,
　　Hy lady mother, ho lady mother,
That's the blood of my grey hound,
　　Because it wadnae rule by me.

O but that blood it is ower clear,
　　My son David, ho son David,
That blood it is ower clear—
　　Come promise tell me true.
O but that's the blood of my brother John,
　　Hy lady mother, ho lady mother,
That's the blood of my brother John,
　　Because he drew his sword tae me.

meir: mare

[1] This version of the ballad Edward was collected by Hamish Henderson
for the School of Scottish Studies of Edinburgh University from Mrs.
Jeannie Robertson, to all of whom we are indebted.

.   .   .   .

.   .   .   .   .   .

.   .   .   .

.   .   .   .   .   .

O but I'm gaun awa' in a bottomless boat,
    In a bottomless boat, in a bottomless boat—
But I'm gaun awa' in a bottomless boat,
    And I'll never return again.

O but when will you come back again,
    My son David, ho son David?
When will you come back again—
    Come promise tell me true.
When the sun and the moon meet in yon glen,
    Hy lady mother, ho lady mother,
When the sun and the moon meets in yon glen:
    'Fore I'll return again.

103   *The Bonnie Laddie's Lang a-Grouwin'*[1]

THE trees are a' ivied, the leaves they are green,
    And past are the mony times that I hae seen;
In the lang winter's nicht it's I maun lie mylane,
    For my bonnie laddie's lang, lang a-grouwin'.

O faither, dear faither, ye've duin me muckle wrang,
    For ye hae mairried me on a lad that's owre young;
He is but twelve, and I'm thirteen,
    And the bonnie laddie's lang, lang a-grouwin'.

mylane: alone

[1] This version of one of the few ballads Child missed was heard *circa* 1960 in Edinburgh by one of the editors, and is almost certainly the result of the then current folk-song revival.

O dochter, dear dochter, I've duin ye nae wrang,
   For I hae mairried ye on a noble lord's son:
And he shall be the lord, and ye will wait on,
   And a' the time your lad'll be a-grouwin'.

O faither, dear faither, and if ye see fit,
   We'll send him tae the schuil a year or twa yit;
And we'll set a lang ribbon roond aboot his bannet,
   And that'll be a token that he's mairried.

O faither, dear faither, and if it pleases ye,
   I'll tie my lang hair abuin my bree,
And this coat and breeks I'll glaidly pit on,
   And I tae the schuil will gang wi him.

In his twelfth year, he was a mairried man,
   In his thirteenth, he had gotten her a son;
But in his fourteenth, his grave it grew green,
   And that pit an end tae his grouwin'.

104   *The Dowie Houms o' Yarrow*

LATE at e'en, drinkin' the wine,
   And ere they paid the lawin',
They set a combat them between,
   To fight it in the dawin'.

'O stay at hame, my noble lord!
   O stay at hame, my marrow!
My cruel brother will you betray,
   On the dowie houms o' Yarrow.'

houms: banks, braes   lawin': owing   marrow: mate
dowie: sad, tragic

'O fare ye weel, my lady gaye!
   O fare ye well, my Sarah!
For I maun gae, tho' I ne'er return
   Frae the dowie banks o' Yarrow.'

She kiss'd his cheek, she kamed his hair,
   As she had done before, O;
She belted on his noble brand,
   An' he's awa to Yarrow.

O he's gane up yon high, high hill—
   I wat he gaed wi' sorrow—
An' in a den spied nine arm'd men,
   I' the dowie houms o' Yarrow.

'O ir ye come to drink the wine,
   As ye hae doon before, O?
Or ir ye come to wield the brand,
   On the bonnie banks o' Yarrow?'

'I am no come to drink the wine,
   As I hae done before, O,
But I am come to wield the brand,
   On the dowie houms o' Yarrow.

'If I see all, ye're nine to ane;
   And that's an unequal marrow;
Yet will I fight, while lasts my brand,
   On the bonnie banks of Yarrow.'

Four he hurt, an' five he slew,
   On the dowie houms o' Yarrow,
Till that stubborn knight came him behind,
   An' ran his body thorrow.

     ir: are   thorrow: through

'Gae hame, gae hame, good-brother John,
  An' tell your sister Sarah
To come an' lift her noble lord,
  Who's sleepin' sound on Yarrow.'

'Yestreen I dream'd a dolefu' dream;
  I ken'd there wad be sorrow;
I dream'd I pu'd the heather green,
  On the dowie banks o' Yarrow.'

She gaed up yon high, high hill—
  I wat she gaed wi sorrow—
An' in a den spy'd nine dead men,
  On the dowie houms o' Yarrow.

She kiss'd his cheek, she kaim'd his hair,
  As oft she did before, O;
She drank the red blood frae him ran,
  On the dowie houms o' Yarrow.

'O haud your tongue, my douchter dear,
  For what needs a' this sorrow?
I'll wed you on a better lord
  Than him you lost on Yarrow.'

'O haud your tongue, my father dear,
  An' dinna grieve your Sarah;
A better lord was never born
  Than him I lost on Yarrow.

'Tak hame your ousen, tak hame your kye,
  For they hae bred our sorrow;
I wiss that they had a' gane mad
  When they cam first to Yarrow.'

           ousen: oxen   kye: cattle

105 *True Thomas*

TRUE Thomas lay on Huntlie bank;
  A ferlie he spied wi' his ee;
And there he saw a ladye bright,
  Come riding down by the Eildon Tree.

Her shirt was o' the grass-green silk,
  Her mantle o' the velvet fyne;
At ilka tett of her horse's mane,
  Hung fifty siller bells and nine.

True Thomas, he pull'd aff his cap,
  And louted low down to his knee,
'All hail, thou mighty Queen of Heaven!
  For thy peer on earth I never did see.'

'O no, O no, Thomas,' she said,
  'That name does not belong to me;
I am but the Queen of fair Elfland,
  That am hither come to visit thee.

'Harp and carp, Thomas,' she said,
  'Harp and carp along wi' me;
And if ye dare to kiss my lips,
  Sure of your bodie I will be.'

'Betide me weal, betide me woe,
  That weird shall never daunton me;'
Syne he has kiss'd her rosy lips,
  All underneath the Eildon Tree.

ferlie: marvel, wonder   Eildon: magic   tett: tassle
louted: stooped   carp: converse   weird: fate

'Now, ye maun go wi' me, ' she said,
  'True Thomas, ye maun go wi' me;
And ye maun serve me seven years,
  Thro' weal or woe as may chance to be.'

She's mounted on her milk-white steed;
  She's ta'en true Thomas up behind:
And aye, whene'er her bridle rung,
  The steed flew swifter than the wind.

O they rade on, and farther on;
  The steed gaed swifter than the wind;
Until they reach'd a desert wide,
  And living land was left behind.

'Light down, light down, now, true Thomas,
  And lean your head upon my knee;
Abide and rest a little space,
  And I will show you ferlies three.

'O see ye not yon narrow road,
  So thick beset with thorns and briers?
That is the path of righteousness,
  Though after it but few enquires.'

'And see ye not that braid, braid road,
  That lies across that lily leven?
That is the path of wickedness,
  Though some call it the road to Heaven.

'And see not ye that bonny road
  That winds about the fernie brae?
That is the road to fair Elfland,
  Where thou and I this night maun gae.

'But Thomas, ye maun hold your tongue,
Whatever ye may hear or see;
For if you speak word in Elflyn land
Ye'll ne'er get back to your ain countrie.'

O they rade on, and farther on,
And they waded through rivers aboon the knee;
And they saw neither sun nor moon,
But they heard the roaring of the sea.

It was mirk, mirk night, and there was nae stern light,
And they waded through red blude to the knee;
For a' the blude that's shed on earth
Rins through the springs o' that countrie.

Syne they came to a garden green,
And she pu'd an apple frae a tre—
'Take this for they wages, true Thomas;
It will give thee the tongue that can never lie.'

'My tongue is mine ain,' true Thomas said;
'A gudely gift ye wad gie to me!
I neither dought to buy nor sell
At fair or tryst where I may be.

'I dought neither speak to prince or peer,
Nor ask of grace from fair ladye!'—
'Now hold thy peace!" the lady said,
'For as I say, so must it be.'

He has gotten a coat of the even cloth,
And a pair of shoes of velvet green;
And till seven years were gane and past,
True Thomas on earth was never seen.

stern: star   dought: fear

ROBERT SEMPILL OF BELTREES

? 1590–? 1660

106   *The Life and Death of Habbie Simson,*
            the Piper of Kilbarchan

KILBARCHAN now may say alas!
    For she hath lost her game and grace,
Both *Trixie* and *The Maiden Trace*;
    But what remead?
For no man can supply his place:
    Hab Simson's dead.

Now who shall play *The Day it Dawis*,
Or *Hunt's Up*, when the cock he craws?
Or who can for our kirk-town cause
    Stand us in stead?
On bagpipes now nobody blaws
    Sen Habbie's dead.

Or wha will cause our shearers shear?
Wha will bend up the brags of weir,
Bring in the bells, or good play-meir
    In time of need?
Hab Simson could, what needs you speir?
    But now he's dead.

So kindly to his neighbours neist
At Beltan and St. Barchan's feast
He blew, and then held up his breast,
    As he were weid:
But now we need not him arrest,
    For Habbie's dead.

sen: since   bend up the brags of weir: play this tune   speir:
ask   neist: beside   weid: mad

305

At fairs he play'd before the spear-men,
All gaily graithed in their gear men:
Steel bonnets, jacks, and swords so clear then
   Like any bead:
Now wha shall play before such weir-men
   Sen Habbie's dead?

At clark-plays when he wont to come,
His Pipe played trimly to the drum;
Like bikes of bees he gart it bum,
   And tun'd his reed:
Now all our pipers may sing dumb,
   Sen Habbie's dead.

And at horse races many a day,
Before the black, the brown, the gray,
He gart his pipe, when he did play,
   Baith skirl and skreed:
Now all such pastime's quite away
   Sen Habbie's dead.

He counted was a waled wight-man,
And fiercely at football he ran:
At every game the gree he wan
   For pith and speed.
The like of Habbie was na than,
   But now he's dead.

And then, besides his valiant acts,
At bridals he wan many placks;

graithed: attired   weir-men: men of war   bikes: hives
gart it bum: made it buzz   gart: compelled   skirl and skreed:
shrill and screech   waled wight-man: chosen stalwart   the
gree he wan: the prize he won   pith: power   placks: coins

He bobbit ay behind folk's backs
  And shook his head.
Now we want many merry cracks
  Sen Habbie's dead.

He was convoyer of the bride,
With Kittock hinging at his side;
About the kirk he thought a pride
  The ring to lead:
But now we may gae but a guide,
  For Habbie's dead.

So well's he keepèd his decorum,
And all the stots of *Whig-meg-morum;*
He slew a man, and wae's me for him,
  And bure the fead!
But yet the man wan hame before him,
  And was not dead.

Ay whan he play'd, the lasses leugh
To see him teethless, auld, and teugh,
He wan his pipes besides Barcleugh,
  Withouten dread!
Which after wan him gear eneugh;
  But now he's dead.

Ay when he play'd the gaitlings gedder'd,
And when he spake the carl bleddered,

cracks: capers   Kittock: Katie, purse   hinging: hanging
gae but: go without   stots of *Whig-meg-morum*: gelded bulls of politics
bure the fead: bore the feud   ay: always   leugh: laughed
teugh: tough   wan him gear eneugh: won him wealth enough
gaitlings: children   gedder'd: gathered   carl bleddered: old man
gossiped

On Sabbath days his cap was fedder'd,
    A seemly weid;
In the kirk-yeard his mare stood tedder'd
    Where he lies dead.

Alas! for him my heart is sair,
For of his spring I gat a skair,
At every play, race, feast, and fair,
    But guile or greed;
We need not look for piping mair,
    Sen Habbie's dead.

fedder'd: feathered   weid: garment   skair: share

ANONYMOUS

107

Maggie Lauder

WHA wadna be in love
    Wi' bonnie Maggie Lauder?
A piper met her gaun to Fife,
    And speir'd what was't they ca'd her.
Right scornfully she answered him,
    'Begone, ye hallanshaker,
Jog on your gate, you bladderskate,
    My name is Maggie Lauder.'

'Maggie,' quoth he, 'and by my bags,
    I'm fidging fain to see thee;
Sit down by me, my bonnie bird,
    In troth I winna steer thee;

fidging fain: excited   steer: interfere with

For I'm a piper to my trade,
　My name is Rob the Ranter;
The lasses loup as they were daft,
　When I blaw up my chanter.'

'Piper,' quoth Meg, 'hae ye your bags,
　Or is your drone in order?
If you be Rob, I've heard o' you;
　Live you upo' the Border?
The lasses a', baith far and near,
　Have heard o' Rob the Ranter;
I'll shake my foot wi' right good will,
　Gif ye'll blaw up your chanter.'

Then to his bags he flew wi' speed,
　About the drone he twisted;
Meg up and wallop'd owre the green,
　For brawly could she frisk it.
'Weel done,' quoth he: 'Play up,' quoth she:
　'Weel bobbed,' quoth Rob the Ranter;
' 'Tis worth my while to play indeed,
　When I hae sic a dancer.'

'Weel hae ye play'd your part,' quoth Meg,
　'Your cheeks are like the crimson;
There's nane in Scotland plays sae weel
　Sin' we lost Habbie Simson.
I've lived in Fife, baith maid and wife,
　These ten years and a quarter;
Gin ye should come to Enster Fair,
　Speir ye for Maggie Lauder.

loup: leap　　　　chanter: pipe of bagpipes　　　　drone: drone of
pipe　　　　bobbed: danced　　　　Enster Fair: Anstruther Fair
speir: ask

108   ## The Gaberlunzie Man

THE pawky auld carle cam ower the lea
   Wi' mony good-e'ens and days to me,
Saying, 'Gudewife, for your courtesie,
   Will you lodge a silly poor man?'
The night was cauld, the carle was wat,
And down ayont the ingle he sat;
My dochter's shoulders he 'gan to clap,
   And cadgily ranted and sang.

'O wow!' quo' he, 'were I as free
As first when I saw this countrie,
How blyth and merry wad I be!
   And I wad nevir think lang.'
He grew canty, and she grew fain,
But little did her auld minny ken
What thir slee twa to gither were say'n
   When wooing they were sa thrang.

'An' O!' quo' he, 'an ye were as black
As e'er the crown of my daddy's hat,
'Tis I wad lay thee by my back,
   And awa' wi' me thou sould gang.'
'An' O!' quo' she, 'an' I were as white
As e'er the snaw lay on the dike,
I'd clead me braw and lady-like,
   And awa' wi' thee I would gang.'

gaberlunzie: wallet   carle: old man   clap: caress   cadgily:
gaily   canty: merry   fain: willing   minny: mother   thir
slee twa: this sly pair   thrang: busy   gang: go   dike: wall
clead: clothe

Between the twa was made a plot;
They raise a wee before the cock,
And wilily they shot the lock,
   And fast to the bent are they gane.
Up in the morn the auld wife raise,
And at her leisure put on her claise,
Syne to the servant's bed she gaes,
   To speir for the silly poor man.

She gaed to the bed where the beggar lay,
The strae was cauld, he was away;
She clapt her hand, cried 'Waladay!
   For some of our gear will be gane.'
Some ran to coffers and some to kist,
But nought was stown, that could be mist;
She danced her lane, cried 'Praise be blest,
   I have lodg'd a leal poor man.

'Since naething's awa' as we can learn,
The kirn's to kirn and milk to earn;
Gae but the house, lass, and waken my bairn,
   And bid her come quickly ben.'
The servant gaed where the dochter lay,
The sheets were cauld, she was away,
And fast to her goodwife did say,
   'She's aff with the gaberlunzie man.'

'O fy gar ride and fy gar rin,
And haste ye find these traitors again;
For she's be burnt, and he's be slain,
   The wearifu' gaberlunzie man.'

bent: moor	claise: clothes	syne: then	speir: inquire
gear: belongings	kist: chest	stown: stolen	leal: loyal
kirn: churn	but: inside	ben: through	O fy gar ride:
O shame, make ride		wearifu': bothersome	

Some rade upo' horse, some ran afit,
The wife was wud, and out o' her wit:
She could na gang, nor yet could she sit,
    But aye she curs'd and she bann'd.

Meantime far 'hind out o'er the lea,
Fu' snug in a glen, where nane could see,
The twa, with kindly sport and glee,
    Cut frae a new cheese a whang:
The priving was gude, it pleas'd them baith,
To lo'e her for ay, he ga'e her his aith.
Quo' she, 'To leave thee I will be laith,
    My winsome gaberlunzie man.

'O kend my minny I were wi' you,
Ill-fardly wad she crook her mou';
Sic a poor man she'd never trow,
    After the gaberlunzie man.'
'My dear,' quo' he, 'ye're yet ower young,
And hae na learned the beggar's tongue,
To follow me frae toun to toun,
    And carry the gaberlunzie on.

'Wi' cauk and keel I'll win your bread,
And spindles and whorls for them wha need,
Whilk is a gentle trade indeed,
    To carry the gaberlunzie on.
I'll bow my leg, and crook my knee,
And draw a black clout ower my e'e;
A cripple or blind they will ca' me,
    While we sall be merry and sing.'

wud: mad   bann'd: swore   whang: slice   priving: tasting
kend: knew   ill-fardly: bad-temperedly   cauk: chalk   keel:
ruddle   whilk: which   clout: cloth

109   *Tak' Your Auld Cloak About Ye*

IN winter when the rain rain'd cauld,
    And frost and snaw on ilka hill;
And Boreas wi' his blasts sae bauld
    Was threat'ning a' our kye to kill.
Then Bell, my wife, wha lo'es na strife,
    She said to me right hastily,
'Get up, gudeman, save crummie's life,
    And tak' your auld cloak about ye.

'My crummie is a usefu' cow,
    An' she has come o' a gude kin',
Aft has she wet the bairns' mou',
    And I am laith that she should tyne.
Get up, gudeman, it is fu' time,
    The sun shines in the lift sae hie;
Sloth never made a gracious end,
    Gae tak' your auld cloak about ye.'

'My cloak was ance a gude grey cloak,
    When it was fitting for my wear;
But now 'tis scantly worth a groat,
    For I ha'e worn't this thretty year.
Let's spend the gear that we ha'e won,
    We little ken the day we'll dee;
Then I'll be proud, sin' I ha'e sworn
    To ha'e a new cloak about me.'

'In days when our King Robert rang,
    His trews they cost but half-a-croun;
He said they were a groat ower dear,
    And ca'd the tailor thief and loon.

ilka: each   kye: cattle   crummie: pet-cow   thretty:
thirty   dee: die   rang: reigned   trews: trousers

He was the king that wore the croun,
    And thou'rt a man of laich degree;
'Tis pride puts a' the country doun,
    Sae tak' thy auld cloak about thee.'

'Every land has its ain laugh,
    Ilk' kind o' corn it has its hool;
I think the warld is a' run wrang,
    When ilka wife her man wad rule.
Do ye no see Rob, Jock, and Hab,
    How they are girded gallantlie;
While I sit hurklin' i' the ase?
    I'll ha'e a new cloak about me!'

'Gudeman, I wat 'tis thretty year
    Sin' we did ane anither ken;
An' we ha'e had atween us twa
    Of lads and bonnie lasses ten;
Now they are women grown and men,
    I wish and pray weel may they be;
And if you prove a good husband,
    E'en tak' your auld cloak about ye.'

Bell, my wife, she lo'es na strife,
    But she would guide me if she can;
And to maintain an easy life,
    I aft maun yield, though I'm gudeman.
Nocht's to be won at woman's han',
    Unless you gie her a' the plea;
Then I'll leave aff where I began,
    And tak' my auld cloak about me.

laich: low	hool: husk	girded gallantlie: well dressed
hurklin': hunched-up	ase: ash	a' the plea: the right of the
argument		

110   *Get Up and Bar the Door*

IT fell about the Martinmas time,
    And a gay time it was then,
When our goodwife got puddings to make,
    And she's boil'd them in the pan.

The wind sae cauld blew south and north,
    And blew into the floor;
Quoth our goodman to our goodwife,
    'Gae out and bar the door.'—

'My hand is in my hussyfskap,
    Goodman, as ye may see;
An' it shou'dna be barr'd this hundred year,
    It's no be barr'd for me.'

They made a paction 'tweeen them twa,
    They made it firm and sure,
That the first word wha'er shou'd speak,
    Shou'd rise and bar the door.

Then by there came two gentlemen,
    At twelve o'clock at night,
And they could neither see house no hall,
    Nor coal nor candle-light.

'Now whether is this a rich man's house,
    Or whether is it a poor?'
But ne'er a word wad ane o' them speak,
    For barring of the door.

    hussyfskap: holdall   it's no: it will not

And first they ate the white puddings,
   And then they ate the black.
Tho' muckle thought the goodwife to hersel'
   Yet ne'er a word she spake.

Then said the one unto the other,
   'Here, man, tak ye my knife;
Do ye tak aff the auld man's beard,
   And I'll kiss the goodwife.'—

'But there 's nae water in the house,
   And what shall we do then?'
'What ails ye at the pudding-broo,
   That boils into the pan?'

O up then started oor goodman,
   An angry man was he:
'Will ye kiss my wife before my een
   And scald me wi' pudding-bree?'

Then up and started our goodwife,
   Gied three skips on the floor:
'Goodman, you've spoken the foremost word!
   Get up and bar the door.'

111   *Waly, Waly*

O WALY, waly up the bank!
   And waly, waly, down the brae!
And waly, waly yon burn-side,
   Where I and my love wont to gae!

waly: woefully

I lean'd my back unto an aik,
  I thought it was a trusty tree;
But first it bow'd, and syne it brak,
  Sae my true-love did lightly me.

O waly, waly! but love be bony
  A little time, while it is new;
But when 'tis auld, it waxeth cauld,
  And fades away like morning dew.

O wherefore shoud I busk my head?
  Or wherefore shoud I kame my hair?
For my true-love has me forsook,
  And says he'll never love me mair.

Now Arthur-Seat shall be my bed,
  The sheets shall ne'er be fyl'd by me;
Saint Anton's well shall be my drink,
  Since my true-love has forsaken me.

Martinmas wind, when wilt thou blaw,
  And shake the green leaves off the tree?
O gentle death, when wilt thou come?
  For of my life I am weary.

'Tis not the frost that freezes fell,
  Nor blawing snaw's inclemency;
'Tis not sic cauld that makes me cry,
  But my love's heart grown cauld to me.

aik: oak	syne: then	brak: broke	lightly: scorn
busk: deck	mair: more	Arthur-Seat: hill outside Edinburgh	
fyl'd: defiled	fell: intensely, lethally		

When we came in by Glasgow town,
  We were a comely sight to see;
My love was cled in the black velvet,
  And I my sell in cramasie.

But had I wist, before I kiss'd,
  That l love had been sae ill to win,
I'd lock'd my heart in a case of gold,
  And pin'd it with a silver pin.

Oh, oh, if my young babe were born,
  And set upon the nurse's knee,
And I my sell were dead and gane!
  For a maid again I'll never be.

cramasie: crimson

112   *The Bonnie House o' Airlie*

IT fell on a day, and a bonny simmer day,
  When green grew aits and barley,
That there fell out a great dispute
  Between Argyll and Airlie.

Argyll has raised an hunder men,
  An hunder harnessed rarely,
And he's awa by the back of Dunkell,
  To plunder the castle of Airlie.

Lady Ogilvie looks o'er her bower-window,
  And oh, but she looks weary!
And there she spy'd the great Argyll,
  Come to plunder the bonny house of Airlie.

aits: oats

ANONYMOUS

'Come down, come down, my Lady Ogilvie,
   Come down, and kiss me fairly:'
'O I winna kiss the fause Argyll,
   If he should na leave a standing stane in Airlie.'

He hath taken her by the left shoulder,
   Says, 'Dame where lies they dowry?'
'O it 's east and west yon wan water side,
   And it 's down by the banks of the Airlie.'

They hae sought it up, they hae sought it down,
   They hae sought it maist severely,
Till they fand it in the fair plumb-tree
   That shines on the bowling-green of Airlie.

He hath take her by the middle sae small,
   And O, but she grat sairly!
And laid her down by the bonny burn-side,
   Till they plundered the castle of Airlie.

'Gif my gude lord war here this night,
   As he is with King Charlie,
Neither you, nor ony ither Scottish lord,
   Durst avow to the plundering of Airlie.

'Gif my gude lord war now at hame,
   As he is with his king,
There durst nae a Campbell in a' Argyll
   Set fit on Airlie green.

'Ten bonny sons I have born unto him,
   The eleventh ne'er saw his daddy;
But though I had an hundred mair,
   I'd gie them a' to King Charlie.'

              grat: wept   gif: if

ALLAN RAMSAY

1684/5–1758

The Twa Books

TWA Books, near Neighbours in a Shop,
   The tane a guilded *Turky* Fop,
The tither's Face was weather-beaten,
And Caf-skin Jacket sair worm-eaten.
The Corky, proud of his braw Suit,
Curl'd up his Nose, and thus cry'd out,
'Ah! place me on some fresher Binks,
'Figh! how this mouldy Creature stinks!
'How can a gentle Book like me
'Endure sic scoundrel Company?
'What may Fowk say to see me cling
' Sae close to this auld ugly thing;
'But that I'm of a simple Spirit,
'And disregard my proper Merit?'

  Quoth Gray-baird, '*Whisht, Sir, with your Din,*
'*For a' your meritorious Skin,*
'*I doubt if you be worth within,*
'*For as auld-fashion'd as I look,*
'*May be I am the better Book.*

  'O Heavens! I canna thole the Clash
'Of this impertinent auld Hash;
'I winna stay ae Moment langer.'
'*My Lord, please to command your Anger;*
'*Pray only let me tell you that—*"
'What wad this Insolent be at!

tane: one   Turky: fancy-leather-bound   tither: other
binks: shelves   clash: talk   hash: mess

'Rot out your Tongue—Pray, Master *Symmer*,
'Remove me frae this dinsome *Rhimer*:
'If you regard your Reputation,
'And us of a distinguish'd Station,
'Hence frae this Beast let me be hurried,
'For with his Stour and Stink I'm worried.'

Scarce had he shook his paughty Crap,
When in a Customer did pap;
He up douse *Stanza* lifts, and ey's him,
Turns o'er his Leaves, admires, and buys him:
'*This Book*', said he, '*is good and scarce,
The Saul of Sense in sweetest Verse.*'
But reading Title of gilt cleathing,
Cries, '*Gods! wha buys this bonny naithing?
Nought duller e'er was put in Print:
Wow! what a deal of Turky's tint!*'

Now, Sir, t'apply what we've invented,
You are the Buyer represented:
And, may your Servant hope
My Lays shall merit your Regard,
I'll thank the Gods for my Reward,
And smile at ilka Fop.

paughty crap: proud head   pap: pop

114 *My Peggy is a Young Thing*

MY Peggy is a young thing,
　　Just enter'd in her teens,
Fair as the day, and sweet as May,
Fair as the day, and always gay:
My Peggy is a young thing,
　　And I'm not very auld,
Yet well I like to meet her at
　　The wauking of the fauld.

My Peggy speaks sae sweetly,
　　Whene'er we meet alane,
I wish nae mair to lay my care,
I wish nae mair of a' that's rare,
My Peggy speaks sae sweetly,
　　To all the lave I'm cauld;
But she gars a' my spirits glow,
　　At wauking of the fauld.

My Peggy smiles sae kindly,
　　Whene'er I whisper love,
That I look down on a' the town,
That I look down upon a crown.
My Peggy smiles sae kindly,
　　It makes me blyth and bauld;
And nathing gi'es me sic delight
　　As wauking of the fauld.

My Peggy sings sae saftly,
　　When on my pipe I play,
By a' the rest it is confest,
By a' the rest that she sings best.

wauking: watching　　　fauld: fold　　　gars: compels

My Peggy sings sae saftly,
    And in her sangs are tald,
With innocence the wale of sense,
    At wauking of the fauld.

wale: choice; pick

115   *The Carle He Came O'er the Croft*

THE carle he came o'er the croft,
    And his beard new shaven,
He look'd at me as he'd been daft,
    The carle trows that I wad hae him.
Howt awa! I winna hae him,
    Na forsooth I winna hae him,
For a' his beard's new shaven,
    Ne'er a bit will I hae him.

A siller broach he gae me niest,
    To fasten on my curtchea nooked;
I wor'd a wee upon my breast,
    But soon, alake! the tongue o't crooked;
And sae may his: I winna hae him;
    Na forsooth I winna hae him;
Ane twice a bairn's a lass's jest;
    Sae ony fool for me may hae him.

The carle has nae fault but ane,
    For he has land and dollars plenty;
But waes me for him! skin and bane
    Is no for a plump lass of twenty.

carle: old man   curtchea: cap   nooked: twisted

Howt awa! I winna hae him,
  Na forsooth I winna hae him;
What signifies his dirty riggs
  And cash without a man with them?

But shou'd my canker'd daddy gar
  Me take him 'gainst my inclination,
I warn the fumbler to beware,
  That antlers dinna claim their station
Howt awa! I winna hae him,
  Na forsooth I winna hae him;
I'm flee'd to crack the haly band,
  Sae Lawty says I shou'd na hae him.

canker'd: sour   gar: compel   antlers: horns of cuckold
flee'd: afraid   haly band: marriage-bond   Lawty: honesty

ALEXANDER ROSS
1699–1784

116   *Woo'd and Married and A'*

WOOED and married and a',
  Married and wooed and a';
The dandilly toast of the parish
  Is wooed and married and a'.
The wooers will now ride thinner,
  And by, when they wonted to ca';
'Tis needless to speer for the lassie
  That 's wooed and married and a'.

dandilly: over-admired

324

The girss had na freedom of growing
    As lang as she wasna awa',
Nor in the town could there be stowing
    For wooers that wanted to ca'.
For drinking and dancing and brulyies,
    And boxing and shaking of fa's,
The town was for ever in tulyies;
    But now the lassie's awa'.

But had they but ken'd her as I did,
    Their errand it wad ha'e been sma';
She neither kent spinning nor carding,
    Nor brewing nor baking ava'.
But wooers ran all mad upon her,
    Because she was bonnie and braw,
And sae I dread will be seen on her,
    When she's byhand and awa'.

He'll roose her but sma' that has married her,
    Now when he's gotten her a',
And wish, I fear, he had miscarry'd her,
    Tocher and ribbons and a'.
For her art it lay all in her dressing;
    But gin her braws ance were awa',
I fear she'll turn out o' the fashion,
    And knit up her moggans with straw.

For yesterday I yeed to see her,
    And O she was wonderous braw,
Yet she cried to her husband to gie her
    An ell of red ribbons or twa.

girss: grass	brulyies: broils	tulyies: turmoils	byhand:
decided	tocher: dowry	moggans: stockings	yeed:
went			

He up and he set doun beside her
   A reel and a wheelie to ca';
She said, Was he this gate to guide her?
   And out at the door and awa'.

Her neist road was hame till her mither,
   Who speer'd at her now, How was a'?
She says till her, 'Was't for nae ither
   That I was married awa',
But gae and sit down to a wheelie,
   And at it baith night and day ca',
And ha'e the yarn reeled by a cheelie,
   That ever was crying to draw?'

Her mother says till her, 'Hech, lassie,
   He's wisest, I fear, of the twa;
Ye'll ha'e little to put in the bassie,
   Gin ye be backward to draw.
'Tis now ye should work like a tiger
   And at it baith wallop and ca',
As lang's ye ha'e youthhead and vigour,
   And little anes and debt are awa'.

'Sae swythe awa' hame to your hadding,
   Mair fool than when ye came awa';
Ye maunna now keep ilka wedding,
   Nor gae sae clean-fingered and braw;
But mind with a neiper you're yokit,
   And that ye your end o't maun draw,
Or else ye deserve to be dockit;
   Sae that is an answer for a'.'

ca': drive   cheelie: youngster   swythe: quickly   hadding: holding   neiper: neighbour   dockit: spanked

Young lucky now finds herself nidder'd,
   And wist na well what gate to ca';
But with hersel even considered
   That hamewith were better to draw,
And e'en tak her chance of her landing,
   However the matter might fa';
Folk need not on frets to be standing
   That 's wooed and married and a'.

   lucky: housewife   nidder'd: held down   gate: way, manner
frets: petty wrongs

JAMES THOMSON

1700–1748

117   From *Winter* [lines 41–105]

NOW, when the cheerless empire of the sky
   To Capricorn the Centaur-Archer yields,
And fierce Aquarius stains the inverted year;
Hung o'er the farthest verge of heaven, the sun
Scarce spreads o'er ether the dejected day.
Faint are his gleams, and ineffectual shoot
His struggling rays in horizontal lines
Through the thick air; as, clothed in cloudy storm,
Weak, wan, and broad, he skirts the southern sky;
And, soon-descending, to the long dark night,
Wide-shading all, the prostrate world resigns.
Nor is the night unwished; while vital heat,
Light, life, and joy, the dubious day forsake.

Meantime, in sable cincture, shadows vast,
Deep-tinged and damp, and congregated clouds,
And all the vapoury turbulence of heaven
Involve the face of things. Thus Winter falls,
A heavy gloom oppressive o'er the world,
Through Nature shedding influence malign,
And rouses up the seeds of dark disease.
The soul of man dies in him, loathing life,
And black with more than melancholy views.
The cattle droop; and o'er the furrowed land,
Fresh from the plough, the dun-discoloured flocks,
Untended spreading, crop the wholesome root.
Along the woods, along the moorish fens,
Sighs the sad genius of the coming storm;
And up among the loose disjointed cliffs
And fractured mountains wild, the brawling brook
And cave, presageful, send a hollow moan,
Resounding long in listening fancy's ear.

　　Then comes the father of the tempest forth,
Wrapt in black glooms. First, joyless rains obscure
Drive through the mingling skies with vapour foul,
Dash on the mountain's brow, and shake the woods
That grumbling wave below. The unsightly plain
Lies a brown deluge; as the low-bent clouds
Pour flood on flood, yet unexhausted still
Combine, and, deepening into night, shut up
The day's fair face. The wanderers of heaven,
Each to his home, retire; save those that love
To take their pastime in the troubled air,
Or skimming flutter round the dimply pool.
The cattle from the untasted fields return,
And ask, with meaning low, their wonted stalls,
Or ruminate in the contiguous shade.
Thither the household feathery people crowd—

The crested cock, with all his female train,
Pensive and dripping; while the cottage hind
Hangs o'er the enlivening blaze, and taleful there,
Recounts his simple frolic: much he talks,
And much he laughs, nor recks the storm that blows
Without, and rattles on his humble roof.

Wide o'er the brim, with many a torrent swelled,
And the mixed ruin of its banks o'erspread,
At last the roused-up river pours along:
Resistless, roaring, dreadful, down it comes,
From the rude mountain, and the mossy wild,
Tumbling through rocks abrupt, and sounding far;
Then o'er the sanded valley floating spreads,
Calm, sluggish, silent; till again, constrained
Between two meeting hills, it bursts a way
Where rocks and woods o'erhang the turbid stream;
There, gathering triple force, rapid and deep,
It boils, and wheels, and foams, and thunders through.

118   [lines 118–174]

When from the pallid sky the sun descends,
With many a spot, that o'er his glaring orb
Uncertain wanders, stained; red fiery streaks
Begin to flush around. The reeling clouds
Stagger with dizzy poise, as doubting yet
Which master to obey; while rising slow,
Blank in the leaden-coloured east, the moon
Wears a wan circle round her blunted horns.
Seen through the turbid, fluctuating air,
The stars obtuse emit a shivering ray;
Or frequent seem to shoot athwart the gloom,
And long behind them trail the whitening blaze.

Snatched in short eddies, plays the withered leaf;
And on the flood the dancing feather floats.
With broadened nostrils to the sky upturned,
The conscious heifer snuffs the stormy gale.
Even as the matron, at her nightly task,
With pensive labour draws the flaxen thread,
The wasted taper and the crackling flame
Foretell the blast. But chief the plumy race,
The tenants of the sky, its changes speak.
Retiring from the downs, where all day long
They picked their scanty fare, a blackening train
Of clamorous rooks thick-urge their weary flight
And seek the closing shelter of the grove.
Assiduous, in his bower, the wailing owl
Plies his sad song. The cormorant on high
Wheels from the deep, and screams along the land.
Loud shrieks the soaring hern; and with wild wing
The circling sea-fowl cleave the flaky clouds.
Ocean, unequal pressed, with broken tide
And blind commotion heaves; while from the shore,
Eat into caverns by the restless wave,
And forest-rustling mountain, comes a voice,
That solemn-sounding bids the world prepare.
Then comes forth the storm with sudden burst
And hurls the whole precipitated air
Down in a torrent. On the passive main
Descends the ethereal force, and with strong gust
Turns from its bottom the discoloured deep.
Through the black night that sits immense around,
Lashed into foam, the fierce conflicting brine
Seems o'er a thousand raging waves to burn.
Meantime the mountain-billows, to the clouds
In dreadful tumult swelled, surge above surge,
Burst into chaos with tremendous roar,

And anchored navies from their stations drive,
Wild as the winds across the howling waste
Of mighty waters: now the inflated wave
Straining they scale, and now impetuous shoot
Into the secret chambers of the deep,
The wintry Baltic thundering o'er their head.
Emerging thence again, before the breath
Of full-exerted heaven they wing their course,
And dart on distant coasts—if some sharp rock,
Or shoal insidious, break not their career,
And in loose fragments fling them floating round.

119   [lines 714–759]

What art thou, frost? and whence are thy keen stores
Derived, thou secret all-invading power,
Whom even the illusive fluid cannot fly?
Is not thy potent energy, unseen,
Myriads of little salts, or hooked, or shaped
Like double wedges, and diffused, immense,
Through water, earth, and ether? Hence at eve,
Steamed eager from the red horizon round,
With the fierce rage of Winter deep suffused,
An icy gale, oft shifting, o'er the pool
Breathes a blue film, and in its mid career
Arrests the bickering stream. The loosened ice,
Let down the flood and half dissolved by day,
Rustles no more; but to the sedgy bank
Fast grows, or gathers round the pointed stone,
A crystal pavement, by the breath of heaven
Cemented firm; till, seized from shore to shore,
The whole imprisoned river growls below.

Loud rings the frozen earth, and hard reflects
A double noise; while, at his evening watch,
The village dog deters the nightly thief;
The heifer lows; the distant water-fall
Swells in the breeze; and, with the hasty tread
Of traveller, the hollow-sounding plain
Shakes from afar. The full ethereal round,
Infinite worlds disclosing to the view,
Shines out intensely keen; and, all one cope
Of starry glitter, glows from pole to pole.
From pole to pole the rigid influence falls
Through the still night, incessant, heavy, strong,
And seizes nature fast. It freezes on;
Till morn, late-rising o'er the drooping world,
Lifts her pale eye unjoyous. Then appears
The various labour of the silent night:
Prone from the dripping eave, and dumb cascade,
Whose idle torrents only seem to roar,
The pendent icicle; the frost-work fair,
Where transient hues, and fancied figures rise;
Wide spouted o'er the hill, the frozen brook,
A livid tract, cold-gleaming on the morn;
The forest bent beneath the plumy wave;
And by the frost refined the whiter snow,
Incrusted hard, and sounding to the tread
Of early shepherd, as he pensive seeks
His pining flock, or from the mountain top,
Pleased with the slippery surface, swift descends.

ADAM SKIRVING

1719–1803

Johnnie Cope

HEY, Johnnie Cope, are ye wauking yet?
  Or are your drums a-beating yet?
If ye were wauking I wad wait
  To gang to the coals i' the morning.

Cope sent a challenge frae Dunbar:
'Charlie, meet me an ye daur,
And I'll learn you the art o' war
  If you'll meet me i' the morning.'

When Charlie looked the letter upon
He drew his sword the scabbard from:
'Come, follow me, my merry, merry men,
  And we'll meet Johnnie Cope i' the morning!

'Now, Johnnie, be as good's your word;
Come, let us try both fire and sword;
And dinna rin like a frighted bird,
  That's chased frae its nest i' the morning.'

When Johnnie Cope he heard of this,
He thought it wadna be amiss
To hae a horse in readiness
  To flee awa' i' the morning.

Fy now, Johnnie, get up and rin;
The Highland bagpipes mak a din;
It's best to sleep in a hale skin,
  For 'twill be a bluidy morning.

wauking: waking

When Johnnie Cope to Dunbar came,
They speered at him, 'Where's a' your men?'
'The deil confound me gin I ken,
     For I left them a' i' the morning.'

'Now Johnnie, troth, ye are na blate
To come wi' the news o' your ain defeat,
And leave your men in sic a strait
     Sae early in the morning.'

'I' faith,' quo' Johnnie, 'I got a fleg
Wi' their claymores and philabegs;
If I face them again, deil break my legs!
     So I wish you a gude morning.'

speered: inquired   blate: shy   fleg: fright   philabegs:
kilts

JOHN SKINNER

1721–1807

121   *Tullochgorum*

COME gie's a sang, Montgomery cry'd,
     And lay your disputes all aside,
What signifies 't for folks to chide
     For what was done before them:
Let Whig and Tory all agree,
     Whig and Tory, Whig and Tory,

Whig and Tory all agree,
　　To drop their Whig-mig-morum;
Let Whig and Tory all agree
To spend the night wi' mirth and glee,
And cheerful sing alang wi' me
　　The Reel o' Tullochgorum.

O Tullochgorum's my delight,
It gars us a' in ane unite,
And ony sumph that keeps a spite,
　　In conscience I abhor him:
For blythe and cheerie we 's be a',
　　Blythe and cheerie, blythe and cheerie,
　　Blythe and cheerie we 's be a',
　　　　And make a happy quorum,
For blythe and cheerie we 's be a'
As lang as we hae breath to draw,
And dance till we be like to fa'
　　The Reel o' Tullochgorum.

What needs there be sae great a fraise
Wi' dringing dull Italian lays,
I wadna gie our ain Strathspeys
　　For half a hunder score o' them;
They're dowf and dowie at the best,
　　Dowf and dowie, dowf and dowie,
　　Dowf and dowie at the best,
　　　　Wi' a' their variorum;
They're dowf and dowie at the best,
Their *allegros* and a' the rest,
They canna' please a Scottish taste
　　Compar'd wi' Tullochgorum.

whig-mig-morum: politics　　　　gars: compels　　　　fraise: fracas
dringing: wearisome　　　dowf: woeful　　　dowie: sad

Let warldly worms their minds oppress
Wi' fears o' want and double cess,
And sullen sots themsells distress
    Wi' keeping up decorum:
Shall we sae sour and sulky sit,
  Sour and sulky, sour and sulky,
  Sour and sulky shall we sit
    Like old philosophorum!
Shall we sae sour and sulky sit,
Wi' neither sense, nor mirth, nor wit,
Nor ever try to shake a fit
    To th' Reel o' Tullochgorum?

May choicest blessings ay attend
Each honest, open-hearted friend,
And calm and quiet be his end,
    And a' that 's good watch o'er him;
May peace and plenty be his lot,
  Peace and plenty, peace and plenty,
  Peace and plenty be his lot,
    And dainties a great store o' them;
May peace and plenty be his lot,
Unstain'd by any vicious spot,
And may he never want a groat,
    That 's fond o' Tullochgorum!

But for the sullen frumpish fool,
That loves to be oppression's tool,
May envy gnaw his rotten soul,
    And discontent devour him;
May dool and sorrow be his chance,
  Dool and sorrow, dool and sorrow,

        dool: grief

Dool and sorrow be his chance,
 And nane say, wae 's me for him!
May dool and sorrow be his chance,
Wi' a' the ills that come frae France,
Wha e'er he be that winna dance
 The Reel o' Tullochgorum.

JEAN ELLIOT

1727–1805

122 *The Flowers of the Forest*

I'VE heard the lilting at our yowe-milking,
 Lasses a-lilting before the dawn o' day;
But now they are moaning on ilka green loaning:
 'The Flowers of the Forest are a' wede away.'

At buchts, in the morning, nae blythe lads are scorning;
 The lasses are lonely, and dowie, and wae;
Nae daffin', nae gabbin', but sighing and sabbing:
 Ilk ane lifts her leglen, and hies her away.

In hairst, at the shearing, nae youths now are jeering,
 The bandsters are lyart, and runkled and grey;
At fair or at preaching, nae wooing, nae fleeching:
 The Flowers of the Forest are a' wede away.

yowe: ewe wede: withered buchts: cattle-pens dowie:
sad daffin': dallying leglen: stool hairst: harvest bandsters: binders lyart: hoary fleeching: coaxing, flattering

At e'en, in the gloaming, nae swankies are roaming
   'Bout stacks wi' the lasses at bogle to play,
But ilk ane sits drearie, lamenting her dearie:
   The Flowers of the Forest are a' wede away.

Dule and wae for the order sent our lads to the Border;
   The English, for ance, by guile wan the day;
The Flowers of the Forest, that foucht aye the foremost,
   The prime o' our land, are cauld in the clay.

We'll hear nae mair lilting at our yowe-milking,
   Women and bairns are heartless and wae;
Sighing and moaning on ilka green loaning:
   'The Flowers of the Forest are a' wede away.'

swankies: young bucks   bogle: peek-a-bo   dule: grief

JAMES BEATTIE
1735–1803

123   *To Mr. Alexander Ross*

O ROSS, thou wale of hearty cocks,
   Sae crouse and canty with thy jokes!
Thy hamely auldwarl'd muse provokes
    Me for awhile
To ape our guid plain countra' folks
    In verse and stile.

wale: choice(st)   crouse: keen   canty: merry

JAMES BEATTIE

Sure never carle was haff sae gabby
E'er since the winsome days o' Habby:
O mayst thou ne'er gang clung, or shabby,
 Nor miss thy snaker!
Or I'll ca' fortune nasty drabby,
 And say—pox take her!

O may the roupe ne'er roust thy weason,
May thirst thy thrapple never gizzen!
But bottled ale in mony a dizzen,
 Aye lade thy gantry!
And fouth o' vivres a' in season,
 Plenish thy pantry!

Lang may thy stevin fill wi' glee
The glens and mountains of Lochlee,
Which were right gowsty but for thee,
 Whase sangs enamour
Ilk lass, and teach wi' melody
 The rocks to yamour.

Ye shak your head, but, o' my fegs,
Ye've set old Scota on her legs,
Lang had she lyen wi' beffs and flegs,
 Bumbaz'd and dizzie;
Her fiddle wanted strings and pegs,
 Waes me! poor hizzie!

carle: old man gabby: gossippy Habby: Habbie Simson
clung: empty, hungry snaker: ? sly drink roupe: head-cold
roust: rust weason: throat thrapple: gullet gizzen:
parch lade: load fouth: plenty vivres: food stevin:
vocal noise gowsty: desolate yamour: clamour fegs:
faith beffs: blows flegs: strokes bumbaz'd: confused

Since Allan's death naebody car'd
For anes to speer how Scota far'd,
Nor plack nor thristled turner war'd
    To quench her drouth;
For frae the cottar to the laird
    We a' rin South.

The Southland chiels indeed hae mettle,
And brawley at a sang can ettle,
Yet we right couthily might settle
    O' this side Forth.
The devil pay them wi' a pettle
    That slight the North.

Our countra leed is far frae barren,
It 's even right pithy and aulfarren,
Oursells are neiper-like, I warran,
    For sense and smergh;
In kittle times when faes are yarring,
    We're no thought ergh.

Oh! bonny are our greensward hows,
Where through the birks the birny rows,
And the bee bums, and the ox lows,
    And saft winds rusle;
And shepherd lads on sunny knows
    Blaw the blythe fusle.

plack: small coin   turner: small coin   war'd: spent
chiels: fellows   ettle: attempt   couthily: cosily   pettle:
plough-staff   leed: language   aulfarren: old-fashioned
neiper-like: neighbourly   smergh: marrow   kittle: ticklish
yarring: snarling   ergh: timid   hows: hollows   birny:
brooklet   rows: rolls   knows: knolls   fusle:
whistle

It 's true, we Norlans manna fa'
To eat sae nice or gang sae bra',
As they that come from far awa,
　　Yet sma's our skaith;
We've peace (and that 's well worth it a')
　　And meat and claith.

Our fine newfangle sparks, I grant ye,
Gi'e poor auld Scotland mony a taunty;
They're grown sae ugertfu' and vaunty,
　　And capernoited,
They guide her like a canker'd aunty
　　That 's deaf and doited.

Sae comes of ignorance I trow,
It 's this that crooks their ill fa'r'd mou'
Wi' jokes sae course, they gar fouk spue
　　For downright skonner;
For Scotland wants na sons enew
　　To do her honour.

I here might gie a skreed o' names,
Dawties of Heliconian dames!
The foremost place Gawin Douglas claims,
　　That canty priest;
And wha can match the fifth King James
　　For sang or jest?

Montgomery grave, and Ramsay gay,
Dunbar, Scot, Hawthornden, and mae

fa': happen　　　　skaith: harm　　　　sparks: wits　　　　ugertfu':
squeamish　　　　capernoited: ill-tempered　　　　doited: half-mad
fa'r'd: fashioned　　　spue: vomit　　　skonner: disgust　　　enew:
enough　　　skreed: list　　　dawties: darlings

Than I can tell; for o' my fae,
    I maun break aff;
'Twould take a live lang simmer day
    To name the haff.

The saucy chiels—I think they ca' them
Criticks, the muckle sorrow claw them,
(For mense nor manners ne'er could awe them
    Frae their presumption)
They need nae try thy jokes to fathom;
    They want rumgumption.

But ilka Mearns and Angus bearn,
Thy tales and sangs by heart shall learn,
And chiels shall come frae yont the Cairn—
    —Amounth, right yousty,
If Ross will be so kind as share in
    Their pint at Drousty.[1]

[1] Alehouse in Lochlee.

muckle: great   mense: good sense   rumgumption: initiative
bearn: man   yousty: talkative

ALEXANDER GEDDES

1737–1802

124 From the *Epistle to the President, Vice-Presidents, and Members of the Scottish Society of Antiquaries: On Being Chosen a Correspondent Member*

NOR will the search be hard or long:
For tho' 'tis true that Mither-tongue
Has had the melancholy fate
To be neglekit by the great,
She still has fun an open door
Amang the uncurruptit poor,
Wha be na weent to treat wi' scorn
A gentlewoman bred and born,
But bid her, thoch in tatters drest,
A hearty welcome to their best.

There aft on benmaist bink she sits,
And sharps the edge of cuintry wits,
Wi' routh of gabby saws, an' says,
An' jokes, an' gibes of uther days:
That gi'e si'k gust to rustic sport,
And gar the langsome night leuk short.

At uther times in some warm neuk
She to the cutchok ha'ds a beuk,
And reids in si'k a magic tone,
The deeds that our forebeirs ha' done:

fun: found   weent: wont   benmaist: innermost   bink:
bench   cuintry: country   routh: plenty   si'k: such   gar:
compel   cutchok: fire   ha'ds: holds

That—as 'tis said of that faim't Greek
Wha gaed to hell his wife to seek,
Sa sweet he sang, Ixion's wheel
And Sysiphus's stane stood still:
Nay mair; those greedy gleds, that iver
'Till nou had peck't Prometheus' Liver,
Forgat their prey, op't wide their throats,
And lent their lugs to Orpheus' notes.
Sa here, gif ye attention gi'e,
Si'k auld-warld wunders ye may see;
May see the maiden stap her wheel;
The mistress cease to turn the reel;
Lizzy, wi' laddle in her hand,
Til pot boil over, gapand stand:
Ev'n hungry Gib his speun depose
And, for a mament, spare his brose.

Let bragart England in disdain
Ha'd ilka lingo, but her a'in:
Her a'in, we wat, say what she can,
Is like her true-born Englishman,[1]
A vile promiscuous mungrel[2] seed
Of Danish, Dutch, an' Norman breed,
An' prostituted, since, to a'
The jargons on this earthly ba'!
Bedek't, 'tis true, an' made fu' smart
Wi' mekil learning, pains an' art;
An' taught to baik, an' benge, an' bou
As dogs an' dancin'-masters do:

[1] Defoe. [2] *Hybrida quidem lingua Anglicana est.* Hickes.

gleds: kites   lugs: ears   stap: stop   gapand: gaping
brose: kind of broth   benge: fawn

Wi' fardit cheeks an' pouder't hair,
An' brazen confidential stare—
While ours, a blate an' bashfu' maid
Conceals her blushes wi' her plaid;
And is unwillan' to display
Her beuties in the face o' day.

Bot strip them baith—an' see wha's shape
Has least the semblance of an ape?
Wha's lim's are straughtest? Wha can sheu
The whiter skin, an' fairer heu;
An' whilk, in short, is the mair fit
To gender genuine manly wit?
I'll pledge my pen, you'll judgment pass
In favor of the Scottis lass.

fardit: painted   blate: shy   whilk: which

ROBERT FERGUSSON

1750–1774

125   *Braid Claith*

YE wha are fain to hae your name
    Wrote in the bonny book of fame,
Let merit nae pretension claim
        To laurel'd wreath,
But hap ye weel, baith back and wame,
        In gude Braid Claith.

hap: wrap   wame: belly

345

He that some ells o' this may fa,
An' slae-black hat on pow like snaw,
Bids bauld to bear the gree awa',
  Wi' a' this graith,
Whan bienly clad wi' shell fu' braw
   O' gude Braid Claith.

Waesuck for him wha has na fek o't!
For he's a gowk they're sure to geck at,
A chiel that ne'er will be respekit
  While he draws breath,
Till his four quarters are bedeckit
   Wi' gude Braid Claith.

On Sabbath-days the barber spark,
When he has done wi' scrapin wark,
Wi' siller broachie in his sark,
  Gangs trigly, faith!
Or to the Meadow, or the Park,
   In gude Braid Claith.

Weel might ye trow, to see them there,
That they to shave your haffits bare,
Or curl an' sleek a pickle hair,
  Wou'd be right laith,
Whan pacing wi' a gawsy air
   In gude Braid Claith.

If ony mettl'd stirrah green
For favour frae a lady's ein

pow: head	gree: prize	graith: attire	bienly:
respectably	waesuck: pity	fek: plenty	chiel: fellow
spark: chap	sark: shirt	haffits: side-whiskers	pickle: little
laith: loath	gawsy: proud	stirrah: gallant	green: yearn

He maunna care for being seen
      Before he sheath
His body in a scabbard clean
      O' gude Braid Claith.

For, gin he come wi' coat thread-bare,
A feg for him she winna care,
But crook her bonny mou' fu' sair,
      And scald him baith.
Wooers shou'd ay their travel spare
      Without Braid Claith.

Braid Claith lends fock an unco heese,
Makes mony kail-worms butter-flies,
Gies mony a doctor his degrees
      For little skaith:
In short, you may be what you please
      Wi' gude Braid Claith.

For thof ye had as wise a snout on
As *Shakespeare* or *Sir Isaac Newton*,
Your judgment fouk wou'd hae a doubt on,
      I'll tak my aith,
Till they cou'd see ye wi' a suit on
      O' gude Braid Claith.

feg: jot   scald: scold   heese: uplift   kail-worms:
caterpillars   skaith: pains

126

Hallow-Fair

AT *Hallowmas*, whan nights grow lang,
  And *starnies* shine fu' clear,
Whan fock, the nippin cald to bang,
  Their winter *hap-warms* wear,
Near Edinbrough a fair there hads,
  I wat there's nane whase name is,
For strappin dames and sturdy lads,
  And cap and stoup, mair famous
      Than it that day.

Upo' the tap o' ilka lum
  The sun began to keek,
And bad the trig made maidens come
  A sightly joe to seek
At *Hallow-fair*, whare browsters rare
  Keep gude ale on the gantries,
And dinna scrimp ye o' a skair
  O' kebbucks frae their pantries,
      Fu' saut that day.

Here country John in bonnet blue,
  An' eke his Sunday claise on,
Rins efter Meg wi' *rokelay* new,
  An' sappy kisses lays on;
She'll tauntin say, Ye silly coof!
  Be o' your gab mair spairin;
He'll tak the hint, and criesh her loof
  Wi' what will buy her fairin,
      To chow that day.

starnies: little stars   bang: defeat   hads: holds   cap: cup
mair: more   lum: chimney   joe: lover   browsters: brewers
skair: share   kebbucks: cheeses   fu' saut: very salt   rokelay:
mantle   coof: fool   gab: mouth   criesh: grease   loof:
palm   fairin: lunch

Here chapman billies tak their stand,
  An' shaw their *bonny wallies*;
Wow, but they lie fu' gleg aff hand
  To trick the silly fallows:
Heh, Sirs! what cairds and tinklers come,
  An' *ne'er-do-weel* horse-coupers,
An' spae-wives fenzying to be dumb,
  Wi' a' siclike landloupers,
          To thrive that day.

Here Sawny cries, frae Aberdeen;
  'Come ye to me fa need:
The brawest *shanks* that e'er were seen
  I'll sell ye cheap an' guid.
I wyt they are as protty hose
  As come fae *weyr* or *leem*:
Here tak a rug, and shaw's your pose:
  Forseeth, my ain's but teem
          An' light this day.'

Ye wives, as ye gang thro' the fair,
  O mak your bargains hooly!
O' a' thir wylie lowns beware,
  Or fegs they will ye spulzie.
For fairn-year *Meg Thamson* got,
  Frae thir mischievous villains,
A scaw'd bit o' a penny note,
  That lost a score o' shillins
          To her that day.

---

chapman billies: packman fellows   wallies: wares   gleg: readily   spae-wives: fortune-tellers   landloupers: vagabonds fa: who   shanks: hose   weyr: wire   leem: loom   rug: bargain   pose: money   ain: own   teem: empty   gang: go   thir: these   lowns: fellows, lads   spulzie: spoil fairn-year: last year   scaw'd bit: worthless thing

The dinlin drums alarm our ears,
   The serjeant screechs fu' loud,
'A' gentlemen and volunteers
   That wish your country gude,
Come here to me, and I shall gie
   Twa guineas and a crown,
A bowl o' *punch*, that like the sea
   Will soum a lang dragoon
      Wi' ease this day.'

Without the cuissers prance and nicker,
   An' our the ley-rig scud;
In tents the carles bend the bicker,
   An' rant an' roar like wud.
Then there 's sic yellowchin and din,
   Wi' wives and wee-anes gablin,
That ane might true they were a-kin
   To a' the tongues at Babylon,
      Confus'd that day.

Whan *Phoebus* ligs in *Thetis* lap,
   Auld Reekie gies them shelter,
Whare cadgily they kiss the cap,
   An' ca't round helter-skelter.
Jock Bell gaed furth to play his freaks,
   Great cause he had to rue it,
For frae a stark Lochaber aix
   He gat a *clamihewit*
      Fu' sair that night.

---

soum: swim   cuissers: lancers   ley-rig: grass field   scud:
drive   carles: old men   bicker: tankard   wud: mad
yellowchin: yelling   wee-anes: children   true: believe
cadgily: gaily   freaks: pranks   clamihewit: heavy blow

350

'Ohon!' quo' he, 'I'd rather be
   By *sword* or *bagnet* stickit,
Than hae my crown or body wi'
   Sic deadly weapons nicket.'
Wi' that he gat anither straik
   Mair weighty than before,
That gar'd his feckless body aik,
   An' spew the reikin gore,
      Fu' red that night.

He peching on the cawsey lay,
   O' kicks and cuffs weel sair'd;
A *Highland* aith the serjeant gae,
   'She maun pe see our guard.'
Out spak the weirlike corporal,
   'Pring in ta drunken sot.'
They trail'd him ben, an' by my saul,
   He paid his drunken groat,
      For that neist day.

Good fock, as ye come frae the fair,
   Bide yont frae this black squad;
There's nae sic savages elsewhere
   Allow'd to wear cockade.
Than the strong lion's hungry maw,
   Or tusk o' Russian bear,
Frae their wanruly fellin paw
   Mair cause ye hae to fear
      Your death that day.

bagnet: bayonet   nicket: cut   straik: stroke   feckless:
useless   reikin: steaming   cawsey: pavement   sair'd: served
maun pe see: must be seing   weirlike: warlike   ben: in
groat: small coin   bide yont: stay far from   wanruly: unruly

A wee soup drink dis unco weel
    To had the heart aboon;
It 's good as lang's a canny chiel
    Can stand steeve in his shoon.
But gin a birkie 's owr weel sair'd,
    It gars him aften stammer
To *pleys* that bring him to the guard,
    An' eke the *Council-chawmir*,
        Wi' shame that day.

unco weel: very well   aboon: above   steeve: upright
birkie: chap

---

127   *The Rising of the Session*

TO a' men living be it kend,
    The SESSION now is at an end:
Writers, your finger-nebbs unbend,
        And quatt the pen,
Till *Time* wi' lyart pow shall send
        Blythe June again.

Tir'd o' the law, and a' its phrases,
The wylie *writers*, rich as *Croesus*,
Hurl frae the town in hackney chaises,
        For country cheer:
The *powny* that in spring-time grazes,
        Thrives a' the year.

kend: known   quatt: quit   lyart pow: hoary head   powny:
pony

Ye lawyers, bid fareweel to lies,
Fareweel to din, fareweel to fees,
The canny hours o' rest may please
      Instead o' siller:
Hain'd *multer* hads the *mill* at ease,
      And finds the *miller*.

Blyth they may be wha wanton play
In *fortune's* bonny blinkin ray,
Fu' weel can they ding dool away
      Wi' comrades couthy,
And never dree a hungert day,
      Or e'ening drouthy.

Ohon the day for him that's laid,
In dowie *poortith's* caldrife shade,
Ablins owr honest for his trade,
      He racks his wits,
How he may get his buick weel clad,
      And fill his guts.

The farmers sons, as yap as sparrows,
Are glad, I trow, to flee the barras,
And whistle to the plough and harrows
      At barley seed:
What writer wadna gang as far as
      He cou'd for bread.

After their yokin, I wat weel
They'll stoo the kebbuck to the keel;

siller: silver	hain'd multer: saved meal	ding: drive
dool: care	dree: endure drouthy: thirsty	dowie: sad
ablins: perhaps	owr: over, too yap: bold	barras: enclosure
stoo: nibble	kebbuck: cheese keel: rind	

Eith can the plough-stilts gar a chiel
        Be unco vogie,
Clean to lick aff his crowdy-meal,
        And scart his *cogie*.

Now mony a fallow's dung adrift
To a' the blasts beneath the lift,
And tho' their stamack's aft in tift
        In vacance time,
Yet seenil do they ken the rift
        O' stappit weym.

Now gin a *Notar* shou'd be wanted,
You'll find the *pillars* gayly planted;
For little thing *protests* are granted
        Upo' a bill,
And weightiest matters covenanted
        For haf a gill.

Nae body takes a morning dribb
O' *Holland gin* frae *Robin Gibb*;
And tho' a dram to Rob's mair sib
        Than is his wife,
He maun take time to daut his *Rib*
        Till siller's rife.

This *vacance* is a heavy doom
On *Indian Peter's* coffee-room,
For a' his china pigs are toom;
        Nor do we see
In wine the sucker biskets soom
        As light's a flee.

eith: easily	vogie: glad	scart: scrape	cogie: dish
dung: struck	lift: sky	in tift: upset	seenil: seldom
stappit weym: full belly	dribb: drop	sib: close, akin	daut: pet
vacance: vacation	toom: empty	soom: swim	flee: fly

ROBERT FERGUSSON

But stop, my Muse, nor make a main,
Pate disna fend on that alane;
He can fell twa dogs wi ae bane,
    While ither fock
Maun rest themselves content wi' ane,
    Nor farer trock.

Ye changehouse keepers never grumble
Tho' you a while your bickers whumble,
Be unco patientfu' and humble,
    Nor make a din,
Tho' gude *joot* binna kend to rumble
    Your weym within.

You needna grudge to draw your breath
For little mair than haf a reath,
Than, gin we a' be spar'd frae death,
    We'll gladly prie
Fresh noggans o' your reaming graith
    Wi' blythsome glee.

main: moan	ae bane: one bone	trock: deal	whumble:
turn down	joot: liquor	weym: belly	haf a reath:
quarter-year	prie: taste	reaming graith: fulsome goods	

128   *The Ghaists: A Kirk-yard Eclogue*

> *Did you not say, on good ANN'S day,*
> *And vow and did protest, Sir,*
> *That when HANOVER should come o'er,*
> *We surely should be blest, Sir?*
>   An auld Sang made new again.

WHARE the braid planes in dowy murmurs wave
      Their antient taps out o'er the cald, cald grave,
Whare *Geordie Girdwood*, mony a lang-spun day,
Houkit for gentlest banes the humblest clay,
Twa sheeted ghaists, sae grizly and sae wan,
'Mang lanely tombs their douff discourse began.

WATSON

Cauld blaws the nippin north wi' angry sough,
And showers his hailstanes frae the Castle Cleugh
O'er the Greyfriars, whare, at mirkest hour,
Bogles and spectres wont to tak their tour,
Harlin the pows and shanks to hidden cairns,
Amang the hamlocks wild, and sun-burnt fearns
But nane the night save you and I hae come
Frae the dern mansions of the midnight tomb,
Now whan the dawning's near, whan cock maun craw,
And wi' his angry bougil gar's withdraw,
Ayont the kirk we'll stap, and there tak bield,
While the black hours our nightly freedom yield.

dowy: sad   houkit: dug   ghaists: ghosts   douff: mournful
Cleugh: cliff   bogles: ghosts   harlin: dragging   **pows:**
heads   dern: secret   bougil: bugle   bield: shelter

356

HERRIOT

I'm weel content; but binna cassen down,
Nor trow the cock will ca' ye hame o'er soon,
For tho' the eastern lift betakens day,
Changing her rokelay black for mantle grey,
Nae weirlike bird our knell of parting rings,
Nor sheds the caller moisture frae his wings.
NATURE has chang'd her course; the birds o' day
Dosin' in silence on the bending spray,
While owlets round the craigs at noon-tide flee,
And bludey bawks sit singand on the tree.
Ah, CALEDON! the land I yence held dear,
Sair mane mak I for thy destruction near;
And thou, EDINA! anes my dear abode,
Whan royal JAMIE sway'd the sovereign rod,
In thae blest days, weel did I think bestow'd,
To blaw thy poortith by wi' heaps o' gowd;
To mak thee sonsy seem wi' mony a gift,
And gar thy stately turrets speel the lift:
In vain did Danish Jones, wi' gimcrack pains,
In Gothic sculpture fret the pliant stanes:
In vain did he affix my statue here,
Brawly to busk wi' flow'rs ilk coming year;
My tow'rs are sunk, my lands are barren now,
My fame, my honour, like my flow'rs maun dow.

WATSON

Sure *Major Weir*, or some sic warlock wight,
Has flung beguilin' glamer o'er your sight;

lift: sky	rokelay: cloak	weirlike: warlike	caller:
fresh	craigs: rocks	bawks: bats	sair mane: sore moan
anes: once	thae: those	poortith: poverty	sonsy:
wealthy	speel: climb	busk: deck	dow: fade

Or else some kittle cantrup thrown, I ween,
Has bound in mirlygoes my ain twa ein,
If ever aught frae sense cou'd be believed
(And seenil hae my senses been deceiv'd),
This moment, o'er the tap of Adam's tomb,
Fu' easy can I see your chiefest dome:
Nae corbie fleein' there, nor croupin' craws,
Seem to forspeak the ruin of thy haws,
But a' your tow'rs in wonted order stand,
Steeve as the rocks that hem our native land.

HERRIOT

Think na I vent my well-a-day in vain,
Kent ye the cause, ye sure wad join my mane.
Black be the day that e'er to England's ground
Scotland was eikit by the UNION's bond;
For mony a menzie of destructive ills
The country now maun brook frae *mortmain bills*,
That void our test'ments, and can freely gie
Sic will and scoup to the ordain'd trustee,
That he may tir our stateliest riggins bare,
Nor acres, houses, woods, nor fishins spare,
Till he can lend the stoitering state a lift
Wi' gowd in gowpins as a grassum gift;
In lieu o' whilk, we maun be weel content
To tyne the capital at three *per cent*.
A doughty sum indeed, whan now-a-days
They raise provisions as the stents they raise,
Yoke hard the poor, and lat the rich chiels be,
Pamper'd at ease by ither's industry.

kittle: ticklish   cantrup: trick   mirlygoes: delusions   seenil: seldom   corbie: crow   haws: halls   steeve: hard   menzie: crowd   scoup: scope   tir: strip   stoitering: staggering   tyne: lose   stents: lots   chiels: fellows

Hale interest for my fund can scantly now
Cleed a' my callants backs, and stap their mou'.
How maun their weyms wi' sairest hunger slack,
Their duds in targets flaff upo' their back,
Whan they are doom'd to keep a lasting Lent,
Starving for England's weel at *three per cent.*

WATSON

AULD REEKIE than may bless the gowden times,
Whan honesty and poortith baith are crimes;
She little kend, whan you and I endow'd
Our hospitals for back-gaun burghers gude,
That e'er our siller or our lands shou'd bring
A gude bien living to a back-gaun king.
Wha, thanks to ministry! is grown sae wise,
He douna chew the bitter cud of vice;
For gin, frae Castlehill to Netherbow,
Wad honest houses baudy-houses grow,
The crown wad never spier the price o' sin,
Nor hinder younkers to the de'il to rin;
But gif some mortal grien for pious fame,
And leave the poor man's pray'r to sane his name,
His geer maun a' be scatter'd by the claws
O' ruthless, ravenous, and harpy laws.
Yet, shou'd I think, altho' the bill tak place,
The council winna lack sae meikle grace
As lat our heritage at wanworth gang,
Or the succeeding generations wrang
O' braw bien maintenance and walth o' lear,
Whilk else had drappit to their children's skair;

cleed: clothe	callants: boys	weyms: bellies	duds:
clothes	targets: rags	back-gaun: needy	siller: silver
bien: ample	douna: dare not	spier: ask for	grien: yearn
sane: bless	geer: goods	meikle: much	at wanworth
gang: go worthless	lear: learning	skair: share	

For mony a deep, and mony a rare engyne
Ha'e sprung frae Herriot's wark, and sprung frae mine.

HERRIOT

I find, my friend, that ye but little ken,
There's einow on the earth a set o' men,
Wha, if they get their private pouches lin'd,
Gie na a winnelstrae for a' mankind;
They'll sell their country, flae their conscience bare,
To gar the weigh-bauk turn a single hair.
The government need only bait the line
Wi' the prevailing flee, the gowden coin,
Then our executors, and wise trustees,
Will sell them fishes in forbidden seas,
Upo' their dwining country girn in sport,
Laugh in their sleeve, and get a place at court.

WATSON

Ere that day come, I'll 'mang our spirits pick
Some ghaist that trokes and conjures wi' Auld Nick,
To gar the wind wi' rougher rumbles blaw,
And weightier thuds than ever mortal saw:
Fire-flaught and hail, wi' tenfald fury's fires,
Shall lay yird-laigh Edina's airy spires:
Tweed shall rin rowtin' down his banks out o'er,
Till Scotland's out o' reach o' England's pow'r;
Upo' the briny Borean jaws to float,
And mourn in dowy saughs her dowy lot.

---

engyne: genius   einow: even now   weigh-bauk: scales
flee: fly   dwining: dwindling   girn: complain   trokes:
deals   fire-flaught: lightning   yird-laigh: earth-low
rowtin': roaring   saughs: willows

HERRIOT

Yonder's the tomb of wise *Mackenzie* fam'd,
Whase laws rebellions bigotry reclaim'd,
Freed the hail land frae covenanting fools,
Wha erst ha'e fash'd us wi' unnumber'd dools;
Till night we'll tak the swaird aboon our pows,
And than, whan she her ebon chariot rows,
We'll travel to the vaut wi' stealing stap,
And wauk Mackenzie frae his quiet nap:
Tell him our ails, that he, wi' wonted skill,
May fleg the schemers o' the *mortmain-bill*.

> fash'd: annoyed   fleg: frighten

129 Epigram on a Lawyer's desiring one of the Tribe to look with respect to a Gibbet

THE Lawyers may revere that tree
  Where thieves so oft have swung,
Since, by the Law's most wise decree,
  Her thieves are never hung.

THOMAS MERCER

floruit 1770's

130   From *Arthur's Seat*

WHERE is the gallant race that rose
  Like old Antaeus on their foes?
Whose valour, thro the world renown'd,
Contracted oft the Roman bound;

And still to fierce invader gave
His father's fate, a bloody grave;
'Till Danish rover fear'd to land,
And, troubling, view'd the Scottish strand.

Where is the lofty spirit fled
Of Honour, Virtue, Freedom bred;
Indignant-spurning, English yoke;
And taught oppressors proud to yield
In many a well-contested field?
—Eclips'd, eclips'd, alas! appears
The glory of a thousand years!
Debas'd, debas'd the nation lyes
In gloom fanatic, cant, and lies!

JOHN MAYNE

1759–1836

131 *Logan Braes*

BY Logan's streams that rin sae deep
Fu' aft, wi' glee, I've herded sheep—
I've herded sheep, or gathered slaes
Wi' my dear lad on Logan Braes.
But wae 's my heart, thae days are gane
And fu' o' grief, I herd my lane,
While my dear lad maun face his faes,
Far, far frae me and Logan Braes.

aft: oft   slaes: sloes   my lane: alone   faes: foes

JOHN MAYNE

Nae mair, at Logan Kirk will he,
Atween the preachings, meet wi' me—
Meet wi' me, or, when it 's mirk,
Convoy me hame frae Logan Kirk.
I weel may sing, thae days are gane;
Frae kirk and fair I come alane,
While my dear lad maun face his faes,
Far, far frae me and Logan Braes.

At e'en, when hope amaist is gane,
I dander dowie and forlane,
Or sit beneath the trysting tree,
Where first he spak' o' love to me.
O! could I see thae days again,
My lover skaithless and my ain,
Revered by friends, and far frae faes,
We'd live in bliss on Logan Braes.

thae: those   dander: saunter   dowie: sad   forlane: forlorn
skaithless: harmless

ROBERT BURNS

1759–1796

132   *Address to the Deil*

O THOU! whatever title suit thee—
    Auld Hornie, Satan, Nick, or clootie—
Wha in yon cavern grim an' sootie,
            Clos'd under hatches,
Spairges about the brunstane cootie,
            To scaud poor wretches!

spairges: spatters   brunstane: brimstone   cootie: a vessel

Hear me, Auld Hangie, for a wee,
An' let poor, damnèd bodies be;
I'm sure sma' pleasure it can gie
    Ev'n to a deil,
To skelp an' scaud poor dogs like me
    An' hear us squeal.

Great is thy pow'r, an' great thy fame;
Far kend an' noted is thy name;
An' tho' yon lowan heugh's thy hame,
    Thou travels far;
An' faith! thou's neither lag, nor lame,
    Nor blate, nor scaur.

Whyles, ranging like a roaran lion,
For prey, a' holes an' corners tryin;
Whyles, on the strong-wing'd tempest flyin,
    Tirlan the kirks;
Whyles, in the human bosom pryin,
    Unseen thou lurks.

I've heard my rev'rend graunie say,
In lanely glens ye like to stray;
Or, where auld, ruin'd castles, grey
    Nod to the moon,
Ye fright the nightly wand'rer's way,
    Wi' eldritch croon.

When twilight did my graunie summon,
To say her pray'rs, douse, honest woman,
Aft yont the dyke she's heard you bumman
    Wi' eerie drone;
Or, rustlin, thro' the boortrees coman,
    Wi' heavy groan.

scaud: scald   heugh: hollow   blate: shy   scaur: scared
tirlan: striking   eldritch: unearthly   douse: decent   bumman: buzzing   boortrees: elder-trees

Ae dreary, windy, winter night,
The stars shot down wi' sklentan light,
Wi' you, mysel, I gat a fright:
     Ayont the lough,
Ye, like a rass-buss, stood in sight,
      Wi' waving sugh.

The cudgel in my nieve did shake,
Each bristl'd hair stood like a stake;
When wi' an eldritch stoor, 'quaick, quaick',
     Amang the springs,
Awa ye squatter'd like a drake,
      On whistling wings.

Let warlocks grim, an' wither'd hags,
Tell how wi' you, on ragweed nags,
They skim the muirs an' dizzy crags,
     Wi' wicked speed;
And in kirk-yards renew their leagues,
      Owre howkit dead.

Thence, countra wives, wi' toil an' pain,
May plunge an' plunge the kirn in vain;
For O! the yellow treasure's taen
     By witching skill;
An' dawtet, twal-pint hawkie's gane
      As yell's the bill.

Thence, mystic knots mak great abuse
On young guidmen, fond, keen an' croose;

sklentan: glancing   lough: lake   sugh: breeze-whisper
nieve: fist   stoor: noise   howkit: dug-up   kirn: churn
dawtet: petted   hawkie: cow   guidmen: husbands   croose:
confident

When the best wark-lume i' the house,
　　　By cantraip wit,
Is instant made no worth a louse,
　　　Just at the bit.

When thowes dissolve the snawy hoord,
An' float the jinglan icy boord,
Then, water-kelpies haunt the foord,
　　　By your direction,
An' nighted trav'llers are allured
　　　　To their destruction.

And aft your moss-traversing spunkies
Decoy the wight that late an' drunk is:
The bleezan, curst, mischievous monkies
　　　Delude his eyes,
Till in some miry slough he sunk is
　　　Ne'er mair to rise.

When Masons' mystic words an' grip
In storms an' tempests raise you up,
Some cock or cat your rage maun stop,
　　　Or, strange to tell,
The youngest brother ye wad whip
　　　Aff straught to Hell.

Lang syne in Eden's bonie yard,
When youthfu' lovers first were pair'd,
An' all the soul of love they shar'd,
　　　The raptur'd hour
Sweet on the fragrant flow'ry swaird,
　　　In shady bow'r;

| wark-lume: tool | cantraip: trick(y) | thowes: thaws |
| kelpies: water-spirits | spunkies: will-o'-the-wisps | |

Then you, ye auld, snick-drawing dog!
Ye cam to Paradise incog,
An' play'd on man a cursed brogue
   (Black be your fa'!),
An' gied the infant warld a shog,
   'Maist ruin'd a'.

D'ye mind that day when in a bizz
Wi' reeket duds, an' reestet gizz,
Ye did present your smoutie phiz
   'Mang better folk;
An' sklented on the man of Uzz
   Your spitefu' joke?

An' how ye gat him i' your thrall,
An' brak him out o' house an' hal',
While scabs an' botches did him gall,
   Wi' bitter claw;
An' lows'd his ill-tongu'd, wicked scaul—
   Was warst ava?

But a' your doings to rehearse,
Your wily snares an' fechtin fierce,
Sin' that day Michael did you pierce
   Down to this time,
Wad ding a Lallan tongue, or Erse,
   In prose or rhyme.

An' now, Auld Cloots, I ken ye're thinkan,
A certain Bardie's rantin, drinkin,
Some luckless hour will send him linkan
   To your black Pit;
But, faith! he'll turn a corner jinkan,
   An' cheat you yet.

brogue: trick   shog: jolt   smoutie phiz: smutty face
sklented on: turned upon   scaul: scold   ding: defeat

But fare-you-weel, Auld Nickie-Ben!
O, wad ye tak a thought an' men'!
Ye aiblins micht—I dinna ken—
      Still hae a stake:
I'm wae to think upo' yon den,
        Ev'n for your sake!

      aiblins: perhaps

133   *The Vision*

      [From *Duan first*]

THE sun had clos'd the winter-day,
   The Curlers quat their roaring play,
And hunger'd Maukin taen her way
      To kail-yards green,
While faithless snaws ilk step betray
      Whare she has been.

The Thresher's weary flingin-tree,
The lee-lang day had tir'd me;
And when the Day had clos'd his e'e,
      Far i' the West,
Ben i' the Spence, right pensivelie,
      I gaed to rest.

There, lanely, by the ingle-cheek,
I sat and ey'd the spewing reek,
That fill'd, wi' hoast-provoking smeek,
      The auld, clay biggin;
And heard the restless rattons squeak
      About the riggin.

quat: quitted   Maukin: a hare   kail-yards: cabbage-plots
flingin-tree: flail   spence: parlour   reek: smoke   biggin:
building   rattons: rats

All in this mottie, misty clime,
I backward mus'd on wasted time,
How I had spent my youthfu' prime
          An' done nae-thing,
But stringing blethers up in rhyme
          For fools to sing.

Had I to guid advice but harket,
I might, by this, hae led a market,
Or strutted in a Bank and clarket
          My Cast-Account;
While here, half-mad, half-fed, half-sarket,
          Is a' th' amount.

I started, mutt'ring blockhead! coof!
And heav'd on high my wauket loof,
To swear by a' yon starry roof,
          Or some rash aith,
That I, henceforth, would be rhyme-proof
          Till my last breath—

When click! the string the snick did draw;
And jee! the door gaed to the wa';
And by my ingle-lowe I saw,
          Now bleezan bright,
A tight, outlandish Hizzie braw,
          Come full in sight.

Ye need na doubt, I held my whisht;
The infant aith, half-form'd, was crusht;

mottie: cloudy   blethers: clap-trap   half-sarket: half-shirted
coof: fool   loof: palm   aith: oath   snick: latch   ingle-
lowe: fireplace flame   Hizzie: hussy   whisht: silence

369

I glowr'd as eerie's I'd been dusht,
        In some wild glen;
When sweet, like modest Worth, she blusht,
        And stepped ben.

Green, slender, leaf-clad Hollyboughs
Were twisted, gracefu', round her brows,
I took her for some SCOTTISH MUSE
        By that same token;
And come to stop those reckless vows,
        Would soon been broken.

A 'hare-brain'd, sentimental trace'
Was strongly marked in her face;
A wildly-witty, rustic grace
        Shone full upon her;
Her eye, ev'n turned on empty space,
        Beam'd keen with Honor.

Down flow'd her robe, a tartan sheen,
Till half a leg was scrimply seen;
And such a leg! my BESS, I ween,
        Could only peer it;
Sae straught, sae taper, tight and clean,
        Nane else came near it.

Her Mantle large, of greenish hue,
My gazing wonder chiefly drew;
Deep lights and shades, bold-mingling, threw
        A lustre grand;
And seem'd, to my astonish'd view,
        A well-known Land.

dusht: attacked   scrimply: barely

Here, rivers in the sea were lost;
There, mountains to the skies were tost:
Here, tumbling billows mark'd the coast,
      With surging foam;
There, distant shone, Art's lofty boast,
      The lordly dome.

Here, DOON pour'd down his far-fetch'd floods;
There, well-fed IRWINE stately thuds:
Auld hermit AIRE staw thro' his woods,
      On to the shore;
And many a lesser torrent scuds,
      With seeming roar.

Low, in a sandy valley spread,
An ancient BOROUGH rear'd her head;
Still, as in Scottish Story read,
      She boasts a Race,
To ev'ry nobler virtue bred,
      And polish'd grace.

134   *To a Mouse*

*On turning her up in her nest
with the plough, November 1785*

WEE, sleeket, cowran, tim'rous beastie,
    O, what a panic's in thy breastie!
Thou need na start awa sae hasty
      Wi' bickering brattle!
I wad be laith to rin an' chase thee,
      Wi' murdering pattle!

bickerin brattle: anxious chiding   pattle: plough-staff

I'm truly sorry man's dominion
Has broken Nature's social union,
An' justifies that ill opinion
  Which makes thee startle
At me, thy poor, earth-born companion
  An' fellow mortal!

I doubt na, whyles, but thou may thieve;
What then? poor beastie, thou maun live!
A daimen icker in a thrave
  'S a sma' request;
I'll get a blessin wi' the lave,
  An' never miss't!

Thy wee bit housie, too, in ruin!
Its silly wa's the win's are strewin!
An' naething, now, to big a new ane,
  O' foggage green!
An' bleak December's win's ensuin,
  Baith snell an' keen!

Thou saw the fields laid bare an' wast,
An' weary winter comin fast,
An' cozie here, beneath the blast,
  Thou thought to dwell,
Till crash! the cruel coulter past
  Out thro' thy cell.

That wee-bit heap o' leaves an' stibble,
Has cost thee monie a wearie nibble!

---

whyles: at times   daimen icker: stray ear   thrave: sheaf
lave: remainder   big: build   foggage: foliage   coulter:
plough-share blade

Now thou's turned out, for a' thy trouble,
    But house or hald,
To thole the winter's sleety dribble,
    An' cranreuch cauld!

But Mousie, thou art no thy lane,
In proving foresight may be vain:
The best-laid schemes o' Mice an' Men
    Gang aft agley,
An' lea'e us nocht but grief an pain,
    For promis'd joy!

Still thou art blest, compar'd wi' me!
The present only toucheth thee:
But och! I backward cast my e'e,
    On prospects drear!
An' forward, tho' I canna see,
    I guess an' fear!

hald: holding	thole: endure	cranreuch: frosty
no thy lane: not alone	gang aft agley: go aft awry	

135   *To a Louse*

*On seeing one on a Lady's
Bonnet at Church*

HA! whare ye gaun, ye crowlan ferlie!
  Your impudence protects you fairly:
I canna say but ye strunt rarely,
    Owre gawze and lace;
Tho' faith, I fear ye dine but sparely
    On sic a place.

crowlan ferlie: crawling wonder   strunt: strut

Ye ugly, creepan, blastet wonner,
Detestet, shunn'd, by saunt an' sinner,
How daur ye set your fit upon her,
      Sae fine a Lady!
Gae somewhere else and seek your dinner,
      On some poor body.

Swith, in some beggar's haffet squattle;
There ye may creep, and sprawl, and sprattle,
Wi' ither kindred, jumping cattle,
      In shoals and nations;
Whare horn nor bane ne'er daur unsettle
      Your thick plantations.

Now haud you there, ye're out o' sight,
Below the fatt'rels, snug and tight,
Na faith yet! ye'll no be right,
      Till ye've got on it,
The vera tapmost, towrin height
      O' Miss's bonnet.

My sooth! right bauld ye set your nose out,
As plump an' gray as onie grozet:
O for some rank, mercurial rozet,
      Or fell, red smeddum,
I'd gie you sic a hearty dose o't,
      Wad dress your droddum!

I wad na been surpriz'd to spy
You on an auld wife's flainen toy;

wonner: wonder, creature	fit: foot	swith: quick
haffet: whisker	fatt'rels: ribbons	grozet: gooseberry
rozet: resin	smeddum: a powder	droddum: backside
flainen toy: flannel mutch-cap		

Or aiblins some bit duddie boy,
        On's wylecoat;
But Miss's fine Lunardi, fye!
        How daur ye do't?

O Jenny dinna toss your head,
An' set your beauties a' abread!
Ye little ken what cursed speed
        The blastie's makin!
Thae winks and finger-ends, I dread,
        Are notice takin!

O wad some Pow'r the giftie gie us
To see oursels as others see us!
It wad frae monie a blunder free us
        An' foolish notion:
What airs in dress an' gait wad lea'e us,
        And ev'n Devotion!

aiblins: perhaps	duddie: ragged	wylecoat: waistcoat
a' abread: all abroad	blastie: dwarf	

136   *To William Simpson, Ochiltree*

I GAT your letter, winsome Willie;
Wi' gratefu' heart I thank you brawlie;
Tho' I maun say't, I wad be silly,
        An' unco vain,
Should I believe, my coaxin billie,
        Your flatterin strain.

billie: fellow

But I'se believe ye kindly meant it,
I sud be laith to think ye hinted
Ironic satire, sidelins sklented,
      On my poor Musie;
Tho' in sic phraisin terms ye've penn'd it,
      I scarce excuse ye.

My senses wad be in a creel,
Should I but dare a hope to speel,
Wi' Allan, or wi' Gilbertfield,
      The braes o' fame;
Or Ferguson, the writer-chiel,
      A deathless name.

(O Ferguson! thy glorious parts,
Ill-suited law's dry, musty arts!
My curse upon your whunstane hearts,
      Ye Enbrugh Gentry!
The tythe o' what ye waste at cartes
      Wad stow'd his pantry!)

Yet when a tale comes i' my head,
Or lasses gie my heart a screed,
As whiles they're like to be my dead,
      (O sad disease!)
I kittle up my rustic reed;
      It gies me ease.

Auld COILA, now, may fidge fu' fain,
She's gotten Bardies o' her ain,

sklented: angled   phraisin: flattering   creel: basket   speel:
climb   cartes: cards   screed: turn   kittle: tickle

Chiels wha their chanters winna hain,
   But tune their lays,
Till echoes a' resound again
   Her weel-sung praise.

Nae Poet thought her worth his while,
To set her name in measur'd style;
She lay like some unkend-of isle
   Beside New Holland,
Or whare wild-meeting oceans boil
   Besouth Magellan.

Ramsay an' famous Ferguson
Gied Forth an' Tay a lift aboon;
Yarrow an' Tweed, to mony a tune
   Owre Scotland rings,
While Irwin, Lugar, Aire, an' Doon,
   Naebody sings.

Th' Illissus, Tiber, Thames an' Seine,
Glide sweet in monie a tunefu' line;
But Willie set your fit to mine,
   An' cock your crest,
We'll gar our streams an' burnies shine
   Up wi' the best.

We'll sing auld Coila's plains an' fells,
Her moors red brown wi' heather bells,
Her banks an' braes, her dens an' dells,
   Where glorious WALLACE
Aft bure the gree, as story tells,
   Frae Suthron billies.

hain: spare   bure the gree: bore off the prize

ROBERT BURNS

At WALLACE' name, what Scottish blood,
But boils up in a spring-time flood!
Oft have our fearless fathers strode
      By WALLACE' side,
Still pressing onward, red-wat-shod,
      Or glorious dy'd!

O sweet are COILA's haughs an' woods,
When lintwhites chant amang the buds,
And jinkin hares, in amorous whids,
      Their loves enjoy,
While thro' the braes the cushat croods
      With wailfu' cry!

Ev'n winter bleak has charms to me
When winds rave thro' the naked tree;
Or frosts on hills of Ochiltree
      Are hoary gray;
Or blinding drifts wild-furious flee,
      Dark'ning the day!

O NATURE! a' thy shews an' forms
To feeling, pensive hearts hae charms!
Whether the Summer kindly warms,
      Wi' life an' light,
Or Winter howls, in gusty storms,
      The lang, dark night!

The Muse, nae Poet ever fand her,
Till by himsel he learn'd to wander,
Adown some trottin burn's meander
      An' no think lang;
O sweet, to stray an' pensive ponder
      A heart-felt sang!

haughs: meadows   lintwhites: linnets   croods: croons

The warly race may drudge an' drive,
Hog-shouther, jundie, stretch an' strive,
Let me fair NATURE's face descrive,
              And I, wi' pleasure,
Shall let the busy, grumbling hive
              Bum owre their treasure.

Fareweel, 'my rhyme-composing' brither!
We've been owre lang unkenn'd to ither:
Now let us lay our heads thegither
              In love fraternal:
May Envy wallop in a tether,
              Black fiend, infernal!

While Highlandmen hate tolls an' taxes;
While moorlan herds like guid, fat braxies;
While Terra firma, on her axis,
              Diurnal turns,
Count on a friend, in faith an' practice,
              In ROBERT BURNS.

              jundie: jostle   braxies: sheep

137   *Death and Doctor Hornbook*

                    A true Story

SOME books are lies frae end to end,
    And some great lies were never penn'd:
Ev'n ministers, they hae been kend,
              In holy rapture,
A rousing whid at times to vend,
              And nail't wi' Scripture.

              whid: lie

But this that I am gaun to tell,
Which lately on a night befel,
Is just as true's the Deil's in hell
        Or Dublin city:
That e'er he nearer comes oursel
        'S a muckle pity!

The clachan yill had made me canty,
I was na fou, but just had plenty:
I stacher'd whyles, but took tent ay
        To free the ditches;
An' hillocks, stanes, an' bushes, kend ay
        Frae ghaists an' witches.

The rising moon began to glowr
The distant Cumnock Hills out-owre:
To count her horns, wi' a' my pow'r
        I set mysel;
But whether she had three or four
        I cou'd na tell.

I was come round about the hill,
And todlin down on Willie's mill,
Setting my staff wi' a' my skill
        To keep me sicker;
Tho' leeward whyles, against my will,
        I took a bicker.

I there wi' *Something* does forgather,
That pat me in an eerie swither;
An awfu' scythe, out-owre ae shouther,
        Clear-dangling, hang;
A three-tae'd leister on the ither
        Lay, large and lang.

yill: ale   fou: drunk   tent: care   bicker: lurch   swither:
doubt   leister: trident

380

Its stature seem'd lang Scotch ells twa;
The queerest shape that e'er I saw,
For fient a wame it had ava;
        And then its shanks,
They were as thin, as sharp an' sma'
        As cheeks o' branks.

'Guid-een,' quo I; 'Friend! hae ye been mawin,
When ither folk are busy sawin?'
It seem'd to mak a kind o' stan',
        But naething spak.
At length, says I: 'Friend! whare ye gaun?
        Will ye go back?'

It spak right howe: 'My name is Death,
But be na' fley'd.' Quoth I: 'Guid faith,
Ye're may be come to stap my breath;
        But tent me, billie:
I red ye weel, take care o' skaith,
        See, there's a gully!'

'Gudeman,' quo' he, 'put up your whittle,
I'm no design'd to try its mettle;
But if I did, I wad be kittle
        To be mislear'd:
I wad na mind it, no that spittle
        Out-owre my beard.'

'Weel, weel!' says I, 'a bargain be't;
Come, gie's your hand, an' say we're gree't:

---

fient a wame, etc.: no belly it had at all   branks: bridles   howe:
hollow   fley'd: afraid   red: advise   skaith: hurt   whittle:
knife   kittle: amused

We'll ease our shanks, an' tak a seat:
        Come, gie's your news:
This while ye hae been monie a gate,
        At monie a house.'

'Ay, ay!' quo' he, an' shook his head,
'It 's e'en a lang, lang time indeed
Sin' I began to nick the thread
        An' choke the breath:
Folk maun do something for their bread,
        An' sae maun Death.

'Sax thousand years are near-hand fled
Sin' I was to the butching bred,
An' monie a scheme in vain's been laid
        To stap or scar me;
Till ane Hornbook's ta'en up the trade,
        And faith! he'll waur me.

'Ye ken Jock Hornbook i' the clachan?
Deil mak his king's-hood in a spleuchan!—
He's grown sae weel acquaint wi' *Buchan*
        And ither chaps,
The weans haud out their fingers laughin,
        An' pouk my hips.

'See, here 's a scythe, an' there 's a dart,
They hae pierc'd monie a gallant heart;
But Doctor Hornbook wi' his art
        An' cursed skill,
Has made them baith no worth a fart,
        Damn'd haet they'll kill!

maun: must   waur: outdo   haet: jot

' 'Twas but yestreen, nae farther gane,
I threw a noble throw at ane;
Wi' less, I'm sure, I've hundreds slain;
   But Deil-ma-care!
It just played dirl on the bane,
   But did nae mair.

'Hornbook was by wi' ready art,
An' had sae fortify'd the part,
That when I lookèd to my dart,
   It was sae blunt,
Fient haet o't wad hae pierced the heart
   Of a kail-runt.

'I drew my scythe in sic a fury,
I near-hand cowpit wi' my hurry,
But yet the bauld Apothecary
   Withstood the shock:
I might as well hae try'd a quarry
   O' hard whin-rock.

'Ev'n them he canna get attended,
Altho' their face he ne'er had kend it,
Just shit in a kail-blade an' send it,
   As soon's he smells't,
Baith their disease and what will mend it,
   At once he tells't.

'And then a' doctors saws and whittles
Of a' dimensions, shapes, an' mettles,
A' kinds o' boxes, mugs, and bottles,
   He's sure to hae;
Their Latin names as fast he rattles
   As A B C.

kail-runt: cabbage-stalk   cowpit: upset

'Calces o' fossils, earth, and trees;
True *sal-marinum* o' the seas;
The *farina* of beans an' pease,
   He has't in plenty;
Aqua-fontis, what you please,
   He can content ye.

'Forbye some new, uncommon weapons,
Urinus spiritus of capons;
Or mite-horn shavings, filings, scrapings,
   Distill'd *per se*;
Sal-alkali o' midge-tail-clippings,
   And monie mae.'

'Waes me for Johnie Ged's Hole now,'
Quoth I, 'if that thae news be true!
His braw calf-ward where gowans grew
   Sae white and bonie,
Nae doubt they'll rive it wi' the plew:
   They'll ruin Johnie!'

The creature grain'd an eldritch laugh,
And says: 'Ye nedna yoke the pleugh,
Kirkyards will soon be till'd eneugh,
   Tak ye nae fear:
They'll a' be trenched wi monie a sheugh
   In twa-three year.

'Whare I kill'd ane, a fair strae death
By loss o' blood or want o' breath,
This night I'm free to tak my aith,
   That Hornbook's skill
Has clad a score i' their last claith
   By drap an' pill.

gowans: daisies rive: tear eldritch: unearthly sheugh:
drill strae: straw drap: drop

'An honest wabster to his trade,
Whase wife's twa nieves were scarce weel-bred,
Gat tippence-worth to mend her head
      When it was sair;
The wife slade cannie to her bed
      But ne'er spak mair.

'A countra laird had taen the batts,
Or some curmurring in his guts,
His only son for Hornbook sets,
      An' pays him well:
The lad, for twa guid gimmer-pets,
      Was laird himsel.

'A bonie lass—ye kend her name—
Some ill-brewn drink had hoved her wame;
She trusts hersel, to hide the shame,
      In Hornbook's care;
Horn sent her aff to her lang hame
      To hide it there.

'That's just a swatch o' Hornbook's way;
Thus goes he on from day to day,
Thus does he poison, kill, an' slay,
      An's weel paid for't;
Yet stops me o' my lawfu' prey
      Wi' his damn'd dirt:

'But hark! I'll tell you of a plot,
Tho' dinna ye be speakin o't:

wabster: weaver   nieves: fists   slade cannie: slid gently   batts:
colic   curmurring: rumbling   gimmer-pets: ewes   hoved:
swelled

I'll nail the self-conceited sot,
   As dead's a herrin;
Neist time we meet, I'll wad a groat,
   He gets his fairin!'

But just as he began to tell,
The auld kirk-hammer strak the bell
Some wee short hour ayont the twal,
   Which raised us baith:
I took the way that pleas'd mysel,
   And sae did Death.

    groat: small coin

138   *Address to the Unco Guid*

 MY son, these maxims make a rule,
  An' lump them ay thegither:
 The Rigid Righteous is a fool,
  The Rigid Wise anither;
 The cleanest corn that e'er was dight
  May hae some pyles o' caff in;
 So ne'er a fellow-creature slight
  For random fits o' daffin.

     SOLOMON (Eccles. vii. 16)

O YE, wha are sae guid yoursel,
  Sae pious and sae holy,
Ye've nought to do but mark and tell
  Your neebours' fauts and folly;
Whase life is like a weel-gaun mill,
  Supplied wi' store o' water;
The heapet happer 's ebbing still,
  An' still the clap plays clatter!

 caff: chaff   daffin: dalliance   happer: hopper

Hear me, ye venerable core,
 As counsel for poor mortals
That frequent pass douce Wisdom's door
 For glaikit Folly's portals:
I for their thoughtless, careless sakes
 Would here propone defences—
Their donsie tricks, their black mistakes,
 Their failings and mischances.

Ye see your state wi' theirs compared,
 And shudder at the niffer;
But cast a moment's fair regard,
 What makes the mighty differ?
Discount what scant occasion gave;
 That purity ye pride in;
And (what's aft mair than a' the lave)
 Your better art o' hidin.

Think, when your castigated pulse
 Gies now and then a wallop,
What ragings must his veins convulse,
 That still eternal gallop!
Wi' wind and tide fair i' your tail,
 Right on ye scud your sea-way;
But in the teeth o' baith to sail,
 It maks an unco lee-way.

See Social-life and Glee sit down
 All joyous and unthinking,
Till, quite transmugrify'd, they're grown
 Debauchery and Drinking:

glaikit: moronic   donsie: smart   niffer: difference

O, would they stay to calculate,
　Th'eternal consequences,
Or—your more dreaded hell to state—
　Damnation of expenses!

Ye high, exalted, virtuous dames,
　Tied up in godly laces,
Before ye gie poor Frailty names,
　Suppose a change o' cases:
A dear-lov'd lad, convenience snug,
　A treach'rous inclination—
But, let me whisper i' your lug,
　Ye're aiblins nae temptation.

Then gently scan your brother man,
　Still gentler sister woman;
Tho' they may gang a kennin wrang,
　To step aside is human:
One point must still be greatly dark,
　The moving *why* they do it;
And just as lamely can ye mark
　How far perhaps they rue it.

Who made the heart, 'tis He alone
　Decidedly can try us:
He knows each chord, its various tone
　Each spring, its various bias:
Then at the balance let's be mute,
　We never can adjust it;
What's done we partly may compute,
　But know not what's resisted.

　　　　lug: ear　　　　aiblins: perhaps

388

Tam o' Shanter

A Tale

> Of Brownys and of Bogillis full is this Buke.
> Gawin Douglas.

WHEN chapman billies leave the street,
  And drouthy neebors neebors meet;
As market-days are wearing late,
An' folk begin to tak the gate;
While we sit bousing at the nappy,
An' getting fou and unco happy,
We think na on the lang Scots miles,
The mosses, waters, slaps, and styles,
That lie between us and our hame
Whare sits our sulky sullen dame,
Gathering her brows like gathering storm,
Nursing her wrath to keep it warm.
This truth fand honest Tam o' Shanter,
As he frae Ayr ae night did canter:
(Auld Ayr, wham ne'er a town surpasses,
For honest men and bonie lasses).

O Tam, had'st thou but been sae wise,
As taen thy ain wife Kate's advice!
She tauld thee weel thou was a skellum,
A blethering, blustering, drunken blellum;
That frae November till October,
Ae market-day thou was na sober;
That ilka melder wi' the miller,
Thou sat as lang as thou had siller;

chapman billies: hawkers   drouthy: thirsty   gate: way
nappy: ale   skellum: no-good   blellum: babbler   melder:
grain-lot

That ev'ry naig was ca'd a shoe on,
The smith and thee gat roaring fou on;
That at the Lord's house, even on Sunday,
Thou drank wi' Kirkton Jean till Monday.
She prophesied, that, late or soon,
Thou would be found deep drown'd in Doon,
Or catch'd wi' warlocks in the mirk
By Alloway's auld, haunted kirk.

Ah! gentle dames, it gars me greet,
To think how monie counsels sweet,
How monie lengthen'd, sage advices
The husband frae the wife despises!

But to our tale:— Ae market-night,
Tam had got planted unco right,
Fast by an ingle, bleezing finely,
Wi' reaming swats, that drank divinely;
And at his elbow, Souter Johnie,
His ancient, trusty, drouthy cronie:
Tam lo'ed him like a very brither;
They had been fou for weeks thegither.
The night drave on wi' sangs and clatter;
And ay the ale was growing better:
The landlady and Tam grew gracious
Wi' secret favours, sweet and precious:
The Souter tauld his queerest stories;
The landlord's laugh was ready chorus:
The storm without might rair and rustle,
Tam did na mind the storm a whistle.

ca'd: knocked　　　gars: compels　　　greet: weep　　　reaming
swats: frothing drinks　　　Souter: shoemaker　　　cronie: comrade
clatter: chat

Care, mad to see a man sae happy,
E'en drown'd himsel amang the nappy.
As bees flee hame wi' lades o' treasure,
The minutes wing'd their way wi' pleasure:
Kings may be blest but Tam was glorious,
O'er a' the ills o' life victorious!

But pleasures are like poppies spread:
You seize the flow'r, its bloom is shed;
Or like the snow falls in the river,
A moment white—then melts for ever;
Or like the borealis race,
That flit ere you can point their place;
Or like the rainbow's lovely form
Evanishing amid the storm.
Nae man can tether time or tide;
The hour approaches Tam maun ride:
That hour, o' night's black arch the key-stane,
That dreary hour Tam mounts his beast in,
And sic a night he taks the road in,
As ne'er poor sinner was abroad in.

The wind blew as 'twad blawn its last;
The rattling showers rose on the blast;
The speedy gleams the darkness swallow'd;
Loud, deep, and lang the thunder bellow'd:
That night, a child might understand,
The Deil had business on his hand.

Weel mounted on his gray mare Meg,
A better never lifted leg,
Tam skelpit on thro' dub and mire,
Despising wind, and rain, and fire;
Whiles holding fast his guid blue bonnet,
Whiles crooning o'er some auld Scots sonnet,

Whiles glow'ring round wi' prudent cares,
Lest bogles catch him unawares:
Kirk-Alloway was drawing nigh,
Whare ghaists and houlets nightly cry.

By this time he was cross the ford,
Whare in the snaw the chapman smoor'd;
And past the birks and meikle stane,
Whare drunken Charlie brak's neck-bane;
And thro' the whins, and by the cairn,
Where hunters fand the murder'd bairn;
And near the thorn, aboon the well,
Whare Mungo's mither hang'd hersel.
Before him Doon pours all his floods;
The doubling storm roars thro' the woods;
The lightnings flash from pole to pole;
Near and more near the thunders roll:
When, glimmering thro' the groaning trees,
Kirk-Alloway seem'd in a bleeze,
Thro' ilka bore the beams were glancing,
And loud resounded mirth and dancing.

Inspiring bold John Barleycorn,
What dangers thou canst make us scorn!
Wi' tippenny, we fear nae evil;
Wi' usquabae, we'll face the Devil!
The swats sae reamed in Tammie's noddle,
Fair play, he car'd na deils a boddle.
But Maggie stood, right sair astonish'd,
Till, by the heel and hand admonish'd,
She ventur'd forward on the light;
And, wow! Tam saw an unco sight!

houlets: owls   smoor'd: smothered   birks: birches
tippenny: beer   usquabae: whisky   boddle: small coin

Warlocks and witches in a dance:
Nae cotillion, brent new frae France,
But hornpipes, jigs, strathspeys, and reels,
Put life and mettle in their heels.
A winnock-bunker in the east,
There sat Auld Nick, in shape o' beast;
A tousie tyke, black, grim, and large,
To gie them music was his charge:
He screw'd the pipes and gart them skirl,
Till roof and rafters a' did dirl.
Coffins stood round, like open presses,
That shaw'd the dead in their last dresses;
And, by some devilish cantraip sleight,
Each in its cauld hand held a light:
By which heroic Tam was able
To note upon the haly table,
A murderer's banes, in gibbet-airns;
Twa span-lang, wee, unchristen'd bairns;
A thief new-cutted frae a rape—
Wi' his last gasp his gab did gape;
Five tomahawks wi' bluid red-rusted;
Five scimitars wi' murder crusted;
A garter which a babe had strangled;
A knife a father's throat had mangled—
Whom his ain son o' life bereft—
The grey hairs yet stack to the heft;
Wi' mair o' horrible and awfu',
Which even to name wad be unlawfu'.
Three lawyers' tongues, turned inside out,
Wi' lies seamed like a beggar's clout;
Three Priests' hearts, rotten, black as muck,
Lay stinking, vile, in every neuk.

winnock-bunker: window-seat   tyke: cur   dirl: resound
cantraip: trick   airns: irons   rape: rope

As Tammie glowr'd, amazed, and curious,
The mirth and fun grew fast and furious;
The piper loud and louder blew,
The dancers quick and quicker flew,
They reel'd, they set, they cross'd, they cleekit,
Till ilka carlin swat and reekit,
And coost her duddies to the wark,
And linket at it in her sark!

Now Tam, O Tam! had thae been queans,
A' plump and strapping in their teens!
Their sarks, instead o' creeshie flannen,
Been snaw-white seventeen hunder linen!—
Thir breeks o' mine, my only pair,
That ance were plush, o' guid blue hair,
I wad hae gi'en them off my hurdies
For ae blink o' the bonie burdies!

But wither'd beldams, auld and droll,
Rigwoodie hags wad spean a foal,
Louping and flinging on a crummock,
I wonder did na turn thy stomach!

But Tam kend what was what fu' brawlie:
There was ae winsome wench and wawlie,
That night enlisted in the core,
Lang after kend on Garrick shore
(For monie a beast to dead she shot,
An' perish'd monie a bonie boat,
And shook baith meikle corn and bear
And kept the country-side in fear).

swat: sweated   reekit: steamed   duddies: rags   sark:
shirt   creeshie flannen: greasy flannel   hurdies: hips   rigwoodie:
stringy   spean: wean   crummock: staff   wawlie: spirited
bear: barley

Her cutty sark, o' Paisley harn,
That while a lassie she had worn,
In longitude tho' sorely scanty,
It was her best, and she was vauntie. . . .
Ah! little kend thy reverend grannie,
That sark she coft for her wee Nannie,
Wi' twa pund Scots ('twas a' her riches),
Wad ever grac'd a dance o' witches!

But here my Muse her wing maun cour,
Sic flights are far beyond her power:
To sing how Nannie lap and flang
(A souple jad she was and strang),
And how Tam stood like ane bewitch'd,
And thought his very een enrich'd;
Ev'n Satan glowr'd, and fidg'd fu' fain,
And hotch'd and blew wi' might and main;
Till first ae caper, syne anither,
Tam tint his reason a' thegither,
And roars out: 'Weel done, Cutty-sark!'
And in an instant all was dark;
And scarcely had he Maggie rallied,
When out the hellish legion sallied.

As bees bizz out wi' angry fyke,
When plundering herds assail their byke;
As open pussie's mortal foes,
When, pop! she starts before their nose;
As eager runs the market-crowd,
When 'Catch the thief!' resounds aloud:
So Maggie runs, the witches follow,
Wi' monie an eldritch skriech and hollo.

cutty sark: short shirt   harn: linen   vauntie: proud   coft: bought
cour: cower   fidg'd: itched   fyke: fuss   byke: hive
pussie: a hare   eldritch: unearthly

Ah, Tam! Ah, Tam! thou'll get thy fairin!
In hell they'll roast thee like a herrin!
In vain thy Kate awaits thy comin!
Kate soon will be a woefu' woman!
Now, do thy speedy utmost, Meg,
And win the key-stane of the brig;
There, at them thou thy tail may toss,
A running stream they dare na cross!
But ere the key-stane she could make,
The fient a tail she had to shake;
For Nannie, far before the rest,
Hard upon noble Maggie prest,
And flew at Tam wi' furious ettle;
But little wist she Maggie's mettle!
Ae spring brought off her master hale,
But left behind her ain grey tail:
The carlin claught her by the rump,
And left poor Maggie scarce a stump.

Now, wha this tale o' truth shall read,
Ilk man, and mother's son, take heed:
Whene'er to drink you are inclin'd,
Or cutty sarks run in your mind,
Think! ye may buy the joys o'er dear:
Remember Tam o' Shanter's mare.

fairin: reward   fient a tail: no tail   ettle: intent   carlin: witch

Holy Willie's Prayer

And send the godly in a pet to pray. Pope.

O THOU that in the Heavens dost dwell,
   Wha, as it pleases best Thysel,
Sends ane to Heaven an' ten to Hell
      A' for thy glory,
And no for onie guid or ill
      They've done before Thee!

I bless and praise Thy matchless might,
When thousands Thou has left in night,
That I am here before Thy sight
      For gifts an' grace
A burning and a shining light
      To a' this place.

What was I, or my generation,
That I should get sic exaltation?
I, wha deserv'd most just damnation
      For broken laws
Sax thousand years ere my creation,
      Thro' Adam's cause!

When from my mither's womb I fell,
Thou might hae plung'd me deep in hell
To gnash my gooms, and weep, and wail
      In burning lakes,
Where damned devils roar and yell,
      Chain'd to their stakes.

    onie: any   gooms: gums

Yet I am here, a chosen sample,
To show Thy grace is great and ample:
I'm here a pillar o' Thy temple,
      Strong as a rock,
A guide, a buckler, and example
      To a' Thy flock!

But yet, O Lord! confess I must:
At times I'm fash'd wi' fleshly lust;
An' sometimes, too, in warldly trust
      Vile self gets in;
But Thou remembers we are dust,
      Defiled wi' sin.

O Lord! yestreen, Thou kens, wi' Meg—
Thy pardon I sincerely beg—
O, may't ne'er be a living plague
      To my dishonour!
An' I'll ne'er lift a lawless leg
      Again upon her.

Besides, I farther maun avow—
Wi' Leezie's lass, three times, I trow—
But, Lord, that Friday I was fou,
      When I cam near her,
Or else, Thou kens, Thy servant true
      Wad never steer her.

Maybe Thou lets this fleshly thorn
Buffet Thy servant e'en and morn,
Lest he owre-proud and high should turn
      That he's sae gifted:
If sae, Thy han' maun e'en be borne
      Until Thou lift it.

fash'd: troubled   fou: drunk

Lord, bless Thy chosen in this place,
For here Thou has a chosen race!
But God confound their stubborn face
      An' blast their name,
Wha brings Thy elders to disgrace
      An' open shame!

Lord, mind Gau'n Hamilton's deserts:
He drinks, an' swears, an' plays at cartes,
Yet has sae monie takin arts
      Wi' great and sma',
Frae God's ain Priest the people's hearts
      He steals awa.

And when we chasten'd him therefore,
Thou kens how he bred sic a splore,
And set the warld in a roar
      O' laughin at us:
Curse Thou his basket and his store,
      Kail an' potatoes!

Lord, hear my earnest cry and pray'r
Against that Presbyt'ry of Ayr!
Thy strong right hand, Lord, make it bare
      Upo' their heads!
Lord, visit them, an' dinna spare
      For their misdeeds!

O Lord, my God! that glib-tongu'd Aiken,
My vera heart and flesh are quakin
To think how we stood sweatin, shakin,
      An' pish'd wi' dread,
While he, wi' hingin lip an' snakin,
      Held up his head.

cartes: cards   splore: riot

Lord, in Thy day o' vengeance try him!
Lord, visit him wha did employ him!
And pass not in Thy mercy by them
        Nor hear their pray'r,
But for Thy people's sake destroy them,
        An' dinna spare!

But Lord, remember me and mine
Wi' mercies temporal and divine,
That I for grace an' gear may shine
        Excell'd by nane;
And a' the glory shall be Thine—
        Amen, Amen!

141   *Corn Riggs*

IT was upon a Lammas night
  When corn riggs are bonie,
Beneath the moon's unclouded light,
  I held awa to Annie:
The time flew by, wi' tentless heed,
  Till 'tween the late and early;
Wi' sma' persuasion she agreed,
  To see me thro' the barley.

The sky was blue, the wind was still,
  The moon was shining clearly;
I set her down, wi' right good will,
  Amang the rigs o' barley:
I ken't her heart wa a' my ain;
  I lov'd her most sincerely;
I kiss'd her owre and owre again,
  Amang the rigs o' barley.

       riggs: fields   tentless: careless

I lock'd her in my fond embrace;
   Her heart was beating rarely:
My blessing on that happy place,
   Amang the rigs o' barley!
But by the moon and stars so bright,
   That shone that night so clearly!
She ay shall bless that happy night,
   Amang the rigs o' barley.

I hae been blythe wi' comrades dear;
   I hae been merry drinking;
I hae been joyfu' gath'rin gear;
   I hae been happy thinking:
But a' the pleasures e'er I saw,
   Tho' three times doubl'd fairly,
That happy night was worth them a',
   Amang the rigs o' barley.

    Corn rigs, an' barley rigs,
      An' corn rigs are bonie:
    I'll ne'er forget that happy night,
      Amang the rigs wi' Annie.

       gear: goods

142   *Of A' the Airts*

OF a' the airts the wind can blaw
   I dearly like the west,
For there the bonie lassie lives,
   The lassie I lo'e best.
There wild woods grow, and rivers row,
   And monie a hill between,
But day and night my fancy's flight
   Is ever wi' my Jean.

   airts: points of compass   row: roll

I see her in the dewy flowers—
  I see her sweet and fair.
I hear her in the tunefu' birds—
  I hear her charm the air.
There's not a bonie flower that springs
  By fountain, shaw, or green,
There's not a bonie bird that sings,
  But minds me o' my Jean.

shaw: grove

143   *Whistle O'er the Lave o't*

FIRST when Maggie was my care,
  Heav'n I thought, was in her air;
Now we're married, spier nae mair,
  But—whistle o'er the lave o't!
Meg was meek, and Meg was mild,
Sweet and harmless as a child:
Wiser men than me's beguiled—
  Whistle o'er the lave o't!

How we live, my Meg and me,
How we love, and how we gree,
I care na by how few may see—
  Whistle o'er the lave o't!
Wha I wish were maggot's meat,
Dish'd up in her winding-sheet,
I could write (but Meg wad see't)—
  Whistle o'er the lave o't.

spier: inquire   lave: rest   care na by: care nothing

ROBERT BURNS

144 *Willie Brew'd a Peck o' Maut*

O WILLIE brew'd a peck o' maut,
    And Rob and Allan cam to see.
Three blyther hearts that lee-lang night
    Ye wad na found in Christendie.

We are na fou, we're nae that fou,
    But just a drappie in our e'e!
The cock may craw, the day may daw,
    And ay we'll taste the barley-bree!

Here are we met three merry boys,
    Three merry boys I trow are we;
And monie a night we've merry been,
    And monie mae we hope to be!

It is the moon, I ken her horn,
    That's blinkin in the lift sae hie:
She shines sae bright to wyle us hame,
    But, by my sooth, she'll wait a wee!

Wha first shall rise to gang awa,
    A cuckold, coward loun is he!
Wha first beside his chair shall fa',
    He is the King amang us three!

maut: malt   fou: drunk   bree: broth   wyle: entice

145 *Tam Glen*

MY heart is a-breaking, dear tittie,
    Some counsel unto me come len'.
To anger them a' is a pity,
    But what will I do wi' Tam Glen?

tittie: sister

403

I'm thinking, wi' sic a braw fellow,
    In poortith I might mak a fen'.
What care I in riches to wallow,
    If I mauna marry Tam Glen?

There's Lowrie the laird o' Dumeller:
    'Guid day to you', brute! he comes ben.
He brags and he blaws o' his siller,
    But when will he dance like Tam Glen?

My minnie does constantly deave me,
    And bids me beware o' young men.
They flatter, she says, to deceive me—
    But wha can think sae o' Tam Glen?

My daddie says, gin I'll forsake him,
    He'd gie guid hunder marks ten.
But if it's ordain'd I maun take him,
    O' wha will I get but Tam Glen?

Yestreen at the valentines' dealing,
    My heart to my mou gied a sten,
For thrice I drew ane without failing,
    And thrice it was written 'Tam Glen'!

The last Halloween I was waukin
    My droukit sark-sleeve, as ye ken—
His likeness came up the house staukin,
    And the very grey breeks o' Tam Glen!

Come, counsel, dear tittie, don't tarry!
    I'll gie ye my bonie black hen,
Gif ye will advise me to marry
    The lad I lo'e dearly, Tam Glen.

poortith: poverty   mak' a fen: manage   minnie: mother
deave: harp at   sten: start   waukin: drying   droukit: drenched

146   *Such a Parcel of Rogues in a Nation*

FAREWEEL to a' our Scottish fame,
    Fareweel our ancient glory!
Fareweel ev'n to the Scottish name,
    Sae famed in martial story!
Now Sark rins over Solway sands,
    An' Tweed rins to the ocean,
To mark where England's province stands—
    Such a parcel of rogues in a nation!

What force or guile could not subdue
    Thro' many warlike ages
Is wrought now by a coward few
    For hireling traitor's wages.
The English steel we could disdain,
    Secure in valour's station;
But English gold has been our bane—
    Such a parcel of rogues in a nation!

O, would, or I had seen the day
    That Treason thus could sell us,
My auld grey head had lien in clay
    Wi' Bruce and loyal Wallace!
But pith and power, till my last hour
    I'll mak this declaration:—
'We're bought and sold for English gold'—
    Such a parcel of rogues in a nation!

147 *A Red, Red, Rose*

O MY luve is like a red, red rose,
   That's newly sprung in June.
O, my luve is like the melodie,
   That's sweetly play'd in tune.

As fair art thou, my bonnie lass,
   So deep in luve am I,
And I will luve thee still, my dear,
   Till a' the seas gang dry.

Till a' the seas gang dry, my dear,
   And the rocks melt wi' the sun!
And I will luve thee still, my dear,
   While the sands o' life shall run.

And fare thee weel, my only luve,
   And fare thee weel a while!
And I will come again, my luve,
   Tho' it were ten thousand mile!

148 *Comin Thro' the Rye*

C OMIN thro' the rye, poor body
   Comin thro' the rye,
She draigl't a' her petticoatie,
   Comin thro' the rye!

   O, Jenny's a' weet, poor body,
      Jenny's seldom dry:
   She draigl't a' her petticoatie,
      Comin thro' the rye!

draigl't: bemired   body: person

406

Gin a body meet a body
    Comin thro' the rye,
Gin a body kiss a body,
    Need a body cry?

O, Jenny 's a' weet, etc.

Gin a body meet a body
    Comin thro' the glen,
Gin a body kiss a body,
    Need the warld ken?

O, Jenny 's a' weet, etc.

149   *Saw Ye Bonie Lesley*

O SAW ye bonie Lesley,
    As she gaed o'er the Border?
She's gane, like Alexander,
    To spread her conquests farther!

To see her is to love her,
    And love but her for ever;
For Nature made her what she is,
    And never made anither!

Thou art a queen, fair Lesley—
    Thy subjects, we before thee!
Thou art divine, fair Lesley—
    The hearts o' men adore thee.

The Deil he could na skaith thee,
　　Or aught that wad belang thee:
He'd look into thy bonie face,
　　And say:— 'I canna wrang thee!'

The Powers aboon will tent thee,
　　Misfortune sha'na steer thee:
Thou'rt like themsel' sae lovely,
　　That ill they'll ne'er let near thee.

Return again, fair Lesley,
　　Return to Caledonie!
That we may brag we hae a lass
　　There's nane again sae bonie.

　　skaith: harm　　　　tent: tend

150　　　*A Man's a Man For A' That*

IS there for honest poverty
　　That hings his head, an' a' that?
The coward slave, we pass him by—
　　We dare be poor for a' that!
For a' that, an' a' that!
　　Our toils obscure, an' a' that,
The rank is but the guinea's stamp,
　　The man 's the gowd for a' that.

What though on hamely fare we dine,
　　Wear hoddin grey an' a' that?
Gie fools their silks, and knaves their wine—
　　A man's a man for a' that.

　　　　hoddin grey: tweed

For a' that, an' a' that,
  Their tinsel show, an' a' that,
The honest man, tho' e'er sae poor,
  Is king o' men for a' that.

Ye see yon birkie ca'd 'a lord',
  Wha struts, an' stares, an' a' that?
Tho' hundreds worship at his word,
  He's but a cuif for a' that.
For a' that, an' a' that,
  His ribband, star, an' a' that,
The man o' independent mind,
  He looks an' laughs at a' that.

A prince can mak a belted knight,
  A marquis, duke, an' a' that!
But an honest man's aboon his might—
  Guid faith, he mauna fa' that.
For a' that, an' a' that,
  Their dignities, an' a' that,
The pith o' sense an' pride o' worth
  Are higher rank than a' that.

Then let us pray that come it may
  (As come it will for a' that)
That Sense and Worth o'er a' the earth
  Shall bear the gree an' a' that!
For a' that, an' a' that,
  It's comin yet for a' that,
That man to man the world o'er
  Shall brithers be for a' that.

birkie: dandy   cuif: fool   fa': do   bear the gree: take
the prize

151   *Mary Morison*

O MARY, at thy window be!
　　It is the wish'd, the trysted hour.
Those smiles and glances let me see,
　　That make the miser's treasure poor.
　　How blithely wad I bide the stoure,
A weary slave frae sun to sun,
　　Could I the rich reward secure—
The lovely Mary Morison.

Yestreen, when to the trembling string
　　The dance gaed thro' the lighted ha',
To thee my fancy took its wing,
　　I sat, but neither heard nor saw:
　　Tho' this was fair, and that was braw,
And yon the toast of a' the town,
　　I sigh'd and said amang them a':—
'Ye are na Mary Morison!'

O, Mary canst thou wreck his peace
　　Wha for thy sake wad gladly die?
Or canst thou break that heart of his
　　Whase only faut is loving thee?
　　If love for love thou wilt na gie,
At least be pity to me shown:
　　A thought ungentle canna be
The thought o' Mary Morison.

152

Rantin, Rovin Robin

THERE was a lad was born in Kyle,
　But what na day o' what na style,
I doubt it 's hardly worth the while
　To be sae nice wi' Robin.

　　Robin was a rovin boy,
　　　Rantin, rovin, rantin, rovin,
　　Robin was a rovin boy,
　　　Rantin, rovin Robin!

Our monarch's hindmost year but ane
Was five-and-twenty days begun,
'Twas then a blast o' Janwar' win'
　Blew hansel in on Robin!

　　Robin was a rovin boy, etc.

The gossip keekit in his loof,
Quo' she:—'Wha lives 'll see the proof,
This waly boy will be nae coof:
　I think we'll ca' him Robin.'

　　Robin was a rovin boy, etc.

'He'll hae misfortunes great an' sma',
But ay a heart aboon them a'.
He'll gie his Daddie's name a blaw,
　We'll a' be proud o' Robin.'

　　Robin was a rovin boy, etc.

hansel: birth-gift　　　gossip: midwife　　　loof: palm　　　coof:
fool

411

'But sure as three times three mak nine,
I see by ilka score and line,
This chap will dearly like our kin',
    Sae leeze me on thee, Robin!'

        Robin was a rovin boy, etc.

'Guid faith', quo' she, 'I doubt you, Stir,
Ye'll gar the lassies lie aspar,
But twenty fauts ye may hae waur—
    So blessins on thee, Robin.'

        Robin was a rovin boy, etc.

aspar: astride

153 *O, Wert Thou in the Cauld Blast*

O WERT thou in the cauld blast
    On yonder lea, on yonder lea,
My plaidie to the angry airt,
    I'd shelter thee, I'd shelter thee.
Or did Misfortune's bitter storms
    Around thee blaw, around thee blaw,
Thy bield should be my bosom,
    To share it a', to share it a'.

Or were I in the wildest waste,
    Sae black and bare, sae black and bare,
The desert were a Paradise,
    If thou wert there, if thou wert there.
Or were I monarch of the globe,
    Wi' thee to reign, wi' thee to reign,
The brightest jewel in my crown
    Wad be my queen, wad be my queen.

bield: shelter

ROBERT BURNS

Scots, Wha Hae

SCOTS, wha hae wi' Wallace bled,
　Scots, wham Bruce has aften led,
Welcome to your gory bed
　　　Or to victorie!

Now's the day, and now's the hour:
See the front o' battle lour,
See approach proud Edward's power—
　　　Chains and slaverie!

Wha will be a traitor knave?
Wha can fill a coward's grave?
Wha sae base as be a slave?—
　　　Let him turn, and flee!

Wha for Scotland's King and Law
Feedom's sword will strongly draw,
Freeman stand, or freeman fa',
　　　Let him follow me!

By Oppression's woes and pains,
By your sons in servile chains,
We will drain our dearest veins
　　　But they shall be free!

Lay the proud usurpers low!
Tyrants fall in every foe!
Liberty's in every blow!
　　　Let us do, or die!

Auld Lang Syne

SHOULD auld acquaintance be forgot,
  And never brought to mind?
Should auld acquaintance be forgot,
  And auld lang syne?

    For auld lang syne, my jo,
     For auld lang syne,
    We'll tak a cup o' kindness yet
     For auld lang syne.

And surely you'll be your pint-stowp,
  And surely I'll be mine,
And we'll tak a cup o' kindness yet
  For auld lang syne!

    For auld lang syne, etc.

We twa hae run about the braes,
  And pou'd the gowans fine,
But we've wander'd monie a weary fit
  Sin' auld lang syne.

    For auld lang syne, etc.

We twa hae paidl'd in the burn
  Frae morning sun till dine,
But seas between us braid hae roar'd
  Sin' auld lang syne.

    For auld lang syne, etc.

And there's a hand, my trusty fiere,
   And gie's a hand o' thine,
And we'll tak a right guid-willie waught
   For auld lang syne!

     For auld lang syne, etc.

guid-willie waught: good-will drink

LADY NAIRNE

1766–1845

156   *Caller Herrin'*

WHA'LL buy my caller herrin'?
   They're bonnie fish and halesome farin';
Wha'll buy my caller herrin',
   New drawn frae the Forth.

When ye were sleepin' on your pillows,
   Dream'd ye aught o' our puir fellows,
Darkling as they fac'd the billows,
   A' to fill the woven willows?
     Buy my caller herrin',
     New drawn frae the Forth.

Wha'll buy my caller herrin'?
   They're no brought here without brave darin';
Buy my caller herrin',
   Haul'd through wind and rain.
     Wha'll buy my caller herrin'? etc.

caller: fresh   halesome farin': healthy food

Wha'll buy my caller herrin'?
  Oh, ye may ca' them vulgar farin'—
Wives and mithers, maist despairin',
  Ca' them lives o' men.
    Wha'll buy my caller herrin'? etc.

When the creel o' herrin' passes,
  Ladies, clad in silks and laces,
Gather in their braw pelisses,
  Cast their heads and screw their faces,
    Wha'll buy my caller herrin'? etc.

Caller herrin's no got lightlie:—
  Ye can trip the spring fu' tightlie;
Spite o' tauntin', flauntin', flingin',
  Gow has set you a' a-singing
    Wha'll buy my caller herrin'? etc.

Neebour wives, now tent my tellin';
  When the bonnie fish ye're sellin',
At ae word be in yere dealin'—
  Truth will stand when a' thing 's failin',
    Wha'll buy my caller herrin'?
      They're bonnie fish and halesome farin',
      Wha'll buy my caller herrin',
      New drawn frae the Forth?

The Land o' the Leal

I'M wearin' awa', John,
Like snaw-wreaths in thaw, John,
I'm wearin' awa'
    To the land o' the leal.
There's nae sorrow there, John,
There's neither cauld nor care, John,
The day is aye fair
    In the land o' the leal.

Our bonnie bairn 's there, John,
She was baith gude and fair, John,
And, oh! we grudged her sair
    To the land o' the leal.
But sorrow's sel' wears past, John,
And joy is comin' fast, John,
The joy that's aye to last
    In the land o' the leal.

Sae dear's that joy was bought, John,
Sae free the battle fought, John,
That sinfu' man e'er brought
    To the land o' the leal.
Oh! dry your glist'nin' e'e, John,
My saul langs to be free, John,
And angels beckon me
    To the land o' the leal.

Oh! haud ye leal an' true, John,
Your day it 's wearin' thro', John,
And I'll welcome you
    To the land o' the leal.

leal: loyal

Now fare ye weel, my ain John,
This warld's cares are vain, John,
We'll meet, and we'll be fain,
    In the land o' the leal.

ANONYMOUS
18th Century

158   *John Anderson, My Jo*

JOHN Anderson, my jo, John,
    I wonder what ye mean,
To lie sae lang i' the mornin',
    And sit sae late at e'en?
Ye'll bleer a' your een, John,
    And why do ye so?
Come sooner to your bed at een,
    John Anderson, my jo.

John Anderson, my jo, John,
    When first that ye began,
Ye had as good a tail-tree,
    As ony ither man;
But now its waxen wan, John,
    And wrinkles to and fro;
I've twa gae-ups for ae gae-down,
    John Anderson, my jo.

I'm backit like a salmon,
    I'm breastit like a swan;
My wame it is a down-cod,
    My middle ye may span:

        down-cod: bolster

Frae my tap-knot to my tae, John,
  I'm like the new-fa'n snow;
And it's a' for your convenience,
  John Anderson, my jo.

O it is a fine thing
  To keep out o'er the dyke;
But it's a meikle finer thing,
  To see your hurdies fyke;
To see your hurdies fyke, John,
  And hit the rising blow;
It's then I like your chanter-pipe,
  John Anderson, my jo.

When ye come on before, John,
  See that ye do your best;
When ye begin to haud me,
  See that ye grip me fast;
See that ye grip me fast, John,
  Until that I cry 'Oh!'
Your back shall crack or I do that,
  John Anderson, my jo.

John Anderson, my jo, John,
  Ye're welcome when ye please;
It's either in the warm bed
  Or else aboon the claes:
Or ye shall hae the horns, John,
  Upon your head to grow;
An' that's the cuckold's mallison,
  John Anderson, my jo.

    hurdies: hips   fyke: jerk

159   *Ca' the Yowes to the Knowes*

C A' the yowes to the knowes,
   Ca' them where the heather grows,
Ca' them where the burnie rowes,
   My bonnie dearie.

'Will ye gang down yon water-side,
That thro' the glen does saftly glide.
And I shall rowe thee in my plaid,
   My bonnie dearie?'

'Ye sall hae rings and ribbons meet,
Calf-leather shoon upon your feet,
And in my bosom ye sall sleep,
   My bonnie dearie.'

'I was brought up at nae sic school,
My shepherd lad, to play the fool,
Nor sit the livelong day in dool,
   Lanely and eerie.'

'Yon yowes and lammies on the plain,
Wi' a' the gear my dad did hain,
I'se gie thee, if thou'lt be mine ain,
   My bonnie dearie.'

'Come weel, come wae, whate'er betide,
Gin ye'll prove true, I'se be your bride,
And ye sall rowe me in your plaid,
   My winsome dearie.'

yowes: ewes   knowes: knolls   rowes: rolls   hain: save

Somebody

OCH hon for somebody!
　　Och hey for somebody!
I wad do—what wad I not,
　　For the sake o' somebody?

My heart is sair, I daurna tell
My heart is sair for somebody;
I wad walk a winter's night,
　　For a sight o' somebody.

If somebody were come again,
Then somebody maun cross the main,
And ilka ane will get his ain,
　　And I will see my somebody.

What need I kame my tresses bright,
Or why should coal or candle-light
E'er shine in my bower day or night,
　　Since gane is my dear somebody?

Oh! I hae grutten mony a day
For ane that's banished far away;
I canna sing, and maunna say
　　How sair I grieve for somebody.

grutten: wept　　　somebody: the Stewart king

161   *Canadian Boat Song*

FAIR these broad meads—these hoary woods are grand;
   But we are exiles from our fathers' land.

Listen to me, as when ye heard our father
   Sing long ago the song of other shores—
Listen to me, and then in chorus gather
   All your deep voices, as ye pull your oars.

From the lone shieling of the misty island
   Mountains divide us, and the waste of seas—
Yet still the blood is strong, the heart is Highland,
   And we in dreams behold the Hebrides.

We ne'er shall tread the fancy-haunted valley,
   Where 'tween the dark hills creeps the small clear stream,
In arms around the patriarch banner rally,
   Nor see the moon on royal tombstones gleam.

When the bold kindred, in the time long vanish'd,
   Conquer'd the soil and fortified the keep—
No seer foretold the children would be banish'd,
   That a degenerate lord might boast his sheep.

Come foreign rage—let Discord burst in slaughter!
   O then for clansman true, and stern claymore—
The hearts that would have given their blood like water,
   Beat heavily beyond the Atlantic roar.

shieling: cottage

162   *The Piper o' Dundee*

AND wasna he a roguey,
 A roguey, a roguey,
And wasna he a roguey,
    The piper o' Dundee?

The piper came to our town,
To our town, to our town,
The piper came to our town,
    And he played bonnilie.
He played a spring the laird to please,
A spring brent new frae yont the seas;
And then he ga'e his bags a wheeze,
    And played anither key.

He played *The welcome owre the main*,
And *Ye'se be fou and I'se be fain*,
And *Auld Stuarts back again*,
    Wi' muckle mirth and glee.
He played *The Kirk*, he played *The Quier*,
The Mullin Dhu and *Chevalier*,
And *Lang awa', but welcome here*,
    Sae sweet, sae bonnilie.

It 's some gat swords, and some gat nane,
And some were dancing mad their lane,
And mony a vow o' weir was ta'en
    That night at Amulrie!
There was Tullibardine and Burleigh,
And Struan, Keith, and Ogilvie,
And brave Carnegie, wha but he,
    The piper o' Dundee?

JAMES HOGG

1770–1835

163   *When the Kye Comes Hame*

COME all ye jolly shepherds
    That whistle through the glen,
I'll tell ye of a secret
    That courtiers dinna ken:
What is the greatest bliss
    That the tongue o' man can name?
'Tis to woo a bonny lassie
    When the kye comes hame.
      When the kye comes hame,
      When the kye comes hame,
      'Tween the gloaming and the mirk,
      When the kye comes hame.

'Tis not beneath the coronet,
    Nor canopy of state,
'Tis not on couch of velvet,
    Nor arbour of the great—
'Tis beneath the spreading birk,
    In the glen without the name,
Wi' a bonny, bonny lassie,
    When the kye comes hame.
      When the kye comes hame, etc.

There the blackbird bigs his nest
    For the mate he loes to see,
And on the topmost bough,
    O, a happy bird is he;

        kye: cattle   bigs: builds

Where he pours his melting ditty,
   And love is a' the theme,
And he'll woo his bonny lassie
   When the kye comes hame.
     When the kye comes hame, etc.

When the blewart bears a pearl,
   And the daisy turns a pea,
And the bonny lucken gowan
   Has fauldit up her ee,
Then the laverock frae the blue lift
   Drops down, an' thinks nae shame
To woo his bonny lassie
   When the kye comes hame.
     When the kye comes hame, etc.

See yonder pawkie shepherd,
   That lingers on the hill,
His ewes are in the fauld,
   An' his lambs are lying still;
Yet he downa gang to bed,
   For his heart is in a flame,
To meet his bonny lassie
   When the kye comes hame.
     When the kye comes hame, etc.

When the little wee bit heart
   Rises high in the breast,
An' the little wee bit starn
   Rises red in the east,

blewart: bluebell   lucken gowan: globe-flower   laverock:
lark   lift: sky

O there's a joy sae dear,
　　That the heart can hardly frame,
Wi' a bonny, bonny lassie,
　　When the kye comes hame!
　　　When the kye comes hame, etc.

Then since all nature joins
　　In this love without alloy,
O, wha wad prove a traitor
　　To Nature's dearest joy?
Or wha wad choose a crown,
　　Wi' its perils and its fame,
And *miss* his bonny lassie
　　When the kye comes hame?
　　　When the kye comes hame,
　　　When the kye comes hame,
　　　'Tween the gloaming and the mirk,
　　　When the kye comes hame!

164　　　　　　*McLean's Welcome*

✓ COME o'er the stream, Charlie, dear Charlie, brave Charlie;
　　Come o'er the stream, Charlie, and dine with McLean;
And though you be weary, we'll make your heart cheery,
And welcome our Charlie, and his loyal train.
We'll bring down the track deer, we'll bring down the black steer,
The lamb from the braken, and doe from the glen,
The salt sea we'll harry, and bring to our Charlie
The cream from the bothy and curd from the pen.

Come o'er the stream, Charlie, dear Charlie, brave Charlie;
Come o'er the sea, Charlie, and dine with McLean;
And you shall drink freely the dews of Glen-sheerly,
That stream in the starlight when kings do not ken,
And deep be your meed of the wine that is red,
To drink to your sire, and his friend the McLean.

Come o'er the stream, Charlie, dear Charlie, brave Charlie;
Come o'er the stream, Charlie, and dine with McLean;
O'er heath-bells shall trace you the maids to embrace you,
And deck your blue bonnet with flowers of the brae;
And the loveliest Mari in all Glen M'Quarry
Shall lie in your bosom till break of the day.

Come o'er the stream, Charlie, dear Charlie, brave Charlie;
Come o'er the stream, Charlie, and dine with McLean;
If aught will invite you, or more will delight you,
'Tis ready, a troop of our bold Highlandmen,
All ranged on the heather, with bonnet and feather,
Strong arms and broad claymores, three hundred and ten!

165   *Lock the Door, Lariston*

LOCK the door, Lariston, lion of Liddisdale,
  Lock the door, Lariston, Lowther comes on,
    The Armstrongs are flying,
    Their widows are crying,
The Castletown's burning, and Oliver's gone;
Lock the door, Lariston—high on the weather gleam
See how the Saxon plumes bob on the sky,
    Yeoman and carbineer,
    Billman and halberdier;
Fierce is the foray, and far is the cry.

Bewcastle brandishes high his broad scimitar,
Ridley is riding his fleet-footed grey,
    Hedley and Howard there,
    Wandale and Windermere,—
Lock the door, Lariston, hold them at bay.
Why dost thou smile, noble Elliot of Lariston?
Why do the joy-candles gleam in thine eye?
    Thou bold Border ranger,
    Beware of thy danger—
Thy foes are relentless, determined, and nigh.

Jock Elliot raised up his steel bonnet and lookit,
His hand grasp'd the sword with a nervous embrace;
    'Ah, welcome, brave foemen,
    On earth there are no men
More gallant to meet in the foray or chase!
Little know you of the hearts I have hidden here,
Little know you of our moss-troopers' might,—
    Linhope and Sorbie true,
    Sundhope and Milburn too,
Gentle in manner, but lions in fight!

'I've Mangerton, Ogilvie, Raeburn, and Netherby,
Old Sim of Whitram, and all his array;
    Come all Northumberland,
    Teesdale and Cumberland,
Here at the Breaken Tower end shall the fray.'
Scowl'd the broad sun o'er the links of green Liddisdale,
Red as the beacon-light tipp'd he the wold;
    Many a bold martial eye
    Mirror'd that morning sky,
Never more oped on his orbit of gold!

Shrill was the bugle's note, dreadful the warrior shout,
Lances and halberds in splinters were borne;
    Halberd and hauberk then
    Braved the claymore in vain,
Buckler and armlet in shivers were shorn.
See how they wane, the proud files of the Windermere,
Howard—Ah! woe to thy hopes of the day!
    Hear the wide welkin rend,
    While the Scots' shouts ascend,
'Elliot of Lariston, Elliot for aye!'

WALTER SCOTT

1771–1832

166   From *The Lay of the Last Minstrel*

[Canto VI. i]

BREATHES there the man with soul so dead,
  Who never to himself hath said,
    This is my own, my native land!
Whose heart hath ne'er within him burn'd,
As home his footsteps he hath turn'd
    From wandering on a foreign strand!
If such there breathe, go, mark him well;
For him no Minstrel raptures swell;
High though his titles, proud his name,
Boundless his wealth as wish can claim;
Despite those titles, power, and pelf,
The wretch, concentred all in self,
Living, shall forfeit fair renown,
And, doubly dying, shall go down
To the vile dust, from whence he sprung,
Unwept, unhonour'd, and unsung.

167   *Lochinvar*

[Marmion v. xii]

O YOUNG Lochinvar is come out of the west,
    Through all the wide Border his steed was the best;
And save his good broadsword he weapons had none,
He rode all unarm'd, and he rode all alone.
So faithful in love, and so dauntless in war,
There never was knight like the young Lochinvar.

He staid not for brake, and he stopp'd not for stone,
He swam the Eske river where ford there was none;
But ere he alighted at Netherby gate,
The bride had consented, the gallant came late:
For a laggard in love, and a dastard in war,
Was to wed the fair Ellen of brave Lochinvar.

So boldly he enter'd the Netherby Hall,
Among bride's-men, and kinsmen, and brothers and all:
Then spoke the bride's father, his hand on his sword,
(For the poor craven bridegroom said never a word,)
'O come ye in peace here, or come ye in war,
Or to dance at our bridal, young Lord Lochinvar?'

'I long woo'd your daughter, my suit you denied;—
Love swells like the Solway, but ebbs like its tide—
And now I am come, with this lost love of mine,
To lead but one measure, drink one cup of wine.
There are maidens in Scotland more lovely by far,
That would gladly be bride to the young Lochinvar.'

The bride kiss'd the goblet: the knight took it up,
He quaff'd off the wine, and he threw down the cup.

She look'd down to blush, and she look'd up to sigh,
With a smile on her lips and a tear in her eye.
He took her soft hand, ere her mother could bar,—
'Now tread we a measure!' said young Lochinvar.

So stately his form, and so lovely her face,
That never a hall such a galliard did grace;
While her mother did fret, and her father did fume,
And the bridegroom stood dangling his bonnet and plume;
And the bride-maidens whisper'd, ' 'twere better by far
To have match'd our fair cousin with young Lochinvar.'

One touch to her hand, and one word in her ear,
When they reach'd the hall-door, and the charger stood near;
So light to the croupe the fair lady he swung,
So light to the saddle before her he sprung!
'She is won! we are gone, over bank, bush, and scaur;
They'll have fleet steeds that follow', quoth young Lochinvar.

There was mounting 'mong Graemes of the Netherby clan;
Forsters, Fenwicks, and Musgraves, they rode and they ran:
There was racing and chasing on Cannobie Lee,
But the lost bride of Netherby ne'er did they see.
So daring in love, and so dauntless in war,
Have ye e'er heard of gallant like young Lochinvar?

168   From *The Lady of the Lake*

[v. xvi]

'NOW, yield thee, or by Him who made
     The world, thy heart's blood dyes my blade!'
'Thy threats, thy mercy, I defy!
Let recreant yield, who fears to die.'

Like adder darting from his coil,
Like wolf that dashes through the toil,
Like mountain-cat who guards her young,
Full at Fitz-James's throat he sprung;
Received, but reck'd not of a wound,
And lock'd his arms his foeman round.
Now, gallant Saxon, hold thine own!
No maiden's hand is round thee thrown!
That desperate grasp thy frame might feel
Through bars of brass and triple steel!
They tug, they strain! down, down they go,
The Gael above, Fitz-James below.
The Chieftain's gripe his throat compress'd,
His knee was planted in his breast;
His clotted locks he backward threw,
Across his brow his hand he drew,
From blood and mist to clear his sight,
Then gleam'd aloft his dagger bright!
But hate and fury ill supplied
The stream of life's exhausted tide,
And all too late the advantage came,
To turn the odds of deadly game;
For, while the dagger gleam'd on high,
Reel'd soul and sense, reel'd brain and eye.
Down came the blow—but in the heath;
The erring blade found bloodless sheath.
The struggling foe may now unclasp
The fainting Chief's relaxing grasp;
Unwounded from the dreadful close,
But breathless all, Fitz-James arose.

169 *Jock of Hazeldean*

'WHY weep ye by the tide, ladie,
  Why weep ye by the tide?
I'll wed ye to my youngest son,
  And ye sall be his bride:
And ye sall be his bride, ladie,
  Sae comely to be seen'—
But aye she loot the tears down fa'
  For Jock of Hazeldean.

'Now let this wilfu' grief be done,
  And dry that cheek so pale;
Young Frank is chief of Errington,
  And lord of Langley-dale;
His step is first in peaceful ha',
  His sword in battle keen'—
But aye she loot the tears down fa'
  For Jock of Hazeldean.

The kirk was deck'd at morning-tide,
  The tapers glimmer'd fair;
The priest and bridegroom wait the bride,
  And dame and knight are there.
They sought her baith by bower and ha';
  The ladie was not seen!
She's o'er the Border, and awa'
  Wi' Jock of Hazeldean.

Pibroch of Donuil Dhu

PIBROCH of Donuil Dhu,
    Pibroch of Donuil,
Wake thy wild voice anew,
    Summon Clan-Conuil.
Come away, come away,
    Hark to the summons!
Come in your war array,
    Gentles and commons.

Come from deep glen, and
    From mountain so rocky,
The war-pipe and pennon
    Are at Inverlochy.
Come every hill-plaid, and
    True heart that wears one,
Come every steel blade, and
    Strong hand that bears one.

Leave untended the herd,
    The flock without shelter;
Leave the corpse uninterr'd,
    The bride at the altar;
Leave the deer, leave the steer,
    Leave nets and barges:
Come with your fighting gear,
    Broadswords and targes.

Come as the winds come, when
    Forests are rended,
Come as the waves come, when
    Navies are stranded:

Faster come, faster come
    Faster and faster,
Chief, vassal, page and groom,
    Tenant and master.

Fast they come, fast they come;
    See how they gather!
Wild waves the eagle plume,
    Blended with heather.
Cast your plaids, draw your blades,
    Forward, each man, set!
Pibroch of Donuil Dhu,
    Knell for the onset!

171   *MacGregor's Gathering*

THE moon's on the lake, and the mist's on the brae,
   And the clan has a name that is nameless by day;
    Then gather, gather, gather, Grigalach!
    Gather, gather, gather, etc.

Our signal for fight, that from monarchs we drew,
Must be heard but by night in our vengeful haloo!
    Then haloo, Grigalach! haloo, Grigalach!
    Haloo, haloo, haloo, Grigalach, etc.

Glen Orchy's proud mountains, Coalchuirn and her towers,
Glenstrae and Glenlyon no longer are ours;
    We're landless, landless, landless, Grigalach!
    Landless, landless, landless, etc.

But doom'd and devoted by vassal and lord,
MacGregor has still both his heart and his sword!
    Then courage, courage, courage, Grigalach!
    Courage, courage, courage, etc.

If they rob us of hame, and pursue us with beagles
Give their roofs to the flame, and their flesh to the eagles!
 Then vengeance, vengeance, vengeance, Grigalach!
 Vengeance, vengeance, vengeance, etc.

While there's leaves in the forest, and foam on the river,
MacGregor, despite them, shall flourish for ever!
 Come then, Grigalach, come then, Grigalach,
 Come then, come then, come then, etc.

Through the depths of Loch Katrine the steed shall career,
O'er the peak of Ben-Lomond the galley shall steer,
And the rocks of Craig-Royston like icicles melt,
Ere our wrongs be forgot, or our vengeance unfelt!
 Then gather, gather, gather, Grigalach!
 Gather, gather, gather, etc.

172   *Lucy Ashton's Song*

LOOK not thou on beauty's charming,
 Sit thou still when kings are arming,
Taste not when the wine-cup glistens,
Speak not when the people listens,
Stop thine ear against the singer,
From the red gold keep thy finger;
Vacant heart and hand and eye,
Easy live and quiet die.

173 *Proud Maisie*

PROUD Maisie is in the wood,
    Walking so early;
Sweet Robin sits on the bush,
    Singing so rarely.

'Tell me, thou bonny bird,
    When shall I marry me?'
'When six braw gentlemen
    Kirkward shall carry ye.'

'Who makes the bridal bed,
    Birdie, say truly?'
'The grey-headed sexton
    That delves the grave duly.

'The glow-worm o'er grave and stone
    Shall light thee steady.
The owl from the steeple sing,
    "Welcome, proud lady".'

174 *Blue Bonnets over the Border*

MARCH, march, Ettrick and Teviotdale,
    Why the deil dinna ye march forward in order?
March, march, Eskdale and Liddesdale,
All the Blue Bonnets are bound for the Border.
    Many a banner spread
    Flutters above your head,
Many a crest that is famous in story.
    Mount and make ready then,
    Sons of the mountain glen,
Fight for the Queen and the old Scottish glory.

Come from the hills where your hirsels are grazing,
Come from the glen of the buck and the roe;
Come to the crag where the beacon is blazing,
Come with the buckler, the lance, and the bow.
      Trumpets are sounding,
      War-steeds are bounding,
Stand to your arms then, and march in good order;
      England shall many a day
      Tell of the bloody fray,
When the Blue Bonnets came over the Border.

175   From *Bonny Dundee*

TO the Lords of Convention 'twas Claver'se who spoke,
  'Ere the King's crown shall fall there are crowns to be broke;
So let each Cavalier who loves honour and me,
Come follow the bonnet of Bonny Dundee.'

    'Come fill up my cup, come fill up my can,
    Come saddle your horses, and call up your men;
    Come open the West Port, and let me gang free,
    And it 's room for the bonnets of Bonny Dundee!'

Dundee he is mounted, he rides up the street,
The bells are rung backward, the drums they are beat;
But the Provost, douce man, said 'Just e'en let him be,
The Gude Town is weel quit of that Deil of Dundee'.

    'Come fill up my cup', etc.

As he rode down the sanctified bends of the Bow,
Ilk carline was flyting and shaking her pow;
But the young plants of grace they look'd couthie and slee,
Thinking, 'Luck to thy bonnet, thou Bonny Dundee'.

    'Come fill up my cup', etc.

ROBERT TANNAHILL

1774–1810

O! Are Ye Sleepin, Maggie?

'O! ARE ye sleepin, Maggie?
   O! are ye sleepin, Maggie?
Let me in, for loud the linn
   Is roarin o'er the warlock craigie!

'Mirk an rainy is the nicht,
   No a starn in a the carry;
Lightnin's gleam athwart the lift,
   An win's drive wi winter's fury.

'Fearfu' soughs the boor-tree bank,
   The rifted wood roars wild an dreary,
Loud the iron yett does clank,
   The cry o howlets mak's me eerie.

'Aboon my breath I daurna speak,
   For fear I rouse your waukrif daddie.
Caul 's the blast upon my cheek,—
   O rise, rise my bonnie ladie!'

She oped the door, she loot him in:
   He cuist aside his dreepin plaidie:
'Blaw your warst, ye rain an win,
   Since, Maggie, now I'm in aside ye.

linn: weir   craigie: rock   boor-tree: elder-tree   yett: gate
howlets: owls   waukrif: wakeful

'Now, since ye're waukin, Maggie,
 Now, since ye're waukin, Maggie,
What care I for howlet's cry,
 For boor-tree bank, or warlock craigie?'

GEORGE GORDON (LORD) BYRON

1788–1824

177   *Lachin Y Gair*

AWAY, ye gay landscapes, ye gardens of roses!
 In you let the minions of luxury rove;
Restore me the rocks where the snow-flake reposes,
 Though still they are sacred to freedom and love:
Yet, Caledonia, beloved are thy mountains,
 Round their white summits though elements war;
Though cataracts foam 'stead of smooth-flowing fountains,
 I sigh for the valley of dark Loch na Garr.

Ah! there my young footsteps in infancy wander'd;
 My cap was the bonnet, my cloak was the plaid;
On chieftains long perish'd my memory ponder'd,
 As daily I strode through the pine-cover'd glade;
I sought not my home till the day's dying glory
 Gave place to the rays of the bright polar star;
For fancy was cheer'd by traditional story,
 Disclos'd by the natives of dark Loch na Garr.

'Shades of the dead! have I not heard your voices
    Rise on the night-rolling breath of the gale?'
Surely the soul of the hero rejoices
    And rides on the wind o'er his own highland vale.
Round Loch na Garr while the stormy mist gathers,
    Winter presides in his cold icy car:
Clouds there encircle the forms of my fathers;
    They dwell in the tempests of dark Loch na Garr.

'Ill-starr'd, though brave, did no visions foreboding
    Tell you that fate had forsaken your cause?'
Ah! were you destin'd to die at Culloden,
    Victory crown'd not your fall with applause:
Still were you happy in death's earthly slumber,
    You rest with your clan in the caves of Braemar;
The pibroch resounds to the piper's loud number,
    Your deeds on the echoes of dark Loch na Garr.

Years have roll'd on, Loch na Garr, since I left you,
    Years must elapse ere I tread you again:
Nature of verdure and flowers has bereft you,
    Yet still are you dearer than Albion's plain.
England! thy beauties are tame and domestic
    To one who has roved o'er the mountains afar:
Oh for the crags that are wild and majestic!
    The steep frowning glories of dark Loch na Garr.

178   *So, We'll Go No More a Roving*

So, we'll go no more a roving
    So late into the night,
Though the heart be still as loving,
    And the moon be still as bright.

For the sword outwears its sheath,
    And the soul wears out the breast,
And the heart must pause to breathe,
    And love itself have rest.

Though the night was made for loving,
    And the day returns too soon,
Yet we'll go no more a roving
    By the light of the moon.

JAMES THOMSON

1834–1882

179   From *The City of Dreadful Night*

PROEM

LO, thus, as prostrate, 'In the dust I write
    My heart's deep languor and my soul's sad tears'.
Yet why evoke the spectres of black night
    To blot the sunshine of exultant years?
Why disinter dead faith from mouldering hidden?
Why break the seals of mute despair unbidden,
    And wail life's discords into careless ears?

Because a cold rage seizes one at whiles
    To show the bitter old and wrinkled truth
Stripped naked of all vesture that beguiles,
    False dreams, false hopes, false masks and modes of youth;
Because it gives some sense of power and passion
In helpless impotence to try to fashion
    Our woe in living words howe'er uncouth.

442

Surely I write not for the hopeful young,
   Or those who deem their happiness of worth,
Or such as pasture and grow fat among
   The shows of life and feel nor doubt nor dearth,
Or pious spirits with a God above them
To sanctify and glorify and love them,
   Or sages who foresee a heaven on earth.

For none of these I write, and none of these
   Could read the writing if they deigned to try:
So may they flourish, in their due degrees,
   On our sweet earth and in their unplaced sky.
If any cares for the weak words here written,
It must be some one desolate, Fate-smitten,
   Whose faith and hope are dead, and who would die.

Yes, here and there some weary wanderer
   In that same city of tremendous night,
Will understand the speech, and feel a stir
   Of fellowship in all-disastrous fight;
'I suffer mute and lonely, yet another
Uplifts his voice to let me know a brother
   Travels the same wild paths though out of sight'.

O sad Fraternity, do I unfold
   Your dolorous mysteries shrouded from of yore?
Nay, be assured; no secret can be told
   To any who divined it not before:
None uninitiate by many a presage
Will comprehend the language of the message,
   Although proclaimed aloud for evermore.

DAVID GRAY

1838–1861

180 *Where the Lilies Used to Spring*

WHEN the place was green with the shaky grass,
  And the windy trees were high;
When the leaflets told each other tales,
  And the stars were in the sky;
When the silent crows hid their ebon beaks
  Beneath their ruffled wing—
Then the fairies watered the glancing spot
  Where the lilies used to spring!

When the sun is high in the summer sky,
  And the lake is deep with clouds;
When gadflies bite the prancing kine,
  And light the lark enshrouds—
Then the butterfly, like a feather dropped
  From the tip of an angel's wing,
Floats wavering on to the glancing spot
  Where the lilies used to spring!

When the wheat is shorn and the burns run brown,
  And the moon shines clear at night;
When wains are heaped with rustling corn,
  And the swallows take their flight;
When the trees begin to cast their leaves,
  And the birds, new-feathered, sing—
Then comes the bee to the glancing spot
  Where the lilies used to spring!

DAVID GRAY

When the sky is grey and the trees are bare,
    And the grass is long and brown,
And black moss clothes the soft damp thatch,
    And the rain comes weary down,
And countless droplets on the pond
    Their widening orbits ring—
Then bleak and cold is the silent spot
    Where the lilies used to spring!

181   From *In the Shadows* [Sonnet 1]

IF it must be; if it must be, O God!
    That I die young, and make no further moans;
That, underneath the unrespective sod,
    In unescutcheoned privacy, my bones
Shall crumble soon,—then give me strength to bear
    The last convulsive throe of too sweet breath!
I tremble from the edge of life, to dare
    The dark and fatal leap, having no faith,
No glorious yearning for the Apocalypse;
    But like a child that in the night-time cries
For light, I cry; forgetting the eclipse
    Of knowledge and our human destinies.
O peevish and uncertain soul! obey
The law of life in patience till the Day.

ROBERT LOUIS STEVENSON

1850–1894

182   *A Mile an' a Bittock*

A MILE an' a bittock, a mile or twa,
   Abune the burn, ayont the law
Davie an' Donal' an' Cherlie an' a',
    An' the müne was shinin' clearly!

Ane went hame wi' the ither, an' then
The ither went hame wi' the ither twa men,
An' baith wad return him the service again,
    An' the müne was shinin' clearly!

The clocks were chappin' in house an' ha',
Eleeven, twal' an' ane an' twa;
An' the guidman's face was turnt to the wa',
    An' the müne was shinin' clearly!

A wind got up frae affa the sea,
It blew the stars as clear's could be,
It blew in the een of a' o' the three,
    An' the müne was shinin' clearly!

Noo, Davie was first to get sleep in his head,
'The best o' frien's maun twine,' he said;
'I'm weariet, an' here I'm awa' to my bed.'
    An' the müne was shinin' clearly!

Twa o' them walkin' an' crackin' their lane,
The mornin' licht cam grey an' plain,
An' the birds they yammert on stick an' stane,
    An' the müne was shinin' clearly!

law: hill   yammert: warbled

O years ayont, O years awa',
My lads, ye'll mind whate'er befa'—
My lads, ye'll mind on the bield o' the law
    When the müne was shinin' clearly.

bield: shelter

183   *Ille Terrarum*

FRAE nirly, nippin', Eas'lan' breeze,
Frae Norlan' snaw, an' haar o' seas,
Weel happit in your gairden trees,
    A bonny bit,
Atween the muckle Pentland's knees,
    Secure ye sit.

Beeches an' aiks entwine their theek,
An' firs, a stench, auld-farrant clique,
A' simmer day, your chimleys reek,
    Couthy and bien;
An' here an' there your windies keek
    Amang the green.

A pickle plats an' paths an' posies,
A wheen auld gillyflowers an' roses:
A ring o' wa's the hale encloses
    Frae sheep or men;
An' there the auld housie beeks an' dozes,
    A' by her lane.

aiks: oaks   theek: thatch   auld-farrant: old-fashioned
reek: smoke   couthy: cosy   bien: comfortable   beeks: bakes

447

The gairdner crooks his weary back
A' day in the pitaty-track,
Or mebbe stops awhile to crack
    Wi' Jane the cook,
Or at some buss, worm-eaten-black,
    To gie a look.

Frae the high hills the curlew ca's;
The sheep gang baaing by the wa's;
Or whiles a clan o' roosty craws
    Cangle thegether;
The wild bees seek the gairden raws,
    Weariet wi' heather.

Or in the gloamin' douce an' grey
The sweet-throat mavis tunes her lay;
The herd comes linkin' doun the brae;
    An' by degrees
The muckle siller müne maks way
    Amang the trees.

Here aft hae I, wi' sober heart,
For meditation sat apairt,
When orra loves or kittle art
    Perplexed my mind;
Here socht a balm for ilka smart
    O' humankind.

Here aft, weel neukit by my lane,
Wi' Horace, or perhaps Montaigne,
The mornin' hours hae come an' gane
    Abüne my heid—
I wadnae gi'en a chucky-stane
    For a' I'd read.

pitaty: potato   crack: gossip   buss: bush

But noo the auld city, street by street,
An' winter fu' o' snaw an' sleet,
Awhile shut in my gangrel feet
          An' goavin' mettle;
Noo is the soopit ingle sweet,
          An' liltin' kettle.

An' noo the winter winds complain;
Cauld lies the glaur in ilka lane;
On draigled hizzie, tautit wean
          An' drucken lads,
In the mirk nicht, the winter rain
          Dribbles an' blads.

Whan bugles frae the Castle rock,
An' beaten drums wi' dowie shock,
Wauken, at cauld-rife sax o'clock,
          My chitterin' frame,
I mind me on the kintry cock,
          The kintry hame.

I mind me on yon bonny bield;
An' Fancy traivels far afield
To gaither a' that gairdens yield
          O' sun an' Simmer:
To hearten up a dowie chield,
          Fancy's the limmer!

gangrel: vagrant   goavin': staring   soopit: swept   glaur:
mud   tautit: brawling   wean: brat   blads: splashes
dowie: sad   cauld-rife: chilly   chitterin': shivering   kintry:
country   bield: hut, shelter   child: chap   limmer: flirt

184   *The Spaewife*

O I WAD like to ken—to the beggar-wife says I—
 Why chops are guid to brander and nane sae guid to fry.
An' siller, that's sae braw to keep, is brawer still to gie.
   It's gey an' easy speirin', says the beggar-wife to me.

O, I wad like to ken—to the beggar-wife says I—
Hoo a' things come to be whaur we find them when we try,
The lasses in their claes an' the fishes in the sea.
—*It's gey an' easy speirin'*, says the beggar-wife to me.

O, I wad like to ken—to the beggar-wife says I—
Why lads are a' to sell an' lasses a' to buy;
An' naebody for dacency but barely twa or three
—*It's gey an' easy speirin'*, says the beggar-wife to me.

O, I wad like to ken—to the beggar-wife says I—
Gin death as shüre to men as killin' is to kye,
Why God has filled the yearth sae fu' o' tasty things to pree.
—*It's gey an' easy speirin'*, says the beggar-wife to me.

O, I wad like to ken—to the beggar-wife says I—
The reason o' the cause an' the wherefore o' the why,
Wi' mony anither riddle brings the tear into my e'e.
—*It's gey an' easy speirin'*, says the beggar-wife to me.

   gey an': very   speirin': inquiring   pree: taste

185 *In the Highlands*

IN the highlands, in the country places,
Where the old plain men have rosy faces,
And the young fair maidens
    Quiet eyes;
Where essential silence cheers and blesses,
And for ever in the hill-recesses
Her more lovely music
    Broods and dies.

O to mount again where erst I haunted;
Where the old red hills are bird-enchanted,
And the low green meadows
    Bright with sward;
And when even dies, the million-tinted,
And the night has come, and planets glinted,
Lo, the valley hollow
    Lamp-bestarred!

O to dream, O to awake and wander
There, and with delight to take and render,
Through the trance of silence,
    Quiet breath;
Lo! for there, among the flowers and grasses,
Only the mightier movement sounds and passes;
Only winds and rivers,
    Life and death.

PITTENDRIGH MACGILLIVRAY

1856–1938

186   *The Return*

(A Piper's Vaunting)

OCH hey! for the splendour of tartans!
    And hey for the dirk and the targe!
The race that was as the Spartans
    Shall return again to the the charge:

Shall come back again to the heather,
    Like eagles, with beak and with claws
To take and to scatter for ever
    The Sasunnach thieves and their laws.

Och, then, for the bonnet and feather!—
    The Pipe and its vaunting clear:
Och, then, for the glens and the heather!
    And all that the Gael holds dear.

JOHN DAVIDSON

1857–1909

187   *Thirty Bob a Week*

I COULDN'T touch a stop and turn a screw,
    And set the blooming world a-work for me
Like such as cut their teeth——I hope, like you——
    On the handle of a skeleton gold key;
I cut mine on a leek, which I eat it every week:
    I'm a clerk at thirty bob as you can see.

But I don't allow it's luck and all a toss;
  There's no such thing as being starred and crossed;
It's just the power of some to be a boss,
  And the bally power of others to be bossed:
I face the music, sir; you bet I ain't a cur;
  Strike me lucky if I don't believe I'm lost!

For like a mole I journey in the dark,
  A-travelling along the underground
From my Pillar'd Halls and broad Suburban Park,
  To come the daily dull official round;
And home again at night with my pipe all alight,
  A-scheming how to count ten bob a pound.

And it's often very cold and very wet,
  And my missis stitches towels for a hunks;
And the Pillar'd Halls is half of it to let—
  Three rooms about the size of travelling trunks.
And we cough, my wife and I, to dislocate a sigh,
  When the noisy little kids are in their bunks.

But you never hear her do a growl or whine,
  For she's made of flint and roses, very odd;
And I've got to cut my meaning rather fine,
  Or I'd blubber, for I'm made of greens and sod:
So p'r'aps we are in Hell for all that I can tell,
  And lost and damn'd and served up hot to God.

I ain't blaspheming, Mr. Silver-tongue;
  I'm saying things a bit beyond your art:
Of all the rummy starts you ever sprung,
  Thirty bob a week's the rummiest start!
With your science and your books and your the'ries about spooks,
  Did you ever hear of looking in your heart?

I didn't mean your pocket, Mr, no:
  I mean that having children and a wife,
With thirty bob on which to come and go,
  Isn't dancing to the tabor and the fife:
When it doesn't make you drink, by Heaven! it makes you think,
  And notice curious items about life.

I step into my heart and there I meet
  A god-almighty devil singing small,
Who would like to shout and whistle in the street,
  And squelch the passers flat against the wall;
If the whole world was a cake he had the power to take,
  He would take it, ask for more, and eat it all.

And I meet a sort of simpleton beside,
  The kind that life is always giving beans;
With thirty bob a week to keep a bride
  He fell in love and married in his teens:
At thirty bob he stuck; but he knows it isn't luck:
  He knows the seas are deeper than tureens.

And the god-almighty devil and the fool
  That meet me in the High Street on the strike,
When I walk about my heart a-gathering wool,
  Are my good and evil angels if you like.
And both of them together in every kind of weather
  Ride me like a double-seated bike.

That's rough a bit and needs its meaning curled.
  But I have a high old hot un in my mind—
A most engrugious notion of the world,
  That leaves your lightning 'rithmetic behind—
I give it at a glance when I say 'There ain't no chance,
  Nor nothing of the lucky-lottery kind.'

And it's this way that I make it out to be:
  No fathers, mothers, countries, climates—none;
Not Adam was responsible for me,
  Nor society, nor systems, nary one:
A little sleeping seed, I woke—I did, indeed—
  A million years before the blooming sun.

I woke because I thought the time had come ;
  Beyond my will there was no other cause;
And everywhere I found myself at home,
  Because I chose to be the thing I was;
And in whatever shape of mollusc or of ape
  I always went according to the laws.

I was the love that chose my mother out;
  I joined two lives and from the union burst;
My weakness and my strength without a doubt
  Are mine alone for ever from the first:
It's just the very same with difference in the name
  As 'Thy will be done'. You say it if you durst!

They say it daily up and down the land
  As easy as you take a drink, it's true;
But the difficultest go to understand,
  And the difficultest job a man can do,
Is to come it brave and meek with thirty bob a week,
  And feel that that's the proper thing for you.

It's a naked child against a hungry wolf;
  It's playing bowls upon a splitting wreck;
It's walking on a string across a gulf
  With millstones fore-and-aft about your neck;
But the thing is daily done by many and many a one;
  And we fall, face forward, fighting, on the deck.

FRANCIS LAUDERDALE ADAMS

1862–1893

188   *William Wallace*

(For the Ballarat statue of him)

THIS is Scotch William Wallace. It was he
  Who in dark hours first raised his face to see:
  Who watched the English tyrant nobles spurn,
Steel-clad, with iron hoofs the Scottish free:

  Who armed and drilled the simple footman Kern,
  Yea, bade in blood and rout the proud Knight learn
His Feudalism was dead, and Scotland stand
  Dauntless to wait the day of Bannockburn!

O Wallace, peerless lover of thy land
We need thee still, thy moulding brain and hand!
  For us, thy poor, again proud tyrants spurn,
The robber rich, a yet more hateful band!

189   *Jesus*

WHERE is poor Jesus gone?
    He sits with Dives now,
And not even the crumbs are flung
  To Lazarus below.

Where is poor Jesus gone?
  Is he with Magdalen?
He doles her one by one
  Her wages of shame!

456

Where is poor Jesus gone?
  The good Samaritan,
What does he there alone?
  He stabs the wounded man!

Where is poor Jesus gone,
  The lamb they sacrificed?
They've made God of his carrion
  And labelled it 'Christ!'

190
To the Christians

TAKE, then, your paltry Christ,
  Your gentleman God.
We want the carpenter's son,
  With his saw and hod.

We want the man who loved
  The poor and oppressed,
Who hated the rich man and king
  And the scribe and the priest.

We want the Galilean
  Who knew cross and rod.
It's your 'good taste' that prefers
  A bastard God!

191
Hagar

SHE went along the road,
  Her baby in her arms.
  The night and its alarms
Made deadlier her load.

Her shrunken breasts were dry;
　　She felt the hunger bite.
　　She lay down in the night,
She and the child, to die.

But it would wail. and wail.
　　And wail. She crept away.
　　She had no word to say,
Yet still she heard the wail.

She took a jagged stone;
　　She wished it to be dead.
　　She beat it on the head;
It only gave one moan.

She has no word to say;
　　She sits there in the night.
　　The east sky glints with light,
And it is Christmas Day!

192　　　　*Evening Hymn in the Hovels*

'WE sow the fertile seed and then we reap it;
　　We thresh the golden grain; we knead the bread.
Others that eat are glad. In store they keep it,
　　While we hunger outside with hearts like lead.
　　　　Hallelujah!

'We hew the stone and saw it, rear the city.
　　Others inhabit there in pleasant ease.
We have no thing to ask of them save pity,
　　No answer they to give but what they please.
　　　　Hallelujah!

'Is it for ever, fathers, say, and mothers,
  That we must toil and never know the light?
Is it for ever, sisters, say, and brothers,
  That they must grind us dead here in the night?
      Hallelujah!

'O we who sow, reap, knead, shall we not also
  Have strength and pleasure of the food we make?
O we who hew, build, deck, shall we not also
  The happiness that we have given partake?
      Hallelujah!'

VIOLET JACOB

1863–1946

193   *The Last o' the Tinkler*

LAY me in yon place, lad,
    The gloamin's thick wi' nicht;
I canna see yer face, lad,
    For my een's no richt.
But it's owre late for leein'
An' I ken fine I'm deein'
Like an auld craw fleein'
    Tae the last o' the licht.

The kye gang tae the byre, lad,
　The sheep tae the fauld,
Ye'll mak a spunk o' fire, lad,
　For my hert's turned cauld;
And whaur the trees are meetin'
There's a sound like waters beatin'
An' the bird seems near tae greetin'
　That was aye singin' bauld.

There's just the tent tae leave, lad,
　I've gaithered little gear,
There's just yersel' tae grieve, lad,
　And the auld dog here;
But when the morn comes creepin'
And the waukin' birds are cheepin'
It'll find me lyin' sleepin'
　As I've slept saxty year.

Ye'll rise tae meet the sun, lad,
　And baith be trayv'lin' west
But me that's auld an' done, lad,
　I'll bide an' tak my rest;
For the grey heid is bendin'
And the auld shune's needin' mendin',
But the trayv'lin's near its endin',
　An' the end's aye the best.

shune: shoes

194

Pride

DID ivver ye see the like o' that?
　The warld's fair fashioned to winder at!
Heuch—dinna tell me! Yon's Fishie Pete
That cried the haddies in Ferry Street
Set up wi' his coats an' his grand cigars
In ane o' thae stinkin' motor-cars!

I mind the time (an' it's no far past)
When he wasna for fleein' alang sae fast,
An' doon i' the causey his cairt wad stand
As he roared oot 'Haddies!' below his hand;
Ye'd up wi' yer windy an' doon he'd loup
Frae the shaft o' the cairt by the sheltie's doup.

Ay, muckle cheenges an' little sense,
A bawbee's wit an' a poond's pretence!
For there's him noo wi' his neb to the sky
I' yon deil's machinery swiggit by,
An' me, that whiles gied him a piece to eat,
Tramps aye to the kirk on my ain twa feet.

And neebours, mind ye, the warld's agley
Or we couldna see what we've seen the day;
Guid fortune's blate whaur she's weel desairv't
The sinner fu' and the godly stairv't,
An' fowk like me an' my auld guidman
Jist wearied daein' the best we can!

blate: shy

461

I've kept my lips an' my tongue frae guile
An' kept mysel' to mysel' the while;
Agin a' wastrels I've aye been set
And I'm no for seekin' to thole them yet;
A grand example I've been through life,
A righteous liver, a thrifty wife.

But oh! the hert o' a body bleeds
For favours sclarried on sinfu' heids.
Wait you a whilie! Ye needna think
They'll no gang frae him wi' cairds an' drink!
They'll bring nae blessin', they winna bide,
For the warst sin, neebours, is pride, ay, pride!

thole: put up with   sclarried: spilt

CHARLES MURRAY

1864–1941

195   *The Whistle*

HE cut a sappy sucker from the muckle rodden-tree
    He trimmed it, an' he wet it, an' he thumped it on his knee;
He never heard the teuchat when the harrow broke her eggs,
He missed the craggit heron nabbin' puddocks in the seggs,
He forgot to hound the collie at the cattle when they strayed,
But you should hae seen the whistle that the wee herd made!

rodden tree: rowan tree   teuchat: lapwing   puddocks: frogs

462

He wheepled on't at mornin' and he tweetled on't at nicht,
He puffed his freckled cheeks until his nose sank oot o sicht,
The kye were late for milkin' when he piped them up the closs,
The kitlin's got his supper syne, an' he was beddit boss;
But he cared na doit nor docken what they did or thocht or said,
There was comfort in the whistle that the wee herd made.

For lyin' lang o' mornin's he had clawed the caup for weeks,
But noo he had his bonnet on afore the lave had breeks;
He was whistlin' to the porridge that were hott'rin on the fire
He was whistlin' ower the travise to the baillie in the byre;
Nae a blackbird nor a mavis that hae pipin' for their trade
Was a marrow for the whistle that the wee herd made.

He played a march to battle, it cam' dirlin' through the mist,
Till the halflin squared his shoulders an' made up his mind to
    'list;
He tried a spring for wooers, though he wistna what it meant,
But the kitchen-lass was lauchin' an' he thocht she maybe kent;
He got ream an' buttered bannocks for the lovin' lilt he played
Wasna that a cheery whistle that the wee herd made?

He blew them rants sae lively, schottisches, reels an' jigs,
The foalie flang his muckle legs an' capered ower the rigs,
The grey-tailed futtrat bobbit oot to hear his ain strathspey,
The bawd cam' loupin' through the corn to 'Clean Pease Strae';
The feet o' ilka man an' beast gat youkie when he played—
Hae ye ever heard o' whistle like the wee herd made?

kye: cows   boss: snug   doit: small coin   docken: anything
of small value   clawed the caup: cleaned the dish   lave: rest
mavis: thrush   halflin: apprentice   ream: cream   futtrat:
weasel   bawd: hare

But the snaw it stopped the herdin' an' the winter brocht him
  dool,
When in spite o' hacks an' chilblains he was shod again for
  school;
He couldna sough the catechis nor pipe the rule o' three,
He was keepit in an' lickit when the ither loons got free;
But he aften played the truant—'twas the only thing he played,
For the maister brunt the whistle that the wee herd made!

  licket: beaten   brunt: burnt

MARION ANGUS

1866–1946

196   *Alas! Poor Queen*

S HE was skilled in music and the dance
  And the old arts of love
At the court of the poisoned rose
And the perfumed glove,
And gave her beautiful hand
To the pale Dauphin
A triple crown to win—
And she loved little dogs
          And parrots
        And red-legged partridges
And the golden fishes of the Duc de Guise
And a pigeon with a blue ruff
She had from Monsieur d'Elbœuf.

Master John Knox was no friend to her;
She spoke him soft and kind,
Her honeyed words were Satan's lure
The unwary soul to blind.
'Good sir, doth a lissome shape
And a comely face
Offend your God His Grace
Whose Wisdom maketh these
Golden fishes of the Duc de Guise?'

She rode through Liddesdale with a song;
'Ye streams sae wondrous strang,
Oh, mak' me a wrack as I come back
But spare me as I gang,'
While a hill-bird cried and cried
Like a spirit lost
By the grey storm-wind tost.

Consider the way she had to go.
Think of the hungry snare,
The net she herself had woven,
Aware or unaware,
Of the dancing feet grown still,
The blinded eyes—
Queens should be cold and wise,
And she loved little things,
        Parrots
    And red-legged partridges
And the golden fishes of the Duc de Guise
And the pigeon with the blue ruff
She had from Monsieur d'Elbœuf.

LEWIS SPENCE

1874–1955

197   *The Prows o' Reekie*

O WAD this braw hie-heapit toun
   Sail aff like an enchanted ship,
Drift owre the warld's seas up and doun
And kiss wi' Venice lip to lip,
Or anchor into Naples Bay
A misty island far astray,
Or set her rock to Athens' wa',
Pillar to pillar, stane to stane,
The cruikit spell o' her backbane,
Yon shadow-mile o' spire and vane,
Wad ding them a'! Wad ding them a'!
Cadiz wad tine the admiralty
O' yonder emerod fair sea,
Gibraltar frown for frown exchange
Wi' Nigel's Crags at elbuck-range,
The rose-red banks o' Lisbon make
Mair room in Tagus for her sake.

A hoose is but a puppet-box
To keep life's images frae knocks,
But mannikins scrieve oot their sauls
Upon its craw-steps and its walls:
Whaur hae they writ them mair sublime
Than on yon gable-ends o' time?

Reekie: Edinburgh   ding: defeat   tine: lose   elbuck:
elbow   scrieve: write

ALEXANDER GRAY

1882–

Scotland

HERE in the uplands
    The soil is ungrateful;
The fields, red with sorrel,
Are stony and bare.
A few trees, wind-twisted—
Or are they but bushes?—
Stand stubbornly guarding
A home here and there.

Scooped out like a saucer,
The land lies before me;
The waters, once scattered,
Flow orderedly now
Through fields where the ghosts
Of the marsh and the moorland
Still ride the old marches,
Despising the plough.

The marsh and the moorland
Are not to be banished;
The bracken and heather,
The glory of broom,
Usurp all the balks
And the fields' broken fringes,
And claim from the sower
Their portion of room.

This is my country,
The land that begat me.
These windy spaces
Are surely my own.
And those who here toil
In the sweat of their faces
Are flesh of my flesh,
And bone of my bone.

Hard is the day's task
Scotland, stern Mother—
Wherewith at all times
Thy sons have been faced:
Labour by day,
And scant rest in the gloaming
With Want an attendant,
Not lightly outpaced.

Yet do thy children
Honour and love thee.
Harsh is thy schooling,
Yet great is the gain:
True hearts and strong limbs,
The beauty of faces,
Kissed by the wind
And caressed by the rain.

ALEXANDER GRAY

(Heine in Scots)

199   *Lassie, What Mair Wad You Hae?*
          (Du hast Diamanten und Perlen)

O YOU'RE braw wi' your pearls and your diamonds,
     You've routh o' a' thing, you may say,
And there's nane has got bonnier een, Kate:
     'Od, lassie, what mair wad you hae?

I've written a hantle o' verses,
     That'll live till the Hendmost Day;
And they're a' in praise o' your een, Kate:
     'Od, lassie, what mair wad you hae?

Your een, sae blue and sae bonny,
     Have plagued me till I am fey,
'Deed, I hardly think I can live, Kate:
     'Od, lassie, what mair wad you hae?

               routh: plenty   hantle: handful

ANDREW YOUNG

1885–

200   *The Falls of Glomach*

RAIN drifts forever in this place
     Tossed from the long white lace
The Falls trail on the black rocks below,
And golden-rod and rose-root shake
In wind that they forever make;
So though they wear their own rainbow
It's not in hope, but just for show,
For rain and wind together
Here through the summer make a chill wet weather.

201 *Suilven*

IT rose dark as a stack of peat
With mountains at its feet,
Till a bright flush of evening swept
And on to its high shoulder leapt
And Suilven, a great ruby, shone;
And though that evening light is dead
The mountain in my mind burns on,
As though I were the foul toad, said
To bear a precious jewel in his head.

202 *Culbin Sands*

HERE lay a fair fat land;
But now its townships, kirks, graveyards
Beneath bald hills of sand
Lie buried deep as Babylonian shards.

But gales may blow again;
And like a sand-glass turned about
The hills in a dry rain
Will flow away and the old land look out;

And where now hedgehog delves
And conies hollow their long caves
Houses will build themselves
And tombstones rewrite names on dead men's graves.

HELEN B. CRUICKSHANK

1886–

203 *Comfort in Puirtith*

THE man that mates wi' Poverty,
   An' clasps her tae his banes,
Will faither lean an' lively thochts,
   A host o eident weans—
But wow! they'll warstle tae the fore
   Wi' hunger-sharpit brains!

But he that lies wi' creeshy W'alth
   Will breed a pudden thrang,
Owre cosh tae ken their foziness,
   Owre bien tae mak' a sang—
A routh o' donnert feckless fules
   Wha dinna coont a dang!

eident weans: diligent brats   creeshy: fat   thrang: throng
cosh: snug   foziness: stupidity   bien: well-off   donnert: stupefied

204 *Shy Geordie*

UP the Noran Water
   In by Inglismaddy,
Annie's got a bairnie
That hasna got a daddy.
Some say it 's Tammas's,
An' some say it 's Chay's;
An' naebody expec'it it,
Wi' Annie's quiet ways.

471

Up the Noran Water
The bonny little mannie
Is dandled an' cuddled close
By Inglismaddy's Annie.
Wha the bairnie's daddy is
The lassie never says;
But some think it 's Tammas's,
An' some think it 's Chay's.

Up the Noran Water
The country folk are kind;
An' wha the bairnie's daddy is
They dinna muckle mind.
But oh! the bairn at Annie's breist,
The love in Annie's e'e—
They mak' me wish wi' a' my micht
The lucky lad was me!

EDWIN MUIR

1887–1959

205

Merlin

O MERLIN in your crystal cave
　Deep in the diamond of the day,
Will there ever be a singer
Whose music will smooth away
The furrow drawn by Adam's finger
Across the meadow and the wave?
Or a runner who'll outrun
Man's long shadow driving on,

Break through the gate of memory
And hang the apple on the tree?
Will your magic ever show
The sleeping bride shut in her bower,
The day wreathed in its mound of snow
And Time locked in his tower?

206   *Scotland's Winter*

NOW the ice lays its smooth claws on the sill,
    The sun looks from the hill
Helmed in his winter casket,
And sweeps his arctic sword across the sky.
The water at the mill
Sounds more hoarse and dull.
The miller's daughter walking by
With frozen fingers soldered to her basket
Seems to be knocking
Upon a hundred leagues of floor
With her light heels, and mocking
Percy and Douglas dead,
And Bruce on his burial bed,
Where he lies white as may
With wars and leprosy,
And all the kings before
This land was kingless,
And all the singers before
This land was songless,
This land that with its dead and living waits the Judgment Day.
But they, the powerless dead,
Listening can hear no more
Than a hard tapping on the floor
A little overhead

Of common heels that do not know
Whence they come or where they go
And are content
With their poor frozen life and shallow banishment.

207 *The Mythical Journey*

FIRST in the North. The black sea-tangled beaches,
Brine-bitter stillness, tablet-strewn morass,
Tall women against the sky with heads covered,
The witch's house below the black-toothed mountain,
Wave-echo in the roofless chapel,
The twice-dead castle on the swamp-green mound,
Darkness at noon-day, wheel of fire at midnight,
The level sun and the wild shooting shadows.

How long ago? Then sailing up to summer
Over the edge of the world. Black hill of water,
Rivers of running gold. The sun! The sun!
Then the free summer isles.
But the ship hastened on and brought him to
The towering walls of life and the great kingdom.

Where long he wandered seeking that which sought him
Through all the little hills and shallow valleys.
One whose form and features,
Race and speech he did not know, shapeless, tongueless,
Known to him only by the impotent heart,
And whether at all on earth the place of meeting,
Beyond all knowledge. Only the little hills,
Head-high, and the winding valleys,
Turning, returning, till there grew a pattern,
And it was held. And there stood both in their stations
With the hills between them. And that was the meaning.

Though sometimes through the wavering light and shadow
He thought he saw it a moment as he watched
The red deer walking by the riverside
At evening, when the bells were ringing,
And the bright stream leapt silent from the mountain
Far in the sunset. But as he looked, nothing
Was there but lights and shadows.

                      And then the vision
Of the conclusion without fulfilment.
The plain of glass and in the crystal grave
That which he had sought, that which had sought him,
Glittering in death. And all the dead scattered
Like fallen stars, clustered like leaves hanging
From the sad boughs of the mountainous tree of Adam
Planted far down in Eden. And on the hills
The gods reclined and conversed with each other
From summit to summit.

                 Conclusion
Without fulfilment. Thence the dream rose upward,
The living dream sprung from dying vision,
Overarching all. Beneath its branches
He builds in faith and doubt his shaking house.

208   *Scotland 1941*

WE were a tribe, a family, a people.
     Wallace and Bruce guard now a painted field,
And all may read the folio of our fable,
Peruse the sword, the sceptre and the shield.
A simple sky roofed in that rustic day,

The busy corn-fields and the haunted holms,
The green road winding up the ferny brae.
But Knox and Melville clapped their preaching palms
And bundled all the harvesters away,
Hoodicrow Peden in the blighted corn
Hacked with his rusty beak the starving haulms.
Out of that desolation we were born.

Courage beyond the point and obdurate pride
Made us a nation, robbed us of a nation.
Defiance absolute and myriad-eyed
That could not pluck the palm plucked our damnation.
We with such courage and the bitter wit
To fell the ancient oak of loyalty,
And strip the peopled hill and altar bare,
And crush the poet with an iron text,
How could we read our souls and learn to be?
Here a dull drove of faces harsh and vexed,
We watch our cities burning in their pit,
To salve our souls grinding dull lucre out,
We, fanatics of the frustrate and the half,
Who once set Purgatory Hill in doubt.
Now smoke and dearth and money everywhere,
Mean heirlooms of each fainter generation,
And mummied housegods in their musty niches,
Burns and Scott, sham bards of a sham nation,
And spiritual defeat wrapped warm in riches,
No pride but pride of pelf. Long since the young
Fought in great bloody battles to carve out
This towering pulpit of the Golden Calf,
Montrose, Mackail, Argyle, perverse and brave,
Twisted the stream, unhooped the ancestral hill.
Never had Dee or Don or Yarrow or Till
Huddled such thriftless honour in a grave.

Such wasted bravery idle as a song,
Such hard-won ill might prove Time's verdict wrong,
And melt to pity the annalist's iron tongue.

209 *Robert the Bruce*

(To Douglas in dying)

'MY life is done, yet all remains,
 The breath has gone, the image not,
The furious shapes once forged in heat
 Live on though now no longer hot.

'Steadily the shining swords
 In order rise, in order fall,
In order on the beaten field
 The faithful trumpets call.

'The women weeping for the dead
 Are not sad now but dutiful,
The dead men stiffening in their place
 Proclaim the ancient rule.

'Great Wallace's body hewn in four,
 So altered, stays as it must be.
O Douglas do not leave me now,
 For past your head I see

'My dagger sheathed in Comyn's heart
 And nothing there to praise or blame,
Nothing but order which must be
 Itself and still the same.

477

'But that Christ hung upon the Cross,
        Comyn would rot until time's end
And bury my sin in boundless dust,
        For there is no amend

'In order; yet in order run
        All things by unreturning ways.
If Christ live not, nothing is there
        For sorrow or for praise.'

So the king spoke to Douglas once
        A little while before his death,
Having outfaced three English kings
        And kept a people's faith.

210   *The Confirmation*

YES, yours, my love, is the right human face.
        I in my mind had waited for this long,
Seeing the false and searching for the true,
Then found you as a traveller finds a place
Of welcome suddenly amid the wrong
Valleys and rocks and twisting roads. But you,
What shall I call you? A fountain in a waste,
A well of water in a country dry,
Or anything that's honest and good, an eye
That makes the whole world bright. Your open heart,
Simple with giving, gives the primal deed,
The first good world, the blossom, the blowing seed,
The hearth, the steadfast land, the wandering sea,
Not beautiful or rare in every part,
But like yourself, as they were meant to be.

The Fathers

OUR fathers all were poor,
  Poorer our fathers' fathers;
Beyond, we dare not look.
We, the sons, keep store
Of tarnished gold that gathers
Around us from the night,
Record it in this book
That, when the line is drawn,
Credit and creditor gone,
Column and figure flown,
Will open into light.

Archaic fevers shake
Our healthy flesh and blood
Plumped in the passing day
And fed with pleasant food.
The fathers' anger and ache
Will not, will not away
And leave the living alone,
But on our careless brows
Faintly their furrows engrave
Like veinings in a stone,
Breathe in the sunny house
Nightmare of blackened bone,
Cellar and choking cave.

Panics and furies fly
Through our unhurried veins,
Heavenly lights and rains
Purify heart and eye,
Past agonies purify

And lay the sullen dust.
The angers will not away.
We hold our fathers' trust,
Wrong, riches, sorrow and all
Until they topple and fall,
And fallen let in the day.

212   *The Transfiguration*

SO from the ground we felt that virtue branch
Through all our veins till we were whole, our wrists
As fresh and pure as water from a well,
Our hands made new to handle holy things,
The source of all our seeing rinsed and cleansed
Till earth and light and water entering there
Gave back to us the clear unfallen world.
We would have thrown our clothes away for lightness,
But that even they, though sour and travel stained,
Seemed, like our flesh, made of immortal substance,
And the soiled flax and wool lay light upon us
Like friendly wonders, flower and flock entwined
As in a morning field. Was it a vision?
Or did we see that day the unseeable
One glory of the everlasting world
Perpetually at work, though never seen
Since Eden locked the gate that 's everywhere
And nowhere? Was the change in us alone,
And the enormous earth still left forlorn,
An exile or a prisoner? Yet the world
We saw that day made this unreal, for all
Was in its place. The painted animals
Assembled there in gentle congregations,
Or sought apart their leafy oratories,

Or walked in peace, the wild and tame together,
As if, also for them, the day had come.
The Shepherds' hovels shone clean at the heart
As on the starting-day. The refuse heaps
Were grained with that fine dust that made the world;
For he had said, 'To the pure all things are pure'.
And when we went into the town, he with us,
The lurkers under doorways, murderers,
With rags tied round their feet for silence, came
Out of themselves to us and were with us,
And those who hide within the labyrinth
Of their own loneliness and greatness came,
And those tangled in their own devices,
The silent and the garrulous liars, all
Stepped out of their dungeons and were free.
Reality or vision, this we have seen.
If it had lasted but another moment
It might have held for ever! But the world
Rolled back into its place, and we are here,
And all that radiant kingdom lies forlorn,
As if it had never stirred; no human voice
Is heard among its meadows, but it speaks
To itself alone, alone it flowers and shines
And blossoms for itself while time runs on.

But he will come again, it 's said, though not
Unwanted and unsummoned; for all things,
Beasts of the field, and woods, and rocks, and seas,
And all mankind from end to end of the earth
Will call him with one voice. In our own time,
Some say, or at a time when time is ripe.
Then he will come, Christ the uncrucified,
Christ the discrucified, his death undone,
His agony unmade, his cross dismantled—

Glad to be so—and the tormented wood
Will cure its hurt and grow into a tree
In a green springing corner of young Eden,
And Judas damned take his long journey backward
From darkness into light and be a child
Beside his mother's knee, and the betrayal
Be quite undone and never more be done.

BESSIE J. B. MACARTHUR

1889–

213 *Nocht o' Mortal Sicht* (1942)

A' DAY aboot the hoose I work,
My hands are rouch, my banes are sair,
Though it's a ghaist comes doon at daw,
A ghaist at nicht that clims the stair.

For nocht o' mortal sicht I see—
But warrin tanks on ilka hand,
And twistit men that lie sae still
And sma', upon the desert sand.

And nocht I hear the leelang day
But skirl o' shell and growl o' gun,
And owre my heid the bombers roar
Reid-hot aneath the Libyan sun.

But when the licht is on the wane,
And antrin winds gae whinnerin by,
It's snaw comes swirlin round my feet
And drifts in cluds across the sky.

daw: dawn

BESSIE J. B. MACARTHUR

And syne it 's straikit owre wi' bluid,
And syne the wind is hairse wi' cries,
And syne abune the Russian snaws
I see the Kremlin towers rise.

While round the city, mile on mile,
The grim battalions tak their stand,
And deid men streik from aff the grund
To grup their comrades by the hand.

And sae it haps that ilka day
Frae mornin' licht to gloamin' fa',
It is a ghaist that walks the hoose
And casts its shadow on the wa'.

hairse: hoarse

MARGARET WINEFRIDE SIMPSON

1893–

Villanelle

O WINTER wind, lat grievin be,
Lat grievin be, and murn nae mair:
Simmer sall set thy sorrow free.

New hurt the heavy hert sall dree;
Thy weariness awa sall wear:
O winter wind, lat grievin be.

Wi a' the waes the warld sall see
What wae hast thou that can compare?
Simmer sall set thy sorrow free,

Yet what delicht sall puirtith pree
When time sall solace thy despair?
O winter wind, lat grievin be.

What fear onkent can trouble thee,
What misery that nane can share?
Simmer sall set thy sorrow free,

But man in dule doth live and dee;
A birn mair brief is thine to bear:
O winter wind, lat grievin be:

Simmer sall set thy sorrow free!

puirtith: poverty   pree: taste   dule: grief   birn: burden

HUGH MACDIARMID
1892–

215   *Crowdieknowe*

OH to be at Crowdieknowe
    When the last trump blaws,
An' see the deid come loupin' owre
The auld grey wa's.

Muckle men wi' tousled beards
I grat at as a bairn
'll scramble frae the croodit clay
Wi' feck o' swearin'.

loupin': leaping   grat: wept   croodit: crowded   feck:
plenty

An' glower at God an' a' his gang
O' angels i' the lift
—Thae trashy bleezin' French-like folk
Wha gar'd them shift!

Fain the weemun-folk'll seek
To mak' them haud their row
—*Fegs, God's no blate gin he stirs up*
The men o' Crowdieknowe!

blate: shy

216   *The Fleggit Bride*

SEIL o' yer face! the send has come.
  I ken, I ken, but awa' ye gan,
An' dinna fash, for what's i' yer hert
A' weemun ken an' nae man can.

Seil o' yer face! Ye needna seek
For comfort gin ye show yer plight.
To Gods an' men, coorse callants baith,
A fleggit bride 's the seilfu' sicht.

fleggit: frightened   seil, etc.: look happy!   send: summons
fash: worry   callants: fellows

217   *Cophetua*

OH! The King's gane gyte,
  Puir auld man, puir auld man,
An' an ashypet lassie
Is Queen o' the lan'.

gyte: mad   ashypet lassie: kitchen-maid

Wi' a scoogie o' silk
An' a bucket o' siller
She's showin' the haill coort
The smeddum intil her!

scoogie: apron   smeddum: gumption

218   *The Innumerable Christ*

'Other stars may have their Bethlehem, and their Calvary, too.'
Professor J. Y. Simpson.

WHA kens on whatna Bethlehems
  Earth twinkles like a star the nicht,
An' whatna shepherds lift their heids
  In its unearthly licht?

'Yont a' the stars oor een can see
An' farther than their lichts can fly
I' mony an unco warl' the nicht
  The fatefu' bairnies cry.

I' mony an unco warl' the nicht
The lift gaes black as pitch at noon,
An' sideways on their chests the heids
  O' endless Christs roll doon.

An' when the earth's as cauld's the mune
An' a' its folk are lang syne deid,
On coontless stars the Babe maun cry
  An' the Crucified maun bleed.

unco: strange   mune: moon

486

219   *Empty Vessel*

I MET ayont the cairney
A lass wi' tousie hair
Singin' till a bairnie
That was nae langer there.

Wunds wi' warlds to swing
Dinna sing sae sweet,
The licht that bends owre a' thing
Is less ta'en up wi't.

220   *O Wha's the Bride?*

O WHA 'S the bride that cairries the bunch
O' thistles blinterin' white?
Her cuckold bridegroom little dreids
What he sall ken this nicht.

For closer than gudeman can come
And closer to'r than hersel',
Wha didna need her maidenheid
Has wrocht his purpose fell.

O wha 's been here afore me, lass,
And hoo did he get in?
—*A man that dee'd or I was born*
This evil thing has din.

And left, as it were on a corpse,
Your maidenheid to me?
—*Nae lass, gudeman, sin' Time began*
's had ony mair to gi'e.

      blinterin': gleaming   dreids: dreads

But I can gi'e ye kindness, lad,
And a pair o' willin' hands,
And you sall ha'e my breists like stars,
My limbs like willow wands.

And on my lips ye'll heed nae mair,
And in my hair forget,
The seed o' a' the men that in
My virgin womb ha'e met. . . .

nae mair: no more

221 *The Great Wheel*

I'M weary o' the rose as o' my brain,
And for a deeper knowledge I am fain
Than frae this noddin' object I can gain.

Beauty is a'e thing, but it tines anither
(For, fegs, they never can be f'und thegither),
And 'twixt the twa it 's no' for me to swither.

As frae the grun' sae thocht frae men springs oot,
A ferlie that tells little o' its source, I doot,
And has nae vera fundamental root.

And cauld agen my hert are laid
The words o' Plato when he said,
'God o' geometry is made'.

Frae my ain mind I fa' away,
That never yet was feared to say
What turned the souls o' men to clay,

tines: loses   fegs: faith   swither: hesitate   ferlie: wonder

HUGH MACDIARMID

Nor cared gin truth frae me ootsprung
In ne'er a leed o' ony tongue
That ever in a heid was hung.

I ken hoo much oor life is fated
Aince its first cell is animated,
The fount frae which the flesh is jetted.

I ken hoo lourd the body lies
Upon the spirit when it flies
And fain abune its stars 'ud rise.

And see I noo a great wheel move,
And a' the notions that I love
Drap into stented groove and groove?

It maitters not my mind the day,
Nocht matters that I strive to dae
—For the wheel moves on in its ain way.

I sall be moved as it decides
To look at Life frae ither sides:
Rejoice, rebel, its turn abides.

And as I see the great wheel spin
There flees a licht frae't lang and thin
That Earth is like a snaw-ba' in.

(To the uncanny thocht I clutch
—The nature o' man's soul is such
That it can ne'er wi' life tine touch.

leed: language   lourd: heavy   stented: appointed   tine: lose

489

Man's mind is in God's image made,
And in its wildest dreams arrayed
In pairt o' Truth is still displayed.

Then suddenly I see as weel
As me spun roon' within the wheel
The helpless forms o' God and Deil.

And on a birlin' edge I see
Wee Scotland squattin' like a flea,
(And dizzy wi' the speed, and me!)

I've often thrawn the warld frae me,
Into the Pool o' Space, to see
The Circles o' Infinity

Or like a flat stone gar'd it skite,
A Morse code message writ in licht
That yet I couldna read aricht.

The skippin' sparks, the ripples, rit
Like skritches o' a grain o' grit
'neth Juggernaut in which I sit.

Twenty-six thousand years it tak's
Afore a'e single roond it mak's,
And syne it melts as it were wax.

The Phoenix guise 't'll rise in syne
Is mair than Euclid or Einstein
Can dream o' or's in dreams o' mine.

gar'd: compelled   skite: skate   rit: rasp

HUGH MACDIARMID

Upon the huge circumference are
As neebor points the Heavenly War
That dung doun Lucifer sae far,

And that upheaval in which I
Sodgered 'neth the Grecian sky
And in Italy and Marseilles,

And there isna room for men
Wha the haill o' history ken
To pit a pin twixt then and then.

Whaur are Bannockburn and Flodden?
—O' a'e grain like facets hod'n,
Little wars (twixt that which God in

Focht and won, and that which He
Took baith sides in hopelessly),
Less than God or I can see

By whatna cry o' mine oottopped
Sall be a' men ha'e sung and hoped
When to a'e note they're telescoped?

And Jesus and a nameless ape
Collide and share the selfsame shape
That nocht terrestrial can escape?

But less than this nae man need try.
He'd better be content to eye
The wheel in silence whirlin' by.

dung: struck   hod'n: holding

491

Nae verse is worth a haet until
It can join issue wi' the Will
That raised the Wheel and spins it still,

But a' the music that mankind
's made yet is to the Earth confined,
Pooerless to reach the general mind,

Pooerless to reach the neist star e'en,
That as a pairt o'ts sel is seen,
And only men can tell between.

Yet I exult oor sang has yet
To grow wings that'll cairry it
Ayont its native speck o' grit.

And I exult to find in me
The thocht that this can ever be,
A hope still for humanity.

For gin the sun and mune at last
Are as a neebor's lintel passed,
The wheel'll tine its stature fast,

And birl in time inside oor heids
Till we can thraw oot conscious gleids
That draw an answer to oor needs,

Or if nae answer still we find
Brichten till a' thing is defined
In the huge licht-beams o' oor kind,

haet: jot   neist: next   birl: revolve

And if we still can find nae trace
Ahint the Wheel o' ony Face,
There'll be a glory in the place,

And we may aiblins swing content
Upon the wheel in which we're pent
In adequate enlightenment.

Nae ither thocht can mitigate
The horror o' the endless Fate
A'thing 's whirled in predestinate.

O whiles I'd fain be blin' to it,
As men wha through the ages sit,
And never move frae aff the bit,

Wha hear a Burns or Shakespear sing,
Yet still their ain bit jingles string,
As they were worth the fashioning.

Whatever Scotland is to me,
Be it aye pairt o' a' men see
O' Earth and o' Eternity

Wha winna hide their heids in't till
It seems the haill o' Space to fill,
As 'twere an unsurmounted hill.

He canna Scotland see wha yet
Canna see the Infinite,
And Scotland in true scale to it.

Nor blame I muckle, wham atour
Earth's countries blaw, a pickle stour,
To sort wha's grains they ha's nae pooer.

aiblins: perhaps   atour: around

E'en stars are seen thegither in
A'e skime o' licht as grey as tin
Flyin' on the wheel as 'twere a pin.

Syne ither systems ray on ray
Skinkle past in quick array
While it is still the self-same day,

A'e day o' a' the million days
Through which the soul o' man can gaze
Upon the wheel's incessant blaze,

Upon the wheel's incessant blaze
As it were on a single place
That twinklin' filled the howe o' space.

A'e point is a' that it can be,
I wis nae man'll ever see
The rest o' the rotundity.

Impersonality sall blaw
Through me as 'twere a bluffert o' snaw
To scour me o' my sense o' awe,

A bluffert o' snaw the licht that flees
Within the Wheel, and freedom gi'es
Frae Dust and Daith and a' disease,

—The drumlie doom that only weighs
On them wha ha'ena seen their place
Yet in creation's lichtnin' race,

skime: gleam   bluffert: squall   drumlie: turbid

494

In the movement that includes
As a tide's resistless floods
A' their movements and their moods,—

Until disinterested we,
O' a' oor auld delusions free,
Lowe in the wheel's serenity

As conscious items in the licht,
And keen to keep it clear and richt
In which the haill machine is dicht,

The licht nae man has ever seen
Till he has felt that he's been gi'en
The stars themsels insteed o' e'en,

And often wi' the sun has glowered
At the white mune until it cowered
As when by new thocht auld 's owrepowered.

Oor universe is like an e'e
Turned in, man's benmaist hert to see,
And swamped in subjectivity.

But whether it can use its sicht
To bring what lies withoot to licht
To answer 's still ayont my micht.

But when that inturned look has brocht
To licht what still in vain it 's socht
Ootward maun be the bent o' thocht.

lowe: glow   benmaist: inmost

And organs may develop syne
Responsive to the need divine
O' single-minded humankin'.

The function, as it seems to me,
O' Poetry is to bring to be
At lang, lang last that unity...

But wae 's me on the weary wheel!
Higgledy-piggledy in't we reel,
And little it cares hoo we may feel.

Twenty-six thoosand years 't'll tak'
For it to threid the Zodiac;
—A single roond o' the wheel to mak'!

Lately it turned—I saw mysel'
In sic a company doomed to mell
I micht ha'e been in Dante's Hell.

It shows hoo little the best o' men
E'en o' them sels at times can ken,
—I sune saw that when I gaed ben

The lesser wheel within the big
That moves as merry as a grig
Wi' mankind in its whirligig

And hasna turned a'e circle yet
Tho' as it turns we slide in it,
And needs maun tak' the place we get,

syne: yet   sune: soon   gaed ben: went inside

496

I felt it turn, and syne I saw
John Knox and Clavers in my raw.
And Mary Queen o' Scots ana',

And Rabbie Burns and Weelum Wallace,
And Carlyle lookin' unco gallus,
And Harry Lauder (to enthrall us).

And as I looked I saw them a',
A' the Scots baith big and sma',
That e'er the braith o' life did draw.

'Mercy o' Gode, I canna thole
Wi' sic an orra mob to roll.'
—'Wheesht! It 's for the guid o' your soul.'

'But what 's the meanin', what 's the sense?'
'—Men shift but by experience,
'Twixt Scots there is nae difference.

They canna learn, sae canna move,
But stick for aye to their auld groove
—The only race in History who've

Bidden in the same category
Frae start to present o' their story,
And deem their ignorance their glory.

The mair they differ, mair the same,
The wheel can whummle a' but them,
—They ca' their obstinacy 'Hame',

And 'Puir auld Scotland' bleat wi' pride,
And wi' their minds made up to bide
A thorn in a' the wide world's side.

thole: endure   orra: incongruous   whummle: overturn

497

There ha'e been Scots wha ha'e ha'en thochts
They're strewn through maist o' the various lots
—Sic traitors are nae langer Scots!'

'But in this huge ineducable
Heterogeneous hotch and rabble,
Why am *I* condemned to squabble?'

'*A Scottish poet maun assume*
The burden o' his people's doom,
And dee to brak' their livin' tomb.

Mony ha'e tried, but a' ha'e failed.
Their sacrifice has nocht availed.
Upon the thistle they're impaled.

You maun choose but gin ye'd see
Anither category ye
Maun tine your nationality.'

And I look at a' the random
Band the wheel leaves whaur it fand 'em.
                              'Auch, to Hell,
I'll tak it to avizandum. . .'

        avizandum: defer decision (law)

222   *The Parrot Cry*

TELL me the auld, auld story
     O' hoo the Union brocht
Puir Scotland into being
As a country worth a thocht.

498

England, frae whom a' blessings flow
What could we dae withoot ye?
Then dinna threep it doon oor throats
As gin we e'er could doot ye!
 My feelings lang wi' gratitude
 Ha'e been sae sairly harrowed
 That dod! I think it's time
 The claith was owre the parrot!

Tell me o' Scottish enterprise
And canniness and thrift,
And hoo we're baith less Scots and mair
Than ever under George the Fifth,
And hoo to 'wider interests'
Oor ain we sacrifice
And yet tine naething by it
As aye the parrot cries.
 Syne gi'es a chance to think it oot
 Aince we're a' weel awaur o't,
 For, losh, I think it's time
 The claith was owre the parrot!

Tell me o' love o' country
Content to see't decay,
And ony ither paradox
Ye think o' by the way.
I doot it needs a Hegel
Sic opposites to fuse;
Oor education's failin'
And canna gi'es the views
 That were peculiar to us
 Afore our vision narrowed
 And gar'd us think it time
 The claith was owre the parrot!

  threep: force tine: lose

A parrot's weel eneuch at times
But whiles we'd leifer hear
A blackbird or a mavis
Singin' fu' blythe and clear.
Fetch ony native Scottish bird
Frae the eagle to the wren,
And faith! you'd hear a different sang
Frae this painted foreigner's then.

> The marine that brocht it owre
> Believed its every word
> —But we're a' deeved to daith
> Wi' his infernal bird.

It's possible that Scotland yet
May hear its ain voice speak
If only we can silence
This endless chatterin' beak.
The blessing wi' the black
Selvedge is the clout!
It's silenced Scotland lang eneuch,
Gi'e England turn aboot.

> For the puir bird needs its rest—
> Wha else'll be the waur o't?
> And it's lang past the time
> The claith was owre the parrot.

And gin that disna dae, lads,
We e'en maun draw its neck
And heist its body on a stick
A' ither pests to check.
I'd raither keep't alive, and whiles
Let bairns keek in and hear

leifer: rather   deeved: deafened   blessing wi'
the black selvedge: Union of 1707   heist: hoist

What the Balliol accent used to be
Frae the Predominant Pairtner here!
　　—But save to please the bairns
　　I'd absolutely bar it
　　For fegs, it's aye high time
　　The claith was owre the parrot!

fegs: faith

EDITH ANNE ROBERTSON

223　　*The Deean Tractorman, Deleerit*

MA lass by munelicht fesht me frae the fail
　A chime o fey blue bells, fleur, stem and ruit,
Laid them on ma deith-pillow; aa the wee bells wail,
O canna ye drive yir tractor hame afore she skids awa?

A kelpie frae the burn cam in and set
Aiverins ontill ma dish, and whan I'd supped,
Ye're futtered, he roared, nou futter the brake yir fit!
O canna ye drive the tractor hame afore she skids awa?

I never thocht they'd shut the iron gate:
Is yon ma bluid or is't the gentil dew
Or is't ma lassie's tears? God hear me say't,
I canna drive ma tractor hame afore I skid awa!

Ma lass and me sclims up the Lairig Gru,
It's me's the shadda on the hurricane
Reft frae her side til tattered haar and spew,
For I maun drive the tractor hame afore she skids awa.

fail: sward　　kelpie: water-spirit　　aiverins: berries　　futtered:
useless　　　sclims: climbs

501

It 's me's the Merry Dancer, leaps to drain
The luift o mirk, ma million million rays
Hae lichted a loesome hauf, a dwallian
For her and me, I'll drive her there afore she skids awa.

luift: sky   dwallian: dwelling

224   *The Deean Tractorman, Clear*

I LOED you for yir kindness
    Til a cameral like me,
For yir swete thrawn blindness
    Til fauts ye cud but see;
        But mair nor aa that
        Sin yestreen ye grat.

I loed you for yir coolness
    On mony a simmer's daw,
And for yir thochts like gypsies
    Vaigan faur awa;
        But mair nor aa that
        Sin yestreen ye grat.

Och, yir chaft wiz puddelt wi tears,
    And yir e'en swown and sair,
And deed ye luiked yir years,
    And a fell puckle mair,
        But dash aa that!
        It wiz for me ye grat!

cameral: poor fish   grat: wept   vaigan: straying   chaft:
cheek   swown: swollen   puckle: great deal

JOE CORRIE

1894–

225 *The Image o' God*

CRAWLIN' aboot like a snail in the mud,
    Covered wi' clammy blae,
ME, made after the image o' God—
    Jings! but it's laughable, tae.

Howkin' awa' 'neath a mountain o' stane,
    Gaspin' for want o' air,
The sweat makin' streams doon my bare back-bane
    And my knees a' hauckit and sair.

Strainin' and cursin' the hale shift through,
    Half-starved, half-blin', half-mad;
And the gaffer he says, 'Less dirt in that coal
    Or ye go up the pit, my lad!'

So I gi'e my life to the Nimmo squad
    For eicht and fower a day;
Me! made after the image o' God—
    Jings! but it's laughable, tae.

clammy blae: blue mud   howkin': digging   hauckit: hacked
hale: whole   gaffer: foreman

226 *Miners' Wives*

WE have borne good sons to broken men,
    Nurtured them on our hungry breast,
And given them to our masters when
    Their day of life was at its best.

We have dried their clammy clothes by the fire,
   Solaced them, cheered them, tended them well,
Watched the wheels raising them from the mire,
   Watched the wheels lowering them to Hell.

We have prayed for them in a Godless way
   (We never could fathom the ways of God),
We have sung with them on their wedding day,
   Knowing the journey and the road.

We have stood through the naked night to watch
   The silent wheels that raised the dead;
We have gone before to raise the latch,
   And lay the pillow beneath their head.

We have done all this for our masters' sake,
   Did it in rags and did not mind;
What more do they want? what more can they take?
   Unless our eyes, and leaves us blind.

WILLIAM JEFFREY
1896–1946

227   *Stones*

THE stones in Jordan's stream
   Perceived the dove descend
In its lily of light:
That glory entered
Their interminable dream.

The stones in Edom's wilderness
Observed the fiend
Take five of their number
And build a cairn thereof,
And beckoning to Jesus
He pointed to the stones and said:
Make bread.
But because of his great love
For the uniqueness of created things,
The confraternity in disparity
Of plant and rock, of flesh and wings,
Jesus would not translate the stones
Out of their immobile immortality
Into that dynasty of death,
Decaying bread:

The stones upon Golgotha's hill
Took the shadow of the cross
Upon them like the scorch of ice:
And they felt the flick of dice
And Jesus' blood mingling with his mother's tears;
And these made indelible stains;
And some of them were taken up
And with curses thrown
At that rejected throne,
And others felt the clamorous butts of Roman spears:
And the pity, horror, and love within them pent
Welled out and shook the earth.
And the veil was rent.

The great stones of the tomb
Enfolded Jesus' body
In silence and deep gloom.

They had him to themselves alone,
That shard of him, sinew and bone,
Transient dust on their immortality.
And now their inanimate heart
Yearned over that shrouded form:
And while three midnights passed
They made of that tomb
A womb:

The fragile bones renewed their strength,
The flesh trembled and moved,
The glory of the dove
Re-descended from above
And with the break of day
The door was rolled away:
The function of the stones was done:
His second birth
Achieved on earth,
Jesus walked into the sun.

228   From *ON GLAISTER'S HILL*

Carlyle on Burns

OOR best-lo'ed makar has but late grown cauld.
Yirdit by the Nith, in St. Michael's fauld;
We micht wi' reverence ha'e ta'en his han'
Had life preserved him, and the psalmist's span
Tied snoods o' cranreuch til his shapely pow;
But laich he's streak'd, under the birken bough.
Ayont the Rhinns there lie the holms o' Ayr,
The garths and shaws and emerant hillocks bare,

makar: poet   yirdit: buried   cranreuch: frost   laich: low

WILLIAM JEFFREY

The liltin' burns and rivers skaddow deep
In glens o' birk and aik, whaur owlets sleep.
In that kintra, that wastlin seaboard clime
He steer'd his gait intil the flume o' time;
At ferm wark, owre the pleugh, his banes were bent,
His youngsome years in clarty cornrigs pent,
Nae boast his cronies nor his callachs braw;
Nathless his ingyne leam'd as blackthorn snaw:
The hert was as a garth in whilk he wonned
Embowerit in a rosier sweet and fair,
Wi' birdies at their sangschule, and the air
Upon the siller streams and wellsprings thron'd.
And aye his harns wi' smeddum birl'd aroun
And spied the maist fause-herted in his toun,
And heez'd them up on laughter's gallows tree.
At lowsen time, when beasts wi' noddin' bree
Gaed schauchlin by, and scal'd frae braes and laws
Cam hamewart doos and blattering o' craws,
At lowsen time, frae lea rigs on Mossgiel,
He'd herd his dreams and tae his chalmer spiel
Atween the rantle-trees, and there wi' words
Jaunty as spatrels frae the waukrife birds,
Or hinny-sweet, like gloamin's croodle-doo,
He twined them, firstlings o' his sang. Till dew
Dwined frae his mou', and daith's untimely shoon
Resoundit on the sun-flumes o' his noon,
And ne'er misguidit, e'en by board or bed,
He followit whaure'er the Scots leid led.

clarty: muddy   cronies: chums   callachs: girls   ingyne:
genius   garth: garden   wonned: lived   harns: brains
smeddum: gumption   lowsen time: knocking-off time   schauchlin: shuffling   rantle-trees: cross-beams   spatrels: notes
doo: dove   dwined: dwindled   leid: tongue

Had he ayont the coulter flash espied
The emerant hills o' vision, and applied
Their musardry and fullsomeness tae sang,
He had been foremaist in the makars' thrang
And Weimar bigg'd aneath the wastlin lift;
But his the hamely bay, the darnit drift
O' burnies drammling frae Valclusa's fountain,
Not his the rosin licht o' Sion's mountain.
And why compleen on't? Suld folk greet and wail
Syne that the gowdspink 's no the nichtingale?
There micht hae been, that mirkin Januar morn,
Anither cottar chiel in Scotia born,
Twa hauns tae ser' the bestial and nae mair,
But oot o' natur's bountith cam this rare
By-ordnar man. Alack! syne he's awa
The people's hert lies dour and quate, like snaw
In shilpit Februar ahint a dyke:
Their ingyne noo is smoorit, as when fyke
Lies mirk and wabbit on the braes and hills.
The skaddow o' the dirk mechanic mills
Snoovles its ghaistly girth owre strath and glen,
And hantles there o' braw upstanding men
Are gruppit in its corp-and-kist-like nieve
And herdit intil stane-land, close and vennel,
And sinder'd far frae growthlie tides that deave,
Frae gowans sinder'd, and frae fog and fennel.
O mirk, mirk, mirk! Spy ye the years tae be?
Spy ye the ootcome o' this wizardry,

coulter: plough-share-blade	musardry: poetry	thrang: throng
bigg'd: built lift: sky	darnit: hidden	drammling:
gurgling gowdspink: goldfinch	chiel: chap	hauns: hands
shilpit: feeble	fyke: burnt heather	wabbit: exhausted
snoovles: glides	hantles: handfuls kist: coffin	nieve: fist
deave: deafen	gowans: daisies	

This maisterhood owre nature? Bluid and glaur,
Castor and Pollux of unhaly war:
Frae whilk a thousand widows mourn, and tint
Are bairns a thousand frae the bonnie glint
O' love within a faither's e'e. Whaur lie
The wings o' ernes that succour? or the cry
Resounding like a bronze in freemen's ears?
Alack, there's naething but the waukrife cheep
O' Smith, Ricardo, Bentham and their peers.

glaur: mud   tint: lost   ernes: eagles   waukrife: wakeful

WILLIAM SOUTAR

1898–1943

229   *Scotland*

ATWEEN the world o' licht
And the world that is to be
A man wi' unco sicht
Sees whaur he canna see:

Gangs whaur he canna walk:
Recks whaur he canna read:
Hauds what he canna tak:
Mells wi' the unborn dead.

Atween the world o' licht
And the world that is to be
A man wi' unco sicht
Monie a saul maun see:

unco: supernatural   mells: mingles

Sauls that are stark and nesh:
Sauls that wud dree the day:
Sauls that are fain for flesh
But canna win the wey.

Hae ye the unco sicht
That sees atween and atween
This world that lowes in licht:
Yon world that hasna been?

It is owre late for fear,
Owre early for disclaim;
Whan ye come hameless here
And ken ye are at hame.

nesh: fine   dree: endure   lowes: glows

230   *A Whigmaleerie*

THERE was an Auchtergaven mouse
   (I canna mind his name)
Wha met in wi' a hirplin louse
Sair trauchl'd for her hame.

'My friend, I'm hippit; and nae doot
Ye'll heist me on my wey.'
The mouse but squinted doun his snoot
And wi' a breenge was by.

Or lang he cam to his ain door
Doun be a condie-hole;
And thocht, as he was stappan owre:
Vermin are ill to thole.

hirplin: limping   trauchl'd: troubled   hippit: lamed   heist:
aid   condie: drain   thole: suffer

231

Supper

STEEPIES for the bairnie
Sae moolie in the mou':
Parritch for a strappan lad
To mak his beard grow.

Stovies for a muckle man
To keep him stout and hale:
A noggin for the auld carl
To gar him sleep weel.

Bless the meat, and bless the drink,
And the hand that steers the pat:
And be guid to beggar-bodies
Whan they come to your yett.

steepies: saps   moolie: squashy   stovies: stove-potatoes
yett: gate

232

Auld Sang

I BROCHT my love a cherry
That hadna onie stane:
I brocht my love a birdie
That hadna onie bane:
I brocht my love a wauchtie
That wasna sour nor sweet:
I brocht my love a bairnie
That didna girn nor greet.

wauchtie: drink

The cherry that I gien him
Was flauntin in the fleur:
The birdie that I taen him
Was nested no an hour:
The wauchtie that I socht him
Cam glintin frae the grund:
The bairnie that I brocht him
Had lang been sleepin sound.

233 *A Riddle*

YON laddie wi' the gowdan pow
　Sae braw in the simmer sün
Will wag a head as white as tow
Afore the year is düne.

The leaf will fa'; and the blusty blaw
That birls the leaf in the air
Will rive his linty locks awa
And lave him bell and bare. (a dandelion.)

gowden: golden   pow: head   tow: flax   birls: whirls
rive: tear   bell: bald

234 *The Tryst*

OLUELY, luely, cam she in,
　and luely she lay doun:
I kent her by her caller lips
and her breists sae smaa and round.

caller: cool-fresh

Aa throu the nicht we spak nae word
nor sindered bane frae bane:
aa throu the nicht I heard her hert
gang soundin wi my ain.

It was about the waukrif hour
whan cocks begin to craw
that she smooled saftly throu the mirk
afore the day wad daw.

Sae luely, luely, cam she in,
sae luely was she gane;
and wi her aa my simmer days
like they had never been.

waukrif: waking   smooled: glided

235   *The Makar*

NAE man wha loves the lawland tongue
   but warstles wi the thocht—
there are mair sangs that bide unsung
nor aa that hae been wrocht.

Ablow the wastery o the years
the thorter o himsel,
deep buried in his bluid he hears
a music that is leal.

And wi this lealness gangs his ain;
and there's nae ither gait
though aa his feres were fremmit men
wha cry: *Owre late, owre late.*

thorter: frustration   leal: genuine, loyal   gait: way
fremmit: estranged

The Auld House

THERE 'S a puckle lairds in the auld house
    wha haud the waas thegither:
there's no muckle graith in the auld house
    nor smeddum aither.

It was aince a braw and bauld house
    and guid for onie weather:
kings and lords thranged in the auld house
    or it gaed a'smither.

There were kings and lords in the auld house
    and birds o monie a feather:
there were sangs and swords in the auld house
    that rattled ane anither.

It was aince a braw and bauld house
    and guid for onie weather:
but it's noo a scruntit and cauld house
    whaur lairdies forgaither.

Lat's caa in the folk to the auld house,
    the puir folk aa thegither:
it's sunkit on rock is the auld house,
    and the rock's their brither.

It was aince a braw and bauld house
    and guid for onie weather:
but the folk maun funder the auld house
    and bigg up anither.

puckle: good few   waas: walls   graith: furniture   smeddum: gumption   bauld: bold   a'smither: to pieces   scruntit: stunted   funder: uproot   bigg: build

237 *The Permanence of the Young Men*

NO man outlives the grief of war
Though he outlive its wreck:
Upon the memory a scar
Through all his years will ache.

Hopes will revive when horrors cease;
And dreaming dread be stilled;
But there shall dwell within his peace
A sadness unannulled.

Upon his world shall hang a sign
Which summer cannot hide:
The permanence of the young men
Who are not by his side.

238 *Song*

WHAUR yon broken brig hings owre,
Whaur yon water maks nae soun',
Babylon blaws by in stour:
Gang doun wi a sang, gang doun.

Deep, owre deep, for onie drouth,
Wan eneuch an ye wud droun,
Saut, or seelfu', for the mouth:
Gang doun wi a sang, gang doun.

Babylon blaws by in stour
Whaur yon water maks nae soun':
Darkness is your only door;
Gang doun wi a sang, gang doun.

brig: bridge   saut: salt   seelfu': sweet

ROBERT RENDALL
1898–

239   *The Planticru*

WHAUR green abune the banks the links stretch oot
    On tae the sandy noust, lies midway there
An auld-time planticru, smothered aboot
    In weeds—but fu' weel delled, and dressed wi' ware.
Biggid o' sea-worn boolders fae the beach
    A dyke runs roond it, lichened doun the sides,
Scarce keepan leaf and root beyond the reach
    O' winter gales and fierce Atlantic tides.

'Oors lang, an age-bent wife wi' aspect mild
    Stands gazan oot tae sea; or digs a speel,
Slowly, as if by vagrant thowts beguiled,
    And sets her twa'r three tatties i' the dreel;
Nor kens hoo firm she heads b' siklike toil
Man's aald inheritance o' sea and soil.

                              planticru: small kailyard

240   *Shore Tullye*
                (*An experiment in Scaldic metre*)

CROFTERS few but crafty,
    Krugglan doun b' moonlight,
Hidan near the headland,
Hint great congles waited.
Swiftly rude sea-raiders
Stranded, evil-handed:
Scythe blades soon were bleedan,
Skulls crackt in the tullye.

    krugglan: crouching   congles: large boulders

516

ROBERT RENDALL

Stretched the battle beachward;
Bravely back we drave them.
Een fleep fleean hinmost
Fand we maakan landward:
Him apae the hillside
Hewed we doun in feud fight—
Never kam sea-rovers
Seekan back tae Rackwick.

fleep: useless fellow, sluggard

ALICE V. STUART

1899–

Lintie in a Cage

(The poet Fergusson in Darien Madhouse, Edinburgh, 1774.
His attendant speaks)

YON is the laddie lo'ed to daunder far
      Whaur the burnie bickers by the Hermitage
That sits at the fit o Braid; or whaur Dunbar,
      Reid as its rocks, breists the blae Frith's blawn rage.
            Noo, in this waefu den
            Mang puir wit-wandered men,
                  His wandering wits aye sing.
I mind my grannie's owercome, 'Even in a cage
      Linties maun sing'.

Lintie: linnet   blae: blue   owercome: refrain

517

I dinna ken the richts o it: he tummelt doun
   (Or so the clash goes) a fell turnpike stair,
Aiblins a wheen the waur o drink: the stoun
    Whummelt his harns: noo, as ye see, sits there,
      Frae his bedding strae a croun
      Tae set his broo abune,
        Plaiting wi mickle care,
'Crouned or uncrouned,' said my grannie, dovering,
    'The makar's aye a king'.

He's aye read-readin his Bibles: whiles will rail
   Against the miscreant (whilk he swears he kens)
That into oor Lord's body drave the nails.
    Guid-sakes! He thinks him amang leevin men!
      It scunners me tae hear,
      Yet aiblins it's no that queer,
        As Innocence suffered then,
Sinsyne maun the saikless thole frae cruel men
    Their share o yon suffering.

Whiles he havers o his pet starling, an' hoo there crept
   Doun the chimley-breist, aince, in the pit-mirk nicht,
A lean cat, huntin-hungered, that stalked, an' leapt
    On the scartin bird, whase maister wauk tae its fricht
      O cheepings an' flichterings
      Ower late for the bluid-clarted wings
      Sae savaged the while he slept.
'Aye, e'en i' the bield o the hearth will the black Fate spring,'
    Quo' cummer, 'on the cherished wings.'

clash: gossip   aiblins: perhaps   wheen: little   harns:
brains   strae: straw   broo: brow   dovering: dozing
saikless thole: innocent suffer   scartin: scratching   bluid-clarted:
blood-soiled   bield: shelter   cummer: old woman

I ken ye maun wark for their guid agin their will,
    Thae doited craturs, but, sirs, it vexes me sair
Tae mind on the lee they tauld him tae fetch him: still
    I see him steppin oot o thon sedan chair
        Wi the daffin licht in his een,
        Thinkin tae crack wi a freen:
        He wisna sae debonair
At the hinner-end, when we had him bound. Yon ill
    Judas-lee wrings me still.

Aye, mebbe he's juist as weel in yon warld o his ain
    Whaur he sings o young love i' the springtime. Hearken
      the noo,
As blithe as a laverock's liltin, the bonny strain
    Ca'd *The Birks o Invermay*, an' a bonny voice too.
        'Sir Precentor', they ca'd the loon
        I' the taverns o Embro toun.
        Aye warblin, warblin away
Till ye fancy ye smell the flourish on the spray
    Owre the daft heid, crouned wi the strae.

Atweel, it'll no be lang noo; he hoasts that sair,
    I jalouse he will sune win free o yon waesome den,
'Even as a bird out of the fowler's snare',
    As the Psalmist sings; an' better wi God than men.
        'A poet, but brunt his rhymes.'
        Dae ye tell me so? There are times
        When I ken that yon voice sae clear
        Will ring even-on i' my ear
        Till the close o my mortal times.

doited: daft   lee: lie   hoasts: coughs   brunt: burnt

ADAM DRINAN

1902–

From *MEN OF THE ROCKS*

[IV]

BELOW the dancing larches freckled
a pinestump-stool on a hyacinth path.
Cool call of willow-wren:
a clan grief in a shrill laugh.

Old Manus, was it your mother's mother
sick in her croft when the factor came?
'Let the old bitch burn, she has lived enough'
they laughed and left her house in flames.

The charred wood rotted, the pinewood grows,
the son's son of a Duke is rich.
Was this a hundred years ago?
not worth the while reviving it?

Mend the gut for the rich young master!
Chew wood-sorrel leaves and spit!
Acid is persecuted action:
taste of resignation, sweet!

[XI]

FIRE the heather
burn the forest
of the foreign gowk
fluting in the south.
Are his grouse nesting?
his deer breeding?
Drunk as his lord
the factor is snoring.

Twenty days now
fierce the sun's rays
and the foreign gowk
flutes in the south
while the hill-mother
stifled in stiff dress
longs for her children
to nose her breast.

She last summer
burned up the fences
of the foreign gowk
fluting in the south.
All his palings
couldn't avail him.
He put us in the dock.
But she fed our flock.

'Keep you from my forest!
This fence is the farthest!'
fluted the foreign gowk
in the south.

It blazed that night.
Terrible was the lightning!
—or so in the court
not an oath but swore it.

Be again free, mother!
Blaze you, heather!
for all the gowks
that flute in the south.
Under the stubs
green shoots will sprout.
Happy our hill then
feed her children.

[XII]

OUR pastures are bitten and bare
our wool is blown to the winds
our mouths are stopped and dumb
our oatfields weak and thin.
Nobody fishes the loch
nobody stalks the deer.
Let us go down to the sea.
The friendly sea likes to be visited.

Our fathers sleep in the cemetery
their boats, cracked, by their side.
The sea turns round in his sleep
pleasurecraft nod on the tide.
Sea ducks slumber on waves
sea eagles have flown away.
Let us put out to sea.
The fat sea likes to be visited.

ADAM DRINAN

Fat sea, what's on your shelf?
all the grey night we wrestled.
To muscle, to skill, to petrol,
Hook oo rin yo! . . . one herring!
and of that only the head.
Dogfishes had the rest,
a parting-gift from the sea.
The merry sea likes to be visited.

Merry sea, what have you sent us?
a rusty english trawler?
The crew put into the hotel
the engineer overhauls her.
Gulls snatch offal to leeward.
We on the jetty await
gifts of the cod we can't afford. . .
The free sea likes to be visited.

Free were our fathers' boats
whose guts are strewn on the shore.
Steam ships were bought by the rich
cheap from the last war.
They tear our nets to pieces
and the sea gives them our fishes.
Even he favours the rich.
The false sea likes to be visited.

WILLIAM MONTGOMERIE

1904–

245   *Glasgow Street*

OUT of this ugliness may come,
 Some day, so beautiful a flower,
That men will wonder at that hour,
Remembering smoke and flowerless slum,
And ask—glimpsing the agony
Of the slaves who wrestle to be free—
'But why were all the poets dumb?'

246   *Author Unknown*

THUS I come to you,
 A beggar in rags,
And in my hands I hold this gem.
Buy it. But you will not buy it,
You say it is glass.
Look, it shines in the dark.
Your eyes are blind,
And cannot see the glow in the heart of it.
You will not give me money for the gem,
And I am in rags and hungry,
And you go away.
But when I die, they will find me in the dark
By this jewel's light.

247

From *Kinfauns Castle*

IS there no vision in a lovely place?
Has no one in this garden sat to think,
And added to his soul another grace,
Because white arabis at the pond's brink
Glimmered at dusk, or a chaffinch came to drink;
Because about this rockery a bee,
Among the violets flying, seemed to link
All flowers along the valley to the sea,
Enmeshed, as men with men, in one wide mystery?

Is it enough to linger here for hours
Until the black slugs of the evening crawl,
And the last bee kicks into the apple-flowers?
Were it enough, such harmony would fall
Among men from this place, that they would all
To these towers make eternal pilgrimage;
As men to Mecca go, or to the wall
That was Jerusalem—because a sage
Here dwelling taught the wisdom of the coming age.

248

Estuary

THE lamps along the river
Are lilies of light
Rooted with fire.

The evening star
Is a windflower of light.

The crescent moon
Holds the apple of darkness
In a glass.

Three fishermen
Are talking by the drawn-up boats.
They know the dark river
And the sea beyond.

The night is full of mystery,
Whose understanding is
In trying no more to understand.

249   *Epitaph*

(*for 2nd Officer James Montgomerie
of the S.S. Carsbreck, lost at sea*)

MY brother is skull and skeleton now,
Empty of mind behind the brow,
In ribs and pelvis empty space,
Bone-naked, without a face.

On a draughty beach drifting sand,
Clawed by a dry skeleton hand,
Sifts in the hourglass of his head
Time, useless to bones of the dead

Elegy

(*for William Soutar*)

A NARROWING of knowledge to one window to a door
Swinging inward on a man in a windless room
On a man inwardly singing
                        on a singing child
Alone and never alone a lonely child
Singing
        in a mirror dancing to a dancing child
Memory sang and words in a mimic dance
Old words were young and a child sang.

A narrowing of knowledge to one room to a doorway
To a door in a wall swinging bringing him friends
A narrowing of knowledge to
                        an arrow in bone in the marrow
And arrow
            death
                    strung on the string of the spine.

To the live crystal in the palm and the five fingers
To the slow thirty years' pearl in the hand
Shelled in a skull in the live face of a statue
Sea-flowered on the neck of broken marble
Sunken fourteen years in that aquarium.

A. D. MACKIE

1904–

251

A New Spring

THE whins are blythesome on the knowe
   Wi candles bleezan clear,
Forsythia's lichtit lowe on lowe,
   But, lass, ye arena here.

Aside the dyke the catkins growe,
   The tulips are asteer,
The daffie wags its gowden powe
   Ahint its pale green spear.

Winter's lang gane, baith snaw and thowe;
   Bricht brairds anither year;
Aathing comes back—my heart is howe!—
   Aathing but you, my dear.

  knowe: knoll   lowe: flame   daffie: daffodil   thowe:
thaw   brairds: springs   howe: hollow

252 *The Young Man and the Young Nun*

'MY milk-white doo,' said the young man
   To the nun at the convent yett,
'Ahint your maiden snood I scan
   Your hair is like the jet.

       doo: dove   yett: gate

Black, black are the een ye hae
Like boontree berries or the slae,
Wi hints o Hevin and glints as weill
O' the warld, the flesh and the muckle Deil.
Come flee wi me!' said the young man
   To the nun at the convent yett.

'I've gien my vow,' said the young nun
   To the man at the convent yett.
'My race outby in the warld is run:
   Earth's cauld and Hell is het.
Although my maiden snood I hain,
I hae a Guidman o my ain,
I hae a Guidman far mair real,
I hae a Guidman far mair leal
Nor ye can be,' said the young nun
   To the man at the convent yett.

'That's aiblins true,' said the young man
   To the nun at the convent yett,
'But ye're owre young your life to ban
   To be the Godheid's pet.
The veil is for the auld and cauld,
Your youth is for the young and yauld;
Come while the sheen is in your hair,
Come while your cheek is round and fair,
Come and be free!' said the young man
   To the nun at the convent yett.

'That step I'd rue,' said the young nun
   To the man at the convent yett.
'My threid o bewtie's jimplie spun
   And men gey sune forget.

---

boontree: elder-tree   slae: sloe   glints: glances   hain: save
leal: true   aiblins: perhaps   ban: curse, blight   yauld: active

A. D. MACKIE

Whan lyart cranreuch streaks my locks
And my cheeks hing syde as a bubbliejock's,
Whas bluid will steer, whas hert will stound,
Whas luve will stanch auld age's wound?
Nane bleeds but He,' said the young nun
   To the man at the convent yett.

'Ye gar me grue,' said the young man
   To the nun at the convent yett.
'The gait ye gang is no Life's plan,
   And to Life ye're awn a debt.
The morn, the laverock shaks the air
And green comes back to the girss and gair;
Your spell wi the Ghaist's owre sune begood,
It's wi ane like me ye suld tyne your snood—
I speak Life's plea,' said the young man
   To the nun at the convent yett.

'Your een are blue,' said the young nun
   To the man at the convent yett,
'But the luvan een o Mary's Son
   Are starns that will never set.
Whan your gowden powe's like the mune's wan heid,
Whan your cheeks are blae and your een are reid,
My Luve will be young as the bricht new gem
That bleezed in the heck at Bethlehem—
He canna dee,' said the young nun
   To the man at the convent yett.

lyart: hoary   cranreuch: frost   syde: low   bubbliejock: turkey
grue: shudder   gait: way   awn: owing   laverock:
lark   girss: grass   gair: slope   tyne: lose   powe: head
heck: manger

A. D. MACKIE

'Brent is your brou,' said the young man
  To the nun at the convent yett,
'And for nae callant o earthly clan
  Your leesome lane ye'll fret.
For me, there are monie still in bloom:
Owre ye, I needna fash my thoom.
Flyting and fleetching baith hae failed,
And sae fareweill—it's yoursel that's waled
The weird ye'll dree,' said the young man
  To the nun at the convent yett.

'I thank ye nou,' said the young nun
  To the man at the convent yett,
'And though your wauf, wild warld I shun,
  Your warmth I'll no regret.
A barren boon for Christ 'twad be
Gif naebodie socht His bride but He,
But the weird ye wale is waur nor mine,
And doubtless ye'll seek to change it syne—
I'll pray for ye,' said the young nun
  To the man at the convent yett.

brent: smooth   callant: fellow   leesome lane: lonely own
fash: bother   thoom: thumb   flyting: scolding   fleetching:
coaxing   dree: endure   wauf: strayed   wale: choose
waur: worse   nor: than

NORMAN CAMERON

1905–1953

253   *For the Fly-Leaf of a School-Book*

ONE of the more intelligent members
     Of the upper-middle classes
Of the most important country
On the nearest-but-two planet to the sun,
I send my prayer unto Thee.

Now reverse this address,
And carry it further
With sections and quarterings
And split the last atom
And come unto Me.

254   *The Unfinished Race*

NO runner clears the final fence,
     The laurels have long since gone stale.
They must be a cardboard pretence,
These watchers crowded on the rail.

For why should crowds stay watching so
To see a race that has no end?
How many centuries ago
The runners came up round the bend.

Always they balk at this last leap,
And then recoil to try once more.
From pride or custom still they keep
On striving—those once at the fore

Distinguished only from the ruck
By their impressive long run back.

255 *The Disused Temple*

WHEN once the scourging prophet, with his cry
Of 'money-changers' and 'my Father's house',
Had set his mark upon it, men were shy
To enter, and the fane fell in disuse.

Since it was unfrequented and left out
Of living, what was there to do except
Make fast the door, destroy the key (No doubt
One of our number did it while we slept).

It stays as a disquieting encumbrance.
We moved the market-place out of its shade;
But still it overhangs our whole remembrance,
Making us both inquisitive and afraid.

Shrewd acousticians hammer on the door
And study from the echoes what is there;
Meaningless yet familiar, these appear
Much what we would expect—but we're not sure.

Disquiet makes us sleepy; shoddiness
Has come upon our crafts. No question that
We'll shortly have to yield to our distress,
Abandon the whole township, and migrate.

256 *Forgive Me, Sire*

FORGIVE me, Sire, for cheating your intent,
  That I, who should command a regiment,
Do amble amiably here, O God,
One of the neat ones in your awkward squad.

257 *Shepherdess*

ALL day my sheep have mingled with yours. They strayed
  Into your valley seeking a change of ground.
Held and bemused with what they and I had found,
Pastures and wonders, heedlessly I delayed.

Now it is late. The tracks leading home are steep,
The stars and landmarks in your country are strange.
How can I take my sheep back over the range?
Shepherdess, show me now where I may sleep.

258 *The Dirty Little Accuser*

WHO invited him in? What was he doing here,
  That insolent little ruffian, that crapulous lout?
When he quitted a sofa, he left behind him a smear.
My wife says he even tried to paw her about.

What was worse, if, as often happened, we caught him out
Stealing or pinching the maid's backside, he would leer,
With a cigarette on his lip and a shiny snout,
With a hint: 'You and I are all in the same galere.'

Yesterday we ejected him, nearly by force,
To go on the parish, perhaps, or die of starvation;
As to that, we agreed, we felt no kind of remorse.

Yet there's this check on our righteous jubilation:
Now that the little accuser is gone, of course,
We shall never be able to answer his accusation.

J. K. ANNAND

1907–

259   *Arctic Convoy*

INTIL the pit-mirk nicht we northwart sail
  Facin the bleffarts and the gurly seas
That ser' out muckle skaith to mortal men.
Whummlin about like a waukrife feverit bairn
The gude ship snowks the waters o a wave,
Swithers, syne pokes her neb intil the air,
Hings for a wee thing, dinnlin, on the crest,
And clatters in the trouch wi sic a dunt
As gey near rives the platin frae her ribs
And flypes the tripes o unsuspectin man.

Northwart, aye northwart, in the pit-mirk nicht.
A nirlin wind comes blawin frae the ice,
Plays dirdum throu the rails and shrouds and riggin,
Ruggin at bodies clawin at the life-lines.
There's sic a rowth o air that neb and lungs
Juist canna cope wi sic a dirlin onding.

gurly: angry   skaith: harm   waukrife: sleepless   snowks:
noses   neb: nose   dinnlin: trembling   nirlin: freezing
dirdum: havoc   rowth: excess   dirlin onding: battering assault

J. K. ANNAND

Caulder the air becomes, and snell the wind,
The waters, splairgin as she dunts her boo,
Blads in a blatter o hailstanes on the brig
And geals on guns and turrets, masts and spars,
Cleedin the iron and steel wi coat o ice.

Northwart, aye northwart, in the pit-mirk nicht.
The nirlin wind has gane, a lown-ness comes;
The lang slaw swall still minds us o the gale.
Restin aff-watch, a-sweein in our hammocks,
We watch our sleepin messmates' fozy braith
Transmogrify to ice upon the skin
That growes aye thicker on the ship-side plates.
Nae mair we hear the lipper o the water,
Only the dunsh o ice-floes scruntin by,
Floes that in the noon-day gloamin licht
Are lily-leafs upon a lochan dubh.
But nae bricht lily-flouer delytes the ee,
Nae divin bird diverts amang the leafs,
Nae sea-bird to convoy us on our gait.
In ilka deid-lown airt smools Davy Jones,
Ice-tangle marline spikes o fingers gleg
To claught the bodies o unwary sailors
And hike them doun to stap intil his kist.
Whiles 'Arctic reek' taks on the orra shapes
O ghaistly ships-o-war athort our gait,
Garrin us rin ram-stam to action stations
Syne see them melt awa intil the air.

snell: cutting	splairgin: spluttering	blads: hammers
blatter: shower	cleedin: cloathing	lown-ness: calmness
fozy: hoary	dunsh: crunch	scruntin: scraping lochan
dubh: black mere	gait: way	smools: glides gleg: quick
claught: catch	hike: haul kist: chest	orra: odd garrin:
making		

Owre lang this trauchle lasts throu seas o daith
Wi neer a sign o welcome at the port,
Nae 'Libertymen fall in!' to cheer our herts
But sullen sentries at the jetty-heid
And leesome lanesome waitin at our birth.

At length we turn about and sail for hame
Back throu rouch seas, throu ice and snaw and sleet,
Hirdin the draigelt remnants o our flock
Bieldin them weel frae skaith o enemie.
But southwart noo we airt intil the licht
Leavin the perils o the Arctic nicht.

trauchle: trouble   leesome lanesome: totally alone   birth:
berth   draigelt: bedraggled

ROBERT MACLELLAN

1907–

260   *Sang*

THERE'S a reid lowe in yer cheek,
    Mither, and a licht in yer ee,
And ye sing like the shuilfie in the she,
But no' for me.

The man that cam' the day,
Mither, that ye ran to meet,
He drapt his gun and fondlet ye
And I was left to greet.

lowe: flame   shuilfie: chaffinch   greet: weep

Ye served him kail frae the pat,
Mither, and meat frae the bane.
Ye brocht him cherries frae the gean,
And I gat haurdly ane.

And noo he lies in yer bed,
Mither, and the licht grows dim,
And the sang ye sing as ye hap me ower
Is meant for him.

kail: cabbage-soup   gean: wild cherry-tree

KATHLEEN RAINE
1908–

261
To My Mountain

SINCE I must love your north
of darkness, cold, and pain,
the snow, the lovely glen,
let me love true worth,

the strength of the hard rock,
the deafening stream of wind
that carries sense away
swifter than flowing blood.

Heather is harsh to tears
and the rough moors
give the buried face no peace
but make me rise,

and oh, the sweet scent, and purple skies!

262 *Isis Wanderer*

THIS too is an experience of the soul
  The dismembered world that once was the whole god
Whose unbroken fragments now lie dead.
The passing of reality itself is real.

Gathering under my black cloak the remnants of life
That lie dishonoured among people and places
I search the twofold desert of my solitude,
The outward perished world, and the barren mind.

Once he was present, numinous, in the house of the world,
Wearing day like a garment, his beauty manifest
In corn and man as he journeyed down the fertile river.
With love he filled my distances of night.

I trace the contour of his hand fading upon a cloud,
And this his blood flows from a dying soldier's wound,
In broken fields his body is scattered and his limbs lie
Spreadeagled like wrecked fuselage in the sand.

His skull is a dead cathedral, and his crown's rays
Glitter from worthless tins and broken glass.
His blue eyes are reflected from pools in the gutter,
And his strength is the desolate stone of fallen cities.

Oh in the kitchen-midden of my dreams
Turning over the potsherds of past days
Shall I uncover his loved desecrated face?
Are the unfathomed depths of sleep his grave?

Beyond the looming dangerous end of night
Beneath the vaults of fear do his bones lie,
And does the maze of nightmare lead to the power within?
Do menacing nether waters cover the fish king?

I piece the divine fragments into the mandala
Whose centre is the lost creative power,
The sun, the heart of God, the lotus, the electron
That pulses world upon world, ray upon ray
That he who lived on the first may rise on the last day.

263   *Spell of Creation*

WITHIN the flower there lies a seed,
    Within the seed there springs a tree,
Within the tree there spreads a wood.

In the wood there burns a fire,
And in the fire there melts a stone,
Within the stone a ring of iron.

Within the ring there lies an O
Within the O there looks an eye,
In the eye there swims a sea,

And in the sea reflected sky,
And in the sky there shines the sun,
Within the sun a bird of gold.

Within the bird there beats a heart,
And from the heart there flows a song,
And in the song there sings a word.

In the word there speaks a world,
A word of joy, a world of grief,
From joy and grief there springs my love.

Oh love, my love, there springs a world,
And on the world there shines a sun
And in the sun there burns a fire,

Within the fire consumes my heart
And in my heart there beats a bird,
And in the bird there wakes an eye,

Within the eye, earth, sea and sky,
Earth, sky and sea within an O
Lie like the seed within the flower.

264

From *BEINN NAOMH*

IV. The Summit

FARTHER than I have been
All is changed: no water for moist souls,
Wind and stone
Is the world of the summit, stone and rain,
Stone wind and cold, only the oldest things remain,
And wind unceasing has blown,
Without beginning or ending the wind has blown.

Noise of wind on rock cries to the soul 'Away,
'Away, what wilt thou do?' The butterfly
Blown up against the summit meets the snow.
Those who rise there endure
Dragon of stone and dragon of air.
'We become what we behold', by wind irresistible
Hurled, or still as stone, the long way
A dream while the wing of a bird
Brushes a grain of quartz from the unmoved hill.

ROBERT GARIOCH

1908–

265 *Embro to the Ploy*

IN simmer, whan aa sorts foregether
in Embro to the ploy,
folk seek out friens to hae a blether,
or faes they'd fain annoy;
smorit wi British Railways' reek
frae Glesca or Glen Roy
or Wick, they come to hae a week
of cultivated joy

or three,
in Embro to the ploy.

Americans wi routh of dollars,
wha drink our whisky neat,
wi Sasunachs and Oxford Scholars
are eydent for the treat

simmer: summer   ploy: festival   blether: gossip   smorit:
smothered   reek: smoke   routh: plenty   eydent: eager

of music sedulously high-tie
at thirty-bob a seat;
Wop opera performed in Eyetie
to them's richt up their street,
         they say,
in Embro to the ploy.

Furthgangan Embro folk come hame
for three weeks in the year,
and find Auld Reekie no the same,
fu sturrit in a steir.
The stane-faced biggins whaur they froze
and suppit puirshous lear
of cultural cauld-kale and brose
see cantraips unco queer
         thae days
in Embro to the ploy.

The tartan tred wad gar ye lauch;
nae problem is owre teuch.
Your surname needna end in -*och*;
they'll cleik ye up the cleuch.
A puckle dollar bills will aye
preive Hiram Teufelsdrockh
a septary of Clan McKay,
it's maybe richt eneuch,
         verfluch!
in Embro to the ploy.

  furthgangan: emigrant   sturrit in a steir: stirred in confusion
biggins: buildings   puirshous lear: poor-house learning   cauld-kale:
cabbage soup   cantraips: tricks   gar ye lauch: make you laugh
teuch: tough   cleik ye up the cleuch: lead you up the rock (i.e. castle
rock)

The auld High Schule, whaur monie a skelp
of triple-tonguit tawse
has gien a heist-up and a help
towards Doctorates of Laws,
nou hears, for Ramsay's cantie rhyme,
loud pawmies of applause
frae folk that pey a pund a time
to sit on wudden raws
                              gey hard
in Embro to the ploy.

The haly kirk's Assembly-haa
nou fairly coups the creel
wi Lindsay's Three Estaitis, braw
devices of the Deil.
About our heids the satire stots
like hailstanes till we reel;
the bawrs are in auld-farrant Scots,
it 's maybe jist as weill,
                              imphm,
in Embro to the ploy.

The Epworth Haa wi wonder did
behold a pipers' bicker;
wi *hadarid* and *hindarid*
the air gat thick and thicker.
Cumha na Cloinna pleyed on strings
torments a piper quicker
to get his dander up, by jings,
than thirty u.p. liquor,
                              hooch aye!
in Embro to the ploy.

tawse: belt   cantie: merry   pawmies: blows on palms
coups: upsets   bawrs: jokes   auld-farrant: old-time

544

The Northern British Embro Whigs
that stayed in Charlotte Square,
they fairly wad hae tined their wigs
to see the Stuarts there,
the bleeding Earl of Moray and aa
weill-pentit and gey bare;
Our Queen and Princess, buskit braw,
enjoyed the hale affair
                              (see Press)
in Embro to the ploy.

Whan day's anomalies are cled
in decent shades of nicht,
the Castle is transmogrified
by braw electric licht.
The toure that bields the Bruce's croun
presents an unco sicht
mair sib to Wardour Street nor Scone,
wae 's me for Scotland's micht,
                              says I
in Embro to the ploy.

A happening, incident, or splore
affrontit them that saw
a thing they'd never seen afore—
in the McEwan Haa:
a lassie in a wheelie-chair
wi naething on at aa;
jist like my luck! I wasna there,
it 's no the thing ava,
                              tut-tut,
in Embro to the ploy.

tined: lost   gey: rather   buskit: dressed   bields: shelters

The Café Royal and Abbotsford
are filled wi orra folk
whas stock-in-trade's the scrievit word,
or twicet-scrievit joke.
Brains, weak or strang, in heavy beer,
or ordinary, soak.
Quo yin: This yill is aafie dear,
I hae nae clinks in poke,
                    nor fauldan-money,
in Embro to the ploy.

The auld Assembly-rooms, whaur Scott
foregethert wi his fiers,
nou see a gey kenspeckle lot
ablow the chandeliers.
Til Embro drouths the Festival Club
a richt godsend appears;
it's something new to find a pub
that gaes on serving beers
                    eftir hours
in Embro to the ploy.

Jist pitten-out, the drucken mobs
frae howffs in Potterraw,
fleean, to hob-nob wi the Nobs,
ran to this Music Haa,
Register Rachel, Cougait Kate,
nae-neb Nellie and aa
stauchert about amang the Great,
what fun! I never saw
                    the like,
in Embro to the ploy.

orra: strange   aafie: awful   clinks: change   fiers:
peers   kenspeckle: famous   fleean: drunk   stauchert:
staggered

They toddle hame doun lit-up streets
filled wi synthetic joy;
aweill, the year brings few sic treats
and muckle to annoy.
There's monie hartsom braw high-jinks
mixed up in this alloy
in simmer, whan aa sorts foregether
in Embro to the ploy.

266   At Robert Fergusson's Grave, October 1962

(Edinburgh Sonnet 14)

CANOGAIT kirkyaird in the failing year
is auld and grey, the wee roseirs are bare,
five gulls leam white agen the dirty air:
why are they here? There's naething for them here.

Why are we here oursels? We gaither near
the grave. Fergusons mainly, quite a fair
turn-out, respectfu, ill at ease, we stare
at daith—there's an address—I canna hear.

Aweill, we staund bareheidit in the haar,
murnin a man that gaed back til the pool
twa hunner-year afore our time. The glaur

that haps his banes glowres back. Strang present dool
ruggs at my hairt. Lichtlie this gin ye daur:
here Robert Burns knelt and kissed the mool.

roseirs: rose-trees   leam: glow   haar: mist   glaur: mud
glowres: stares   dool: woe   lichtlie: scorn   gin ye daur: if
you dare   mool: mould

267 *Elegy*

(Edinburgh Sonnet 16)

THEY are lang deid, folk that I used to ken,
their firm-set lips aa mowdert and agley,
sherp-tempert een rusting amang the cley:
they are baith deid, thae wycelike, bienlie men,

heidmaisters, that had been in poure for ten
or twenty year afore fate's taiglie wey
brocht me, a young, weill-harnit, blate and fey
new-fledgit dominie, intill their den.

Ane tellt me it was time I learnt to write,
roun-haun, he meant, and saw about my hair:
I mind of him, beld-heidit, wi a kyte.

Ane sneerit quarterly (I cudna square
my savings-bank) and sniftert in his spite.
Weill, gin they arena deid, it's time they were.

mowdert: mouldered   agley: awry   een: eyes   cley: clay
bienlie: good-willed   taiglie: snaring   weill-harnit: brainy
blate: shy   beld-heidit: bald   kyte: paunch

268   *On Seein an Aik-Tree Sprent Wi Galls*

IN Aprile at the hicht of noon,
whan leean hauf-licht there was nane,
nae flichtie ferlie was to blame
for yon queer sicht: an aik in blume.

leean: lying   flichtie ferlie: flighty marvel   aik: oak

Ben ilka flure there bode a worm
in borrowed housie bien and warm;
to bigg its bield the twist was torn
and beauty browden'd it in turn.

My Makar! God wha made me dour
as ony aik, my worm is dear;
oh grant, amang this warldis steir,
that I may florische in the sture.

ben ilka flure: in each flower   bien: snug   bigg: build
bield: shelter   browden'd: pampered   steir: strife   sture:
conflict

GEORGE BRUCE

1909–

269   *My House*

MY house
is granite
It fronts
North,

Where the Firth flows,
East the sea.
My room
Holds the first

Blow from the North,
The first from the East,
Salt upon
The pane.

In the dark
I, a child,
Did not know
The consuming night

And heard
The wind,
Unworried and
Warm—secure.

270   *Sumburgh Heid*

RUMMLE an' dunt o' watter,
    Blatter, jinkin, turn an' rin—
A' there—burst an' yatter
Sea soun an' muckle an' sma win
Heich abune purpie sea, abune reid
Rocks—skraichs. That an' mair's the dirdit
Word—Sumburgh, Sumburgh Heid.

271   *The Singers*

O THALASSA! Thalassa! Where, where
    Are the winged instruments of celebration!
Where are the singers of today?
We did not know that our sea, debauched
By old men's pilferings, sullied by paddling boys,
Was not unsimilar to Homer's ocean,
Our bitter, treacherous coast reminiscent.
We did not know the music of the Ancient World
Whispered with the spindrift at our back door,

Offered its strange acclamation with wintry thunderings
For all who would hear. But we
Would not, could not, had no eyes for the dawn,
No ears for the wavering music of the wind.

The porridge pot is on the fire,
The spelding's frae the rack,
Or we can catch the tide at five
Ower meat we maun be swack.

Charlie's at the pier lang syne
Tae fuel engine an test her.
Hist ye, Meg, the baited lines
And hist ye, lass, ma s'wester.

And the music was there waiting—years back—
For the singers of love and violence
To tell the tale at the roaring night-fire
Into the unborn future.

Drap the anchor Charlie! Dod,
We're tee the gruns noo,
If but the Weather'll only haud
We'll full the boxes foo.

But gin she blaw anither bittock
Or shift a pint tae north
Nae one whiting, cod or haddock,
Nae a maik we're worth.

spelding: kipper   swack: quick   Dod: George   maik: ha'penny

Songs—in a land of the strange and the common—
The irregular crags in the green winter light,
The frozen fall in the secret corrie,
The caves with the sounding waters,
The caves of the dying birds,
The hollow hills and the deadly currents
And the slow sun rising on the ordinary landscape.
The country of low stone dykes and tractable fields,
The man at his labour in the field,
The obedient dog, the sheep on the low hill,
The woman at the baking board,
The children with blue butterflies in the hard sun
On the road to the shore.
A boy with a can of milk walks to the shore,
Returns with shining herring to the dark land.

> Throttle her doon, Dod,
> At thon black rock,
> Tide's runnin strang, Dod,
> We'll coup gin she knock.

> A sair tyave it wis, boy,
> In yon black swell,
> But we're hame wi' a shot, boy,
> Will dee us well.

In the cold of morning as day
Stretches on the hills—the beginning,
The resumption of the tasks of the day,
The woman moving about the house,
The child crying, the cattle heaving

coup: overturn   tyave: struggle

In their stalls. The boat goes from the pier,
The wind creeps to the wide waterways,
The ploughman drives the long furrow,
And in the prime of day—activity.
By the road to the shore in the sun
The sheep's backs are dappled with sweetness.
Happiness spreads like summer.
At night the world is in the mouths of men
Till the flames are down and the embers ash.

> Lat go that rope, loon,
> Watch, she'll brak.
> Smert's the word, loon
> Or she snap.

> Alec John's deid.
> Ae weet nicht
> Slipped, cracked his heid,
> Pitten oot in sma licht.

Our coasts have no laurels—only the white dawn.
Yesterday the seas cavorted, brought
With the thin spume, Alec John's blue mitt.
Yesterday a fankled line took Sandy,
A pot in the wrinkled sand foundered Jack Bayne.
To salvage 'The Water Lily' was a fikey business—
The crew were all young men.
We did not know as the tides came upon us
And our river ran in spate to the sea
Our waters were touched by the Athenian sun.

Where, where are the singers,
Where the winged instruments of celebration?

                    loon: lad

T. A. ROBERTSON ('VAGALAND')

1909–

272   *Tuslag*

WI da lentenin days ida first o da Voar
 Da Mairch wind comes agyin ta da door
At da black frost stekkit wi bolts an bars,
An reesles him open apo da harrs.

We wait, whin da door is open wide,
Fir life ta come ta da world ootside.
Ee day, wi a glöd atween da shooers,
We see da first o da Tuslag flooers.

Whaar last year's girse lies bleached an dowed
Dey sheen laek a nevfoo o yallow gowd.
Whin we see dem apo da eart we kyin
At da Voar is here wi his arles agyin.

Dey're a sign ta men at da Voar can gie
Plenty ta dem at'll earn der fee
Be da toil o der haands an da sweat o der broo,
Wi kishie, an spade, an harrow, an ploo.

Whin dey're kyerried an borrowed an spread an shölled
An delled da leys an harrowed da möld,
Dey can say at last, 'We're döne wir best;
Lord send göd wadder ta dö da rest.'

tuslag: coltsfoot   Voar: spring   stekkit: shut   reesles:
wrests   harrs: hinges   glöd: sunshine   nevfoo: handful
arles: token pay   kishie: peat-basket   borrowed: wheeled
shölled: shovelled   delled: delved   wadder: weather

Dey'll be mael an taeties, an maet fir kye,
Ta pey fir wir wark, an we'll get firbye,
As da year gengs on wi da sun an shooers,
Da colour an scent o a million flooers.

mael: meal   taeties: potatoes   maet: meat   kye: cattle
firbye: as well

NORMAN MACCAIG

1910–

273   *Golden Calf*

IF all the answer's to be the Sinai sort
  The incorruptible lava of the word
Made alphabetic in a stormspout, what
Mere human vocables you've ever heard,
Poor golden calf, could overbear, I wonder,
    The magniloquence of thunder?

You're for another flame. The Moses in me
Looks with a stone face on our gaudy lives.
His fingers, scorched with godhead, point, and loose
An influence of categorical negatives
That make an image of love, a trope of lover.
    Our dancing days are over.

The buckles tarnish at the thought of it.
The winecup shatters. The bragging music chokes
To the funeral silence it was awkward in.
And before the faggot of salvation smokes,
Your knees are loosed, your wreathed neck bows lowly
    In presence of the holy.

What's a disgruntled cloud to you or me?
Listen to my multitudes, and beam for them,
Making a plinth of this dark wilderness.
Utter such rigmaroles an apothegm,
Doing its head-stroke, drowns in such wild water
    And proves itself no matter.

Or where's the desert cat, or hunching shade
That ambles hugely in the dark outside,
Or hospitable anguish beckoning
To its foul ceremony a sorry bride
Could bear the darts struck from your hide by torches
    That guard our pleasure's marches?

Forty years. Small wilderness to unravel
Such an unknotted thread of wandering.
The desert is in Moses' skull, the journey
To the white thalamus whose cradling
Enfolds the foetus of the law—gestation
    Of Moses as a nation.

A chosen people, since they have no choice.
The doors are locked, the flesh-pots on the shelves,
And a long line of lamentation moves
Led by the nose through their own better selves
To buy with blood a land of milk and honey
    Where's no need of money.

The smoke and thunder die. And here I stand
Smelling of gunpowder and holiness.
The great fire does its belly-dance and in it
You shine unharmed, not knowing what's to confess;
And the desert, seeing the issue grows no clearer,
    Takes one long slow step nearer.

Nude in a Fountain

CLIP-CLOP go water-drops and bridles ring—
Or, visually, a gauze of water, blown
About and falling and blown about, discloses
Pudicity herself in shameless stone,
In an unlikely world of shells and roses.

On shaven grass a summer's litter lies
Of paper bags and people. One o'clock
Booms on the leaves with which the trees are quilted
And wades away through the air, making it rock
On flowerbeds that have blazed and dazed and wilted.

Light perches, preening, on the handle of a pram
And gasps on paths and runs along a rail
And whitely, brightly in a soft diffusion
Veils and unveils the naked figure, pale
As marble in her stone and stilled confusion.

And nothing moves except one dog that runs,
A red rag in a black rag, round and round
And that long helmet-plume of water waving,
In which the four elements, hoisted from the ground,
Become this grace, the form of their enslaving.

Meeting and marrying in the midmost air
Is mineral assurance of them all;
White doldrum on blue sky; a pose of meaning
Whose pose is what is explicit; a miracle
Made, and made bearable, by the water's screening.

The drops sigh, singing, and, still sighing, sing
Gently a leaning song. She makes no sound,
They veil her, not with shadows, but with brightness;
Till, gleam within a glitter, they expound
What a tall shadow is when it is whiteness.

A perpetual modification of itself
Going on around her is her; her hand is curled
Round more than a stone breast; and she discloses
The more than likely in an unlikely world
Of dogs and people and stone shells and roses.

275   *Celtic Cross*

THE implicated generations made
    This symbol of their lives, a stone made light
By what is carved on it.
                         The plaiting masks,
But not with involutions of a shade,
What a stone says and what a stone cross asks.

Something that is not mirrored by nor trapped
In webs of water or bag-nets of cloud;
The tangled mesh of weed
                         lets it go by.
Only men's minds could ever have unmapped
Into abstraction such a territory.

No green bay going yellow over sand
Is written on by winds to tell a tale
Of death-dishevelled gull
                         or heron, stiff
As a cruel clerk with gaunt writs in his hand
—Or even of light, that makes its depths a cliff.

Singing responses order otherwise.
The tangled generations ravelled out
In links of song whose sweet
                              strong choruses
Are these stone involutions to the eyes
Given to the ear in abstract vocables.

The stone remains, and the cross, to let us know
Their unjust, hard demands, as symbols do.
But on them twine and grow
                              beneath the dove
Serpents of wisdom whose cool statements show
Such understanding that it seems like love.

Feeding Ducks

ONE duck stood on my toes.
    The others made watery rushes after bread
Thrown by my momentary hand; instead,
She stood duck-still and got far more than those.

An invisible drone boomed by
With a beetle in it; the neighbour's yearning bull
Bugled across the five fields. And an evening full
Of other evenings quietly began to die.

And my everlasting hand
Dropped on my hypocrite duck her grace of bread.
And I thought, 'The first to be fattened, the first to be dead',
Till my gestures enlarged, wide over the darkening land.

277   *By Achmelvich Bridge*

NIGHT stirs the trees
     With breathings of such music that they sway,
Skirts, sleeves, tiaras, in the humming dark,
Their highborn heads tossing in disarray.

A floating owl
Unreels his silence, winding in and out
Of different darknesses. The wind takes up
And scatters a sound of water all about.

No moon need slide
Into the sky to make that water bright;
It ties its swelling self with glassy ropes;
It jumps from stones in smithereens of light.

The mosses on the wall
Plump their fat cushions up. They smell of wells,
Of under bridges and of spoons. They move
More quiveringly than the dazed rims of bells.

A broad cloud drops
A darker darkness. Turning up his stare,
Letting the world pour under him, owl goes off,
His small soft foghorn quavering through the air.

278   *Aspects*

CLEAN in the light, with nothing to remember,
     The fox fur shrivels, the bone beak drops apart;
Sludge on the ground, the dead deer drips his heart.

Clean in the weather, trees crack and lean over;
Mountain bows down and combs its scurfy head
To make a meadow and its own death bed.

Clean in the moon, tides scrub away their islands,
Unpicking gulls. Whales that have learned to drown,
Ballooning up, meet navies circling down.

Clean in the mind, a new mind creeps to being,
Eating the old. . . . Ancestors have no place
In such clean qualities as time and space.

T. S. LAW
1910–

Wemen's Wather

THE reever ryves at the gullie,
the mountain yokes on the plain,
the wuin fae the wast lik a brulyie
o targes is blatterin slaigerin rain—
wemen's wather, I sayt again.

I sayt an sayt again,
thoch oor wemen are shy wi thur shoothers
lik knowes whan the haur's i a glen,
they ken a wheen mair nor yer Luthers,
I sayt again.

Oor wemen in passioun greetin
are rairin wi loe o thur pain,
sae chyldlyke an wyldlyke they meet in

wather: weather	ryves: tears	gullie: knife	wuin: wind
brulyie: uproar	targes: scolds	blatterin: driving	slaigerin:
drenching	shoothers: shoulders	knowes: knolls	haur: mist
wheen mair nor: lot more than		greetin: weeping	rairin: roaring

the howe caad wumman's alane,
wumman's sorrow, you sayt again.

For damn it, oor wemen are baneruif,
no gaizent lik watterless bynes;
nae Virgins, nae Marys sae maenruif
wi faces lik soor tattie scones,
paer things, lik daichie an soor tattie scones.

Oor wemen are straucht as the sun shynes
whan the luft has been gurlie a wee,
as bricht as the bleeze o the leven in trees,
as loesome as rain, the mad til the sane,
the gowk til the wuid,
the curl o a clood,
I sayt an sayt again.

howe caad: hollow called	baneruif: bony	gaizent: wizened
bynes: tubs	maenruif: plaintive	tattic: potato	daichie: flabby
straucht: ?	luft: sky	gurlie: turbulent	leven: lightning
gowk: cuckoo	wuid: wood	clood: cloud

J. F. HENDRY

1912–

280   *The Constant North*

ENCOMPASS me, my lover,
With your eyes' wide calm.
Though noonday shadows are assembling doom,
The sun remains when I remember them.
And death, if it should come,
Must fall like quiet snow from such clear skies.

Minutes we snatched from the unkind winds
Are grown into daffodils by the sea's
Edge, mocking its green miseries;
Yet I seek you hourly still, over
A new Atlantis loneliness, blind
As a restless needle held by the constant north
    we always have in mind.

DOUGLAS YOUNG

1913–

281

Last Lauch

THE Minister said it wad dee,
  the cypress bush I plantit.
But the bush grew til a tree,
naething dauntit.

Hit's growin, stark and heich,
derk and straucht and sinister,
kirkyairdie-like and dreich.
But whaur's the Minister?

282

Winter Homily on the Calton Hill

THESE chill pillars of fluted stone
  shine back the lustre of the leaden sky,
stiff columns clustered on a dolerite hill
in solemn order, an unperfected vision
dimly gleaming. Not at random thrown
like old Greek temples that abandoned lie
with earthquake-riven drums. Rigid and chill
this still-born ruin stands for our derision.

A fine fantasy of the Whig literati
to build a modern Athens in our frore islands,
those elegant oligarchs of the Regency period,
Philhellenic nabobs and the Scots nobility.
As soon expect to meet a bearded Gujerati
stravaiging in a kilt through the uttermost Highlands,
or in Princes Street gardens a coy and blushing Nereid.
Athens proved incapable of such mobility.

Is the thing meaningless, as it is astonishing,
a senseless fantasy, out of time and place?
Apeing foreign fashions is always derisible,
and mimicry, for Plato, was the soul's unmaking.
The ruin is symbolic, a symbol admonishing
Scottish posterity. Seekers after grace
must not imitate the outward and visible.
The culture of Athens was a nation's awaking.

283   *For a Wife in Jizzen*

LASSIE, can ye say
    whaur ye hae been,
whaur ye hae come frae,
whatna ferlies seen?
Eftir the bluid and swyte,
the warsslin o yestreen,
ye ligg forfochten, whyte,
prouder nor onie queen.
Albeid ye hardly see me
I read it i your een,
sae saft blue and dreamy,
mindan whaur ye've been.

jizzen: childbirth   ferlies: wonders   ligg forfochten: lie exhausted

564

Anerly wives ken
the ruits o joy and tene,
the mairch o daith and birth,
the tryst o luve and strife
i the howedumbdeidsunsheen,
fire, air, water, yirth
mellan tae mak new life,
lauchan and greetan, feiman and serene.
Dern frae aa men
the ferlies ye ha seen.

tene: pain   howedombdeidsunsheen: midnight-sunshine
greetan: weeping   feiman: fevered   dern: hidden

R. CROMBIE SAUNDERS

1914–

284

Ressaif My Saul

(A poem in Middle Scots)

MY dolour is ane cup
Held to my lippis up;
So, Lord, I pray fra out that wae
Thy mercie I may sup.
And so fra wantonness contrair
Into they bountitude preclair
Ressaif my saul, that it gang fre
Fra seiknes and infirmitie.

ressaif my saul: receive my soul   wae: woe   preclair:
excellent

Alluterlie my neid
Me to defend fra deid
Is of thy luve, and so abuve
Is succour and remeid;
Quhy then so brukil and affrayit
Suld I gang in the warldis gait?
Ressaif my saul, that it may dree
No langer sic perplexitie.

My hert and mind tak cure
To be thy servitour,
Not for my sin can hope to win
Thy luve be adventur.
So fra this warldis wayis to gain
The favour of my Soveraine,
Ressaif my saul, and lat it be
At ane with thy felicitie.

alluterlie: absolutely   brukil: frail   dree: endure

285   *The Empty Glen*

TIME ticks away the centre of my pride
   Emptying its glen of cattle, crops and song,
Till the deserted headlands are alone
Familiar with the green uncaring tide.

What gave this land to gradual decay?
The rocky field where plovers make their nest
Now undisturbed had once the soil to raise
A happy people, but from day to day

The hamlets failed, the young men sought the towns,
Bewildered age looked from the cottage door
Upon the wreck of all they'd laboured for,
The rotting gate, the bracken on the downs;

And wondered if the future was so black
The children would have stayed but did not dare,
Who might, they hoped, be happy where they are.
And wondered, Are they ever coming back?

G. S. FRASER

1915–

286 *Lean Street*

HERE, where the baby paddles in the gutter,
    Here in the slaty greyness and the gas,
Here where the women wear dark shawls and mutter
    A hasty word as other women pass,

Telling the secret, telling, clucking and tutting,
    Sighing, or saying that it served her right,
The bitch!—the words and weather both are cutting
    In Causewayend, on this November night.

At pavement's end and in the slaty weather
    I stare with glazing eyes at meagre stone,
Rain and the gas are sputtering together
    A dreary tune! O leave my heart alone,

O leave my heart alone, I tell my sorrows,
  For I will soothe you in a softer bed
And I will numb your grief with fat to-morrow
  Who break your milk teeth on this stony bread!

They do not hear. Thought stings me like an adder,
  A doorway's sagging plumb-line squints at me,
The fat sky gurgles like a swollen bladder
  With the foul rain that rains on poverty.

287   *Letter to Anne Ridler*

A BIRD flies and I gum it to a concept,
    You trim your concept to the flying bird,
Your round words plopping open out in rings.
May your love's dreams be innocent and absurd
For dreaming of your verses while he slept
You mastered these oblique and tricky things . . .

But I was a reporter on a paper
And saw death ticked out in a telegram
On grey and shabby sheets with pallid print
So often, that it seemed an evening dram
Of solace for the murderer and the raper
Whose love has grown monstrous through stint.

I was a poet of this century
Pursued by poster-strident images
And headlines as spectacular as a dream
Full of cartoonists' dolls with paper visages;
I had no spare time over for reality,
I took things largely to be what they seem.

I had a headache from the endless drum,
The orator drumming on his private anger,
And the starved young in their accusing group
When I had written and could write no longer
Over my shoulder seemed to peer and stoop.
The adequate perspectives would not come.

It was not real, the news I got from London,
But made the immediate avenue unreal
And sapped my habits of their privileges:
Dreamy the granite in the evening sun
And like a vision, in their swoop and wheel,
The pigeons fluttering at Union Bridge.

The Communists were always playing darts,
The Spanish War survivors would not talk,
The Tory member only talked of peace.
In spring, the ash-buds blossomed in our hearts,
The tangle blossomed on the slimy rock,
The private impulse sought its vain release . . .

And in December on the ballroom floor
The girls in flowering dresses swayed and whirled,
And no girl leant on my protective arm.
From all the height of speculation hurled,
I stood and hesitated by the door;
I felt the pathos and I felt the charm . . .

Oh, I had hardly any will or shape,
Or any motive, but a sort of guilt
That half attracted them and half repelled;
My hand shook, and my glass of sherry spilt,
I wore a sort of silence like a cape.
The old heroic constant pattern held.

And when at midnight in my lonely room
I tried to integrate it all in verse
The headlines seemed as distant as the girls.
If sex was useless, history was worse.
A terrible remoteness seemed my doom
Whether I wrote of bayonets or culls . . .

So the stiff stanzas and the prosy lines
Accumulated on my dusty shelf,
A family joke, like any secret vice;
Dud bombs, damp rockets, unexploded mines,
'This sort of writing isn't really nice.
Oh George, my darling, can't you be yourself?'

You can; and I would praise your studied art,
Dry and stiff-fingered, but more accurate
Than all my brilliant angers and my blind
Hot, hurt perceptions, energized with hate:
Would praise your calm perspectives of the mind
So coloured with the pathos of the heart.

For my slack words were awkwardly heroic,
Your noble mood assumes no airs at all:
A rock of anger in this world unstable,
Me other people's sufferings made a stoic,
But you, a hostess, at our hungry table,
Are kind; your atmosphere is germinal.

Loving the charity of women's love,
Too much a household pet, I see in you
The gentle nurture that now curbs my grief
As I grow tall, beyond that budding grove
Of all the beautiful beyond belief
Within whose shade my windflower passions blew,

Private to me, their shy and secret suns
Who now with other private suns compete
And seek in man's inverted mode such love
As nerves the will to enter and complete
Its terrible initiation of
Man to these virtues that from pain are won.

And the sick novice whimpers for his home
Who shall be hurt and horribly alone
Before the historic vigil lets him sleep.
Yet for such hurt, such pity might atone
And such an Ithaca for those who roam
Far, that they may at last return and weep.

Why do the towers of Troy for ever burn?
Perhaps that old Jew told us, or perhaps
Since women suffer much in bearing us
We also must show courage in our turn,
Among these forks and dreaded thunder-claps,
Against an endless dialectic tearing us . . .

Or freedom, say, from family love and strife
And all the female mystery of a room
That half supports and half imprisons us
May tear a man from mother, sister, wife,
And every soft reminder of the womb.
Dead Freud in lost Vienna argued thus.

I hardly know! But Fritz, who's now interned,
(Sober and well-informed like all his race)
Told me this war might last, say, seven years;
But right would be triumphant then, the tide be turned,
Unless indeed (the night fell on his face)
Our hopes are just illusions like our fears.

Perhaps in London, say, in seven years,
We'll meet, and we will talk of poetry,
And of the piety of homely things,
A common past, the flowering library
In which the awkward spirit perseveres
Until a world of letters shines and sings . . .

Unless the vigilant years have numbed my face,
The long humiliation soured my heart,
The madman's silence boxed my veering mood:
Let time forgive me, if I fall apart,
And fall, as many souls have fallen from grace,
Through just and necessary servitude.

Or if we never meet, remember me
As one voice speaking calmly in the north
Among the muslin veils of northern light;
I bore the seed of poetry from my birth
To flower in rocky ground, sporadically,
Until I sleep in the unlaurelled night.

SYDNEY GOODSIR SMITH

1915–

288   *Epistle to John Guthrie*

(*who had blamed the poet for writing in Scots
'which no one speaks'*)

WE'VE come intil a gey queer time
  Whan scrievin Scots is near a crime,
'There 's no one speaks like that', they fleer,
—But wha the deil spoke like King Lear?

scrievin: writing   fleer: sneer

And onyweys doon Canongate
I'll tak ye slorpin pints till late,
Ye'll hear Scots there as raff and slee—
It's no the point, sae that'll dae.

Ye'll fin the leid, praps no the fowth,
The words're there, praps no the ferlie;
For he wha'ld rant wi Rabbie's mouth
Maun leave his play-pen unco erlie.

Nane cud talk lik Gawen Douglas writes,
He hanna the vocablerie,
Nor cud he flyte as Dunbar flytes—
Yir argy-bargy's tapsalteerie!

Did Johnnie Keats whan he was drouth
Ask 'A beaker full o the warm South'?
Fegs no, he leaned across the bar
An called for 'A point o bitter, Ma!'

But the Suddron's noo a sick man's leid,
Alang the flattest plains it stots;
Tae reach the hills his fantice needs
This bard maun tak the wings o Scots.

And so, dear John, ye jist maun dree
My Scots; for English, man, 's near deid,
See the weeshy-washy London bree
An tell me then whaes bluid is reid!

slorpin: swilling	raff: abundant	slee: witty	leid:
tongue	fowth: whole	ferlie: magic	flytes: scolds
tapsalteerie: upside down	fegs: faith		Suddron: English
fantice: imagination	dree: put up with	bree: brew	

But mind, nae poet eer writes 'common speech',
Ye'll fin eneuch o yon in prose;
His realm is heich abune its reach—
Jeez! wha'ld use ale for Athol Brose?

289 *The Mither's Lament*

WHAT care I for the leagues o sand,
 The prisoners and the gear they've won?
My darlin liggs amang the dunes
Wi mony a mither's son.

Doutless he deed for Scotland's life;
Doutless the statesmen dinna lee;
But och tis sair begrutten pride
And wersh the wine o victorie!

begrutten: tear-stained   wersh: bitter

2 *Ye Mongers aye Need Masks for Cheatrie*

DELACROIX pentit Chopin's heid
 No lik ithers a jessie hauf deid
But true, wi a neb lik a eagle's beak,
Een lik levin frae the thunner's crack,
His rasch face sterk wi pouer and daith
And aa the agonie o Poland's skaith.

mongers: jobbers   pentit: painted   jessie: pansy   levin:
lightning   rasch: vigorous

Wha'll pent trulie Scotland's heid
Nae couthy gloam but mirk and reid?
Skail yir myth o the Union year
Saw mob and riot but deil a cheer?
Syne an Empire 's biggit wi Scottis bluid
—But wha'd hae gane gin hame was guid?

Ye mak a myth o a cheated land
As Chopin 's made a lilly man;
But truth will screich and Scotland rid
Ye mongers as the Irish did;
The bluid ye drave til ilka airt
Sall feed its ain reid sleepan hert.

> skail: scatter   biggit: built

291   *The Ineffable Dou*

WHITE Dou o Truth
    Black Dou o Luve
Perpend, incline
My sang to pruve.

What ye be
Hairt canna tell
Nor mynd nor saul
That in ye mell.

What life I hae's
Hauf mine hauf thine
You speak throu me
But hauf is mine.

> mell: mingle

Dou, come til me
Lea me nocht
For she and ye
Are ane in thocht.

Nae truth but speaks
Throu cloud, as she
Lives in mysel
But isna me.

Learn me, Dou,
To be for her
As she til me
Sae that aawhar

Daith dees to see
The licht we burn
And the blind worm
Forget to girn.

Sae we sall be
Licht burnan licht
The gleid consume
Our final nicht.

Goddess, Dou,
That kills her ain
Grant me a space
To sing again.

Ae final word
And syne gae doun
Hapt in the splendour
Of thy doom

girn: complain   gleid: burning ember

When luve sall kill
At last the wound
That luve gied
Our life to stound.

Then sall our life
Become our luve
And the fell truth
My sang sall pruve.

Sae we sall be
Made ane at last
And luve made truth
Sing frae the dust.

Goddess and Queen
Incline thy face
Our end nae end
But in thy Grace.

292   *Under the Eildon Tree*

(Elegy V)

HERE I ligg, Sydney Slugabed Godless Smith,
   The Smith, the Faber, ποιητής and Makar,
And Oblomov has nocht til lear me,
Auld Oblomov has nocht on me
Liggan my lane in bed at nune
Gantan at gray December haar,

ligg: lie   lear: teach   gantan: yawning   haar: sea mist

A cauld, scummie, hauf-drunk cup o tea
   At my bedside,
     Luntan Virginian fags
—The New World thus I haud in fief
And levie kyndlie tribute. Black men slave
Aneath a distant sun to mak for me
Cheroots at hauf-a-croun the box.
   Wi ase on the sheets, ase on the cod,
And crumbs o toast under my bum,
Scrievan the last great coronach
O' the westren flickeran bourgeois world.
   Eheu fugaces!
           Lacrimae rerum!
Nil nisi et cetera ex cathedra
         Requiescat up your jumper.

O, michtie Stalin i the Aist!
Coud ye but see me nou,
The type, endpynt and final blume
O' decadent capitalistical thirldom
    —It took five hunder year to produce me—
Och, coud ye but see me nou
What a sermon coud ye gie
   Furth frae the Hailie Kremlin
Bummlan and thunderan owre the Steppes,
Athort the mountains o Europe humman
Till Swack! at my front door, the great Schloss Schmidt
That 's Numéro Cinquante (пятьдесят,[1] ye ken)
I' the umquhile pairk o Craigmillar House
Whar Marie Stewart o the snawie blee
Aince plantit ane o a thousand treen.

        [1] *piat' desiat*—fifty.

luntan: smoking	ase: ash	cod: pillow	coronach: lament
endpynt: endpoint	thirldom: slavery	blee: complexion	

Losh, what a sermon yon wad be!
For Knox has nocht on Uncle Joe
And Oblomov has nocht on Smith
 And sae we come by a route maist devious
 Til the far-famed Aist-West Synthesis!
 Beluved by Hugh that's beluved by me
And the baith o us loe the barley-bree—
But wha can afford to drink the stuff?
 Certies no auld Oblomov!
 —And yet he does! Whiles!
 But no as muckle as Uncle Joe—I've smaa dout!
На здоровье,[1] then, auld Muscovite!

Thus are the michtie faaen,
Thus the end o a michtie line,
Dunbar til Smith the Slugabed
Whas luve burns brichter nor them aa
And whas dounfaain is nae less,
 Deid for a ducat deid
By the crueltie o his ain maistress.

 [1] *Na zdorovye*—good health.

293 *Leander Stormbound*

THE auld mune on her back
 In a black luift o rags
That the wind pell-mell
Ryves wi a banshee yell
 And a blaff o hail . . .

luift: sky

Out throu her eldritch rags
The auld mune-hag
Looks on the bylan seas
Whaur sleek as backs o seals
   Curls ilka sweel,

And looks on the tuim promenade
The folk all abed
On this daft nicht, but me
That looks on the stairvan sea
   Wantan ye.

And awa ayont the faem
And the black storm, at hame
Ye're sleepan peacefullie—
Or maybe hear the thunderan sea
   ... Wantan me.

294   *The Mandrake Hert*

YE saw't floueran in my breist
   —My mandrake hert—
And, wi a wild wae look
(O my dear luve!)
Ye reift it screichan out ...
And the bluid rins aye frae the torn ruit.

295

Cokkils

DOUN throu the sea
    Continuallie
A rain o cokkils, shells
    Rains doun
Frae the ceaseless on-ding
O' the reefs abune—
    Continuallie.

Slawlie throu millenia
Biggan on the ocean bed
Their ain subaqueous Himalaya
Wi a fine white rain o shells
Faa'an continuallie
    Wi nae devall.

Sae, in my heid as birdsang
Faas throu simmer treen
Is the thocht o my luve
Like the continual rain
O' cokkils throu the middle seas
    Wi nae devall—
The thocht o my true-luve
    Continuallie.

on-ding: battering   devall: respite

GEORGE CAMPBELL HAY

1915–

(*From the Italian of Cecco Angiolieri*)

296   *Sonnet*

BECKIE, my luve!—What is't, ye twa-faced tod?—
Forgie me, Beckie!—Ye're no worthy o't.—
In God's name pity!—Humbly ye come, by God!—
And aye will sae.—Whar is yere bond for that?—
My ain gude faith.—Gin faith is walth, gang beg.—
For ye I hae't.—Gie owre, ye fraik. Begane!—
What hae I dune?—I hae heard aa, ye cleg.—
Tell me, luve, what?—Leave off! God, war ye gaen!

Ye'd hae me dee?—Livan 's yere weary faut.—
Ye spak fu' ill.—In that ye schuled me weel.—
Then dee I will!—Anither lee, ill fa't!—
May God forgie ye!—What! No' gane? Here still?—
Could I but gang!—I haud ye by the coat?—
Nae, by the hert.—Sae tae yere grief I will.

tod: fox   walth: wealth   fraik: freak   cleg: gadfly
faut: fault   schuled: schooled   lee: lie

297   *Song*

DAY will rise and the sun from eastward,
    the mist in his rays from marsh and plain,
the dew will rise from the bending branches—
    och, when will my own heart rise again?
For a treasure shines on the head that haunts me,
    like old kings' vaults or the spoils of Spain,
gold hair falling about her shoulders,
    the red gold pouring like burning rain.

582

Her mouth is the sun through red wine shining,
    lips that are tender and fine with pride,
white is the neck where the ringlets cluster,
    like a white stone under the running tide,
like a burst of sun on broken water
    when the mad wind scatters the spindrift wide,
or the drifting snow that the wind is blowing,
    whispering, cold on the bare hillside.

By night I travelled rough lonely places,
    and down by Garvalt I took my way,
till I reached at dawning the rocky summit,
    above the toun where my darling lay;
the stars were fading, the sky was paling,
    the cock told loud in her home of day,
I saw the smoke from her hearthstone rising,
    I wept, and sighing I turned away.

From showery meadows the wind comes softly
    with a scent of blossoms and tender grass;
heartsome the breezes from narrow valleys,
    myrtle and heather they breathe, and pass;
but the south wind singing, that comes to lull us,
    from sleepy hillsides and seas of glass,
brings to me thoughts of care and sorrow
    out of the airt where dwells my lass.

298   *Flooer o the Gean*

FLOOER o the gean,
    yere aefauld white she wore yestreen.
Wi gentle glances aye she socht me.
Dwell her thochts whaur dwalt her een?

    gean: wild cherry   yere aefauld: your spotless

Flooer o the broom,
gowden abune the thicket's gloom,
I canna see ye as I pu' ye.
My een are fu', my hert is toom.

Flooeran slae,
white ye are, untried, in May.
When Simmer 's gane, an' hard days rock ye,
yere fruit is black an' bitter tae.

Bloom o the whin,
born frae the stabs an' still their kin,
the een that seek her beauty yearn for
a flooer that wounds are dernan in.

Flooer o the briar,
the haund that socht ye throbs wi fire.
The hert that socht her tholes its searan
tae see her mood grow sweir an' tire.

Flooer o the thorn,
the haund that plucked at ye is torn.
Is anger's edge in ane sae gracious?
Can thon sweet face be sherp wi scorn?

Spray o the pine,
that never fades nor faas tae crine,
green I pu' ye, leal I ken ye.
I'll weir the green I winna tine.

Fior di mento,
la roba vien e va come va il vento.
La bella donna fa l'uomo contento.

toom: empty	slae: sloe	stabs: spines	dernan:
hiding	tholes: endures	sweir: listless	crine: wither
leal: loyal	weir: wear	tine: lose	

Flooer o the mint,
lik wund the warld's goods come an' are tint.
Wumman's beauty gies man true content.

tint: lost

299 *The Two Neighbours*

TWO that through windy nights kept company,
two in the dark, two on the sea at the steering,
with aye one another's bow-wave and wake to see,
the neighbour's light away on the beam plunging and soaring.

Two on blind nights seeking counsel in turn—
'Where will we head now?'—sharing their care and labours,
spoke across plashing waters from stern to stern,
comrades in calm, fellows in storm, night-sea neighbours.

Dark and daybreak, heat and hail had tried
and schooled the two in the master glance for esteeming
the curve of the outgoing net, the set of the tide,
the drift of wind and sea, the airt where the prey was swimming.

Two on the sea. And the one fell sick at last,
'for he was weak, the soul, and old'. And the other
watched long nights by his bed, as on nights that were past
he watched from the stern for his light, sea-neighbour, in ill a
  brother.

Watched by the peep of a lamp long nights by his side;
brightened his mood, talking their sea-nights over;
followed him to Cill Aindreis[1] when he died,
and left him at peace in a lee that would feel no wind for ever.

[1] Cill Aindreis: the graveyard of Tarbert Loch Fyne.

From *The Dark Dialogues*

II

ALMOST I, yes, I hear
 Huge in the small hours
A man's step on the stair
Climbing the pipeclayed flights
And then stop still
Under the stairhead gas
At the lonely tenement top.
The broken mantle roars
Or dims to a green murmur.
One door faces another.
Here, this is the door
With the loud grain and the name
Unreadable in brass.
Knock, but a small knock,
The children are asleep.
I sit here at the fire
And the children are there
And in this poem I am,
Whoever elsewhere I am,
Their mother through his mother.
I sit with the gas turned
Down and time knocking
Somewhere through the wall.
Wheesht, children, and sleep
As I break the raker up,
It is only the stranger
Hissing in the grate.
Only to speak and say
Something, little enough,
Not out of want

Nor out of love, to say
Something and to hear
That someone has heard me.
This is the house I married
Into, a room and kitchen
In a grey tenement,
The top flat of the land,
And I hear them breathe and turn
Over in their sleep
As I sit here becoming
Hardly who I know.
I have seen them hide
And seek and cry come out
Come out whoever you are
You're not het I called
And called across the wide
Wapenshaw of water.
But the place moved away
Beyond the reach of any
Word. Only the dark
Dialogues drew their breath.
Ah how bright the mantel
Brass shines over me.
Black-lead at my elbow,
Pipe-clay at my feet.
Wheesht and go to sleep
And grow up but not
To say mother mother
Where are the great games
I grew up quick to play.

III

Now in the third voice
I am their father through

Nothing more than where
I am made by this word
And this word to occur.
Here I am makeshift made
By artifice to fall
Upon a makeshift time.
But I can't see. I can't
See in the bad light
Moving (Is it moving?)
Between your eye and mine.
Who are you and yet
It doesn't matter only
I thought I heard somewhere
Someone else walking.
Where are the others? Why,
If there is any other,
Have they gone so far ahead?
Here where I am held
With the old rainy oak
And Cartsburn and the Otter's
Burn aroar in the dark
I try to pay for my keep.
I speak as well as I can
Trying to teach my ears
To learn to use their eyes
Even only maybe
In the end to observe
The behaviour of silence.
Who is it and why
Do you walk here so late
And how should you know to take
The left or the right fork
Or the way where, as a boy,
I used to lie crouched

Deep under the flailing
Boughs of the roaring wood?
Or I lay still
Listening while a branch
Squeaked in the resinous dark
And swaying silences.

Otherwise I go
Only as a shell
Of my former self.
I go with my foot feeling
To find the side of the road,
My head inclined, my ears
Feathered to every wind
Blown between the dykes.
The mist is coming home.
I hear the blind horn
Mourning from the firth.
The big wind blows
Over the shore of my child-
Hood in the off season.
The small wind remurmurs
The fathering tenement
And a boy I knew running
The hide and seeking streets.
Or do these winds
In their forces blow
Between the words only?

I am the shell held
To Time's ear and you
May hear the lonely leagues
Of the kittiwake and the fulmar.

301 *Many Without Elegy*

MANY without elegy interpret a famous heart
Held with a searoped saviour to direct
The land. This morning moves aside
Sucking disaster and my bread
On the hooped fields of Eden's mountain
Over the crews of wrecked seagrain.

There they employ me. I rise to the weed that harps
More shipmark to capsizing, more to lament
Under the whitewashed quenched skerries
The washed-away dead. Hullo you mercies
Morning drowns tail and all and bells
Bubble up rigging as the saint falls.

Many dig deeper in joy and are shored with
A profit clasped in a furious swan-necked prow
To sail against spout of this monumental loss
That jibles with no great nobility its cause.
That I can gather, this parched offering
Of a dry hut out of wrong weeping

Saying 'there's my bleached-in-tears opponent
Prone on his brothering bolster in the week
Of love for unbandaged unprayed-for men'.
            Gone to no end but each man's own.
So far they are, creation's whole memory
Now never fears their death or day.

Many out of the shades project a heart
Famous for love and only what they are
To each self's landmark marked among
The dumb scenery of weeping.
I come in sight and duty of these
For food and fuel of a talking blaze.

Here as the morning moves my eyes achieve
Further through elegy. There is the dolphin
Reined with searopes stitching a heart
To swim through blight. No I'll inherit
No keening in my mountainhead or sea
Nor fret for few who die before I do.

MAURICE LINDSAY

1918–

Hurlygush

302

THE hurlygush and hallyoch o the water
a-skinlan i the moveless simmer sun,
harles aff the scaurie mountain wi a yatter
that thru ten-thoosan centuries has run.

Wi cheek against the ash o wither't bracken,
I ligg at peace and hear nae soun at aa
but yonder hurlygush that canna slacken
thru time and space mak never-endan faa:

as if a volley o the soun had brought me
doun tae thon pool whaur timeless things begin,
and e'en this endless faa'an that had caught me
wi ilka ither force was gether't in.

hurlygush: the sound made by falling water   hallyoch: the sound
made by water over stones   harles: peels

303   *The Exiled Heart*

TWO purple pigeons circle a London square
    as darkness blurs and smudges the shadowless light
of a winter evening. I pause on the pavement and stare
at the restless flutter of wings as they gather flight,
like rustling silk, and move out to meet the night.

And my restless thoughts migrate to a Northern city—
fat pigeons stalking the dirty, cobbled quays,
where a sluggish river carries the cold self-pity
of those for whom life has never flowed with ease,
from a granite bridge to the grey Atlantic seas:

the bristling, rough-haired texture of Scottish manners;
the jostled clatter of airless shopping streets
where lumbering tramcars squeal as they turn sharp corners;
the boosy smell from lounging pubs that cheats
the penniless drunkard's thirst with its stale deceits:

where my heart first jigged to the harsh and steady sorrow
of those for whom mostly the world is seldom glad;
who are dogged by the flat-heeled footpad steps of to-morrow;
for whom hope is a dangerous drug, an expensive fad
of the cushioned rich, or the young and lovesick mad:

where chattering women in tea-rooms, swaddled with furs,
pass knife-edged gossip like cakes, and another's skirt
is unstitched with sharp words, and delicate, ladylike slurs
are slashed on the not-quite-nice or the over-smart,
till their cigarette smoke is a lazy prickled hurt.

I remember Glasgow, where sordid and trivial breed
from the same indifferent father; his children side
with the mother whose sour breasts taught them first to feed
on her hot, caressing hates that sear and divide,
or swell the itched, distorting bladder of pride.

Yet my casual smile is the tossed-down beggar's penny
the goaded heart throws out in vain to procure
the comfortable forgetfulness of the many
who lie in content's soft arms, and are safe and sure
in the fabled Grecian wanderers' lotus-lure:

who forget the sullen glare of the wet, grey skies,
and the lashing Northern wind that flicks the skin
where hum-drum poverty's dull and listless eyes
are pressed to the window, hearing the friendly din
of the party, watching the lights and the laughter within.

But oh! I cannot forget! So I wait, and wonder:
how long will the thinly-dividing window hold?
How long will the dancing drown the terrible anger
of those, the unwanted, who peddle their grief in the cold,
wrapped in their own despair's thick and unkindly fold?

Yet evil is no pattern of places
varied, like terraces from town to town.
A city's charms and individual graces
are but the sculptor's bleak and basic stone,
the photographic face without a frown.

The wound is in this bewildered generation,
unfriended, lost within the Freudian wood,
its compass-point no longer veneration
of that lost God who rewarded the simple and good,
vivid and real, now, only in childhood.

For we, the children of this uncertain age,
breathing its huge disasters and sad airs,
have seen that our warm, humanitarian rage
is impotent to soothe war's animal fears,
and cannot quell the lonely exile's tears . . .

So the heart, like a wounded seabird, hungers home
to muffled memories on fainter-beating wings
which once soared over history's clouded foam;
to that first shore where each new hero flings
his careful stone that fades in slow, concentric rings.

WILLIAM J. TAIT

1918–

304   *Gallow Hill*

(*The scene of the last Shetland witch-burning*)

FOR aa da scraimin stars at hing
    Black i' da lourd lift's aze,
For aa da kolkoom möns at kring
    Da skoilts an skurms o' days,

For aa da lapperin blöd 'll swee
    Frae da kirnin sea's owreflowe,
Yit canna slock da blazin tree
    Nor da aaberknot[1] o lowe,

I tank Dee, tank . . . . . but still I stirn.
    O cled me, Christ or Deil,
In sic a sark o fire, I burn
    Trowe Heevin an Aert an Hell!

[1] A mystic knot tied on a sprain, etc., as a cure.

at hing: that hang   lourd lift's aze: heavy sky's blaze   kolkoom:
cindered   kring: tether   skoilts an skurms: shards and shells
lapperin: overflowing   swee: burn, hiss in the fire   kirnin:
churning   slock: slake   tank: thank   stirn: shiver   sic:
such   sark: shirt

THURSO BERWICK

1919–

305 *Idleset (2)*

ILL 'S the airt o the Word the day
It 's in ma heid bit it willna say.
It maks me for its gemme an play.
Ill 's the airt o the Word the day.

Wary the yin contains the Word,
Like ti the tree thit kens nae bird,
Like ti the twa thit kens nae third.
Wary the yin contains the Word.

Ill 's the airt o the Word the day,
An, baudrons-like, baith fauss an fey.
It 's bell-the-cat ir a pickle strae.
Ill 's the airt o the Word the day.

airt: point of compass   gemme: game   baudrons-like: pussy-
like   fey: fated

HAMISH HENDERSON

1920–

306 *First Elegy for the Dead in Cyrenaica*

THERE are many dead in the brutish desert,
        who lie uneasy
among the scrub in this landscape of half-wit
stunted ill-will. For the dead land is insatiate
and necrophilous. The sand is blowing about still.

Many who for various reasons, or because
              of mere unanswerable compulsion, came here
and fought among the clutching gravestones,
            shivered and sweated,
cried out, suffered thirst, were stoically silent, cursed
the spittering machine-guns, were homesick for Europe
and fast embedded in quicksand of Africa
            agonized and died.
And sleep now. Sleep here the sleep of the dust.

There were our own, there were the others.
Their deaths were like their lives, human and animal.
There were no gods and precious few heroes.
What they regretted when they died had nothing to do with
            race and leader, realm indivisible,
laboured Augustan speeches or vague imperial heritage.
(They saw through that guff before the axe fell.)
            Their longing turned to
the lost world glimpsed in the memory of letters:
an evening at the pictures in the friendly dark,
two knowing conspirators smiling and whispering secrets;
            or else
a family gathering in the homely kitchen
with Mum so proud of her boys in uniform:
            their thoughts trembled
between moments of estrangement, and ecstatic moments
of reconciliation: and their desire
crucified itself against the unutterable shadow of someone
whose photo was in their wallets.
Then death made his incision.

There were our own, there were the others.
Therefore, minding the great word of Glencoe's
son, that we should not disfigure ourselves

with villainy of hatred; and seeing that all
have gone down like curs into anonymous silence,
I will bear witness for I knew the others.
Seeing that littoral and interior are alike indifferent
and the birds are drawn again to our welcoming north
why should I not sing *them*, the dead, the innocent?

307 *The Flyting o' Life and Daith*

QUO life, the warld is mine.
   The floo'ers and trees, they're a' my ain.
I am the day, and the sunshine
Quo life, the warld is mine.

Quo daith, the warld is mine.
Your lugs are deef, your een are blin
Your floo'ers maun dwine in my bitter win'
Quo daith, the warld is mine.

Quo life, the warld is mine.
I hae saft win's, and healin' rain
Aipples I hae, an' breid an' wine
Quo life, the warld is mine.

Quo daith, the warld is mine.
Whit sterts in dreid, gangs doon in pain
Bairns wantin' breid are makin' mane
Quo daith, the warld is mine.

Quo life, the warld is mine.
Your deidly wark, I ken it fine
There's maet on earth for ilka wean
Quo life, the warld is mine.

     lugs: ears   dwine: dwindle

Quo daith, the warld is mine.
Your silly sheaves crine in my fire
My worm keeks in your barn and byre
Quo daith, the warld is mine.

Quo life, the warld is mine.
Dule on your een! Ae galliard hert
Can ban tae hell your blackest airt
Quo life, the warld is mine.

Quo daith, the warld is mine.
Your rantin' hert, in duddies braw,
He winna lowp my preeson wa'
Quo daith, the warld is mine.

Quo life, the warld is mine.
Though ye bigg preesons o' marble stane
Hert's luve ye cannae preeson in
Quo life, the warld is mine.

Quo daith, the warld is mine.
I hae dug a grave, I hae dug it deep,
For war an' the pest will gar ye sleep.
Quo daith, the warld is mine.

Quo life, the warld is mine.
An open grave is a furrow syne.
Ye'll no keep my seed frae fa'in in.
Quo life, the warld is mine.

crine: waste away   ban: curse   bigg: build

ALEXANDER SCOTT

1920–

308   *Calvinist Sang*

A HUNDER pipers canna blaw
⠀⠀⠀Our trauchled times awa,
Drams canna droun them out, nor sang
Hap their scarecraw heids for lang.

Gin aa the warld was bleezan fou,
⠀⠀⠀Wh'at gowk wald steer the plou?
Gin cheils were cowpan quines aa day,
They'd mak, but n'ever gaither, hay.

Pit by yir pipes and brak yir gless,
⠀⠀⠀Wi quines, keep aff the gress,
The day ye need a hert and harns
Dour as the diamant, cauld as the starns.

trauchled: troubled⠀⠀⠀hap: cover⠀⠀⠀fou: drunk⠀⠀⠀gowk: fool
cowpan quines: laying girls⠀⠀⠀harns: brains

309   *Coronach*

(*For the Dead of the 5/7th Battalion,
The Gordon Highlanders*)

W AEMENT the deid
⠀⠀⠀I never did,
Ower gled I was ane o the lave
That somewey baid alive
Tae trauchle my thowless hert
Wi ithers' hurt.

coronach: dirge⠀⠀⠀⠀waement: lament⠀⠀⠀⠀thowless: passive

599

But nou that I'm far
Frae the fechtin's fear,
Nou I hae won awa frae aa thon pain
Back til my beuks and my pen,
They croud around me oot o the grave
Whaur luve and langourie and blyeness grieve.

Cryan the cauld words:
'We hae dree'd oor weirds,
But you that byde ahin,
Ayont oor awesome hyne,
You are the flesh we aince had been,
We that are bruckle brokken bane.'

Cryan a drumlie speak:
'You hae the words we spak,
You hae the sang
We canna sing,
Sen daith maun skail
The makar's skill.

'Makar, frae nou ye maun
Be singan for us deid men,
Sing til the warld we loo'd
(For aa that its brichtness lee'd)
And tell hou the sudden nicht
Cam doun and made us nocht.'

Waement the deid
I never did,
But nou I am safe awa
I hear their wae
Greetan greetan dark and daw,
Their dregy ere I dae.

langourie: yearning   blyeness: ? happiness   dree'd: suffered
bruckle: brittle   drumlie: turbid   skail: spill   greetan: weeping
dregy: dirge

310 *Letter to Robert Fergusson*

DEAR Fergusson—They've Ramsay's statue clean,
But yours they cudna touch—ye haena ane,
And wadna hae a stane abune your lair
But Burns, your 'younger brither', laid it there—
For wha's the lad to love a makar's sang
(Whan baxters, bylies, aa the haill jing-bang
O' toun-heid patrons, pass his singin by
For ither makars wi a fremmit cry)
Gif no the scriever, like yoursel a Scot,
That kens *your* scrievin saved *his* page a blot
A hantle whiles, and shawed his words the gait
To lead them fairheid-weys whan they were blate?

Ye spak o music aince, a while sinsyne,
O' 'vile Italian tricks' the warld thocht fine,
O' 'foreign sonnets' hung wi triumph's bays
Whan dubs were dingit doun on hameil lays;
It's aye the same, and no a wheen mair rational,
Though nou we caa the wey o't 'international'
To tak sic tent o tunes frae ither airts
And never fash for Scottish sangs-o-pairts.

What gowk wad praise your 'Birks o Invermay'
Whan Bartok's folksy ferlies stairt to play?
The Scottish reel may tap her taes for lang
Whan Khatchaturian's sabres clank and clang,
Sen nane will dance wi her, nor think it queer
To wiggle their hurdies ower the conga here

lair: grave   makar: poet   baxters: bakers   bylies: baillies
jing-bang: collection   fremmit: foreign   scriever: writer
hantle: handful   gait: way   blate: shy   dubs: mud   hameil:
homely   wheen: lot   tent: care   fash: bother   gowk:
fool   ferlies: wonders   hurdies: hips

And kick and thraw like a herd o doited stots
In onie jigs but them that were made by Scots.

Nae monie seek to hear a tune frae hame
Whan fremmit tooters blaw a fremmit fame
For sangs frae Paris, Budapest and Rome.
Their farness maks them fair, and sae they come
To conquer fowk that love their reputations
(Sae lang as they're the wark o ither nations)
And praise wi pounds a fremmit bard far raither
Nor fling a meck to '*Him*? I kent his faither!'

There 's some wad mak ye out ower fond o drams,
And some declare ye far ower free wi damns
At aathing furth o Alba's coorse-like Eden,
But siccan fauts—gin fauts they were—are needan
Anither defence nor mine, sen I mysel
Hae drunk my dram and damned the warld to hell,
And doutless ye'd your reason wi your rhyme
Gin warld and flesh and deil in aulden time
Were mair or less the warld and flesh and deil
That herrie the hert and the harns o the modern chiel.

For aye we're deaved wi clapper tongues that ding
A dregy ower the sangs we fain wad sing
In Scots or Gaelic ('Saft auldfarrant havers!')
But clink sic peals o praise for Suddron quavers
Ye'd nearhand think they'd read the sangs they blaw,
Though fient the sang-beuk 's on their skelfs ava.
For aye whan heids are tuim the tongues'll tirl,
The daftest mak the loudest din and dirl,

doited stots: crazy cattle   onie: any   meck: ha'penny
coorse: coarse   harns: brains   deaved: deafened   dregy:
dirge   auldfarrant: old-fashioned   fient the: devil the one
ava: at all

And aye what's fremmit's fine and what's our ain
A puir-like thing for makar-gowks to hain.

I'll no deny some fremmit sangs are braw,
But gin mair fowk wad read your sangs an-aa
They'd see—like Burns—a chiel o note (and notes)
Had scrieved atween the Tweed and John o' Groats
And aa the talents werena south and hyne
On Thames or Tiber, fousome Fleet or Rhine;
But gin they neither ken nor praise your fame
There's ane at least will aye cry up your name
(Warse luck that sic a cryin's muckle nott),
And here's my ain—Yours, Alexander Scott.

hain: save   hyne: far   fousome: filthy   nott: needed

SYDNEY TREMAYNE

1920–

311   *Moses*

HEAD in a cloud Moses stands
    Beckoning with explosive hands,
Threatening unpromised lands.

Tutmouse the Pharaoh rather bored
Hears the wind harp through his beard.
His heart is hardened by the Lord.

Superior persons tend to miss
Unreasoning people's deadliness.
Pharaoh is sunk because of this.

Pillar of cloud, pillar of fire,
Songs and timbrels fill the air.
Logic never led so far.

Moses harder than a stone
With the Laws engraved thereon
Knocks the gods and Pharaoh down.

In the desert, furious,
Rules with God's and Pharaoh's voice,
For the chosen have no choice.

EDWIN MORGAN

1920–

312   *The Second Life*

BUT does every man feel like this at forty—
I mean it's like Thomas Wolfe's New York, his
heady light, the stunning plunging canyons, beauty—
pale stars winking hazy downtown quitting-time,
and the winter moon flooding the skyscrapers, northern—
an aspiring place, glory of the bridges, foghorns
are enormous messages, a looming mastery
that lays its hand on the young man's bowels
until he feels in that air, that rising spirit
all things are possible, he rises with it
until he feels that he can never die—
Can it be like this, and is this what it means
in Glasgow now, writing as the aircraft roar
over building sites, in this warm west light
by the daffodil banks that were never so crowded and lavish—

green May, and the slow great blocks rising
under yellow tower cranes, concrete and glass and steel
out of a dour rubble it was and barefoot children gone—
Is it only the slow stirring, a city's renewed life
that stirs me, could it stir me so deeply
as May, but could May have stirred
what I feel of desire and strength
like an arm saluting a sun?

All January, all February the skaters
enjoyed Bingham's pond, the crisp cold evenings,
they swung and flashed among car headlights,
the drivers parked round the unlit pond
to watch them, and give them light, what laughter
and pleasure rose in the rare lulls
of the yards-away stream of wheels along Great Western Road!
The ice broke up, but the boats came out.
The painted boats are ready for pleasure.
The long light needs no headlamps.

Black oar cuts a glitter: it is heaven on earth.

Is it true that we come alive
not once, but many times?
We are drawn back to the image
of the seed in darkness, or the greying skin
of the snake that hides a shining one—
it will push that used-up matter off
and even the film of the eye is sloughed—
That the world may be the same, and we are not
and so the world is not the same,
the second eye is making again
this place, these waters and these towers,
they are rising again

as the eye stands up to the sun,
as the eye salutes the sun.

Many things are unspoken
in the life of a man, and with a place
there is an unspoken love also
in undercurrents, drifting, waiting its time.
A great place and its people are not renewed lightly.
The caked layers of grime
grow warm, like homely coats.
But yet they will be dislodged
and men will still be warm.
The old coats are discarded.
The old ice is loosed.
The old seeds are awake.

Slip out of darkness, it is time.

GEORGE MACKAY BROWN

1927–

The Old Women

313

G O sad or sweet or riotous with beer
Past the old women gossiping by the hour,
They'll fix on you from every close and pier
An acid look to make your veins run sour.

'No help', they say, 'his grandfather that's dead
Was troubled with the same dry-throated curse,
And many a night he made the ditch his bed.
This blood comes welling from the same cracked source.'

On every kind of merriment they frown.
But I have known a gray-eyed sober boy
Sail to the lobsters in a storm and drown.
Over his body dripping on the stones
Those same old hags would weave into their moans
An undersong of terrible holy joy.

314   *December Day, Hoy Sound*

THE unfurled gull on the tide, and over the skerry
    Unfurling waves, and slow unfurling wreckage
—The Sound today a burning sapphire bough
Fretted with mimic spring.

                              The creatures of earth
Have seasons and stations, under the quartered sun
Ploughshare and cornstalk, millwheel and grinning rags.
The December seed kneels at his frosty vigil,
Sword by his side for the long crusade to the light
In trumpeting March, with the legion of lamb and leaf.

The sea grinds his salt behind a riot of masks.

Today on Hoy Sound random blossoms unfurl
Of feather and rust, a harlequin spring.

                              Tomorrow
The wave will weep like a widow on the rock,
Or howl like Lear, or laugh like a green child.

315 *Stars*

TAE be wan o them Kings
That owre the desert rode
Trackan a muckle reid star,
The herald o God!

Tae swivel a crystal eye
Abune a mountain place
And light on an uncan star,
A tinker in space!—

Thought Tammas, rowan his boat
Fae creel tae creel around,
When Venus shook her hair
Owre the Soond.

WILLIAM PRICE TURNER

1927–

316 *Alien*

I MET an honest man today,
    a foreigner, of course.
I knew him in a sudden way
    by the pent force
in his calm gaze, but most
    I suppose, by his song:
    it came from some pure source
before the semantic ghost
confounded builders of wrong.

I hear many a rich man curse
    from his pride's ladder-top,
Life and living's bottomless purse
      for a poor crop,
    but the honest man breeds
    his own fierce truth, among
    the weeds that others chop,
never caring who first heeds
the good of all he has sung.

I see so many men
    who choose the strongest horse,
spurring and urging on, and then
      without remorse
    staking that flesh and more
    for room on a fresh rung.
    The honest man grows hoarse:
I hope he dies before
they teach him a new tongue.

317   *Coronary Thrombosis*

HOW fierce in its loyalties the beat of the heart,
    thudding and thudding, pistoned in faith;
and what a desperate ethic devils us
      to soar through space,
when all the mighty engines men construct
to probe infinity's most abstract pores
wait on the humours of the old blood-pump
      powering even our repose.

How free with its argosies the pride of the mind,
    planning, explaining, fraught with campaign . . .
When progress founders or prejudice destroys,
    fresh lures prevail.
On time's expense account the kinks uncoil:
dynasties rattle down like dominoes
while wheels and ladders theorise the void
    of the rule-grinder's monotone.

How long are these pillories of justice we deal,
    shackles untackled, to be retained?
Divorce's ducking-stool, and legislation's
    erratic snail
strain from their slime in public marathon—
but who, privileged to witness one slow
gas chamber waltz, knowing the score, applauds
    the guillotine as metronome?

How madly determinist the plight of the world,
    massively passive before decay;
windmill politics pounding bones of peace
    concatenate
famine and harvest and the price of beer.
The rice-grain peasant and the champagne bore
frown across columns of one magazine
    where oblique colloquies explode.

How true of our apathy the man on the cross:
    languishing anguish, hanging in grace,
and the squatting prince, uprooted from desire,
    how they translate!
As if the ravages of compromise,
convulsing shrouds to impregnate a ghost,
have primed a faith that heart and brain deny:
    a bastard truth, ashamed of both.

How sure of security the breast in the hand,
    trustingly thrusting, moot for debate;
and what impermanent, randomly pledged debts
    these moods we slake.
The steady poisons of the flesh relent,
the craft of love is scuttled out of port
and both minds paddle rancours of regret
    into poor harbours of their own.

So primitive, this ever-laborious clutch,
    thumping and pumping blood to the brain.
Intellect's miserly budgeting inflicts
    lavish blockades:
so the old craftsman, curator of whims
today no body of men dare afford,
tightens the shutters on integrity,
    the doomed only trade that he knows.

318   *University Curriculum*

IN this factory, here the axe-grinders
are whetted by degrees,
there are courses in log-rolling
and a shortage of trees.

BURNS SINGER

1928–1964

Peterhead in May

SMALL lights pirouette
Among these brisk little boats.
A beam, cool as a butler,
Steps from the lighthouse.

Wheelroom windows are dark
Reflections of light quickly
Skip over them tipsily like
A girl in silk.

One knows there is new paint
And somehow an intense
Suggestion of ornament
Comes into mind.

Imagine elephants here
They'd settle, clumsily sure
Of themselves and of us and of four
Square meals and of water.

Then you will have it. This
Though a grey and quiet place
Finds nothing much amiss.
It keeps its stillness.

There is no wind. A thin
Mist fumbles above it and,
Doing its best to be gone,
Obscures the position.

This place is quiet or,
Better, impersonal. There
Now you have it. No verdict
Is asked for, no answer.

Yet nets will lie all morning,
Limp like stage scenery,
Unused but significant
Of something to come.

320   *Nothing*

THEY say the experimental
    Zero is impossible.
The mind cannot conceive it,
The heart cannot believe it:
That mind meets mind whenever mind
Notions its way through more refined
Lacks of possibility.
And heart meets heart and mind and hand
Although it cannot understand
More than its own immensity.
That every vacuum known to space,
In spite of walls round emptiness,
Must let the heavens' swift particles
Meander through it and displace
Vacuum with vacillation.
But you, my darling, when we meet
It is in a dispassionate
Area outside all relation.
We speak and thus create our silence
Where passion's peace and passion's violence
Combine in an autonomous

613

State that is not between them nor
Explicable by metaphor.
I am the nothingness of us,
And you are me, and we are two
Demonstrations that nothing *is* true.

321   *Marcus Antoninus*
                 cui cognomen erat
                 Aurelius

THE world is Rome; Carnuntum, on the Danube.

A man seated, a tent, three thousand tents, a man,
His skin sponged brown by the Italian summer,
Darkened by shadows and the sun of Egypt,
A face tugged out by winds of the desert, tight from sea-plod,
Contrary to innocence, and gentle:
The posture harsh; the mind alone is active.
Respectfully his, a boy at the back of him squats:
In front, a skeleton enters
(Epictetus, the wise slave, walks):
Then an Immortal
Staggering upwards painfully under
Bundles, for burden,
Of brown sackcloth wings.
The boy and the skeleton grin and are earnest.
That is their nature. His, the duty;
His, the decision: decide.

There is an army and an enemy,
And one in ten but from which century
He tallies purposes and hears them hold
Clamour raised upon clamour,

Rattle of armour, death squeals.
A mind, erratic within
His decent body, carries
Piecemeal a soul which cannot live outside:
Looks out and vanishes ahead of him.

The boy squats pleasant: truthfully he is blind.
The articulated bones are hollow and unkind.
That is the nature of things. His is the empire.
His is the duty. Decide.

The boy, a curt word;
The skeleton vanishes.
There, instead of it, stands
(Alive in that curious negligent flesh
He fears for his own)
No master now but his quiet servant.
Words and an officer,
Words, and a name: it was done,
And the hum of dispatches begun
Two secretaries scribbling, the couriers off,
And a cold walk in the camp,
And a hot meal, and his duty.

Two hours alone he must sit with the truth,
That bitter gentleman all made of teeth,
Listens to cauldrons and the clank of torture,
Screams from the innocent and the unholy:
Then hearing this he must resign himself,
Prepare himself for action and forget
Warmth, with its quiet
Noise of a woman
Who once breathed beside him,
Cold, with its quiet
Clinks of his skeleton's

Vertebrae in him.
It must be done, and it is difficult,
Difficult while soldiers
Aloud about
Tent, bed and table
Query, quip, react
To orders given;
Difficult in his tent,
Difficult in his Empire:
It is difficult to forget and threadbare follow
The thin mind of a slave compelled by masters
To move through all of it without the world.
Beyond all this, he must not ask for comfort.
Others have owned the universe before him
And his destiny yet
Will, fleetfoot, overtake many.

Thus ends his meditation.
Noise, and the tent-flap opens.
Noise, and his name.
He must go out, go sit in judgment,
And he must make haste.
He ponders quietly and asks quick questions.
Mercy must not itself become unjust.
This can have suicide, but that the gallows,
And one is loaded with new innocence.
He breaks a sword and pushes out in silence.
He had no right to judge them, but a duty.

Officially a banquet, therefore sit
Above the ambassadors and drink wine.
Dim memories recur that take time in
But must be battened or constricted for safeguard
Of his immediate purposes in war.
He smiles attentively. He makes a joke.

A long way gone, but not a long way back
To the boy squatting over difficult sums.
Politely he refuses, makes a promise, then
Singling out his enemy confronts the issue.
His empire is about him. His, the duty.
But then go back, and he must be alone,
Prepare for sleep; and it is an emperor's duty
Not to be weary lest he waste his empire:
Barbarians, past the number of sleep,
Wait with long swords for civilisation to nod.
To sleep and not to dream, for in dreams too
Hordes gather against him
And against him bring
That sickness for slaughter
Which history has
Leached into his lineage,
The rattle of armour, death squeals:
And, in his bed, lean hungry longings taunt him,
Pinprick and bite him;
Deep dreams of goodness keep him from sleep.
Why have the heavens not elected him
To be impoverished, alone, unheeded,
Taken all from him but his mind only
And given him freedom, made him a slave?
O Epictetus! Corpses are moving!
The slave he ambitions
Walks and with humble lessons
Proves the futility of all desire;
Fades in the act, accepting happiness,
The red earth round the oblong of his coffin.

Again the emperor shuts his eyes, and sleeps.
Let no scream from the tortured,
No prim innocence in the reprieved,

No cry against the cupidity of his time,
No pity for men in battle nor for his ancestors under the earth,
No lingering on the loveliness of the flesh,
No hungering after good honour,
Not a single prayer,
Not a hope of mercy
Corrupt the darkness in which he is resting:
Let him lie easily until the morning.

Then, to rise up, punctual not previous.
He puts on dignity like a suit of sack-cloth,
Walks in the weather that is sharp and sad.
He calls his commanders to council.
It is time to prepare
Another ambush.

322   *Still and All*

I GIVE my word on it. There is no way
Other than this. There is no other way
Of speaking. I am my name. I find my place
Empty without a word, and my word is
Given again. It is nothing less than all
Given away again, and all still truly
Returned on a belief. Believe me now.
There is no other. There is no other way.

These words run vertical in their slim green tunnels
Without any turning away. They turn into
The first flower and speak from a silent bell.
But underneath it is as always still
Truly awakening, slowly and slowly turning
About a shadow scribbled down by sunlight
And turning about my name. I am in my
Survival's hands. I am my shadow's theme.

My shadow's ground feeds me with roots, and rhymes
My statement over. Its radius feeds my flames
Into a cool tunnel. And I who find your ways
About me (In every part I find your ways
Of speech.) pierce ground and shadow still. The light
Is struck. Its definition makes me my quiet
Survival's answer. All still and all so truly
Wakening underneath me and turning slowly.

It's all so truly still. I'll take you into
The first statement. I'll take you along cool tunnels
That channelled light and petalled an iridescent
Symmetry over my bruised shadow. And yes
I'll take you, and your word will follow me,
Till definitions gather distilled honey
And make their mark the fingerprints of light.
I am, believe me then, the name I write.

I lie here still. Yes, truly still. And all
My deliberate identities have fallen
Away with the word given. I find my place
In every place, in every part of speech,
And lie there still. I let my statements go.
A cool green tunnel has stepped in the light of my shadow
There is no way round it. It leads to the flower
Bell—that swings slowly and slowly over.

IAIN CRICHTON SMITH

1928–

323   *John Knox*

THAT scything wind has cut the rich corn down—
    the satin shades of France spin idly by—
the bells are jangled in St. Andrew's town—
a thunderous God tolls from a northern sky.
He pulls the clouds like bandages awry.
See how the harlot bleeds below her crown.
This lightning stabs her in the heaving thigh—
such siege is deadly for dallying gown.

A peasant's scythe rings churchbells from the stone.
From this harsh battle let the sweet birds fly,
surprised by fields, now barren of their corn.
(Invent, bright friends, theology, or die.)
The shearing naked absolute blade has torn
through false French roses to her foreign cry.

324   *Culloden and After*

YOU understand it? How they returned from Culloden
    over the soggy moors aslant, each cap
at the low ebb no new full tide could pardon:
how they stood silent at the end of the rope
unwound from battle: and to the envelope
of a bedded room came home, polite and sudden.

And how, much later, bards from Tiree and Mull
would write of exile in the hard town
where mills belched English, anger of new school:
how they remembered where the sad and brown
landscapes were dear and distant as the crown
that fuddled Charles might study in his ale.

620

There was a sleep. Long fences leaned across
the vacant croft. The silly cows were heard
mooing their sorrow and their Gaelic loss.
The pleasing thrush would branch upon a sword.
A mind withdrew against its dreamed hoard
as whelks withdraw or crabs their delicate claws.

And nothing to be heard but songs indeed
while wandering Charles would on his olives feed
and from his Minch of sherries mumble laws.

325

For Angus MacLeod

Headmaster, and Editor of Gaelic Poems

TO-DAY they laid him in the earth's cold colour,
a man from Lewis with his seventy-five
years struck from his head. Teacher, scholar,
he had worked a true task when all alive,

building a school, elucidating texts.
The Gaelic shone quite clearly in his bones.
A casket filled with ashes has been mixed
with filtered sunlight and the small stones.

A useful life with pupils and with poems:
sufficient honours (his humour asked no more)
he takes his place in many minds and rooms.
Without their knowing it, his patient care

instructs far hands to turn a new lever,
a voice to speak in a mild-mannered tone.
The deeds we do reverberate forever.
Inveterate justice weighs the flesh and bone.

His best editions are some men and women
who scrutinise each action like a word.
The truest work is learning to be human
definitive texts the poorest can afford.

326 ## For My Mother

SHE is tougher than me, harder.
Elephant body on a miniature stool
keels when rising till the drilled stick
plants it upright. Rock
fills the false room

who has more air about her.
Kneaded life like good butter.
Is at seventy not afraid
of the perished dead
who spit and rear

snarling at me, not her,
though forty years younger.
Not riches do I wish me
nor successful power.
This only I admire

to roll the seventieth sea
as if her voyage were
to truthful Lewis rising,
most loved though most bare,
at the end of a rich season.

INDEX OF AUTHORS

[The references are to the numbers of the poems]

INDEX OF AUTHORS

Morgan, Edwin, 312.
Muir, Edwin, 205–12.
Murray, Charles, 195.

Nairne, Lady, 156, 157.

Raine, Kathleen, 261–4.
Ramsay, Allan, 113–15.
Reid, (?) John, of Stobo, 22.
Rendall, Robert, 239, 240.
Robertson, Edith Anne, 223, 224.
Robertson, T. A., ('Vagaland'), 272.
Rolland, John, 68.
Ross, Alexander, 116.

Saunders, R. Crombie, 284, 285.
Scott, Alexander, 62–67.
Scott, Alexander, 308–10.
Scott, Walter, 166–75.
Sempill, Robert, of Beltrees, 106.
Simpson, Margaret Winefride, 214.
Singer, Burns, 319–22.

Skinner, John, 121.
Skirving, Adam, 120.
Smith, Iain Crichton, 323–6.
Smith, Sydney Goodsir, 288–95.
Souter, William, 229–38.
Spence, Lewis, 197.
Stevenson, Robert Louis, 182–5.
Stewart, John, of Baldynneis, 77.
Stewart, Henry (Lord Darnley), 69, 70.
Stewart, (? William), 40.
Stuart, Alice V., 241.

Tait, William J., 304.
Tannahill, Robert, 176.
? Thomas of Erceldoune, 1.
Thomson, James, 117–19.
Thomson, James, 179.
Tremayne, Sydney, 311.
Turner, William Price, 316–18.

Young, Andrew, 200–2.
Young, Douglas, 281–3.

INDEX OF FIRST LINES

First lines of extracts are printed in italics. The numbers refer to the pages.

INDEX OF FIRST LINES

INDEX OF FIRST LINES

INDEX OF FIRST LINES

PRINTED IN GREAT BRITAIN
AT THE UNIVERSITY PRESS, OXFORD
BY VIVIAN RIDLER
PRINTER TO THE UNIVERSITY